The Weapons Acquisition Process: Economic Incentives

The Weapons Acquisition Process: Economic Incentives

FREDERIC M. SCHERER

Assistant Professor of Economics
Princeton University

Formerly Research Associate
Harvard University

DIVISION OF RESEARCH
GRADUATE SCHOOL OF BUSINESS ADMINISTRATION
HARVARD UNIVERSITY
Boston · 1964

The Weapons Acquisition Process: Economic Incentives

This volume is the second major publication resulting from a research project at the Harvard Business School on the development of advanced weapons. The study is directed toward a dual audience. On the one hand, it deals with problems of interest to those responsible for formulating and executing procurement policies within government and for operating under those policies within contractor organizations. At the same time it explores questions of motivation, risk, uncertainty, and business behavior which concern social scientists.

The author is Frederic M. Scherer, Assistant Professor of Economics at Princeton University and former Research Associate at the Harvard Business School. The over-all research project was directed by Paul W. Cherington, James J. Hill Professor of Transportation.

The development and production of advanced weapon systems in the United States are carried out mainly by private firms under contract to government agencies. Cost, time, and quality uncertainties are substantial in this process; risks are shifted to the government as buyer through such devices as the cost reimbursement or incentive contract; and once a program is underway, buyer and seller are locked together in a bilateral bargaining relationship. This volume explores the government's problem of maintaining incentives for efficient and optimal program execution in this essentially nonmarket environment.

Two broad classes of incentives, differing mainly in the form of the reward, are analyzed in this volume. Competitive incentives, considered in Chapters 2 through 5, involve the correlation of sales rewards with contractor performance. Contractual incentives, examined in Chapters 6 through 10, involve the correlation of contract profits with contractor performance.

When firms seek program support for their weapons within the limited national defense budget, they are in effect attempting to maximize the sales of their products. And since on the average more or less standard profit margins are added onto costs in weapons contracting, sales maximization is a means of maximizing long-run profits. The armed services have placed great emphasis on expected end-product quality (technical performance and reliability) in deciding which of various competing weapons development programs to continue supporting, somewhat less emphasis on time of availability, and relatively little emphasis on cost of development. As a result, during the development stages of programs, close-substitute competition and competition for budgetary support have generated fairly strong incentives for quality maximization and development time minimization, but only weak incentives for cost minimization. Competitive incentives for cost reduction have tended to become more potent in the production stages.

Firms also compete energetically to be chosen to conduct new development programs. In deciding the winner of a source selection competition, greatest weight has usually been assigned to the attractiveness of technical proposals and the availability of suitable human and physical resources, while past performance typically has received little weight. When emphasis is placed on technical proposals, firms are frequently compelled to make overly optimistic technical promises, to divert top technical talent from research and development work to selling activities, to hoard scarce technical talent, and to diversify at government expense into fields often served more effectively by existing specialists.

In the production stages of a weapons program, the government may be able to reap the efficiency benefits of advertised competitive bidding and second sourcing. But use of these types of competition is limited by the cost of setting up new producers and the risk of quality failures.

Automatic contractual incentives for good performance are created when buyer and seller jointly negotiate performance targets and profit-performance correlation formulas before contract execution. In the past, performance targets have been negotiated mainly on the cost dimension, although in recent years the use of multidimensional contractual incentives has increased rapidly.

Because the uncertainties associated with cost, quality, and time predictions are substantial, it is seldom possible to secure agreement on development program contracts with strong profit-performance correlations. Instead, cost-plus-fixed-fee (CPFF) contracts (in which realized profit does not vary with the actual cost outcome) and cost-plus-incentive-fee (CPIF) contracts (with relatively weak profit-cost correlations) have been used most frequently in development. The ability of CPIF contracts to incite development cost reduction is often frustrated by the negotiation of cost targets so optimistic relative to actual cost expectations that the contractor perceives no chance of earning more than its minimum guaranteed fee.

To maximize long-run profits, contractors must deduct from any so-called contractual incentive profits the user costs reflecting expected future sales and profit losses due to current cost reductions effected by sacrificing quality and time. User costs are also incurred by making pure short-run efficiency gains: cost reductions achieved by laying off technical and production staff members may impair a firm's ability to compete successfully for future contracts awarded on the basis of resource availability. Case study evidence indicates that contractors consider these user costs to be quite significant, often overwhelming the incentive profits attainable through development cost reduction actions. As a result, automatic contractual incentives for development cost reduction are often of limited effectiveness, especially when firms have excess capacity. On the other hand, firms confronted with more profit-earning opportunities than their resources can assimilate appear to have a positive incentive for efficiency even under cost-plus-fixed-fee contracts.

Since various kinds of competition generate fairly strong incentives for quality maximization and development time minimization, and since scientists and engineers tend naturally to seek high quality for its own sake, automatic contractual incentives on the quality and time dimensions are in large measure redundant. In addition, the complexity of multidimensional incentive contracts leads to undesirable development flexibility losses. The analysis in this volume suggests that the Department of Defense should reconsider its policy of encouraging maximum multidimensional incentive contract use and should rather focus on the cost dimension to spur needed efficiency.

It is also difficult to secure really strong automatic contractual incentives for cost reduction in weapon system and major subsystem production programs. Due to their superior knowledge of cost factors, contractors have an important bargaining advantage over the government in cost target negotiations. When the government does succeed in setting tight cost targets, contractors respond by attempting to negotiate weak profit-cost correlations, reducing the risk of loss and the incentive for cost reduction. When loose cost targets are established, the incentive for cost reduction is weakened further by the contractor's recognition that realizing high profits can damage its relations with the government and that incremental profits may be recaptured in renegotiation. Relatively weak automatic contractual incentives for production efficiency are often insufficient to overpower the user costs and disutilities connected with cost reduction, and so little cost reduction is incited. Analysis of quantitative data on contract outcomes suggests that variations in the target-setting (bargaining) process were much more important causes of contract cost outcome variations than efficiency shifts motivated by contractual incentives.

Another way of creating contractual incentives for good performance is to award higher negotiated contract profit rates to good performers than to poor performers. But up to 1963, when a change in defense procurement regulations was made, there was little effort to exploit this potential incentive system.

An assessment of the prevailing incentive structure in weapons acquisition concludes that reasonably powerful incentives exist for quality maximization and development time control, but that incentives for cost reduction have been generally inadequate.

To secure stronger and better-balanced incentives, the author proposes an after-the-fact evaluation system of incentives. The over-all performance and cost efficiency of contractors in major development programs would be evaluated retrospectively by a competent and objective board. Profit awards would be related to the contractor's efficiency in performing its development assignment: the more efficient the performance, the higher the profit award. The award of new contracts and subcontracts would be related to the contractor's over-all performance: the better the performance, the more rapidly the contractor's defense sales would be permitted to grow.

A concluding chapter argues that improved incentive systems are required before it will be possible to reverse the trend toward increasingly detailed direct government control and supervision of contractor operations.

(Published by Division of Research, Harvard Business School, Soldiers Field, Boston, Mass. 02163. xxi + 447 pages. 1964, $7.50)

Foreword

This volume, which focuses on contractual and competitive incentives in the development and production of major weapon systems, is the second publication resulting from the School's Weapons Acquisition Research Project. The first volume, *The Weapons Acquisition Process: An Economic Analysis,* by Merton J. Peck and Frederic M. Scherer, was published in the spring of 1962. To some degree, this book follows from and builds on the concepts, data, and findings of the earlier volume. But they have been extended, refined, and substantially added to in the present volume by Professor Scherer.

The Weapons Acquisition Research Project was begun in 1958, under a grant from the Ford Foundation, and had as its basic objective an exploration of the nature of the relationship which exists between government and industry in the weapon systems area. Of the faculty research team which worked on the project, Professor Scherer was a particularly active member for all but one year of its existence. It should be noted that an earlier version of the present volume was written on an independent basis by Professor Scherer as part of the requirements for the doctor's degree in the Department of Economics of Harvard University.

The initial volume by Peck and Scherer described the over-all economic structure within and the process by which weapons acquisition takes place. The primary core of the research material upon which it was based was a series of case histories of 12 major weapon systems. A very considerable amount of additional statistical and factual data gathered from both primary and secondary sources was also used. In the current volume by Professor Scherer, considerable reliance is placed upon this original research material. In addition, however, Professor Scherer has used a new body of material which has come into being since the field research on the Weapons Acquisition Research Project ceased in 1961. In particular, he has analyzed and appraised reports, information, and data stemming from the drive by the Department of Defense for incentive-type contracts and the more recent move by the Office of the Secretary of Defense to establish a system of contractor performance evaluation.

The publication of this volume comes at a time when the questions of incentives and of the relation between incentives on the one hand and controls on the other are particularly timely. Since Robert S. McNamara became Secretary of Defense in the winter of 1961, substantial changes have taken place in management and contractual devices used by the Department in dealing with weapons contractors. In part, these changes involve a growing use of incentive-type contracts, containing specific provisions designed to induce the contractor to control costs, to adhere to schedules, and to meet the technical performance specifications of the weapon system under his charge. Simultaneously, there has been a considerable growth in the number and detail of controls which are imposed by the government upon weapon system contractors and directed to the same three objectives. While the desirability of improved weapon system management as an objective, the need for which was partially documented in the Peck and Scherer volume, is generally not in dispute, the methods by which such improvements are to be achieved and the implementation of these methods have caused and are causing substantial controversy between the government, on the one hand, and industry, on the other. It is hoped that Professor Scherer's detailed discussion of both contractual and competitive incentives will not only add to the literature on the subject, but also contribute to a greater awareness and appreciation of the basic issues involved and the basic alternatives available.

Nevertheless, it should be pointed out here, as well as on the flyleaf, that certain of Professor Scherer's conclusions and recommendations are not in line with the views of various responsible Department of Defense officials. That the Department was, nonetheless, willing to "clear" the volume speaks well for their objective approach to the admittedly difficult problems of incentives.

In his preface, Professor Scherer felt impelled to express his personal doubts as to the morality of contemporary weapons developments and of his own participation in a project which seeks to improve the efficiency of the weapons acquisition process. Because of these expressed views, we must state that they are not those of the Dean of the School, the Director of Research, the Project Director, or, to the best of our knowledge, of any other member of the project staff. This does not mean that we do not deplore, equally with Professor Scherer, the underlying causes which currently necessitate an extensive arms program.

The views expressed by Professor Scherer may raise a question in the minds of some readers, whether they have colored or warped the analysis and conclusions of the text itself. This question has been carefully considered by us, and we believe that his analytical work has not been affected by his moral scruples. Like a skilled surgeon, he may loathe his patient, but he would never think of letting his knife slip on that account. While neither we nor other members of the Faculty agree with each and every conclusion and recommendation, we believe that his volume represents a highly competent and virtually unique analysis of economic incentives in weapons acquisition, is fully worthy of publication, and will serve a useful purpose.

While Professor Scherer has appropriately recorded in his preface the help and cooperation which he received in the preparation of this volume, we should like to indicate here our own thanks on behalf of the project and the Harvard Business School to the many industry and government officials who assisted at all stages of this work, and to the Ford Foundation for the financial support of the research project.

Paul W. Cherington
PROJECT DIRECTOR

Bertrand Fox
DIRECTOR OF RESEARCH

Soldiers Field
Boston, Massachusetts
December 1963

Preface

The publication of this volume terminates a long struggle with my conscience. It is difficult to write a book of this sort without suppressing doubts about the morality of contemporary weapons development and production efforts. But here I wish to articulate the reservations I tried to set aside while performing my job as analyst.

The indiscriminate slaughter of hundreds of millions of innocent persons through total nuclear (or chemical or bacteriological) war would clearly be wrong. In my mind, even resolving to wage total war under some set of conditions poses moral problems. Although I admit numerous doubts, I feel it may even be wrong to participate actively in the creation of improved instruments for waging total war. And my work on this volume certainly constituted participation, however indirect, in the creation of such instruments.

I am troubled more directly by a basic policy premise of this book: that efficiency is a desirable objective in the conduct of advanced weapons development and production programs. It is by no means certain that this is true. The weapons acquisition process may be too efficient already. To be sure, there are gross inefficiencies. But despite them, the process has given mankind all too much power for its own annihilation. One might justify efficiency measures in the hope that freed resources could be devoted to education, exploration of the universe, technical aid to emerging nations, urban redevelopment, etc. Given the pervasive pressures for added arms spending, however, it seems likely that efficiency gains would lead more to increases in our already formidable arsenal than to the reallocation of resources into applications yielding greater social benefit. An efficiency-induced increase in U.S. military strength would in turn, if recent history can be extrapolated, spur the Soviet bloc to intensified efforts in forging new and more powerful countervailing weapons. And I believe that continuation of this arms race will not reduce and probably will increase the already grave risk of nuclear war due to accident, escalation, miscalculation, or madness.

I recognize the existence of compelling arguments for maintaining a powerful military posture in this troubled world. From a short-run viewpoint I find myself agreeing frequently with the advocates of increased military strength. But when I worry about the long run, taking into account the inherently self-defeating dynamics of arms races, my conclusions tend to turn out rather differently. Increasing the efficiency of the weapons acquisition process certainly will not help and, by dulling our appreciation of the economic sacrifices weapons programs require, may well impair the development among decision makers and the average citizen of a more far-sighted perspective.

Why did I persevere in writing this volume despite my reservations? I am not proud of what seem to be my principal motives — intellectual fascination with a complex and challenging problem, the desire to be recognized for proposing an improved analysis of and solution to the problem, and the well-known need in academic circles to publish or perish. These are not uncommon motives in our society, and I believe they also play a role in the arms race. Much of the initial impetus for new weapons developments comes, I think, from the fascination of scientists, engineers, and military planners with the technical challenges posed by new weapons concepts; from the urge to triumph over nature in solving a difficult technical problem; and from the desire to be recognized by one's peers for achieving a successful solution. Stimuli of this sort have long been a driving force in the advance of science, both physical and social. But now, unfortunately, scientific advance seems to contribute more to our capabilities for destroying civilization than to building a better world. The scientist, by tradition reserving judgment on the moral implications of his work, will continue to publish, and perhaps we shall all perish.

Having eased my conscience if not my sense of guilt, let me turn now to the more important function of a preface: expressing my gratitude to the many good people who have advised and assisted me in my work.

I have drawn heavily from a series of weapon system and commercial system development program case histories prepared by members of the Harvard University Weapons Acquisition Research Project. Therefore, I am especially indebted to the many representatives of some 27 corporations and several government agencies who contributed the necessary documentary and interview material. Recognition is also due to my former colleagues Gerald Siegel, Charles Stein, Jr., and M. J. Peck, who shared with me responsibility for collecting the evidence and processing it into the written case studies. My good fortune in having quantitative data on an extensive sample of government contracts is partly the result of efforts by Martin Reinstein of the Office of the Secretary of Defense. Howard Raiffa and John Pratt offered valuable advice on some statistical problems.

In revising the manuscript I have benefited greatly from the comments of Richard Heflebower, M. J. Peck, David Novick, Bertrand Fox, Paul W. Cherington, Graeme C. Bannerman, Gerald Siegel, J. Sterling Livingston, Admiral J. B. Pearson, and William G. Bowen.

Mrs. Nina Dolben has been most helpful in locating hard-to-find information, proofreading the book at several stages in its evolution, and preparing the index. An early version of the manuscript was typed by Mrs. Virginia Pond, Miss Dorcas Holden, and Mrs. Mary Swanson. Mrs. Rochelle Meltz assisted in the final stages by reading page proof. As over-all editor of the volume, Miss Ruth Norton suffered through my last-minute changes and my statistical approach to typographical error control with remarkable restraint.

My deepest debt, however, is to my wife, who unselfishly accepted the annual extensions of what started out to be a one-year commitment into a five-year endurance test, and who encouraged me when the usual setbacks of authorship interacted with my moral reservations to make continued progress seem impossible.

Naturally, I alone accept responsibility for all deficiencies and errors of fact, analysis, and judgment.

F. M. SCHERER

Princeton, New Jersey
November 1963

Table of Contents

CHAPTER PAGE

1. INTRODUCTION 1
   Efficient and Optimal Program Conduct as a Policy Objective . . . The Mechanism of an Incentive System . . . Competitive and Contractual Incentives . . . Methods of Research . . . Organization of the Study

PART I. COMPETITIVE INCENTIVES

2. COMPETITION BETWEEN CLOSE SUBSTITUTE WEAPONS 19
   The Degree of Substitutability . . . Competition and Innovation . . . Competition and Competitive Optimism . . . Competition, Tradeoffs, and Efficiency . . . Competition and Talent Allocation Decisions . . . Competition and Morale . . . The Number of Competitors and the Effects of Competition . . . Conclusion

3. COMPETITION FOR BUDGETARY SUPPORT 51
   The Theory of Incentives from Budgetary Competition . . . The Effects of Budgetary Competition in the 1950's: *Budgetary Pressures and Tradeoff Decisions; Budgetary Pressures and Production Efficiency* . . . The Possibilities for Improved Budgetary Competition Incentives

4. COMPETITION FOR NEW PROGRAMS ON THE BASIS OF REPUTATION 68
   The Role of Past Performance in Selection Decisions: *Poor Performance and the Demise of Defense Contractors; Other Limitations in the Use of Performance Criteria; Contrasting*

Experience in Commercial Practice . . . Contractor Perception of the Consequences of Poor Performance . . . The Feasibility of Basing Program Awards on Past Performance: *Other Conflicts of Objectives; The Problem of Program Weighting; Can Contractor Performance Be Measured?; The Problem of Time, Quality, and Cost Weighting; The Intertwining of Contractor and Government Performance* . . . *Conclusion*

5. COMPETITIVE BIDDING FOR PRODUCTION CONTRACTS . 102

Breakout and Competitive Bidding: *The Effects of Breakout and Competitive Bidding; The Costs of Breakout and Competitive Bidding; Breakout and the Military R & D Base; Breakout, Proprietary Rights, and Bargaining Power; Summary* . . . Second Sourcing: *World War II Progress Curves Under Competition; The Costs of Second Sourcing* . . . Conclusion

PART II. CONTRACTUAL INCENTIVES

6. THE THEORY AND APPLICATION OF AUTOMATIC CONTRACTUAL INCENTIVES 131

The Variety of Contract Types: *The So-Called Incentive Contracts; Redeterminable Fixed-Price Contracts; Other Contract Types* . . . Extent of Use of the Various Contract Types . . . The Choice of a Contract Type: *Government Preferences; Contractor Preferences*

7. AUTOMATIC CONTRACTUAL INCENTIVES IN DEVELOPMENT PROGRAMS 153

Cost Reimbursement Contracts and Cost Overruns . . . Automatic Contractual Incentives and Tradeoff Decisions: *The Suboptimization Problem; Tradeoff Decisions Under Fixed-Price Contracts* . . . The Redundancy of Multidimensional Contractual Incentives: *Department of Defense Policy on Multidimensional Incentive Contracts, The Problems of Negotiating Multidimensional Incentive Contracts* . . . *Automatic Contractual Incentives and Efficiency: Limits on Contractual Incentives for Efficiency; Opportunity Cost and CPFF Incentives for Efficiency* . . . Conclusion

8. AUTOMATIC CONTRACTUAL INCENTIVES IN PRODUC-
TION PROGRAMS 191

The Financial Outcomes of Fixed-Price Type Contracts:
*The Distribution of Individual Cost Outcomes; The Rea-
sons for a Net Underrun Tendency: Some Hypotheses;
Quantitative Evidence on the Alternative Hypotheses* . . .
The Crucial Role of Bargaining: *Knowledge of Costs; Defi-
cient Accounting Systems; Contingency Factors; Analogous
Problems in the Soviet Union; The Government's Bargain-
ing Power; Tightness of Cost Targets and the Choice of a
Contract Type; Further Evidence on the Negotiation of
Sharing Provisions* . . . The Importance of Tight Cost
Targets: *The Reward and Pressure Theories; Evidence from
the Case Studies* . . . Contractual Incentives and Quality
Tradeoffs . . . Contractual Incentives and Efficiency . . .
Diminishing Marginal Utility of Profit . . . The Impact of
Renegotiation: *Renegotiation and Incentives for Efficiency;
The Incremental Nature of Incentive Profits; Cost Padding
and Inefficiency; Case Study Evidence on Renegotiation's
Effects* . . . Automatic Contractual Incentives for Sta-
bilized Production . . . Conclusion

9. VARIATIONS IN NEGOTIATED PROFIT RATES AS AN IN-
CENTIVE APPROACH 271

Actual Profit Rate Variations and Their Causes: *Pricing
Risk; Contractor Investment; Extent of Subcontracting;
Contractor Bargaining Power; The Nature of the Work Performed; Interservice Profit Rate Differences; Past Contractor Performance* . . . The Feasibility of a Negotiated
Profit Rate Incentive System: *Consistent Performance
Evaluations; The Multidimensionality of Performance; Performance Correlations vs. Other Reasons for Profit Rate
Variation; The Extent of Performance-Correlated Variations
and Contractor Behavior; Bargaining and Entry-Exit Considerations* . . . Conclusion

10. OTHER CONTRACTUAL INCENTIVES 300

Paying No Profit on Development Contracts: *Effects on
Contractor Behavior; Effects on Entry and Exit; Conclusion*
. . . Some Special Contractual Incentives

PART III.   INCENTIVES AND GOVERNMENT POLICY

11. EXISTING INCENTIVE SYSTEMS: SUMMARY AND BAL-
     ANCED APPRAISAL 313
     Competitive Incentives and Efficiency . . . Contractual
     Incentives and Efficiency . . . The Balance Problem in
     Multidimensional Incentive Contracting

12. AFTER-THE-FACT EVALUATION: A NEW INCENTIVE
     APPROACH 327
     Evaluating Contractor Performance . . . The Use of
     After-the-Fact Evaluation in Profit Determination: *Over-All
     Performance vs. Efficiency; The Distribution of Profit
     Awards; Application to Production Contract Profit Deter-
     mination; Exemption from Renegotiation; Summary* . . .
     The Use of After-the-Fact Evaluation in Sales Determina-
     tion: *Performance Evaluations as a Basis for Source Selec-
     tion; A Level-of-Effort Incentive System; Performance
     Index Problems; Summary* . . . Publication of Program
     Evaluation Board Rankings . . . Advantages of the After-
     the-Fact Evaluation Approach . . . Objections to the Pro-
     posal: A Critical Appraisal: *Socialism and Unilateralism;
     The Responsibility Issue; The Problem of Objectives; The
     Performance Evaluation Problem* . . . The Program Eval-
     uation Board's Membership . . . Conclusion

13. ALTERNATIVE POLICIES FOR IMPROVED INCENTIVES .. 363
     Improved Automatic Contractual Incentives: *Production
     Contract Incentives; The Problem of Renegotiation* . . .
     Negotiated Profit Rate Incentives . . . Past Performance
     as a Source Selection Criterion . . . Competition Between
     Close Substitutes

14. ALTERNATIVES TO THE INCENTIVES APPROACH 372
     Incentives vs. Controls: *The Government's Specific Roles
     in Program Management; Controls, Initiative, and Respon-
     sibility; Technical Administration and Controls; Conclusion*
     . . . The Arsenal System of Weapons Development: *The
     Production Motive and Innovation; The Development-Pro-
     duction Transition Problem; The Personnel Problem of
     Government Laboratories; Conclusion*

15. CONCLUSION 400

APPENDIX TO CHAPTER 7. A STOCHASTIC USER COST
MODEL 407

APPENDIX TO CHAPTER 8. THE OPTIMAL CHOICE OF A
SHARING PROPORTION 412
The Contractor's Profit Maximization Problem . . . Government Outlay Minimization and Conflicts of Interest

SELECTED BIBLIOGRAPHY 433

INDEX 439

List of Tables

TABLE NO.   PAGE

3.1   U.S. Weapons and Space Development and Procurement Expenditures: 1953–1963   57

3.2   The Level of Aircraft, Aircraft Engines, and Parts Industry Activity: 1952–1962   58

4.1   Summary of Correlations: Contractor Performance Scaling Factors as Dependent Variables and Selected Independent Variables   96

5.1   Progress Curve Data on 5 World War II Aircraft Programs with Second Sourcing Competition . .   120–121

6.1   Classification of Price and Profit Changes in the Redetermination of 207 Army and Navy Contracts   139

6.2   Proportion of Military Procurement Dollars Obligated by Contract Types, Three Services; Fiscal Years 1951–1962   143

6.3   Proportion of Military Procurement Dollars Obligated, by Service and Contract Type, Fiscal Year 1960   144

6.4   Proportion of Military Procurement Dollars Obligated, by Contract Type and Procurement Category, Fiscal Year 1960   148

7.1   The Relationship Between Opportunity Cost and Efficiency in 10 Weapon System Development Programs   187

8.1   Cost Outcomes of 699 Weapons Procurement Contracts   192–193

8.2 Summary of Tests for Normality on Six Distributions of Fixed-Price Type Contract Outcomes .. 195

8.3 Sales, Profit, and Refund Statistics of Renegotiation: 1956–1962 264

8A.1 Government and Contractor Optima under Diverse Assumptions 428

List of Figures

NUMBER   PAGE

8.1   Distribution of Cost Outcomes on 161 Air Force and
      Navy Fixed-Price Incentive Contracts Settled Be-
      tween July 1959 and December 1961 196

8.2   Distribution of Cost Outcomes on 47 Air Force
      Fixed-Price Incentive Contracts with Initially Firm
      Targets Settled Between January 1957 and June
      1959 197

8.3   Distribution of Cost Outcomes on 47 Navy Fixed-
      Price Incentive Contracts Settled Between January
      1957 and December 1959 198

8.4   Distribution of Cost Outcomes on 51 Air Force
      Fixed-Price Incentive Contracts with Delayed Firm
      Targets Settled Between January 1957 and June
      1959 199

8.5   Distribution of Price Outcomes on 156 Army Re-
      determinable Fixed-Price Contracts Redetermined
      During Fiscal Year 1959 200

8.6   Distribution of Price Outcomes on 66 Navy Flexible
      and Maximum Fixed-Price Contracts Redetermined
      During Fiscal Years 1958 and 1959 201

8.7   a. Seventy Percent Efficiency. b. Eighty Percent Effi-
      ciency 233

8.8   Illustrations of Cost Reduction Equilibria 244

8.9   Profit Rates Realized as a Percentage of Actual Cost
      on 47 Navy Aircraft and Guided Missile Fixed-Price
      Incentive Contracts 248

8.10 Profit Rates Realized as a Percentage of Target Cost
      on 47 Navy Aircraft and Guided Missile Fixed-Price
      Incentive Contracts 250

8.11 Cost Reduction Equilibria Under Firm Fixed-Price and Fixed-Price Incentive Contracts 267

9.1 Originally Negotiated Profit Rates on CPFF and CPIF Contracts Held by 22 Major Air Force Contractors and 38 Small Business Concerns in 1957 and 1958 . 275

9.2 Originally Negotiated Profit Rates on 47 Navy Aircraft and Guided Missile Fixed-Price Incentive Contracts 276

9.3 Originally Negotiated Profit Rates on 63 Navy Redeterminable Fixed-Price Contracts With Domestic Firms 277

9.4 Originally Negotiated Profit Rates on 156 Army Ordnance and Signal Corps Redeterminable Fixed-Price Contracts 278

7A.1 Possible Configurations of the $f_t(\triangle C_1)$ Function ... 408

7A.2 The $f_t(\triangle C_1)$ Function with Confidence Bands 410

8A.1 Graph of $U = .2X + .04X^2$ 415

8A.2 Graph of $U = 1.10X + .05X^2$ 418

8A.3 Graph of $U = .2X - .04X^2$ 420

8A.4 Government and Contractor Optimal α as a Function of b 429

CHAPTER 1

Introduction

THE UNITED STATES armed services obtain most of their advanced weapons — in 1962 roughly $16 billion worth of manned bombers and fighters, guided missile systems, reconnaissance satellites, radar and communications systems, and the like — from private industrial contractors. Contracting for conventional ordnance items such as clothing, trucks, and filing cabinets, through advertised competitive bidding has a time-honored place in the activities of government. But the acquisition of advanced weapons poses distinctive problems which lead to buyer-seller relationships quite unlike those associated with the traditional competitive bidding situation.

The weapons acquisition process is defined here to include the conception, development, and early production of technically advanced weapon systems and subsystems. Development activities in particular encounter uncertainties and risks unique in magnitude. Development cost predictions made in the face of uncertainty are susceptible to gross errors; for example, the average development cost prediction error in a sample of 12 U.S. weapons programs was 220%, with a standard deviation of 170%.[1] At the same time, individual research and development programs often assume a gigantic scale. The least costly of the 12 programs had development outlays of $60 million; the median cost was about $400 million; and three of the efforts cost more than $1 billion each. Program size and uncertainty interact in weapons acquisition to compel the shifting of financial risks from contractors to the government through such devices as the cost reimbursement contract.

An additional complication is the fact that once a weapons program is under way, the contractor accumulates specialized experience and physical assets to a degree severely restricting the gov-

[1] Merton J. Peck and Frederic M. Scherer, *The Weapons Acquisition Process: An Economic Analysis* (Boston: Division of Research, Harvard Business School, 1962), pp. 16–45. Cited hereafter as Peck and Scherer. The sample of programs will be discussed in greater detail later.

1

ernment's ability to bring in an alternate contractor. Buyer and seller are locked together in a relationship analogous to bilateral monopoly for the life of the program, and they must deal with each other on a bargaining basis.

These attributes of weapons acquisition preclude reliance on anything like a conventional market system for the procurement of advanced weapons, evoking instead what is best described as a nonmarket, quasi-administrative buyer-seller relationship. In this nonmarket environment the automatic guides and restraints provided by the market's "invisible hand" are absent. To replace them the government must deliberately structure its relations with contractors in such a way as to assure successful weapons program execution.

It has two main ways of doing this. One is through controls — direct participation in the contractor's internal operations through technical and financial administration and decision making. The weapons acquisition process is perhaps unparalleled among U.S. economic activities in the extent to which the buyer intervenes in seller operations. The other way is the incentives approach — harmonizing government and contractor objectives by the rewarding of desirable performance and penalizing of unsatisfactory performance. A properly functioning market system tends automatically to reward good performance and punish poor performance, and in private enterprise economies the incentives approach is the accepted method by which consumer sovereignty is enforced. But the nonmarket environment of weapons acquisition calls for special incentive mechanisms, usually simulating administratively or through bargaining the incentives generated automatically by an impersonal market mechanism.

This volume is concerned almost exclusively with the use of the incentives approach to elicit desirable contractor performance in weapons development and production programs. The controls approach will be examined only briefly as a digression in Chapter 14.

EFFICIENT AND OPTIMAL PROGRAM CONDUCT AS A POLICY OBJECTIVE

Of what does "desirable contractor performance" consist? Two broad objectives will be emphasized in this volume. Contractor performance should be efficient, and it should be optimal. These terms are employed in an unconventional sense, so a word of explanation is in order.

In economic analysis it is customary to use the terms "efficient" and "optimal" synonymously. Here, however, it is convenient to draw a distinction, letting "efficiency" take on a narrower meaning. An efficient program is one which accomplishes a given result — e.g., developing a weapon system with certain qualitative features for operational availability at some particular date — with the minimum possible expenditure of resources, viewed in an *ex ante* and relative sense. The *ex ante* orientation of this efficiency concept deserves special stress. After a research and development effort is completed, one can usually look back and identify many resource-saving opportunities that might have been exploited, had they been foreseen. But technological and strategic uncertainties frequently obscure these opportunities before the fact. The definition of efficiency employed here presupposes not perfect foresight, but only that level of foresight which competent managers, scientists, and engineers can attain in the face of uncertainty. A relativistic notion of efficiency is adopted because it is empirically unrealistic to expect complex organizations made up of fallible human beings to operate continuously at a 100% efficiency level. Rather, we must judge efficiency against the level which capable firms can sustain in actual practice.

The performance problem embraces much more, however, than simply accomplishing certain results at minimum cost. Decisions must also be made on the results to be accomplished. Performance in a weapons program is multidimensional. In the simplest conception, it involves three dimensions: quality, time of availability, and cost. Quality can in turn be subdivided almost indefinitely to measure a weapon system's technical performance in terms of speed, range, accuracy, destructive force, maneuverability, reaction time, and so on; together with its reliability, that is, the probability that the system will in fact sustain its technical performance potential in combat.

Maximizing quality is a desirable objective in weapons development. Differences in the technical performance and reliability of weapons have had a significant role in determining the outcomes of countless military engagements. A small margin of quality could make the difference between success and failure on a combat mission. Minimizing development time is also desirable. The nation which first fields an important new improvement in weapons technology may gain a decisive military advantage, while a weapon system which is available too late will be obsolescent, unable to cope effectively with advanced enemy threats. Finally, minimizing cost is a worthwhile objective. Money costs reflect the scarcity of real resources, and especially of talented engineers and scientists, competent managers, and skilled production workers. Given this scarcity, the uneconomic use of resources in one weapons program deprives other military programs of the resources they require. Or it prevents the satisfaction of nondefense wants in such fields as education, space exploration, and technical aid to emerging nations.

It is generally impossible to move out on any one of these various performance dimensions without encountering conflicts with the other dimensions. One cannot maximize or minimize on every dimension; something must be sacrificed in exchange. Given the state of the scientific and technical art existing at some moment in time, enhancing quality usually requires a longer development time span, or incurring additional resource costs, or both.[2] At a constant level of quality and efficiency, a reduction in development time can be accomplished only by accepting an increase in development cost.[3] A sacrifice on one dimension to secure gains on another dimension is called a tradeoff. Optimal conduct of a weapons program requires striking tradeoffs which tend *ex ante* to maximize the military value attainable with a given over-all defense budget and a given set of time-quality-cost possibilities.[4] Efficiency, on the other hand, is defined here more narrowly to mean achieving any time-quality result — whether it be optimal or not — with the minimum possible expenditure of resources.[5]

[2] *Ibid.*, pp. 266–268 and 467–472.
[3] *Ibid.*, pp. 254–266.
[4] *Ibid.*, pp. 269–285 and 286–287. In practice this is an extremely difficult concept to apply due to fundamental problems in the definition and measurement of military value. At best, only rough approximations can be expected.
[5] *Ibid.*, pp. 255–256 and 509–512. Usually economists assume away the efficiency problem defined here by assuming that all rational producers operate on the so-called production frontier. But we will find that weapons

This volume proceeds from an assumption that in general the U.S. weapons acquisition process has not been conducted as efficiently and optimally as one might reasonably expect. The first volume of this study concluded that weapons program costs have been unnecessarily high because of the inefficient utilization of technical, administrative, and production manpower. Excessive costs have also been due to nonoptimal tradeoff decisions — that is, to the development of qualitative features and increments of technical performance whose cost exceeded their military value.[6]

The inefficiencies and nonoptimal tradeoff decisions observed in weapons acquisition are not attributable entirely to faulty or deficient incentives. Decisions, actions, and inactions of the government as buyer of weapons underlie many problems. The analysis here, however, is primarily concerned with the contractor's active role in weapons development and production. Contractors are responsible, either through direct delegation or by joint participation with government procurement agencies, for the thousands of major and minor tradeoff decisions made during a weapons program. They have direct responsibility for the efficient or inefficient utilization of their human and physical resources. Not all contractor shortcomings are due to ineffective incentive systems, but as we shall discover, many inefficiencies can be traced directly to incentive problems.

The task of this volume therefore is to isolate the conditions under which existing incentives have failed to encourage efficient and optimal performance by contractors and to explore the opportunities for creating a more effective system of incentives.

THE MECHANISM OF AN INCENTIVE SYSTEM

Given this frame of reference, let us establish more precisely what is meant by an incentive and how incentive systems operate. It is not unusual for incentives to be discussed as rewards which one deserves in equity or as "nice to receive" windfalls. Such usages are erroneous. The correct definition of an incentive is "that which incites, or tends to incite, to determination or action." [7]

---

makers do not operate on the frontier, and therefore a more limited concept of efficiency is useful.

[6] *Ibid.,* pp. 593–594.

[7] *Webster's New International Dictionary* (2nd edition).

The notion of inciting to action is crucial; a reward (or penalty) which has no action connection is not an incentive.

Rewards and penalties become incentives when they are correlated in the expectations of individuals or organizations with certain actions or levels of action. Thus, an incentive for efficient performance (the action) exists when weapons makers expect that efficient performance will be rewarded more than inefficient performance, or that inefficient performance will be penalized more than efficient. To have any behavioral effect the reward/penalty correlation with performance must be expected rather than already attained. The carrot provides an incentive only when it is in front of the horse. Once he has it in his mouth, it no longer lures him on; it must be replaced by another if the horse is to go further. The essence therefore of an incentive system is the expectation by potential actors of a correlation between the effectiveness of their actions and the existence or size of future rewards or penalties.

The subjective actor-oriented nature of this correlation cannot be overemphasized. Whether the person or organization doling out rewards and penalties perceives a correlation with performance is essentially irrelevant. A government agency can profess that it will reward contractors who perform efficiently and penalize those who perform inefficiently, but if the contractors do not believe it, the agency's expectation will have created no incentive for efficiency. It is therefore necessary that actors be convinced of a future correlation between their acts and the rewards/penalties they receive.

In one respect only are past rewards and penalties relevant to inciting good current performance: if government agencies have in the past consistently rewarded good performance and penalized poor performance, defense contractors have a historical basis for expecting a similar correlation in the future. In general, the more consistent the past correlation has been, the stronger will be the expectation that future rewards depend upon the efficacy of current performance. Consequently, consistent correlation of rewards/penalties with performance is important to the effective operation of an incentive system — a point to be stressed repeatedly in subsequent chapters.

What are the rewards and penalties through which an incentive system operates? Obviously, a reward can be the attainment of anything desired by the contractor. Penalties are administered by withholding what contractors desire or imposing upon them anything they dislike. What is desired or disliked in this context depends upon the goals held collectively or individually by the persons comprising a contractor organization. Firms bring many different goals into their weapons development and production efforts.[8] Any listing must include at least the following:

Maximization of profits
Organizational survival
Growth of sales and employment
Security of employment, sales, and profits
Freedom from harassment
The desire for public approbation
The desire to contribute usefully to the national defense
The desire to advance science and technology

Some of these goals may be identical or reinforce one another, one serving as a useful proxy for the other; e.g. (as I shall argue shortly), organizational survival, growth, and long-run profit maximization. Others may conflict with one another; e.g., growth and security, or (in certain situations) profit maximization and public approbation. When conflicts do arise, the relative strength of the goals will be an important determinant of the firm's behavior.

Similarly, some goals are held collectively by the individuals comprising a firm, and thus can appropriately be called organizational goals. Others may be important only to certain individuals who do not necessarily correspond to the usual conception of the entrepreneur or top manager, but who are nevertheless able to influence the firm's decisions and actions. The general approach here will be to emphasize organizational goals, or at least those goals pursued by the management of defense contracting organizations. This approach implicitly assumes that if corporate management is strongly motivated to perform well, it will in turn effectively trans-

[8] For a classical discussion of the multiplicity of company goals, see Alfred Marshall, *Principles of Economics* (8th ed., 1920), Appendix D. For a survey of the more recent literature, see A. G. Papandreou, "Some Basic Problems in the Theory of the Firm," in B. F. Haley (ed.), *A Survey of Contemporary Economics*, Vol. II (Homewood: American Economic Association, 1952), especially pp. 205–213.

mit its motivation down through the organization to members who may possess different goal structures. Such an assumption clearly fails to reflect all the complexities of actual organizational behavior, and it will be necessary on occasion to point out cases in which it breaks down badly. Still no better framework for analyzing the operation of economic processes and relationships is available, and the assumption that effective incentives work their way through the organization is undoubtedly a tolerable, even though imperfect, approximation to reality.

This limitation should warn us, however, not to expect too much from the incentives approach. A perfect incentive system by no means guarantees perfect economic performance. A highly motivated organization can produce unsatisfactory results because its technical choices made in the face of uncertainty prove faulty. Likewise, it could fail because its production staff lacks the craftsman's pride so important to high quality workmanship; because its technical people are inexperienced or incompetent; or because its managers do not know how to organize, inspire, and bring out the best in their subordinates. Incentives can, of course, spur organizations to build up their competence through education and training, to promote able new people, and to weed out incompetents. But such changes are accomplished only gradually. And within the defense industry as a whole there is only a limited quantity of first-rate talent; so some groups simply must make do with less than the best.

A system of economic rewards and penalties can also work in another way to correct talent deficiencies within a single sector of the economy such as the defense industry. It may force the exit of those firms which cannot perform well and attract the entry of new, potentially better performers. The problem of motivating entry and exit is nevertheless neglected for two principal reasons. First, specialization of skills, experience, and capital equipment impedes the flow of resources from one field into another, stretching into years the time required to accomplish perceptible changes in defense industry capabilities. Second, the incentives for entry and exit affecting the U.S. weapons industry have been examined at some length in the first volume of this study, and further discussion would be largely redundant.[9] Therefore, this volume focuses

9 Peck and Scherer, pp. 190–221.

petition at the feasibility study and preliminary design stages of a program encourages innovation, besides giving the government a variety of alternatives from which to choose. But the uncertainties associated with a technically ambitious set of military requirements may be so great that government decision makers cannot select the best or near-best technical proposal with any degree of confidence. Further work on computer simulation, breadboard models, and actual prototypes — seldom a part of the technical effort going into management and sometimes even full-blown design competitions — is often needed before these uncertainties are dispelled. And when technical judgments can be made with confidence, it is generally possible to correct the problems in a deficient proposal, as the Air Force and Navy did with General Dynamics' proposal in the TFX competition.[38] The milieu of government technical proposal competitions may also encourage emphasis on trivial but appealing design details (i.e., furnishing detailed layouts of the missile system launch officer's control console) rather than sound engineering analysis and projection. For these reasons technical proposal competitions may yield rather meager statistical benefits; that is, they do not significantly reduce the risk of commitment to an inferior technical approach. As indicated earlier, they also encourage excessively optimistic quality, time, and cost promises. And since innovation can be encouraged in other ways — e.g., by the need to leapfrog competing programs already in development — the incremental behavioral benefits of technical proposal competitions tend to be modest.

Thus, it is not at all certain that the benefits of design and technical proposal competitions outweigh their costs in terms of scarce technical talent and misinformation. A method of selecting development program contractors is needed which provides incentives for innovation and good performance while discouraging undue optimism and minimizing the demands on creative scientific and engineering talent. This problem will be considered further in later chapters.

Once a development program is under way, the appearance of competition usually encourages company management to strengthen the project's manning, if doing so will counteract the competitive

[38] Cf. George C. Wilson, "TFX Board Selected Boeing Four Times," *Aviation Week & Space Technology,* March 4, 1963, pp. 22–24.

threat. For example, when the prime contractor in one program threatened the subcontractor for an important component with contract cancellation and possible "blacklisting" unless its performance improved, the component maker increased its development team from 8 to 18 engineers and shifted to a 54-hour week, all without receiving additional profit on its contract. Similarly, Robert Schlaifer reports that when a competitor challenged Stromberg's dominant position in the aircraft carburetor field, not only was a new technical approach explored,[39] but the company also doubled the size of its development team.[40] Competition also incited enhanced project manning, both qualitatively and quantitatively, in other weapon system and subsystem development efforts and in three commercial product development efforts covered by our case studies.

COMPETITION AND MORALE

Competition is generally assumed to spur the members of an organization to more vigorous efforts. As Hitch and McKean have observed, ". . . there is nothing as stimulating to most people and organizations engaged in research and development as the fear that another company or laboratory will beat it to the objective." [41] However, there is reason to believe the relationship between competition and morale is not quite so simple.

One of the best documented competitions between close substitute weapon systems took place between the Air Force Thor and the Army Jupiter IRBM's from 1956 through 1958. Although interservice rivalry complicated the normal rivalry between development groups, evidence of the Thor-Jupiter competition's effects on morale is nevertheless of interest. About this competition Air Force General Clarence S. Irvine said:

> I think there is nothing healthier for this country than interservice rivalry, so-called. I would say if anything helped the Air Force to work like hell on the Thor it is the fact we knew the Army was clawing at our backs.[42]

[39] Cf. page 24 *supra*.

[40] *Development of Aircraft Engines,* pp. 101, 522, and 543.

[41] *The Economics of Defense in the Nuclear Age,* p. 250.

[42] House, Committee on Government Operations, *Eleventh Report, Organization and Management of Missile Programs* (1959), p. 101.

Similarly, former Secretary of Defense Neil H. McElroy observed:

> I think you could really make a case that the interservice rivalry has speeded up the development of the two, because, as you well know in our competitive economy, a competitive spirit, if it does not run amuck, does something to stimulate people to strive toward a result more than if they do not have that competitive spirit driving them.[43]

General John B. Medaris, chief of the Army's Jupiter development organization, agreed that the sense of urgency created by the Thor-Jupiter competition probably accelerated the development effort.[44] However, he commented further that:

> The primary bottleneck throughout the entire Jupiter program can hardly be called a bottleneck. It is more in the nature of an impediment, it has been that of uncertainty, it has been the fact that the program was under constant examination for possible cancellation. We had lifetimes given to us that varied from 5 months at the beginning to as low as 45 days that we were looking forward to as the lifetime of the project possibly, and this has a very profound psychological effect naturally.[45]

Thus, fear of imminent cancellation seemed to be a psychological impediment in the conduct of the Jupiter program.

Only one of our case studies provided sufficient evidence to explore this question in greater depth. In that program, as in the Thor-Jupiter case, there was a substantial possibility of cancellation because of competition from a close substitute weapon system. Interviews with a number of operating level scientists and engineers working on the challenged program revealed a general reduction of morale as a result of the competition. Some said that the competition led them to doubt whether their work was important or appreciated. Others simply blamed the competitive threat on political influences within the sponsoring service. It was not possible to determine whether this attitude in fact impaired the work of the project group members, but it would not be unreasonable to infer

[43] Senate, Committee on Armed Services, Preparedness Investigating Subcommittee, *Hearings, Inquiry Into Satellite and Missile Programs* (1958), p. 223.

[44] *Ibid.*, p. 572.

[45] *Ibid.*, p. 550. See also John B. Medaris, *Countdown for Decision* (New York: Putnam, 1960), pp. 125, 150, and 178–179.

that it did. Management of the company, on the other hand, seemed much less depressed by the competitive situation and appeared to be exerting every possible effort toward winning the struggle.

One cannot, of course, generalize conclusively from a single case study. Still certain speculative hypotheses appear in order. First, the threat of cancellation in a heated competition may tend to hurt the morale of technical personnel deeply involved in a development project, dampening their enthusiasm and degrading their performance. Second, the principal stimulating effects of competition take place at the project management level, where decisions to reallocate technical resources and modify technical approaches can be taken. Third, the process of management selection tends to screen out those scientists and engineers who react to competition by becoming discouraged. Or alternatively, when a professional person assumes a position in management, he acquires a new point of view and is likely to become less deeply involved psychologically in the projects he manages.

In any event, we cannot simply assume that the effects of competition on organizational morale will all be positive. It is possible that negative effects appear at the operating levels of technical groups. This is a problem deserving further research by sociologists and psychologists.

THE NUMBER OF COMPETITORS AND THE EFFECTS OF COMPETITION

Much of the general theoretical literature in economics emphasizes, as a kind of social optimum, that competition which is characterized by large numbers of competitors. Yet at the weapon systems level the number of development programs under way at any one time which are direct substitutes for one another can usually be counted on one hand, often leaving a couple of fingers to spare. Does this mean that competition in weapons development is less effective than in the economist's "purely" competitive model? And would increasing the number of competing programs increase the effectiveness of competition?

The case for large numbers in economic theory rests largely on three propositions. (1) Assuming *inter alia* that production decisions are made with the goal of maximizing profits given only a

Jupiter intermediate range ballistic missile system (Army)
Nike Ajax surface-to-air guided missile system (Army)
Nike Hercules surface-to-air guided missile system (Army)
Bomarc surface-to-air guided missile system (Air Force)
Talos surface-to-air guided missile system (Navy)
Sparrow III air-to-air guided missile system (Navy)
Nike Zeus ballistic missile defense system (Army)

The commercial product development programs were:

Indian Point atomic power reactor (Consolidated Edison Corporation)
TD–2 microwave radio relay system (A.T. & T.)
TH microwave radio relay system (A.T. & T.)
Van de Graaff tandem particle accelerator (High Voltage Engineering Corporation)
Chemical process plant (Blaw-Knox Corporation)
A family of motor vehicles
An earth-moving vehicle

The case studies explored in some detail the decisions, problems, contractual and competitive environment, institutional arrangements, and outcomes of these 19 programs. They were compiled by examining program records, schedules, and correspondence and by interviewing personnel at several levels of the participating organizations (including both government and contractor groups for the weapons programs).

The weapons case histories include national security classified data, and all contain information proprietary to the organizations involved. To avoid compromising this information, most of the direct references to case study evidence in this volume will be made without naming the specific program and without describing the situation in its full technical and institutional context. This is an unfortunate but necessary expedient.[15]

Certain other limitations in the case study evidence deserve mention. For one, our case study research focused on weapon systems and subsystems development. Little or no attention was paid to independent basic and applied research work and to the development of new elemental components. Therefore, this volume

---

[15] It is anticipated that nonclassified versions of two weapons case studies and two commercial product development studies will be published.

can say little about these latter activities, which play a key role in the process of technological advance by supplying most of the material and conceptual advances exploited in systems development.

Nearly all of the case study and other field research underlying this study was conducted during the late 1950's. Since then many changes have been made in Department of Defense weapons acquisition policies and practices, and in June of 1963, when final substantive revisions to this volume were completed, more changes — especially in the incentives area — were in process. Where appropriate, these changes have been described and analyzed on the basis of published information. But relying upon press releases, trade journal reports, and testimony before Congressional Committees is a poor substitute for careful empirical research. Public statements may convey a false air of finality with respect to plans which have been worked out only tentatively. Describing some of the new policy trends has been like shooting at a rapidly and erratically moving target. And most important, our case study research demonstrated vividly that there is often an enormous disparity between what one reads in public documents (or even what one hears directly from top-ranking government officials) and what is in fact happening at the operating levels of government and contractor organizations. The picture of post-1960 policy developments is therefore incomplete and perhaps inaccurate in points of detail. Still the primary thrust of this volume is analytical rather than descriptive, and the fundamental incentive problems of advanced weapons development have been present in more or less recognizable form for at least two decades. Consequently, case studies of experience during the 1950's undoubtedly retain considerable value for predicting the effects of policies — actual or proposed — of the 1960's.

Naturally, it would be advantageous if careful case studies could have been executed to assess empirically the effects of the most recent policy developments. But this was precluded by inevitable limitations of time and manpower.

ORGANIZATION OF THE STUDY

Parts I and II of this volume are primarily analytical and predictive in orientation. Using the case studies and other material as data, they attempt to identify how various types of incentives have affected contractor behavior in diverse actual program circumstances and to predict the changes in behavior which would result from qualitative and quantitative modifications of existing incentive systems. Chapters 2 through 5 cover four general types of competitive incentives: competition between close substitute weapons, competition for budgetary support, competition for new programs on the basis of reputation, and competitive bidding for production contracts. Chapters 6 through 10 deal with a variety of contractual incentives.

In Part III the emphasis shifts to problems of public policy. Chapter 11 provides an integrated summary of the analytical findings. In Chapters 12 and 13 the most fruitful opportunities for improved incentive policies are explored. Chapter 14 is a digression, considering ways other than the incentives approach for modifying or avoiding the tendencies toward nonoptimal performance found in a contracting system of weapons development. Chapter 15 contains concluding observations on the study's policy implications.

PART I

COMPETITIVE INCENTIVES

CHAPTER 2

Competition Between Close Substitute Weapons

NO WEAPON SYSTEM is immune to the perennial gale of competition from potentially superior technical substitutes. If such a thing were possible, we would still be settling our disputes with clubs, spears fashioned out of bronze, or muzzle loading rifles. Perhaps mankind would be better off in such a case, but the competition of new technical ideas is a fact of our existence.

From the standpoint of weapons program execution, this competition between substitutes affords the government two main benefits, which will be called the statistical benefits and the behavioral benefits. As indicated in Chapter 1, uncertainty is a constant companion to weapons development programs. Predictions of end-product technical performance, time of availability, cost, and military value are subject to substantial errors, especially early in a new program. Therefore, at the outset of a development effort it is often difficult or impossible to choose with any degree of certainty the best of several technical alternatives — "best" being defined in terms of whatever program parameters, such as development time or end-product quality, are considered crucial. By sponsoring the more or less concurrent development of two or more competing weapon systems or key subsystems which represent potential substitutes for filling a presumed military need, the government can hedge against these uncertainties, reducing the risk of being committed to an unsatisfactory approach and increasing the probability of obtaining an acceptable end product. The increased probability of success gained through this type of hedging — that is, the increase in the expected value of weapon system quality or the decrease in the expected value of development time

19

— represents what will be called the statistical benefits of competition.[1]

Statistical benefits would be realized even if the government were to establish parallel projects whose participants were utterly unaware of each other's existence. However, when the groups are aware of their mutual rivalry — when they recognize that only one may be rewarded with further development and/or production contracts — their behavior may change in a variety of ways. These changes are called the behavioral effects (and to the extent that they are favorable, the behavioral benefits) of competition.

This important distinction is not always recognized or drawn clearly in the literature. In their authoritative study Hitch and McKean do distinguish between "duplication" (defined as the pursuit of several routes in a development effort, and thus identical with the definition of statistical benefits used here) and "competition" (which is said to provide a spur to the people and organizations engaged in research and development, and thus implies the concept of behavioral benefits employed here).[2] However, the empirical examples they cite to illustrate the benefits of "competition" — the tendency of one service to correct the mistakes or omissions of the other in aircraft engine development, and the difficulty of picking technical "winners" on the basis of preliminary

---

[1] For a more rigorous analysis, see Peck and Scherer, pp. 261–263 and 488–492. See also Richard R. Nelson, "Uncertainty, Learning, and the Economics of Parallel Research and Development Efforts," *Review of Economics and Statistics,* November 1961, pp. 351–364. However, Nelson's paper is limited almost exclusively to a special and probably unimportant case: carrying forward parallel development efforts to minimize development cost, given some technical objective. As he admits (p. 361), when minimizing development cost is a dominant objective, it can usually be satisfied best by resolving the technical uncertainties step by step through inexpensive applied research before beginning a full-scale development effort. The argument for parallel developments is much stronger (that is, the statistical benefits are much greater) when the government is anxious to minimize development time while accomplishing significant technical advances in the face of uncertainty. But rigorous treatment of this case seems to require very difficult quantitative assumptions about the military value of time increments.

[2] Charles J. Hitch and Roland N. McKean, *The Economics of Defense in the Nuclear Age* (Cambridge: Harvard University Press, 1960), pp. 249–251.

designs — actually reflect the risk-reducing benefits of "duplication," as they use the term.

Isolating competition's behavioral effects usually requires more information than is generally made public by research and development organizations, and this may explain their neglect in the literature. But our 12 weapons program case studies provided considerable qualitative, even if not quantitative, insight. Since our main interest in this volume is the impact of incentives on contractor behavior and since the statistical benefits of competition have been explored elsewhere, emphasis in the following pages will fall on competition's behavioral benefits.

THE DEGREE OF SUBSTITUTABILITY

An important consideration in this analysis is the immediacy and closeness of competition, and especially, the extent to which one firm perceives another firm's product as a direct threat to the sales of its own product. There is no universally valid definition which permits us to distinguish competitive situations from noncompetitive ones, just as in an antitrust proceeding there can be no unambiguous delineation of the relevant "market." This chapter considers the competition between weapon systems or subsystems which are reasonably close substitutes, both technically and operationally, for the performance of a military mission. "Reasonably close substitutes" is defined arbitrarily to include, for example, competition between two or more manned strategic bombers or between different long-range ballistic missiles in either the same or different generations, but not the competition between a manned bomber and an ICBM. Cases of the latter type involving less direct substitution will be included in the next chapter.

Even under this very restrictive definition of "reasonably close substitutes," we find that the weapons acquisition process of the 1950's and 1960's has been generally quite competitive. All of the 12 weapon system programs covered by our case studies were challenged during their development and early production phases by other programs seeking to accomplish the same or a similar mission. Direct challenges sometimes arose during the design stage, sometimes in the course of development, sometimes at the time of initial production decisions, and in several instances continually throughout the program. In addition, the certainty that new challenges would sooner or later materialize, even when they were not immediately in view, constituted an enduring element of potential competition.

To illustrate the bounds and extent of competition as defined in this chapter, the two programs subjected to the least competition from direct substitutes were Polaris and Nike Zeus. Polaris had to oust the nonballistic Regulus II from its potential role as a submarine-launched strategic missile, and although there were no competing Navy ballistic missiles, the Air Force's Atlas, Titan, and Minuteman ICBM's and Thor IRBM and the Army's Jupiter IRBM were in continuous competition for Polaris' role as a strategic deterrent. Up to 1963 no ballistic missile defense systems were being developed to challenge Nike Zeus directly, but tens of millions of dollars were spent each year on studies aimed at finding better substitutes for the Zeus system. At the other extreme, the program facing the largest number of close substitutes was Sparrow III. During various periods that Raytheon air-to-air missile competed for operational assignments with the generally similar Sperry Sparrow I, Douglas-Bendix Sparrow II, Bell Meteor, and Hughes Falcon; with the unguided Douglas Genie; with the much less expensive but less versatile Sidewinder; with the longer range, higher performance Eagle; and with a variety of other air defense missiles.

For reasons brought out in Chapter 1, a common contractor objective is to maximize the expected value of the development and production sales of its product. But the immediate or potential competition of substitute systems or subsystems threatens the firm with program cancellation or reduction in program scale. These threats may affect the firm's behavior in terms of its propensity to innovate, the time-quality-cost tradeoff decisions it makes, its efforts to achieve efficiency, its talent allocation decisions, its morale, etc. What varies from case to case is the immediacy and timing of the competitive threat. This chapter examines the behavioral patterns associated with various degrees of competition at diverse stages in a program's life.

COMPETITION AND INNOVATION

Progress is made by the implementation of new and clearly superior technical ideas; that is, by innovation. What effect does competition have on the conception and acceptance of new devices and concepts in weapon system and subsystem development?

It is not at all clear that competition is a primary or necessary stimulus to the conception of really good new ideas. In fact, the "new ideas" which come out of competitions between proposed operational systems and subsystems are apt to be rather contrived — "Rube Goldberg" creations rather than the fundamental simplifications on which technical progress relies so heavily.

What competition can do is force a technical group to recognize that the solutions it has accepted in the past are inadequate — in Professor Usher's terminology, to cause the perception of an unsatisfactory pattern.[3] But this is only the first essential step in the process of invention. The actual achievement of a significant new insight depends upon many other conditions, including important chance factors, and so the probability that the new ideas arising under competitive pressures will be awkward contrivances rather than fundamental breakthroughs is high. As Usher has written:

> For some, or even many, individuals, successful solution of the problem is unlikely. For a limited number of individuals, successful solution of the problem can occur under special conditions, but these conditions cannot be created deliberately by the individual seeking a solution.[4]

Yet significant improvements in particular weapon systems or subsystems do not usually require wholly new inventions. At least in the recent past many good concepts and devices have emerged from government, university, and industrial laboratories, only to lie idle or not fully exploited because of lack of acceptance. The problem is this: a technical group tends to become committed to a certain approach or solution to a problem, and as long as it works satisfactorily, no serious effort is made to seek fundamentally better solutions. The role of competition is to destroy this satisfaction with the *status quo* by threatening the firm's future sales. In the face of such threats, the search for new approaches may begin. This need not lead to a new invention within the group; in many

---

[3] Abbot Payson Usher, *A History of Mechanical Inventions* (rev. ed.; Cambridge: Harvard University Press, 1954), p. 65.

[4] *Ibid.,* p. 66.

cases acceptance of some superior concept or device already in existence is sufficient to meet the threat successfully.

For example, in one guided missile program covered by our case studies a certain system for subjecting the missile to a pre-launch readiness test had been devised fairly early in the development effort. Little thought was given to making improvements in this system until the government began to consider buying a faster, more reliable system offered by a competing firm. This caused the guided missile producer to re-evaluate its original design and to work out a number of desirable new features, none of which required any original inventions. In another guided missile program the competition of a substitute weapon forced the development group to realize their launching system could be automated considerably, leading to faster operation and the need for fewer attending personnel. Robert Schlaifer cites a similar example in his study of the development of aircraft engines. Even though the floatless carburetor concept had been known for many years, not until a competing firm offered a successful floatless model did the leading carburetor maker begin vigorous efforts first to improve its float-type design and then to develop a floatless model.[5] Schlaifer observes that an important effect of competition is:

> . . . the stimulation it gives to the purely technical thinking of engineers, who are very likely to become set in the belief that a given end should be accomplished by given means, and to be willing to admit that other means are superior only after someone else has shown them to be.[6]

The major variables in these cases were the extent of commitment to prior technical approaches and the severity of the competitive threat. However, a more complete analysis requires the inclusion of two additional variables — the relationship of a particular technical effort to the main stream of a development program, and the timing of the competitive threat.

Some of our case studies disclosed behavior which at first appeared puzzling. Serious competitive threats to a contractor's program would appear — for example, the emergence of a rival

---

[5] Robert Schlaifer, *Development of Aircraft Engines* (Boston: Division of Research, Harvard Business School, 1950), pp. 100–102, 522, 543.

[6] *Ibid.*, p. 102.

program embracing new technical concepts obviously attractive to the buying service. Yet no evidence of an attempt by the challenged firm to improve its product in other than peripheral matters could be found.

In one instance it was apparent that this unwillingness to make changes was due largely to the strength of the development group's commitment to its own concepts. The engineers and scientists associated with a guided missile project believed so strongly in the superiority of their approach that rival programs simply were not perceived as a real technical challenge. Statements by military personnel suggesting the possible value of a rival approach were dismissed as "uninformed" or "politically motivated." Whether this perception of the situation was correct or not is irrelevant; the fact is, the perception existed and the group behaved accordingly. The development team was a thoroughbred with blinders, unable to recognize whether it was running five lengths ahead or neck and neck.

In other situations more "objective" explanations for a group's unwillingness to contemplate its technical approach critically could be found. Nearly every development effort is based upon certain technical concepts which give identity to the project. For example, in the Atlas ICBM project, balloon-type airframe structure and on-the-ground ignition of all rocket engine stages were crucial; in the Nike Ajax and Nike Hercules programs the central concept was radio command guidance, with optimized missile trajectories controlled by a ground-based computer; in the Sparrow III program it was continuous wave doppler homing radar guidance; and in the B–58 program it was the notion of a highly compact delta wing air vehicle with disposable elements.

Once a development effort is under way, it becomes very difficult to abandon or even seriously question basic concepts without seriously disruptive effects. In part this is due to the obvious costs of change: usually a fundamental change requires the development group to begin almost afresh, losing the benefit of much progress already made. Often it is preferable to take one's chances with the future rather than abandon what has already been accomplished, especially when the results in hand may provide a competitive time advantage offsetting technical disadvantages. Perhaps more importantly, intense commitment to certain basic technical concepts is a psychological necessity if a development team is to persevere in the face of inevitable problems. The development group which will readily abandon its basic approaches is probably not a well-motivated group, and is unlikely to succeed in any event.

This does not mean that every idea becomes inviolate once a project is under way. Very many technical features can be changed without threatening the main stream of development, at least in a complex system effort.[7] But for a strongly motivated development group, decisions to change basic concepts which have been accepted and partly executed are often so painful that they will be made only by external authority (e.g., by the government procurement agency for a change in system concept, or by the system designer for a change in subsystem concept) or internally as a result of the clearest and most intense competitive pressures.

We find then that competition spurs the creation or acceptance of new ideas most effectively at the outset of a development effort, before commitments have become strong and while an active search for superior alternatives is still feasible. Two types of competition are most prominent at this early stage. The better known variety is the formal design or technical proposal competition, in which two or more firms compete directly on the basis of proposed technical concepts or designs to conduct a single new development program. Second, to secure the award of a new development contract it is often necessary to leap ahead of substitute weapon systems or subsystems further along in development, even when no other firms are directly seeking the immediate contract. Our case studies indicated that both types of competition can create viable incentives for abandoning old concepts and embracing superior new solutions.

COMPETITION AND COMPETITIVE OPTIMISM

Although competition at the outset of a development program has the desirable property of inciting innovation, it also has important adverse effects. Notably, in their zeal to win new development program assignments firms tend to submit excessively optimistic predictions of the proposed program's quality, time, and cost outcomes.

For purposes of analysis the optimism of contractors in project-

---

[7] Of course, what to the weapon system project manager is peripheral may be central to the computer designer or the test equipment specialist.

ing the multidimensional outcome of a program can be resolved into optimism on the cost dimension as a resultant. That is, firms either overestimate the level of weapon system technical performance which can be achieved with a given amount of resource inputs, or they underestimate the cost of achieving a certain level of technical performance. As we have seen in Chapter 1, actual costs in the 12 weapon system developments covered by our case studies exceeded original contractor predictions by 220% on the average. Actual costs turned out to be less than original predictions in only one program — the program initiated under the least competitive circumstances. The first volume of this study found that competitive optimism was a major (although not the only) cause of these cost prediction errors.[8]

In the past several factors have interacted to encourage "buying into" new development programs with unrealistically optimistic predictions.[9] First, the financial penalties for competitive optimism have been either modest or nonexistent. The worst plight a contractor would typically suffer was to have its optimistic cost estimates negotiated into a cost-plus-fixed-fee contract or some other cost reimbursement contract. As cost increases were revealed, they were fully reimbursed by the government, and at most the contractor sacrificed some incremental profit opportunities. But in many cases even this sacrifice has been unnecessary. When government agencies contract for development on a year-by-year basis, tolerate long delays before development contract cost and profit provisions are negotiated, or are willing to accept so-called "extra scope" contract amendments to cover cost increases — all common practices in the past — contractors are able to secure an additional profit markup on cost increases along with reimbursement of the extra costs. Second, contractors had much to gain through optimism. Since military officials generally place a premium on projected technical achievement in selecting the contractor for a new program, firms have a strong incentive to outdo each other in their promises. At the same time, realistic estimation of the resources needed to meet ambitious technical goals can endanger the financial support of a new program and (when time and quality considerations are more or less equal) impair one's chances of winning the

[8] Cf. Peck and Scherer, pp. 301, 364, 411–420, and 431–444.
[9] This paragraph summarizes pp. 411–420 of Peck and Scherer.

competition. And as the advocates of new programs, government operating agencies have often encouraged contractors to estimate costs optimistically, recognizing that higher headquarters might be shocked out of supporting a program whose true costs were revealed at the outset. They have sought to disclose cost increases only gradually, after programs have gained momentum and cancellation has become difficult. Finally, decision makers at higher levels who were willing to analyze program prospects objectively have often lacked the technical expertise needed to adjust contractor and operating agency cost estimates to a more realistic basis. For all these reasons, most weapon system development programs of the late 1940's and the 1950's began with unduly optimistic quality, time, and/or cost goals. From this optimistic bias in initial estimates often followed erroneous program support decisions and subsequent program execution problems.

In short, besides providing behavioral and statistical benefits, competition at the outset of new programs also can have serious misinformation costs. Top government officials have become well aware of this problem, and in recent years a number of procedural and policy changes have been made to discourage excessive contractor optimism and to ensure that program decisions are based on more realistic projections. For one, a two-stage approach to the competitive selection of contractors has been adopted by the Department of Defense. Under this approach the field of would-be contractors is narrowed to one or a very few in a preliminary competition. Approval of a full-scale development effort and (when appropriate) the selection of a single winning development contractor are then deferred until promising solutions to all anticipated technical problems have been identified and cost and time estimates have been sharpened through a so-called program definition effort. In addition, contracting practices have been altered to incite more realistic cost estimation by contractors.[10] Even though competitive optimism may still run rampant at the outset of new programs, as in the past, the new policy's aim is to have realism prevail by the end of the program definition phase, before substantial financial commitments to full-scale development are made.

Positive assessment of the effectiveness of these recent changes would be premature. However, early experience in one of the

[10] These will be discussed in Chapters 7 and 9.

largest programs initiated under the new system suggests that competitive optimism has by no means been eliminated. The Department of Defense claimed that TFX fighter aircraft cost estimates submitted by General Dynamics and Boeing were unrealistically optimistic, despite an intensive program definition effort lasting nearly a year.[11]

It seems probable that the incentives for competitive optimism in the early stages of development programs will continue to be strong, and therefore that underestimation of program costs by contractors will remain a problem. If this is true, then the avoidance of erroneous program decisions depends upon the government's ability independently to adjust contractor estimates to a more realistic basis. In the past the government has possessed technical competence sufficient to make only very rough corrections. This competence has been gradually increased in recent years, especially in the Office of the Secretary of Defense, where advocacy of new programs is at a minimum and the willingness to examine cost estimates realistically is at a maximum. Whether the Defense Department's scientists, engineers, and cost analysts will be successful in their efforts to compensate for contractors' optimism can be determined conclusively only through the stern test of time.[12]

COMPETITION, TRADEOFFS, AND EFFICIENCY

Competition also affects the decisions a contractor makes with respect to quality-time-cost tradeoffs, given some over-all technical approach, and its efforts to achieve efficiency. Presumably, when two or more contractors are competing to fill certain operational needs of the military, the firm which does the best job in meeting the service's technical performance; reliability; time of availability; and development, production, and operating cost preferences will win the lion's share of subsequent contracts. Along what lines do these government preferences run?

Economic analysis indicates that the government *ought to* maxi-

[11] "McNamara Explains TFX Award Decision" (transcript of testimony before the Senate Permanent Investigations Subcommittee), *Aviation Week & Space Technology*, March 25, 1963, p. 101.

[12] My personal, scarcely expert opinion is that Department of Defense technical personnel have been somewhat optimistic about their ability to identify contractors' optimism.

mize the expected military value of its weapons programs, subject
to the constraints that total program costs equal its weapons budget
and that any given program provide no less value than its cost (assuming value and cost to be commensurable in terms of a dollar
common denominator). To illustrate some conditions for an
optimal program, let V_i be the expected military value of the ith
program and C_i the expected total cost over time of the ith program. The expected value of program i is a function v^i of $j = 1$,
. . . , m weapon system quality (technical performance and reliability) variables q_{ij} and time of availability t_i: [13]

$$V_i = v^i(q_{i1}, \ldots, q_{im}, t_i) = v^i(q_i, t_i).$$

The expected cost of program i is a function c^i of the same variables:

$$C_i = c^i(q_{i1}, \ldots, q_{im}, t_i) = c^i(q_i, t_i).$$

To simplify the presentation, assume that the n programs in which
$V > C$ are known and specified in advance.[14] Then the government wishes to maximize:

$$L = v^1(q_1, t_1) + \cdots + v^n(q_n, t_n) + \lambda[B - c^1(q_1, t_1) - \cdots - c^n(q_n, t_n)].$$

Differentiating for purposes of illustration with respect to the jth
quality variable of the ith program, we obtain as a first order condition:

$$\frac{\partial L}{\partial q_{ij}} = \frac{\partial v^i}{\partial q_{ij}} - \lambda \frac{\partial c^i}{\partial q_{ij}} = 0.$$

Note that in this case:

$$\lambda = \frac{\dfrac{\partial v^i}{\partial q_{ij}}}{\dfrac{\partial c^i}{\partial q_{ij}}};$$

that is, λ equals the increase in value provided by the last dollar
spent on increasing quality variable q_{ij}. If in fact defense budgets
have been inadequate to meet the nation's needs, as many have

[13] This exposition is a variation of Chapter 9 in Peck and Scherer. Assumptions about commensurability, structural relations, and appropriate-
ness of the criteria are discussed there.

[14] Otherwise we would have a problem in nonlinear programming.

argued in recent years, and if military value can be measured in dollar terms, then the value of λ should be greater than unity. In other words, the last dollar spent on the jth quality variable in program i (or on any other quality-increasing or time-decreasing activity in any program) should bring a return in value of more than one dollar. This is the penalty one pays for setting a restrictive budget.

Historical evidence suggests strongly that when competition takes place at the outset of or during the early developmental stages of a program, the military officials deciding which weapon system to choose do not worry about over-all budgetary constraints. Most of the costs are expected to be incurred only several years in the future, when the over-all weapons budget may be larger or smaller than at the time of the competition. In such a case it is not improbable that the officials choose that weapon system which maximizes $\mu = V_i - C_i$, assuming commensurability of the cost and value functions.[15] First order conditions will be:

$$\frac{\partial \mu}{\partial q_{ij}} = \frac{\partial v^i}{\partial q_{ij}} - \frac{\partial c^i}{\partial q_{ij}} = 0;$$

which differ from the conditions for maximization subject to a budgetary constraint only in the absence of the Lagrangian multiplier λ. In other words, the unconstrained maximum is nothing but a special case, with $\lambda = 1$, of the constrained maximum. But using this special unconstrained choice criterion makes an important difference in the tradeoff incentives provided contractors, if the national defense budget really is restrictive (that is, if $\lambda > 1$). Making what appear to be reasonable assumptions about the shapes of the v^i and c^i functions,[16] it can be seen that choosing the winner on the basis of unconstrained maximization encourages contractors to build too much quality into their weapon systems and to conduct the development at too rapid a rate, spending in the process government money which could be used to better advantage in other programs.

[15] This is the criterion used by Peck and Scherer, pp. 275–282 and 486–488.

[16] Namely, that v^i is concave monotonic increasing and c^i is convex monotonic increasing. For support of these assumptions, see *ibid.,* pp. 254–266, 271–273, 467–472, and 632–638.

This theoretical illustration provides one possible explanation for what in practice is a very evident phenomenon. Our case studies repeatedly revealed that enhancing weapon system quality and reducing development time were considered much more important by contractor and service decision makers than minimizing development cost.[17] Nevertheless, the bare model undoubtedly assumes too much knowledge and foresight on the part of weapons program officials. In practice it is most difficult, if not impossible, to quantify the value of any given increment of weapon system quality or development time, and even if quantification were possible, technical and strategic uncertainties would preclude any but the roughest measurements. Several other explanations for the strong emphasis on quality and time appear more plausible.

First, there exists a general belief bordering on faith that the value (v^i) functions associated with advanced weapons programs are normally configured in such a way as to encourage quality increases and time reductions.[18] When additional reliability or technical performance can make the difference between success or failure on a combat mission, or when the race may go to the swiftest in terms of development lead time, military decision makers are not inclined to pinch pennies. Second, cost predictions tend to be subject to much greater errors than quality and time predictions, especially during the early stages of a weapons program.[19] As a result, military officials tend to discount cost predictions and give much greater weight to quality and time factors in competitions to select the contractor for a new development program.[20] For the same reason, less emphasis is placed on cost considerations in tradeoff decisions made once a program is under way. Third, there is a clear propensity (although neither universal nor unlimited) among government technical decision makers not to worry about costs, partly because they are responsible mainly for the technical aspects of a program and partly because the expenditures within any single program manager's compass seem insignificant relative

[17] For an attempt to quantify the relative importance of time, quality, and cost in development programs, see *ibid.*, pp. 288–295. In only 2 of 13 weapons programs did development cost have a weight greater than or equal to quality or time.

[18] *Ibid.*, pp. 294–295.

[19] *Ibid.*, pp. 366–367.

[20] *Ibid.*, pp. 21–24 and 299–303.

to the total availability of national defense resources. Consequently, they tend to ignore the λ factor in their tradeoff decision reviews, or perhaps even to maximize quality for its own sake, disregarding its military value and cost. Concern over costs is left to budget specialists, but the latter seldom have the technical competence needed to weigh the complex issues of a weapons program tradeoff decision.[21] Finally, in at least some programs, our case studies revealed, service officials deliberately refrained from pressing for development cost reductions because they wanted to maintain amicable contractor relations, anticipating that a friendly contractor would turn in a quicker and better development job.

To be sure, development and production costs may make the difference between winning or losing a competition when quality and time of availability are equal, but the latter seldom are equal. The typical dominance of quality over cost is shown in this exchange between Congressman William H. Bates of Massachusetts and J. L. Atwood, President of North American Aviation, Inc.:

MR. BATES.   Let's talk about competition. Yours is not a question of competition for price on production.

MR. ATWOOD.   Not directly. . . . It is technical and design competition; yes sir. That is the emphasis.

* * * * *

MR. BATES.   So we get an altogether different situation than we get in most business, then?

MR. ATWOOD.   We do. Of course price of an airplane does have a direct effect, too. When two generally comparable planes could be made available, the cheapest plane would be bought.

MR. BATES.   Yes. But how often does that situation ever arise?

MR. ATWOOD.   Not very frequently. From time to time it does.

---

[21] *Ibid.,* pp. 440–444, 451, and 476–478. Secretary of Defense Robert S. McNamara illustrated this problem well in testimony on the TFX aircraft competition: ". . . the source selection board, using factors weighted by judgment, made a recommendation which appeared to place greater emphasis on potential bonus factors in certain operational areas, rather than on dependability of development and predictability of costs. This recommendation, understandably, was seconded by the Navy and Air Staffs, since these officers are most vitally interested in obtaining the ultimate in performance in individual weapons systems." "McNamara Explains TFX Award Decision," *Aviation Week & Space Technology,* March 25, 1963, p. 103.

MR. BATES.   What they want is performance?
MR. ATWOOD.   Yes, sir.[22]

Thus, cost considerations come into play only when quality factors are roughly equal. Moreover, small differences in quality can offset fairly large differences in cost. An excellent example is the competition between the Navy's F4H–1 and F8U–3 interceptors in 1958. The choice between these two aircraft, called by Navy officials "the closest competition in modern aircraft history," [23] took place after prototypes were flown, so that technical performance uncertainties had been considerably reduced. Similarly, cost uncertainties were not a serious barrier to comparison, since both prime contractors guaranteed to produce their aircraft at specified firm fixed prices. Time of availability, speed, altitude capability, armament, and other significant factors were deemed roughly equal at the time. However, with two engines the F4H–1 was considered less likely to fail on missions, and its two-seat configuration permitted more human attention to operation of the airplane and its equipment. Navy officials believed that these advantages were worth a 15% to 20% cost premium, and the F4H–1 won the competition.

The importance of quality in competitive situations is also seen in the history of the F–105 tactical fighter-bomber. During the development of that aircraft many improvements over the original design were incorporated (all, of course, with service approval and indeed encouragement). These changes delayed operational availability of the F–105 and added significantly to its development and production costs. Yet without them, the aircraft could not have withstood competition from the F–100, F–101, F–104, and F–107 systems. Nevertheless, production of the F–105 was cancelled somewhat unexpectedly when the Air Force decided in 1961 to purchase the Navy's F4H–1, which was judged superior to the F–105 in rate of climb, altitude, speed, ability to utilize short runways, and other features.[24]

[22] House, Subcommittee for Special Investigation of the Committee on Armed Services, *Hearings, Aircraft Production Costs and Profits* (1956), p. 1373.
[23] "One Had to Lose Out," *Business Week*, December 27, 1958, p. 26.
[24] "Battle Over Fighter Planes," *Business Week*, December 30, 1961, pp. 86–87.

Still another illustration of the importance of quality involves the prime contractor of a guided missile program covered by our case studies, a nonprofit technical advisory group, and the sponsoring government agency, all of which must remain anonymous. The guided missile system was in competition with a close substitute system somewhat further along in development. To offset its time disadvantage, the prime contractor favored advances in performance capability regardless of cost. The nonprofit group, on the other hand, was inclined to make sacrifices in performance in order to bring continually rising development costs under control. However, when conflicts between these groups were presented to the sponsoring agency for resolution, the service typically decided in favor of increased performance.

In all of these cases quality was emphasized over cost and (with some exceptions) development time as a result of competitive pressures. But in other situations time reduction was spurred by competition. For example, while one of our case studies was in progress, the officials of a certain firm observed that they were carrying out exploratory studies in a new and promising field of commercial technology relevant to their main line of business, but that no full development program would be launched until several years of preliminary work had reduced the technical uncertainties. However, only a few months later the firm's competitor commenced a development in that area. As a result, the company immediately accelerated its work and began to develop operational prototypes.

While in commercial projects firms can take the initiative in time-cost tradeoffs, a defense contractor is seldom able to spend additional government money to accelerate its weapons program work without authorization from the sponsoring military agency. But the military services also find themselves under competitive time pressures. For example, in a weapon system program affected by interservice rivalry over roles and missions in a new field of technology, one of the government agencies involved chose a strategy of minimum-time development in order to be first with an operational weapon and thus to stake out a claim to the new mission.

Of course, cases occasionally do arise in which time and quality factors are so equal that cost considerations become competitively decisive. Situations of this nature occur most frequently when a program's development effort has been largely completed, so that quality, time, and even cost uncertainties have declined substantially. Then attention can focus on cost of production. In several of the programs covered by our case studies, contractors gave priority to cost reduction efforts once their weapon systems had progressed to the stage of production for the operational inventory, and when competition from other less expensive weapons threatened the continued receipt of production contracts. Competitive pressures clearly were an incentive for cost reduction in these cases. Even then, however, quality differentials were considered of major importance, and contractors appeared universally unwilling to cut corners on technical performance and reliability in order to reduce production costs.

Thus, surviving actual and potential competition from close substitute weapon systems and subsystems in the past has generally demanded much more emphasis on technical performance, reliability, and development time than on development cost. This means that competitive substitution has been closer on the quality and time dimensions than on the development cost dimension. Indeed, weapon system programs have typically been such distant substitutes for each other on the cost dimension that significant development cost inefficiencies have not adversely affected their competitive status. Only infrequently have programs been terminated merely because of development costs much higher than those of competing programs. A much more common cause of termination has been poor technical performance or serious development schedule slippages. In sum, the competitive incentives in weapons acquisition of the 1950's ran strongly in favor of quality maximization and lead time minimization, but almost negligibly in favor of development cost minimization.

Can these propensities of the 1950's be projected into the 1960's? One might argue that they cannot, for Secretary of Defense Robert S. McNamara announced in 1962 that:

> Shortening development lead time and reducing development costs shall be considered equal in importance to achieving performance in weapon systems and equipment.[25]

---

[25] Philip J. Klass, "Defense to Speed Development, Cut Cost," *Aviation Week & Space Technology*, February 5, 1962, p. 26.

That this was no idle threat was soon demonstrated by the Secretary's decision to award the TFX fighter development contract to General Dynamics — Fort Worth, overriding the military chiefs' repeated recommendations in favor of Boeing. The most widely publicized consideration in this controversial decision was McNamara's belief that substantial cost savings would result from the allegedly greater "commonality" of Air Force and Navy versions in the General Dynamics design. But in addition, McNamara ruled that the superior technical performance features of the Boeing design were not worth the additional cost and risk their development would require. He observed that:

> Boeing had from the very beginning consistently chosen more technically risky tradeoffs in an effort to achieve operational features which exceeded the required performance characteristics. . . . But my judgment . . . clearly indicated that these proposals would, in fact, complicate the development problems, and would require a significantly greater development effort to be expended by Boeing in their solution.[26]

He criticized the tendency of military planners "to forget that every additional bit of complexity you add to your operation tends to degrade the over-all efficiency of the operation," indicating that:

> You cannot make decisions simply by asking yourself whether something might be nice to have. You have to make a judgment on how much is enough.[27]

Differences in judgment about the military value of the performance increments offered by Boeing, as well as skepticism about the alleged cost savings resulting from commonality of parts, were at the heart of the bitter controversy over McNamara's TFX decision. The position of military leaders was made clear by Admiral George W. Anderson, then chief of naval operations:

> As a one-inch longer reach is to a boxer, this (performance) edge often is very small when measured in terms such as altitude,

[26] "McNamara Explains TFX Award Decision," *Aviation Week & Space Technology*, March 25, 1963, p. 101. For an interesting, more general interpretation of the design strategies chosen by Boeing and General Dynamics, see the two articles by R. A. Smith in *Fortune*, March and April 1963.

[27] Jack Raymond, "M'Namara Is Firm on His Decisions," *New York Times*, April 21, 1963, p. 43.

miles per hour, range, time on station, operating depths and the like. . . . Those of us who have learned the hard way of the importance of this edge attach great significance to what might otherwise appear inconsequential differences between two competing pieces of military hardware. I know of no way to attach numbers, weight or scores to such intangibles, but their importance has been written in the record of military history.[28]

Similarly, the vice chief of staff of the Air Force stated that "operational factors should be overriding considerations to all others in choosing between the two systems because these aircraft are being produced for use in event of war." [29]

There the conflict stood in May 1963, when this was written. It is possible only to speculate on the emphasis in quality-time-cost tradeoffs of the future. In all probability, military service decision makers will continue to place great stress on quality and time at the expense of cost. The Office of the Secretary of Defense will remain more cost-conscious. But when the force of the Mc-Namara personality is absent from the Pentagon, as it sooner or later must be, there is apt to be greater reluctance to reject the judgment of military leaders.[30]

Moreover, although increased emphasis will be placed on cost factors in future weapon system technical decisions, technical performance and reliability will still be important and often crucial variables. Notably, Secretary McNamara was willing to spend nearly $1 billion to develop the essential performance advances offered by TFX, even though he would not go all the way to the margin proposed by Boeing. And once a development program is under way, demonstrated quality deficiencies and significant schedule slippages will surely endanger the ability of weapon systems to withstand the competition of substitutes. Therefore, it is likely that competitive incentives for meeting approved quality and time objectives will remain strong.

[28] "Performance Edge Stressed in TFX Quiz," *Aviation Week & Space Technology,* April 15, 1963, p. 28.

[29] Statement of Gen. William F. McKee cited in *ibid.*

[30] As a rule I tend to doubt that a single individual can significantly alter the performance of an organization as vast as the Department of Defense. However, the cult of the McNamara personality in the Pentagon is a most impressive phenomenon, and it probably has made a notable difference.

COMPETITION AND TALENT ALLOCATION DECISIONS

If the market for engineers, scientists, and qualified project managers equated salaries with marginal productivities, there would be no qualitative talent allocation problem in weapons acquisition. But in fact, the market operates very imperfectly. Two $10,000-a-year engineers are usually not the equivalent of one $20,000 engineer. Rather, the highly talented technical and managerial personnel in a weapons firm affect the success or failure of programs to a degree rarely reflected in salary differentials.[31] As a result, talent allocation decisions assume special significance. These decisions are often influenced by competitive pressures.

Just what the effect of competition on allocation decisions will be depends in large measure upon the contractor's perception of its chances of winning and upon the alternatives available. Generally, company executives indicated a preference for allocating top talent into relatively noncompetitive areas whenever possible. Firms with alternative program opportunities tended to put their "second teams" on projects which, because of intense competition, had little prospect of leading to production contracts.[32]

However, an important exception must be noted. In recent years the very best technical talent of defense firms has gravitated into design studies and the preparation of technical proposals for source selection competitions — perhaps the most competitive activity in weapons acquisition, at least in terms of the number of firms seeking a single contract.[33] The reason for this behavior is simple: major defense firms cannot maintain their sales volume without obtaining new development programs, and winning a source selection competition is the principal way by which new programs are obtained.

The emphasis placed by firms on winning such competitions is in many respects undesirable. In order to be fair to all would-be

[31] Peck and Scherer, p. 501.

[32] *Ibid.,* pp. 504–507.

[33] C. F. Horne, Vice President of General Dynamics Corporation, has estimated that 18% of the defense industry's top scientific and engineering talent is working on competitive proposals rather than the actual execution of programs. "The Impact on Business Firms: I," *Research Management,* September 1962, p. 331.

participants and to demonstrate (mainly to Congress [34]) that they
are conducting a vigorously competitive procurement program, as
well as to have available an adequate array of technical alternatives, government agencies encourage widespread participation in
their technical competitions. In a sample of 18 weapon system
design competitions, mostly held shortly after World War II, the
average number of active competitors was 3.9, with a range of
from 2 to 10.[35]   During the late 1950's so-called management
competitions gradually replaced the formal design competition as a
means of limiting the field to one or a very few firms which are
then supported in further program definition and design work.
Attracting from 6 to 31 active entrants, the management competition is supposed to require less technical effort on the part of
competitors.[36]   However, technical criteria are still accorded substantial weight in the source selection decision, and so in order to
win, firms assign their most capable and creative scientists and
engineers to the proposal preparation effort.[37]   Since the number
of winners is at most four and usually fewer, management competitions end with as many as 30 losers.   And at least from the perspective of the losing firms, the creative efforts of their best technical
personnel have been wasted.

To the extent that such competitions yield tangible benefits to
the government as buyer, it would be inaccurate to say that the efforts of losing entrants are really wasted.   As we have seen, com-

---

[34] The intent of Congress to have widespread competition for new program awards was expressed in a 1962 amendment to the *Armed Services
Procurement Act* requiring that "proposals shall be solicited from the maximum number of qualified sources consistent with the nature and requirements of the supplies or services to be procured."   10 U.S.C. 2304(g).

[35] Cf. Peck and Scherer, p. 340.

[36] *Ibid.,* pp. 340–352.   Even more bidders sometimes enter minor subsystem development contract competitions.

[37] As an extreme example, entrants in the competition which narrowed
the TFX fighter development contract field from six to two teams are said
to have spent from $4 million to $7 million on their proposals.   Larry
Booda, "New Delay Raises Doubts on TFX Future," *Aviation Week & Space
Technology,* July 9, 1962, p. 26.   At one point in the competition Boeing
had 1,000 persons working on its proposal preparation effort, and some of
the proposals were as long as 1,500 pages.   R. A. Smith, "The $7-Billion
Contract That Changed the Rules," *Fortune,* March 1963, p. 101, and
April 1963, p. 110.

mainly on incentives for optimal and efficient contractor performance within the context of particular weapons programs, dealing with longer-run entry and exit factors only when they interact significantly with the problems of spurring good performance in the relatively short run.

For all these reasons, it must be re-emphasized that the incentive systems considered here are only one of several important determinants of weapons program outcomes. Thus the present volume is strictly a partial analysis of the over-all weapons acquisition problem.

COMPETITIVE AND CONTRACTUAL INCENTIVES

We shall direct our attention to two general categories of incentive systems: competitive incentives and contractual incentives. Competitive incentives operate through correlations between the level or rate of growth of a firm's sales and its performance. Contractual incentives operate through correlations between the amount and/or rate of profit received on specific contracts and the firm's performance.

This is admittedly an unconventional dichotomy. It has two principal justifications. First, it is consistent with administrative practice in weapons acquisition. The award of contracts (determining sales volume) and the determination of profits on those contracts are separate administrative activities, often reflecting quite different decision-making processes and criteria.

Incentives based upon the correlation of sales with performance might well be called "sales-oriented" incentives rather than "competitive" incentives. But the term "competitive" has been chosen because competition in the weapons acquisition process works its direct effects mainly on sales rather than contract profits. Competition between mutually substitutable weapon systems and competition for budgetary support determine the level and duration of any given defense product's sales. The growth or decline of a defense contractor's sales also depends upon the firm's success in competing for a role in new development efforts. In contrast, except for atypical advertised competitive bidding situations, profit rates on specific contracts are determined only after the government and its contractor are locked together in a relationship approximating bilateral monopoly. Competitive factors do influence profits in the resulting negotiations, but their effects usually enter indirectly through sales-oriented considerations.

Second, the dichotomy between competitive and contractual incentives is drawn because the various reward-performance correlations work through distinguishable corporate goals. In a system of contractual incentives, the desire of firms to maximize accounting profits during the short run of a contract is exploited. Competitive incentives, on the other hand, exploit the desire of firms to survive, to grow, and perhaps to maximize long-run profits.

This classification of corporate goals is apt to evoke protests. In particular, economists may question on both theoretical and empirical grounds whether short-run accounting profit maximization is a true goal of business enterprises. The objection is well taken. Nevertheless, numerous persons responsible for the implementation of incentive systems in weapons programs apparently believe that firms do attempt to maximize accounting profits on specific contracts. I shall argue later that this assumption is a source of many an error in policy and practice. But since the belief is widely held and acted upon, it is useful for expositional reasons to count short-run accounting profit maximization as a possibly distinct goal of weapons makers.

The assertion that competitive incentives exploit the desire of firms to survive and grow in sales volume suggests more general statements in the same vein by William Baumol. Baumol has argued that some form of sales maximization is a primary goal of firms with market power, dominating the partly conflicting profit maximization objective.[10] His views have been criticized by other economists reluctant to abandon the conventional profit maximization model.[11] However, the competitive incentives goal assumptions adopted here require neither outright acceptance nor rejection of the Baumol sales maximization hypothesis.

This is so because in the nonmarket environment of weapons acquisition, perhaps unlike imperfectly or monopolistically com-

---

[10] *Business Behavior, Value, and Growth* (New York: Macmillan, 1959), pp. 45–53; and "On the Theory of Expansion of the Firm," *American Economic Review,* December 1962, pp. 1078–1087.

[11] See the reviews by Franklin Fisher in *Journal of Political Economy,* June 1960, pp. 314–315; and Carl Kaysen, *American Economic Review,* December 1960, pp. 1036–1038.

petitive market situations, maximizing sales tends to be an operational means of maximizing long-run profits. Weapons development and production contracts are priced on a fairly consistent "cost-plus" basis. Even for so-called fixed price contracts, the price is customarily negotiated by adding to a mutually agreed-upon estimate of costs a certain profit percentage. The percentage markup does vary from contract to contract, but at least in current practice the pattern of profit rates applied to any given type of contract held by a certain firm for specific types of work is more or less standard and predictable. The cost estimate to which the profit rate is applied may also vary with bargaining power relationships, but as we shall see, the importance of such variations is minimized by short-term contracting practices,[12] and over the long run the variations probably tend to cancel out randomly. Consequently, the firm which maximizes its defense contract sales can expect, as a good first approximation, also to be maximizing the amount of profit it earns in the long run.[13]

Still this discussion only indicates that sales maximization and long-run profit maximization are good proxies for one another, not whether they are distinct goals, and, if so, which is really more im-

[12] For a more compact discussion of short-term contracting practices than this volume contains, see Peck and Scherer, pp. 416–418.

[13] A related problem should be noted briefly here. Maximizing the long-run amount of profit is not necessarily consistent with maximizing the appropriately discounted present value of long-run profits, or with maximizing the return on a firm's invested capital. These alternative objectives tend to be consistent, however, in a short-run analysis which permits neither net investment nor net disinvestment. This condition is generally met in the kinds of short-run program performance problems considered in this volume. Furthermore, since (at least historically, although less so in recent years) the government often provides much of the incremental fixed and working capital required for new programs, the condition also tends to be satisfied over longer periods. Maximizing the long-run amount of profit is also consistent with return on investment maximization when all incremental investments can be financed at costs lower than the net profit returns they make possible. In fact, at least in the aircraft sector of the weapons industry, on which the best data are available, almost all new investment has been financed through either depreciation, retained earnings, or low-cost debt, at an out-of-pocket cost undoubtedly lower than the incremental returns provided. Cf. Peck and Scherer, pp. 164–167. The analysis here ignores the problem of capital investment's opportunity cost, which will be introduced as a complication only in later chapters.

portant in the hierarchy of corporate goals. If they are distinct, conflicts may occasionally arise, and their relative importance to company decision makers will determine the resulting behavior. If they are distinct and not in conflict, they may be mutually reinforcing. On these questions it is best to keep an open mind until all the evidence has been examined.

Both competitive and contractual incentive systems operate in terms of measurable economic magnitudes — sales in the first instance and contract profits in the second. Other incentives for good performance in weapons programs exist, but they are less susceptible to measurement and administrative variation. For example, an organization which does a good job developing a new and useful weapon system is rewarded by the satisfaction of its desire to contribute to the national defense effort, but this kind of satisfaction cannot be consciously doled out by government agencies. Our attention in this volume will be directed mainly to competitive and contractual incentives, although on occasion it will be possible to point out the role which noneconomic incentives play and to consider some ways of enhancing their effectiveness.

METHODS OF RESEARCH

The subsequent analysis is based on several kinds of data. Published congressional documents and unpublished Department of Defense reports contain much valuable quantitative and qualitative information, and they have been utilized whenever appropriate. A more important source was a collection of detailed historical case studies of 12 advanced weapon system and 7 commercial product development programs prepared during 1958 and 1959 by members of the Harvard University Weapons Acquisition Research Project.[14] The weapons programs were:

B–58 supersonic strategic bomber (Air Force)
F–105 supersonic fighter-bomber (Air Force)
F4H–1 supersonic interceptor (Navy)
Atlas intercontinental ballistic missile system (Air Force)
Polaris intermediate range ballistic missile system (Navy)

[14] When referring to the group of case studies collectively, I will use the term *"our* case studies" to emphasize that they were a joint product of the research group, not of the author alone, and to distinguish them from similar case studies by other organizations such as The RAND Corporation.

price-quantity (demand) function and a cost-quantity (supply) function, both known with certainty, and assuming further no technological change, it can be shown that the optimal allocation of resources results when the number of firms is so large that no single firm believes it can exert a perceptible influence on price.[46] (2) Kenneth Arrow has relaxed the "no technological change" assumption and shown that under the remaining conditions of the first proposition, including perfect foresight, the incentive to make patented cost-reducing inventions is at a maximum when the number of firms is very large.[47] (3) When the number of firms is large, the probability of collusion to raise prices and extract monopoly profits from buyers is at a minimum.

It is hardly necessary to state that proposition (1) is totally inapplicable to advanced weapons development and production. Proposition (2) is more interesting, but it too assumes standardized products sold in a market setting with consideration given only to price-quantity and cost-quantity relationships. Such a market environment does not and cannot exist for weapons acquisition.[48] Proposition (3) comes closest to the mark, for collusive price-fixing is not unknown in government procurement.[49] Nevertheless, the cases of collusion typically involve products such as electric generators, lock nuts, and electronic components purchased to established technical specifications on the basis of price. When

[46] For an excellent summary of the many conditions necessary for this statement to be valid, see J. de V. Graaff, *Theoretical Welfare Economics* (Cambridge: Cambridge University Press, 1957), pp. 142–155.

[47] "Economic Welfare and the Allocation of Resources for Invention," *The Rate and Direction of Inventive Activity,* ed. Richard Nelson, National Bureau of Economic Research conference report (Princeton: Princeton University Press, 1962), pp. 619–622. In a similar vein see William Fellner, "The Influence of Market Structure on Technical Progress," *Quarterly Journal of Economics,* November 1951, pp. 556–577. Fellner adds, however, that the injection of uncertainty may make many-seller industries *less* innovative than few-seller industries.

[48] Cf. Chapter 1 *supra.*

[49] The best-known recent example is, of course, the electrical manufacturers' price conspiracy of the late 1950's. Cf. John G. Fuller, *The Gentlemen Conspirators: The Story of the Price-Fixers in the Electrical Industry* (New York: Grove, 1962). For some less dramatic examples specifically in the field of defense, see "New Study Is Urged for U.S. Trust Laws," *New York Times,* April 12, 1962, p. 21; and "Fastener Firms and Officials Fined," *Aviation Week & Space Technology,* September 23, 1963, p. 40.

the conditions of purchase are multidimensional, including many aspects of quality and time as well as price, independent action on the part of sellers seems much more likely. At least, no cases of collusion in weapon system or subsystem bidding not explicitly approved by the government are known, and all the evidence points to a high degree of independence in competitors' offers and actions.

How then do variations in the number of competitors affect the behavior of research and development contractors? Analysis of the case study evidence suggests that the most important variables are the probability of success, the size of the contracts attainable, the amount of effort required to compete, and the eagerness of individual competitors to retain or win sales.

As a first approximation, the larger the number of competitors, the lower the probability of success is for any given firm, assuming that the government's intent is to choose one or only a few winners once the competition has run its course.[50] This proposition is by no means intuitively obvious. A top-rated distance runner's chances of winning a marathon are not necessarily reduced because many runners known to have less stamina enter the race. But in the early stages of weapons development, uncertainty prevents a firm from knowing when it holds a decisive advantage. Technological uncertainties, as we have seen, make it difficult to identify superior technical solutions in advance of actual testing. Unpredictable changes in the strategic picture may wipe out the advantage of weapon system concepts good in all technical respects. And perhaps most important, contractors are seldom certain which of many possible selection criteria (including not only technical factors, but also political and socioeconomic considerations) government officials will stress in their elimination decisions. Thus, there is an important element of randomness in competitions between close substitute weapons at the design and early development stages. An increase in the number of competitors therefore tends to reduce the chance of winning for any given entrant.

To be sure, the quality and quantity of each competitor's effort also affect its chances of winning, especially when the elimination decision will be deferred until government personnel can make

---

[50] Note that this differs from the conventional assumption of economic analysis that, in equilibrium, all firms selling in a given market will continue to sell there, except for the natural decline and growth of firms.

meaningful judgments on the various entrants' actual performance and prospects.[51] The intensity of a contractor's effort in turn depends at least partly upon its eagerness to retain current contracts and to gain new business.[52] When a firm is threatened with a serious sales decline, it is more apt to compete vigorously to defend its remaining contracts and win new ones than a firm whose order book is full. The following analysis necessarily holds this "eagerness" variable constant, assuming that all or most of the serious entrants in a competition are in roughly similar positions with respect to sales backlogs.

In management competitions, which attract as many as 30 entrants, the relatively low *ex ante* probability of winning does not seem to discourage trying, mainly because the effort required to submit a proposal is quantitatively small and the gain (a large development contract) from winning is high.[53] Our case studies provided detailed information on only three formal design competitions, and from this limited sample it was not possible to conclude whether the vigor of entrants' efforts varied with the number of firms participating. There was at least some evidence that when the number of invitations to participate sent out by the sponsoring agency was high, some firms either decided not to compete at all or submitted only a courtesy proposal embodying little technical effort. Recognizing that, some of the remaining firms saw their chances of winning enhanced and therefore mounted a vigorous design effort. Thus the number of serious competitors in a design competition may tend to be self-limiting because initially widespread participation discourages marginally eager entrants.

Since the selection of firms to do a job in advance of any actual substantive performance is unique to contracting situations, a much

[51] The validity of this proposition is not nearly as certain as one might suppose. An empirical study of three Air Force source selection competitions disclosed that the technical quality of proposals was largely unrelated to the quantitative level of effort entrants expended on the proposals. T. J. Allen, "Problem-Solving by Research Groups: A Study of Factors Influencing the Technical Quality in the Preparation of Proposals for Government Contracts" (unpublished Master's thesis, School of Industrial Management, Massachusetts Institute of Technology, 1963).

[52] For a further discussion of the eagerness variable, see Peck and Scherer, pp. 405–411 and 420–423.

[53] *Ibid.*, pp. 340–343.

more interesting question concerns the effect of variations in the number of competitors on company performance once a development effort is under way. In general, our case study evidence indicated that competitive situations with a large number of more or less equally eager firms working toward the same objective, and hence a correspondingly low probability of winning follow-on contracts for any one firm, were conducive to poor performance. For example, in one high priority program the prime contractor selected ten subcontractors to work on different approaches to a vital subsystem. The firms chosen foresaw little prospect of winning production contracts in the face of this competition, and as a result their efforts were half-hearted. The projects were poorly staffed and there was little innovation, even though the prospects for exploring new ideas were excellent. When the number of competitors was cut to three, efforts of the surviving participants increased significantly. In another situation, the number of companies chosen to perfect a certain gyroscope design was deliberately limited to four so that the prospects of production contracts contingent upon good performance would be attractive enough to induce the firms to assign their more capable engineers.

Furthermore, competition in the limiting case of only two rivals may be just as effective from a behavioral standpoint as competition among a few firms. For instance, the Thor IRBM was considered no less a threat to Jupiter and the F8U–3 to the F4H–1 than competition from Sparrow I, Sparrow II, Falcon, and Sidewinder was to the Sparrow III development group. For optimal incentive effects the number of competitors needs to be only large enough to pose a distinct threat of project cancellation, but should not be so large that the chances of surviving are considered so small that a company finds it preferable to divert its resources to less competitive programs.

Thus, when only one or a few can finish the race successfully and when no one firm has a clearly recognized advantage, competition in research and development has more desirable behavioral effects when the number of rivals is small than when it is large. This generalization is probably valid for most areas of weapon system and subsystem development, as well as for competitions to enter new commercial product markets in which economies of scale limit the number of firms able to survive. It is not applicable to situations in which the market is large enough to absorb all or most of the firms which may enter by developing new products — a condition common in many areas of weapons component technology (e.g., special valves, transistors, resistors, electrical connectors, instruments, etc.).

CONCLUSION

In sum, the case for competition between close substitutes in weapons programs is a complicated one. Competition can encourage innovation, efficiency, and favorable allocation of talent; stimulate people to greater effort; and increase the probability of technical success in the face of uncertainty. But it also may lead to overemphasis on quality-increasing and time-decreasing activities and impair the morale of technical groups whose projects are threatened. Competition also has other unambiguous costs — the resource costs of supporting more than one approach toward an objective, the misinformation costs of competitive optimism, and a tendency for the exchange of technical information to break down among organizations which must cooperate while competing.[54] Too much competition can discourage rather than stimulate vigorous effort. Given these conflicting considerations, it is clear that there are many cases in which the costs of competition between close substitutes outweigh the benefits.

There are no simple rules of thumb which permit a military decision maker to tell when or how much competition is appropriate. All the factors examined in this chapter appear relevant. Nevertheless, a few broad generalizations can be framed.

At the outset of a new program spirited technical concept and design competition can be secured, but only at the cost of diverting industry's top technical talent from actual research and development work into the preparation of technical proposals, only one or a few of which will be accepted. The problems of excessive competitive optimism are also severe. Nevertheless, the level of technical uncertainty early in a weapons program is often so high that the statistical benefits of encouraging several alternative approaches may outweigh the costs of competition, if the alternatives are supported to a stage at which more confident choices can be made.

[54] House, Committee on Government Operations, *Eleventh Report, Organization and Management of Missile Programs* (1959), pp. 110–111.

As a program progresses toward the testing of prototypes, the possibilities for innovation become increasingly limited while other behavioral effects of competition assume more and more significance. During this period competition between close substitutes usually generates strong incentives for quality maximization (subject to the constraint of the broad technical approach taken) and lead time minimization, but not for development cost reduction. Indeed, the pressures of competition may cause firms to seek technical sophistication and perfection not worth their cost. Counterpressures are needed to encourage the cost-consciousness conducive to optimal tradeoff decisions and efficiency. As development progresses the rate of spending increases, and so the resource cost of supporting competing efforts climbs rapidly. At the same time, in technically ambitious programs major uncertainties may not be eliminated until operational prototypes are tested. In such cases the statistical benefits of competition could outweigh their cost. The best-motivated contractor performance on an inferior technical approach will not yield optimal results. These and other factors such as morale and talent allocation effects must be evaluated in determining how much competition is appropriate.

As production of operational equipment begins, contractor emphasis under the pressure of close-substitute competition typically shifts from quality enhancement and lead time minimization to cost reduction. Here too, however, the potential benefits of competition must be weighed against the cost of maintaining duplicate programs.

CHAPTER 3

Competition for Budgetary Support

THE DESIRE TO TRIUMPH over one's acknowledged rivals undoubtedly influences the behavior of some individuals and organizations. However, here the desire of firms to maintain and increase the volume of their sales, rather than to win sales from rivals, is stressed as the basis of competitive incentives. There are two reasons for this emphasis. First, sales maximization as a general goal subsumes the special goal of winning sales for the sake of winning. Second, the weapon system sales of a firm are threatened not only by the competition of close substitute weapons, but also by the competition of other programs for shares of the limited national defense budget. In this chapter the latter kind of competition and its effects on contractor behavior are examined.

The Nike Zeus ballistic missile defense program provides a good example of budgetary competition among weapons which are not close technical and operational substitutes. That program was continually threatened with cancellation from 1959 through 1962 even though, as noted in the last chapter, there were no competing antimissile systems under development. The objections to Nike Zeus centered not on its technical feasibility, although many difficult technical problems had to be overcome, but on the relationship between its expected cost and military value. Zeus critics held that the cost of an offensive ballistic missile was considerably less than the cost of intercepting it. An economic advantage was in the hands of the offense — additional ICBM's and decoys to swamp the Zeus system could be obtained at less cost than the additional Zeus missiles required to intercept them. Therefore, it was argued, the United States would be better off building up its strategic deterrent capabilities — Atlas, Titan, and Minuteman ICBM's, Polaris IRBM's, and manned bombers — than spending billions of dollars

on ballistic missile defense.[1]   Arguments such as this were instrumental in convincing top Defense Department officials for several
years not to support the Army's demands for the accelerated production of operational Nike Zeus units.

The Theory of Incentives from Budgetary Competition

To put the problem of budgetary competition on a sounder theoretical footing, an introductory analogy from the nonweapons
world is useful. All consumer goods are substitutes for one another
to a greater or lesser degree. A Chevrolet is clearly a close substitute for a Ford, and therefore we readily admit that the Ford
Motor Company and the Chevrolet Division of General Motors are
competitors. But Ford must also face recognizable competition of
a less direct sort. In deciding how to spend its income a family may
consider as competing alternatives buying a new automobile (Ford,
Chevrolet, or whatever), taking a vacation trip, remodeling the
house, having a cleaning woman once a week, adding to the savings
account, and so forth almost indefinitely. Sets of consumer budget
choices among such alternatives, taken many millionfold, determine
the elasticity of demand for any given product. The more that substitutes of this sort are able to affect the sales of a particular product over some price range, the more elastic the demand for that
product is said to be. The more elastic the demand schedule faced
by an individual firm is, the more competitive that firm's position
is said to be.

The government as buyer of weapons also has a budget. It must
make the best possible use of its budgeted funds, allocating them
among different weapon system programs, some close substitutes
for one another and some (like Nike Zeus and Polaris) remote substitutes. As suggested in the preceding chapter, this is accomplished
by maximizing the expected military value of its weapons programs
subject to the constraint that total weapons program costs just ex-
haust the weapons budget. The government also will not support

----

[1] See, for example, the testimony of Air Force Assistant Secretary for
Research and Development Richard E. Horner in House, Committee on Appropriations, *Hearings, Department of Defense Appropriations for 1960*
(1959), Part 6, pp. 164–167. For a criticism of this logic see Thornton
Read, "Strategy for Active Defense," *American Economic Review,* May
1961, pp. 465–471.

a program which promises less value than its cost, assuming the two to be somehow commensurable. Moreover, the budgetary problem is not just a question of supporting or not supporting a given program; there are also various possible levels of support. The first volume of this study showed that the greater the surplus of military value over cost a development program offers, the more funds that development should receive.[2] When the time for production of operational units arrives, weapon systems promising high value relative to their cost will be procured in larger dollar volumes than systems affording relatively less value, and the less effective systems may not be produced at all. Thus, something analogous to elasticity of demand also exists for weapon systems, although the existence of only one or at most a few buyers may lead to significant discontinuities in demand schedules.

To the weapons contractor this means that even though its weapon system has no direct competitors in the form of close technical and operational substitutes, competition for budgetary support imposes definite constraints on its program behavior. If quality is permitted to deteriorate or development schedules to slip, the program's military value will fall relative to its cost,[3] and funds will be reallocated to other programs with higher value/cost ratios, or the program may even be cancelled. For example, late operational availability of the Snark long-range cruise missile led to the program's termination after only one operational squadron had been procured. As the commander of the Strategic Air Command said, "Let's face it, it came too late. . . . They have a very limited value to SAC." [4] Likewise, if costs are permitted by a contractor to rise too much relative to value, program cancellation again will result, as in the well-publicized Skybolt missile case.[5]

[2] Peck and Scherer, pp. 280–281.

[3] *Ibid.,* pp. 271–275 and 632–638.

[4] House, Committee on Appropriations, *Hearings, Department of Defense Appropriations for 1960* (1959), Part 2, p. 393.

[5] Note that short of program cancellation, it is impossible to predict without further information how excessively high development costs will affect the contractor's total revenue. As long as the contractor can avoid program cancellation, increases in costs due, for example, to inefficiency or the development of uneconomic performance features may be greater than the decrease in financial support due to conducting the development on a less urgent timetable.

Of course, we might expect this second, "cost push" type of pressure to operate less strongly than quality and time pressures. As indicated in the preceding chapter, quality and time generally receive much greater weight than cost in weapons choice decisions. In terms of the present schema, military value falls off rapidly as time is increased or quality decreased. On the other hand, the significance of development cost is reduced by the difficulty of making commensurable value-cost comparisons, the great uncertainty present in early development program cost predictions, and by the fact that once costs have been incurred, they are "sunk" and are (or at least, should be [6]) irrelevant to program continuation decisions, regardless of their magnitude. Therefore the government's "demand" for a development program is apt to be quite inelastic through a substantial range of development costs.

In top priority programs, whose value is high relative to cost, we should expect the threat of cancellation for budgetary reasons to be slight and the competitive pressure on budgets to be weak.[7] On the other hand, in programs with value/cost relationships near the margin of cancellation in the estimation of government decision makers, we should expect a dual incentive for optimal and efficient performance to be present. To keep a marginal program alive, a contractor must make good use of the resources it is given. At the same time, the government is typically much less generous in providing funds for marginal programs than for high priority efforts, and so the contractor is forced to live austerely.

THE EFFECTS OF BUDGETARY COMPETITION IN THE 1950's

So much for the theory. How severe in fact were budgetary pressures in weapons programs of the 1950's? And how did these pressures affect contractor behavior in terms of tradeoff decisions and efforts to achieve efficiency?

[6] But decision makers do not always act as economists would have them behave. See Peck and Scherer, pp. 320–321.

[7] The high priority Nike Zeus program seems to be an exception. My interpretation of the Zeus program budgeting problem is as follows: The program was so large that a small proportional surplus of expected military value over cost would be absolutely large, motivating the assignment of a high priority. However, given the high level of technical and strategic uncertainty, an unfavorable program outcome which completely eliminated the expected surplus of military value over cost was quite possible.

None of the five high priority efforts among the 12 programs covered by our case studies experienced significant budgetary pressures during their development phases. In most instances officials connected with these programs indicated that funds were readily made available for whatever work they deemed necessary, and sometimes even that they had been given a "blank check" to accomplish their urgent development jobs. On the other hand, the two medium and five relatively low priority programs were subjected to budgetary pressures of varying severity, especially during the period beginning around 1957.[8]

If frugal use of resources is correlated with the severity of budgetary pressures, and if the severity of budgetary pressures is correlated with program priority, we should expect a correlation between efficiency and program priority. High priority programs with "blank check" funding ought to be conducted less efficiently on the average than low priority programs. To test this hypothesis, it was possible to determine with fairly high confidence whether 10 of the 12 development programs were executed relatively efficiently or inefficiently.[9] The results of this classification do not support the hypothesis; indeed, they tend to contradict it. Two of the three high priority programs on which efficiency judgments could be made were conducted relatively efficiently. Five of the seven medium and low priority programs were conducted relatively inefficiently, even though it was predicted that budgetary pressures would afford an incentive for efficiency.

Several factors appear to underlie this result. First, the top priority programs generally were conducted by unusually capable contractor organizations, while some of the lower priority programs were handled by teams of inferior ability. Thus, the competence variable directly correlated with program priority may have been a more important determinant of relative efficiency than the budgetary pressure variable inversely correlated with priority.

Furthermore, none of the programs in our sample held extremely low priorities. All were able to obtain sufficient funds to sustain an active (although not necessarily the planned) rate of development progress. In only three programs was there a serious threat of pro-

8 A program-by-program analysis of the severity and effects of development expenditure limitations is provided in Peck and Scherer, pp. 447–451.

9 See also Chapter 7 *infra*.

gram cancellation due to high development costs or funds shortages, even when the Department of Defense's mid-1957 austerity
drive forced the cancellation of several hundred contracts (mostly
quite small) by the three services.[10]

In many cases the effect of funds limitations such as those imposed in 1957 was the elimination of less essential development and
preproduction activities and the acceptance of minor quality sacrifices rather than the extension of development schedules.[11]   The
mere fact that nonessential activities were under way in these low
priority programs suggests that budgetary pressures for efficiency
had not originally been severe.[12]

Nevertheless, for a number of reasons the budgetary pressures
on medium and low priority development programs became increasingly strong from 1957 through 1960. Many programs which
had been started in the late 1940's and early 1950's and carried
forward at relatively low expenditure levels during the mid-1950's
suddenly reached the point at which greatly increased budgetary
support for final development and production of operational equipment was required. At the same time attractive new technical possibilities opened up, especially in the missile and space fields. Increased awareness of Soviet military and technological capabilities
also led to the inception of many new development programs. Thus,
the demand for budgetary support of weapons programs grew
rapidly during the 1957–1960 period. However, as Table 3.1
shows, total expenditures for weapons and space programs increased fairly slowly from July 1957 through June 1960 — certainly much less rapidly than the expansion in the demand for
funds. Top priority programs had little trouble in obtaining sufficient budgetary support despite increased competition for the
limited number of defense dollars. But firms responsible for lower
priority programs found themselves unable to command the funds
that they considered necessary to maintain competitive development schedules, were faced with imminent program cancellation,
or both.   In terms of the constrained maximization model presented in Chapter 2, the value of λ had risen perceptibly.

[10] House, Committee on Government Operations, *32nd Report, Research
and Development* (1958), pp. 35–41.

[11] Peck and Scherer, pp. 448–451.

[12] *Ibid.,* p. 499.

TABLE 3.1

U.S. Weapons and Space Development and Procurement
Expenditures: 1953–1963
(millions of dollars)

Fiscal Year Ending in June:	Defense Procurement *	Defense RDT&E †	NACA NASA	Total	Percentage Change
1953	17,297	2,148	79	19,524	
1954	15,957	2,187	90	18,234	−6.7
1955	12,838	2,261	74	15,173	−16.8
1956	12,227	2,101	71	14,399	−5.1
1957	13,488	2,406	76	15,970	+10.9
1958	14,083	2,504	89	16,676	+4.4
1959	14,409	2,866	145	17,420	+4.4
1960	13,334	4,710	401	18,445	+5.9
1961	13,095	6,131	740	19,966	+8.2
1962	14,836	6,039	1,380	22,255	+11.4
1963	15,356	6,650	2,400	24,406	+9.7

* Includes the procurement of aircraft, missiles, ships, astronautics; ordnance, vehicles, and related equipment; electronics and communications, and other procurement. Since 1954 "other procurement" was less than 10% of the total.
† Research, development, test, and evaluation.

SOURCES: Defense data are from an Office of the Secretary of Defense, Comptroller, estimate of January 18, 1962, in which an attempt was made to keep the breakdown between Procurement and RDT&E as comparable over the years as possible. NACA–NASA data are from U.S. Bureau of the Census, *Statistical Abstract of the United States: 1962*, p. 544; and Peck and Scherer, p. 100. The figures for 1963 are projected estimates.

With the change in technology of the 1950's came an influx of new firms into the weapons industry and no corresponding exit of established firms.[13]   This new entry, combined with price and wage increases and the hold-the-line policy on defense spending, put special pressure on aircraft producers.   As Table 3.2 shows, the aircraft and parts industry attained peak postwar sales and employment levels in calendar year 1957.   Then a decline set in, and by 1960 sales were 6.5% and employment was 24.7% below the 1957 peaks.

All of the interviews connected with our weapons program case studies took place during this period.   Many executives expressed concern over the growing pressure on program budgets.   Although

[13] *Ibid.*, pp. 220–221.

TABLE 3.2

The Level of Aircraft, Aircraft Engines, and Parts
Industry Activity: 1952–1962

Year	Sales (millions)	Employees	December 31 Backlog (millions)
1952	$ 6,497	670,600	17,653
1953	8,511	795,500	16,753
1954	8,305	782,900	14,852
1955	8,470	761,300	15,702
1956	9,496	837,300	18,350
1957	11,765	895,800	14,531
1958	11,470	783,600	13,171
1959	11,255	755,400	12,120
1960	10,997	673,800	12,496
1961	n.a.	668,900	n.a.

SOURCE: Aerospace Industries Association, *Aerospace Facts and Figures: 1962* (Washington: 1962), pp. 12, 14, and 66. More recent sales and backlog data cannot be obtained because of changes in coverage.

the process was too gradual to permit distinguishing discrete behavioral changes, there was considerable evidence of belt-tightening in old-line sectors such as aircraft and aircraft engines. To be sure, there were institutional lags in industry's adaptation to these new conditions. The first reaction of defense executives was often indignation at the government's reluctance to increase defense spending despite obvious needs, rather than any constructive actions. But as the pressure on program budgets grew stronger, many contractor officials recognized that the liberal funding days of the mid-1950's were passing. Companies began eliminating unproductive overhead personnel, assuming a firmer stand in wage-rate negotiations, taking cost reduction programs seriously (rather than viewing them as an innocuous method of pleasing contracting agencies), and generally tightening up on their operations.[14]

The Eisenhower Administration was subjected to bitter criticism, both partisan and nonpartisan, for attempting to hold the line on defense spending despite rapidly growing program demands. Whether this criticism was justified in terms of over-all national security posture cannot be determined here. It is reasonably clear,

[14] *Ibid.,* pp. 517–528.

however, that these policies had the desirable effect of injecting a greater sense of cost-consciousness into weapons acquisition activities. Nor was this benefit unsolicited. Secretary of Defense Charles E. Wilson recognized that projects of marginal value would not be eliminated by the military services and contractors unless financial pressure was applied. As a House of Representatives committee report said of the 1957 memorandum in which Wilson announced his controversial reduction in funds for development programs:

> . . . The intent behind the August 17, 1957, memorandum was said, therefore, to be to force the military departments to cull such relatively doubtful items out of the P & P program and to force the services to give them a more rigid evaluation. . . .[15]

Wilson himself remarked, with characteristic sarcasm, that "the penalty for saving money isn't as great this year as it was in the past." [16] It is not unlikely that at least some of the criticism heaped upon Wilson by defense industry representatives was motivated by resentment of his role in disturbing what had been a rather good life.

As Table 3.1 shows, expenditures for weapons and space programs began to increase more rapidly after 1960. Again, the scope of the present study precludes any effort to decide whether the increase was in the broad national interest. Since our case study research was concluded in 1959, no direct evidence on the effect of these changes on contractor behavior is available. It is clear that competition among programs for budgetary support remained strong as more and more new projects in fields of weapons and space technology were proposed. Nevertheless, it seems likely that the addition of more than $4 billion to annual weapons and space expenditures during fiscal years 1962 and 1963 relieved some of the financial pressure on defense contractors.

Budgetary Pressures and Tradeoff Decisions

In the five relatively low priority programs covered by our case studies, shortages of funds led to a relaxation of original program

[15] House, Committee on Government Operations, *32nd Report, Research and Development* (1958), p. 139.

[16] Claude Witze, "Services to Get Fiscal 1959 Ceilings," *Aviation Week,* August 12, 1957, p. 26.

objectives, and especially to slippages in development schedules. Typically what happened is as follows. Because of unexpected technical difficulties, initially unrealistic cost predictions, or conscious decisions to seek improved technical performance, additional funds were required to hold the program on schedule. The sponsoring government agency found itself unable to provide some or all of these additional funds. It was faced with the choice of lowering its quality objectives or "stretching out" the development effort over a longer period. Since in these low priority programs there was no urgent need for the weapon systems being developed, the decision in nearly every case was to accept a development schedule slippage.

As a rule the final decision in such situations was made by government officials, although contractor executives played an important supporting role. Yet in several cases one might have expected the contractor to have an option other than schedule slippage or quality reduction, for all but one of the programs confronted with serious choices of this nature were conducted relatively inefficiently. That is, the shortage of funds might have been met by reducing unnecessary costs rather than increasing development time. Such an alternative certainly had its attractions, since in all but one program the schedule slippages led to decreases in the quantity of operational weapon systems procured. Thus, by accepting delays the contractors let their sales expectations decline. Why were the potential competitive incentives for efficiency ineffective in these programs?

Three explanations, not mutually exclusive, appear relevant. First, the explanation is related partly to the definition of inefficiency applied here. That is, a program could have been classified as inefficient because it was "stretched out" too frequently or over too long a period, so that the program's overhead burden was inordinately high relative to its direct technical effort.[17] In one program this was probably the main source of inefficiency, and in another program it was a less important source.

Second, it is possible that company top management and project leaders were doing their best to eliminate inefficiencies, but that their best was not very good. Inefficiency is neither identified nor wiped out easily in an advanced weapons development program,

[17] Cf. Peck and Scherer, p. 265 and note 31 on p. 441 concerning this "overhead effect."

for sophisticated judgments must be made on the number and types of technical tasks to be performed and the number of people needed to complete them. The most highly motivated manager is likely to turn in an inefficient performance if he lacks the ability to detect inefficiency or to obtain the cooperation of often recalcitrant operating level personnel in cost reduction efforts. This was a significant problem in at least four and probably all six of the programs classified as inefficient. In such cases incentives for efficiency can operate only slowly by spurring top management to develop or hire more capable operating level managers and to eliminate weak links.

Finally, firms faced with a shortage of current work may be willing to risk certain kinds of follow-on production contract losses due to schedule slippages and high costs in order to ensure company survival on a broader plane. This is not necessarily short-sighted behavior. The possession of a going organization, with the appropriate complement of development and production skills, is a vital ingredient in the formula for winning new program participation opportunities. When there is not enough work to go around currently on an efficient basis, it is often preferable to sacrifice certain specific future follow-on production contract possibilities rather than break up technical groups and other key capabilities which will be instrumental in competing for new program awards. In other words, future sales expectations in the particular program may be sacrificed to protect other future sales opportunities. Shortages of funds are met by letting current program efforts get out of balance; e.g., by deferring the production of critical long lead time items, by reducing the amount of resources given to specialist subsystem and parts vendors, by pulling subcontracted work back "in-house," [18] and as a last resort by laying off one's own personnel in those departments and activities which do not play a strategic role in the company's longer-run competitive plans. Government personnel are commonly unable to prevent these actions, even when they lead to undesirable schedule slippages and quality deficiencies, because they lack the detailed technical knowledge and insight required to refute contractor claims that the in-house activities not cut back are crucial to program success. Behavior of this sort was apparent in at least three of the five low priority programs covered by our case studies.

Thus, even though budgetary pressures provide an incentive for

[18] For examples, see *ibid.*, pp. 388–394.

efficiency, the incentive may not be sufficient to offset many of the tendencies toward inefficiency present in a development program. And in certain cases contractors may respond to budgetary pressures, not by eliminating avoidable inefficiencies in strategic parts of their organizations, but by letting development schedules slip and perhaps by sacrificing quality.

Budgetary Pressures and Production Efficiency

Competition for budgetary support can also generate incentives for efficiency during the production phases of a weapons program. In two programs characterized by especially vigorous cost reduction efforts, the explanations given by company executives for their economy drives reflected a belief that the long-run price or cost elasticity of demand for their weapon systems was greater than unity. Their reasoning was as follows. Budget allocations for the procurement of their weapons in the next fiscal year were generally fixed. The lower the price per unit quoted, the more units would be ordered with the fixed amount of procurement funds available. This suggests a short-run elasticity of demand of 1.0 for that fiscal year's procurement. Furthermore, company officials believed that by reducing its cost per unit, they could make their weapon system more attractive to the buying service, leading to larger orders in subsequent fiscal years and perhaps even postponement of the program's ultimate termination date. This implies a longer-run elasticity of demand greater than unity for any lasting cost reduction. Since negotiated profit rates on production contracts tend to be roughly constant for a given firm in a given type of program,[19] cost reductions with an elasticity of demand greater than unity increase both sales and profits in the long run.

Obviously, this reasoning is not valid for all procurement situations. When the government requires a fixed number of units, regardless of moderate variations in cost per unit, reducing unit costs will reduce both sales and profits. Such a relationship is probable for subsystems and components which represent only a small part of a weapon system's total cost and which are needed in fixed proportion to the number of weapon systems procured. It may also occur for very high priority weapon systems with no close substitutes. To the extent that contractors believe the cost elasticity

[19] Cf. Chapter 9 *infra*

of demand for their products is less than unity, as suggested in this case, an incentive for inefficiency exists. Our case studies offered no indication of how prevalent such a view was among defense firm executives.

THE POSSIBILITIES FOR IMPROVED BUGETARY COMPETITION INCENTIVES

In both development and production programs, then, competition for budgetary support can under certain conditions supply an incentive for good contractor performance, including good performance on the cost dimension. This cost effect is especially important, given the fact that competition between close substitute weapons provides at best a weak incentive for development cost reduction and more frequently an incentive to enhance quality and reduce time at the expense of cost control. Can better use be made of the budgetary competitive incentive to spur cost consciousness in defense contracting?

If budgetary competition is to generate stronger incentives for development program efficiency, one major condition must be met: program budgets must be sufficiently tight to put pressure on contractor operations. If, on the other hand, development efforts are generously funded, contractors will feel little compulsion to eliminate interesting but unnecessary technical tasks, reject superfluous weapon system features and gadgets, hold overhead costs to austere levels, strive for high worker productivity, allocate specialized tasks to the most efficient subcontractors, and so on. The crucial question, therefore, is this: Can the government establish program budgets which are tight, but not so restrictive that undesirable time and quality sacrifices are forced?

The evidence from our case studies suggests a pessimistic answer. The government agencies responsible for the programs studied had little independent ability to determine how much money a development or early production effort needed. Typically, in high priority programs the contractor stated how much money it required to meet the service's time and quality goals, and although sometimes there were heated arguments, the contractor usually could defend its requests successfully, and all or nearly all of the requested funds were made available. In lower priority programs the contractor often received a good deal less than it requested.

However, as a rule such reductions were enforced not because of any buying service decision that its objectives could be satisfied for less money, but because the service was unable to cover all requests fully within its budget constraint. As a result, sometimes the reductions still left the contractor with considerable budgetary slack, sometimes they applied just the right amount of pressure, and sometimes they led to time and quality sacrifices undesirable to the government — all in a decidedly unknowing, almost random fashion.

Virtually all the detailed cost estimation for weapons program budget decisions of the 1950's was undertaken by contractors. But delegation of this function to industry has two major problems. First and most obvious, unless its program is on the brink of cancellation due to high costs, a company has an incentive in its annual development budget estimates to ensure that all personnel levels, projects, and contingencies are provided for.[20]   The conflict of objectives common under these circumstances is shown by an example from our case studies:

> Believing that a major development effort was being conducted inefficiently, service officials asked the prime contractor to provide a priority-ranked list of development tasks so they could delete unnecessary items. The company refused to comply, claiming that all of its tasks were vital — an assertion disputed by scientists not connected with the contractor organization. The buying agency then sent its own group of technical specialists into the contractor's laboratory to evaluate the tasks, but they were unsuccessful in their attempt to learn which could be eliminated or reduced in size. The buying agency then shifted the burden back to the contractor, making an arbitrary cut in the company's budgetary request and announcing, "We have only so much money. Which jobs can you do?" The contractor then trimmed its work program to conform with the service's budgetary constraint. No time delays or quality sacrifices resulted from this pruning operation.

[20] This is not true of over-all program cost projections, especially those submitted very early in the program, for in such cases the incentive to "buy in" by underestimating costs is very strong. These underestimates are then gradually corrected as contracts are negotiated and as annual budget forecasts are submitted. See Peck and Scherer, pp. 411–418.

A second problem connected with contractor budget estimation is the typically unsatisfactory character of weapons makers' accounting systems. This will be discussed more thoroughly in a later chapter. Here it is sufficient to note that as a rule during the late 1950's, firms were unable to allocate costs to specific development tasks and weapon system elements. Therefore cost projections were normally made by estimating how many scientists, senior engineers, engineers, draftsmen, technicians, and other personnel the *over-all* project would require — a procedure which buries the most important possibilities for cost reduction.

Coupled with these contractor deficiencies has been the inability of government agencies to make detailed independent judgments on the amount of resources required in a development effort to meet time and quality objectives. In all but three of the 12 programs covered by our case studies, there existed within the buying agency no group with the technical competence needed for a thorough independent analysis of contractor budget estimates. In the remaining three programs at least some technically qualified people were assigned to this job, but typically the amount of analysis carried out was quite limited.

Of course, even the most expert budget analysis group cannot determine exactly what is needed and what is unnecessary to meet government objectives in an ambitious development effort. Inherent uncertainties preclude such precision. Nevertheless, estimates much tighter than those common in the 1950's could be obtained by the government if the required independent technical competence were brought to bear.

Progress in this direction has been made within the Department of Defense since 1960. One improvement is the "program package" approach to budgeting, which attempts to identify all costs relevant to a program during the coming five-year period.[21] This procedure should help the government avoid situations in which over-all program costs are badly underestimated at the outset of a program, but the contractor avoids program cancellation by revising its estimates only gradually, after many costs are already

[21] The idea itself is not a new one. It was outlined in some detail by David Novick in *Efficiency and Economy in Government Through New Budgeting and Accounting Procedures,* R–254 (Santa Monica: The RAND Corporation, 1954).

"sunk." In 1962, however, the Defense Department's budgetary groups were still highly dependent upon contractors for basic cost estimate inputs. To correct this deficiency, the Office of the Secretary of Defense and the services initiated programs to train government personnel in the techniques of cost analysis.[22] Whether mere acquisition of techniques, as opposed to the employment of persons thoroughly familiar with the relevant program technology, will lead to significant improvements in the government's cost analysis capabilities remains to be seen. Finally, continuing efforts have been made to obtain improvements in contractor cost accounting systems and to secure the use of such estimation techniques as the PERT/Cost system.[23]

Even if these efforts are highly successful, a substantial and unavoidable element of uncertainty in budget estimation must remain.[24] Disagreements over the amount of resources required to meet time and quality objectives in ambitious development programs will inevitably arise. Will government agencies be willing to overrule their contractors and independently set what they consider to be tight budgets, running the risk of schedule slippages and quality deficiencies? As we have seen, in the past they have been forced by over-all funds shortages to do so in connection with low priority programs. But in top priority programs, our case studies showed, government officials were generally reluctant to cut down what they considered to be excessive contractor funds requests, fearing that by so doing they would lose the contractor's wholehearted support or provide an excuse for possible failure. There is no reason to believe that this problem will be eliminated when and if the government develops an expertise equal to that of contractors in estimating program costs.

[22] See William H. Gregory, "USAF Drive Begins to Improve Forecasts," *Aviation Week & Space Technology,* June 4, 1962, pp. 76–85.

[23] See, for example, Robert Miller, "How to Plan and Control with PERT," *Harvard Business Review,* March–April 1962, pp. 93–104; and William Beller, "PERT's Horizon Beginning to Widen," *Missiles and Rockets,* July 17, 1961, pp. 110 ff. It should be obvious that such techniques as the PERT system are no better than the competence and intent of the contractor personnel supplying underlying time and cost estimates.

[24] For a similar conclusion by the principal architect of the program package approach, see David Novick, *Costing Tomorrow's Weapon Systems,* RM–3170–PR (Santa Monica: The RAND Corporation, 1962), pp. 8–9.

In sum, stronger incentives for efficiency can be achieved by fixing program budgets at levels just sufficient to meet government time and quality goals. To accomplish this, the military services and the Office of the Secretary of Defense must acquire independent competence in estimating program costs. Nevertheless, the budgetary incentives approach is clearly not a complete solution. Difficult problems involving uncertainty and information transmission will remain even if the problem of training competent cost analysts is solved. And under certain conditions, contractors may prefer to incur schedule slippages rather than reduce their costs to efficient levels. Counterbalancing incentives would be needed to prevent undesirable tradeoffs in such situations.

CHAPTER 4

Competition for New Programs on the Basis of Reputation

No weapon system program lasts forever. Sooner or later (and more likely sooner in an era of rapid technological change) a contractor must look to new programs for its survival and growth. This need makes possible a competitive incentive system based upon correlating the award of new programs with past performance.

The theory is simple: firms which have performed well in the past are rewarded with desirable new programs, while firms which have performed poorly are deprived of growth and perhaps survival by the withholding of new programs. Reputation becomes a significant asset in the competition for new programs.

It should be recognized that this type of competitive incentive requires no formal competition for implementation. The first volume of this study showed that in a sample of nearly 100 U.S. aircraft and guided missile system programs, more than half of the principal contractors had been chosen for their roles without formal source selection competition.[1] Nevertheless, what matters from our present point of view is not the form of the selection action, but the substance. Being eliminated from the running in a very informal screening because of poor past performance deprives a firm of new sales just as clearly as being eliminated for the same reason in a full-fledged formal design competition. As long as defense contractors expect their past performance to be an important factor in new program source selection actions, whether formally competitive or noncompetitive, an incentive for good performance exists.

This expectation aspect must be accentuated. If in fact past performance is not considered in source selection decisions but

[1] Peck and Scherer, pp. 326–340. The sample covered roughly 20 years in most categories. It should be noted that more recently the proportion of selection actions involving formal competition has risen.

contractors for some reason believe it is, their behavior will nevertheless be affected. Recognizing this, we must ask two different questions. First, what role have past performance considerations actually played in the choice of contractors for new programs? And second, how do contractors perceive the relationship between past performance and future selection?

THE ROLE OF PAST PERFORMANCE IN SELECTION DECISIONS

In the past relatively little emphasis has been placed on past performance in the selection of contractors for new weapon system and subsystem development programs. The clearest evidence of this is found in formal source selection competitions for which quantitative criterion point lists have been prepared. In a typical selection involving 10 firms, past performance considerations were assigned 10 out of a total of 100 points. This in itself suggests a minor role for past performance. Even more significant, however, was the distribution of points actually awarded within the performance category. All but one of the ten competitors received either nine or ten performance points, the one exception receiving eight points. Thus, the variation due to past performance was one point or at most two. This small difference might, of course, have just tipped the balance in an otherwise marginal situation. But such a distribution of points leads the firm seeking a new program to focus its efforts on those factors which are weighted more heavily and which are more variable, rather than on building up a reputation for good performance.

The "other factors" which normally receive much greater weight in competitive selection actions, including those with implicit rather than explicit criterion weighting, are the technical attractiveness of concepts and designs proposed by the competitors (as discussed in Chapter 2) and the extent to which prospective contractors have suitable technical, managerial, and physical resources available.[2] The exact balance of emphasis depends upon the type of selection action employed, reflecting such variables as the degree of technical uncertainty present and the government's program objectives. In competitions of the design type, attractiveness of proposed technical solutions and concepts is the paramount factor.

[2] For a more complete discussion of how these factors are considered in source selection competitions, see *ibid.,* pp. 362–373.

For instance, Department of Defense officials indicated that the choice of two finalists for the multibillion dollar TFX fighter program award was based "purely on technical evaluations." [3]   In the subsequent TFX run-off competition, the military source selection board assigned two-thirds of its criterion points to technical and operational considerations and one-third to management, production, cost, and logistic elements.[4]   In so-called management competitions, primary emphasis is placed upon the would-be contractors' qualitative and quantitative program execution capabilities — e.g., the availability of experienced technical and managerial personnel and appropriate research, development, and production facilities — although proposed technical concepts also receive considerable stress.   The management competition approach has been favored by the Air Force, as suggested in this statement by General Bernard A. Schriever, Air Force Systems Command chief:

> It is the policy of this Command to evaluate proposals primarily upon the comparative technical and managerial abilities of the proposed contractors responsive to the requirements being procured.[5]

It is widely believed that political pressures play an important role in the award of new government contracts.[6]   However, popular discussions probably exaggerate the influence of congressional politics on particular advanced weapon system and subsystem development contract awards.[7]   To be sure, politics has a significant procedural and ritualistic effect on the source selection process.

[3] Larry Booda, "Boeing Will Change Engine in TFX Bid," *Aviation Week & Space Technology,* February 12, 1962, p. 28.

[4] George C. Wilson, "McNamara Tries to Steer TFX Questions," *Aviation Week & Space Technology,* April 1, 1963, p. 26, summarizing testimony of Air Force Brig. Gen. A. T. Culbertson.   As we have seen in Chapter 2, Secretary of Defense McNamara later reversed the source selection board's decision, mainly because he considered a quite different set of weights appropriate.   But his emphasis was still on essentially technical considerations — e.g., expected cost, commonality of parts, and technical risk — and not on past performance.

[5] Letter to various operating agency commanders dated January 12, 1962.

[6] Cf. "White House Contract Pressure Is Increasing," *Missiles and Rockets,* February 11, 1963, p. 9; and "Sen. Case Seeks Watchdog Unit for Military, Space Contracts," *Aviation Week & Space Technology,* February 25, 1963, p. 34.

[7] "Particular" must be emphasized.   The more general impact of political pressures on firms' survival will be discussed later.

For example, announcement of the Air Force's 120-inch solid rocket engine development contract award decision was delayed until one day after a Florida primary election because the contract had become a political issue.[8]   But the substantive impact appears much smaller.   Our case study research disclosed no selection decisions which could not be justified on nonpolitical grounds, even though political influence had been alleged in several cases.[9]   Two conditions have served to limit the effects of politics.   First, many political pressures cancel out.   By deferring to a congressman from California in a specific contract award decision, military officials risk bringing down the wrath (or at least the counter-demands) of congressmen representing other firms from New York, Michigan, Texas, etc.   Recognizing this, decision makers attempt to avoid political criteria and stress other more suitable criteria in their choices.   And second, the highly technical nature of award decisions permits them to follow this course successfully.   Without an extensive fact-finding investigation, a legislator is seldom able to dispute the Defense Department's claim that a certain contractor was chosen for compelling technical or economic reasons.[10]   As a result, the political sound and fury which accompany large contract awards generally signify little or nothing, as President Kennedy implied in denying the imposition of political pressures on the TFX award:

> . . . Senators and Congressmen who are concerned about unemployment among their citizens, who are concerned about the flow of tax dollars, will continue to press.   But the fact of the matter is we have a Secretary of Defense who is making very honest judgments in these matters, and I know from personal experience that Senators and Congressmen who recently visited Secretary McNamara, asking to prevent plans from being turned down, who happen to be members of my own party, and indeed, even more closely related, have been rejected by the Secretary of Defense.[11]

----

8 Larry Booda, "United Technology Corp. Awarded Contract for 120-in. Solid Motor," *Aviation Week & Space Technology,* May 14, 1962, p. 33.

9 Peck and Scherer, pp. 379–382.

10 It is possible that politics has more influence on contract awards involving no advanced technology, although on this I simply have no evidence.

11 From a press conference transcript in *Wall Street Journal,* March 22, 1963, p. 20. The "even more closely related" phrase was presumably a refer-

Thus, the conclusion stands that criteria relating to technical merit and contractor capabilities were given predominant weight in the vast majority of source selection competitions during the 1950's and early 1960's, while past performance considerations received relatively little weight.

It is quite possible that past performance criteria work their most significant effects in a more informal way. For instance, a high-ranking Department of Defense official observed that a contractor which has turned in an especially unsuccessful performance may be omitted from the lists of firms invited to bid on new contracts.[12] Still this step is apparently resorted to infrequently, and when firms have been "black-listed," the deprivation has generally been for only a short period. Furthermore, the "black-list" approach affords no essential sales-performance correlation once some minimum standard of acceptable performance is exceeded.

It is also possible that superior capability and good past performance are correlated in the assessments of military decision makers. In particular, managers, scientists, and engineers may not be regarded as highly capable unless they have performed well on past and ongoing contracts. But while this relationship undoubtedly holds to some extent, it is by no means universal. A technical group can gain skill by learning from its mistakes as well as from its successes. And as we will see shortly, firms have often built up superior program execution capabilities through inefficient rather than efficient past performance.

One can of course find examples of source selection decisions which were affected by past performance considerations. In the X–22A vertical takeoff and landing research vehicle competition, the Bell Aerospace Company was chosen despite a technical evaluation in favor of Douglas Aircraft Company because Bell's "experience and past performance" were deemed more appropriate.[13]

---

ence to his brother, U.S. Senator Edward M. Kennedy, who campaigned in 1962 on the platform that "he could do more for Massachusetts."

[12] "Constant Reviews Yield Sharp Technical Control," *Missiles and Rockets,* March 25, 1963, p. 45, citing Dr. Harold Brown, Director of Defense Research and Engineering.

[13] George C. Wilson, "Gilpatric Cites Knowledge of X–22A Firms," *Aviation Week & Space Technology,* June 24, 1963, p. 36, recording testimony before the Preparedness Investigating Subcommittee of the Senate Committee on Armed Services.

Yet past experience was apparently weighted much more heavily than past performance in this 1962 decision. Explaining the choice, Deputy Defense Secretary R. L. Gilpatric emphasized that Bell had considerable direct prior experience in the VTOL field, whereas Douglas had virtually none. He noted further that Bell's past record showed a strong research orientation desired in the X–22 program, while Douglas' forte had been transport and fighter production. On the past performance side of the issue, a memorandum evaluating the two competitors pointed out that "Douglas' recent performance in a variety of jobs, notably Skybolt, has been very questionable." However, Gilpatric asserted that "When I came to make my decision in this X–22 matter, I was not influenced by the Skybolt situation." [14]

Our case studies furnished some more clear-cut examples of a role for past performance criteria. Although such matters as lack of scientific capability have been stressed in published discussions,[15] the dissatisfaction of Air Force officials with Convair's performance in the F–102 and other programs also had a bearing on their decision not to let Convair assume full prime contractor responsibilities in the accelerated Atlas ICBM program. In another major guided missile program the buying agency rejected two otherwise favorably placed contenders for the prime contractor's task because of failures in earlier guided missile developments.

Nevertheless, even more cases can be found in which, after turning in a plainly unsatisfactory job, a company has received a very desirable new program award. For instance, when the program in our case study sample with the largest cost overrun and the third largest schedule slippage was drawing to a close, its principal contractor was "rewarded" with one of the most sought-after new programs in that general field. And when major firms *were* rejected in selection actions as a result of poor past performance they have been, with few exceptions, able to maintain their sales volume by entering other competitions in which performance considerations did not make the decisive difference.

[14] *Ibid.*, p. 37.
[15] Cf. House, Committee on Government Operations, *Eleventh Report, Organization and Management of Missile Programs* (1959), pp. 70–79.

Poor Performance and the Demise of Defense Contractors

This finding suggests a broader question: How frequently have the U.S. armed services let a major contractor wither away and die mainly because of poor performance?

The analysis of turnover among the 100 largest U.S. defense prime contractors presented in the first volume of this study shows that many firms have fallen from the ranks of the government's leading weapons vendors.[16] Over a 20-year period from 1940 to 1960, 195 companies appeared at one time or another on three lists of the 100 largest prime contractors. Thirty-seven of World War II's top 100 contractors disappeared from the Korean period list for reasons other than mergers. Forty-one of the Korean period's top 100 were missing from the 1958–1960 list for nonmerger reasons.

Yet more careful scrutiny reveals that factors other than the denial of new contracts due to poor performance largely explain the disappearance of these firms. Consider those 26 companies among the top 50 prime contractors during World War II which had fallen 20 ranks or more by the 1958–1960 period. The positions of automobile makers General Motors, Ford, Nash-Kelvinator (now American Motors), and Studebaker-Packard declined partly because of company decisions to concentrate on automobile production during the periods of pent-up consumer demand following World War II and the Korean conflict, and partly because the demand for military goods shifted from tanks and other vehicles to aircraft, rockets, and electronic systems.[17] Changes in military demand appear mainly responsible for the decline of shipbuilders Henry J. Kaiser, Todd Shipyards, California Shipbuilding, and Bath Iron Works; for Bethlehem Steel, Consolidated Steel, and U.S. Steel and Permanente Metals; for heavy equipment makers International Harvester, American Locomotive, American Car and Foundry, Baldwin Locomotive, Pressed Steel Car, Caterpillar, Allis Chalmers, and Diamond T; and for U.S. Rubber and Sun Oil. DuPont dropped from 15th to 86th place partly because of the shift from conventional to nuclear explosives, but also because of a somewhat unique desire to shed the "merchants of death" im-

[16] Peck and Scherer, pp. 127–128 and 599–620.
[17] *Ibid.*, pp. 191–193.

age with which it had been branded during the interwar period. Only three firms in the aircraft, electronics, and instrumentation fields — Curtiss-Wright, Bell Aircraft, and the Norden Company — declined 20 or more ranks from World War II to 1958–1960. Thus, changes in demand due to changing military technology, rather than poor performance in a given field, appear to explain most of the major declines in market position of leading defense contractors.

The clearest example of a disappearance because of unsatisfactory performance is the case of Brewster Aeronautical Corporation, 84th on the list of prime contractors during World War II. Brewster's wartime record reflects what a congressional investigating committee called "an extreme case" of abuses.[18] The wartime cast of characters at Brewster included a board chairman who insisted on running the company from his farm; two munitions commission brokers who were imprisoned for attempting to sell arms to the enemy; a string of operating executives brought in at Navy request who found themselves with no real authority; a labor union president with extraordinary powers over hiring, firing, work force discipline, job assignments, and draft deferments who remarked on one occasion, "If I had brothers at the front who needed the 10 or 12 planes that were sacrificed I would let them die"; [19] and some 21,000 employees who, according to a War Manpower Commission survey, performed productive work during only one of every three hours for which they were paid.[20] The Brewster Corporation's initial claim to fame was the Buffalo fighter, which in 1938 was the Navy's fastest carrier-based fighter and which was a mainstay of U.S. defenses in the Battle of Midway. By 1942, however, the Buffalo was obsolete and saw little wartime production. Brewster developed a dive bomber for the Navy, but the program was terminated after only 300 units were delivered because of engineering deficiencies and evidence of sabotage on a number of aircraft, and because production fell nearly two years behind schedule due to inadequate material controls and work force

[18] House Committee on Naval Affairs, *Report of the Subcommittee Appointed To Investigate the Causes of Failure of Production of Brewster Aeronautical Corporation Under Its Contracts With the Navy* (1943), p. 3.

[19] *Ibid.*, p. 37.

[20] *Ibid.*, p. 34.

stoppages, slowdowns, and strikes. Those dive bombers which had been delivered were found suitable only for operational training and target towing.

In April 1942 Brewster was taken over and placed under direct Navy management until, a month later, its directors agreed to put their stock in trust for two years. After a succession of five presidents in three years failed to solve the company's problems, Liberty Ship builder Henry J. Kaiser was installed in October 1943, as a congressional committee said, to cleanse "the Augean stables at Brewster." [21] Having lost all of the contracts to produce aircraft of its own design, the company at the time was concentrating on its role as one of three producers of the Vought Corsair Navy fighter — an effort on which Brewster was about a year behind its original schedule. Under Kaiser a production rate of 120 aircraft per month was achieved (against promised deliveries of 150 per month). Nevertheless, Brewster had the highest unit costs of the three Corsair producers, and in May 1944 a reduction in Corsair requirements was met by cancelling Brewster's contract, leaving the company with virtually no work. Many of its employees then staged a sit-in strike to protest the cancellation.[22] But despite vigorous objections by local congressmen, the Navy made only token efforts to give Brewster any further business, and in 1946 the company was liquidated.

The Brewster case is not only a strong example; it is unique. From the time the United States entered World War II through 1962, Brewster has been the only firm specializing in combat aircraft permitted by the government to go completely out of business.[23] The nearest comparable example appears at the subsystem

[21] *Ibid.*, p. 50.

[22] "Brewster Pickets Gibe Only Navy," *New York Times,* May 30, 1944, p. 34.

[23] The only other known instance of a World War II contractor being taken over and managed by the government was the case of the Lord Manufacturing Company, which refused to reprice its contracts despite profits alleged to have been between 66% and 100% of costs. See John Perry Miller, *Pricing of Military Procurements* (New Haven: Yale University Press, 1949), pp. 105–106. In 1962, however, Lord was still active in the same military product line (shock resistant engine and instrument mounts), although its employment had declined to 1,075 from a 1944 level of 3,000. Brewster's troubles with the government were certainly not the same as Lord's — Brewster was one of the rare firms that managed to lose money

level. After an excellent start in the jet engine field, Westinghouse stumbled badly in developing the J–46 and especially the J–40 engines. Despite development expenditures of roughly $100 million, the J–40 fell far short of its thrust specifications, and an underpowered version was beset by reliability and delivery problems. These difficulties delayed the availability of the F3H interceptor, urgently needed for the Korean conflict, until it could be redesigned around another engine. During a 1955 congressional investigation of the J–40 program, Westinghouse jet engine division officials admitted underestimating the magnitude of the task, failing to expand their engineering staff quickly enough, placing inadequate emphasis on basic aerodynamic research, scattering their operations too widely across the country, and various other deficiencies.[24] In its report on the investigation, the House Committee on Government Operations enunciated a thinly veiled threat that:

> . . . Westinghouse's expectation of future Government contracts will be more solidly grounded if it displays a much greater willingness to make investments for research and development of a magnitude commensurate with the role it would like to play in the Nation's military aircraft program.[25]

Even before that report appeared, the Navy began to consider eliminating Westinghouse from the jet engine field.[26] During the late 1950's Westinghouse developed the J–54 engine through 150-hour tests completely at its own expense, but the engine was not accepted for production by the government. After several years of unsuccessful attempts to regain favor, Westinghouse withdrew from the jet engine business in 1960 and returned to the Navy the $137 million plant it had been using.[27]

Although some may exist, cloaked in secrecy, no other cases are known in which the U.S. government carried its displeasure over unsatisfactory performance in major weapon system or subsystem developments as far as in these two examples. As indicated earlier,

---

consistently during World War II despite operation exclusively under defense contracts.

[24] House, Committee on Government Operations, *Tenth Intermediate Report, Navy Jet Engine Procurement Program* (1956), pp. 34–35.

[25] *Ibid.*, p. 35.

[26] *Aviation Week,* February 15, 1954, p. 11.

[27] *Aviation Week & Space Technology,* March 28, 1960, p. 37.

a few firms (such as Curtiss-Wright, Bell Aircraft, and Fairchild) suffered significant defense prime contract position losses even though the broad fields in which they operated were not obliterated by changes in weapons technology.[28]   But the reasons for the decline of Bell, Curtiss-Wright, and Fairchild are certainly complex, perhaps involving no lasting displeasure over past performance at all, and none was completely eliminated from the weapons industry.[29]

Bell Aircraft Company (acquired in 1960 by Textron) dropped from 25th place among defense prime contractors during World War II to 45th place in 1958–1960. Its troubles began when the Bell F–83 interceptor lost out in an informal competition with the Lockheed F–80 during the late 1940's. After that time there were simply fewer new development programs than there were interested firms in the fighter field — Bell's former specialty. Bell then diversified into rocket, missile, and space work, but during the late 1950's it suffered serious sales losses due to the cancellation of several major projects. Whether it will be able to recover its position through new contracts remains to be seen. The company has over the years maintained a leading position in the helicopter field.

Curtiss-Wright, which dropped from second place among prime contractors during World War II to 11th place in the Korean period and 30th in 1958–1960, failed to make the transition into jet aircraft production, possibly because of its continuing emphasis on reciprocating engine and propeller technology. Notably, only one of several postwar fighters designed by Curtiss-Wright (the F–87) took advantage of jet propulsion. The company's Wright Division later modified two British-designed turbojet engines to meet U.S. needs, but this effort was not especially successful, and it led to production contracts of only limited duration. For unknown reasons the company did not move aggressively into rocket engine and

[28] The reasons for bombsight maker Norden's decline and ultimate absorption by United Aircraft are not fully known. For a partial discussion of Norden's disappearance, along with two others not explained by over-all military demand changes, see Peck and Scherer, pp. 125–126.

[29] Westinghouse as a corporation was also not eliminated, although its rank among the top 100 prime contractors declined from 14th in the Korean period (1951–1953) to 19th in 1958–1960, while most electrical and electronics firms were experiencing rank increases.

guided missile system work. A precipitous sales decline after 1957 was probably caused by this inaction, and perhaps also by the deterioration of relations between certain of the company's officers and top military officials.

Fairchild Engine and Airplane Corporation (now Fairchild Stratos Corporation) is not included in the analysis of firms which declined in rank by 20 places or more following World War II, but its history also deserves mention. During the World War II period it was 73rd in the list of prime contractors. With large orders for the production of C–119 (Flying Boxcar) transports it jumped to 38th during the Korean period. It then fell to 52nd place in the 1958–1960 period, partly because the demand for medium transport aircraft declined and partly because it suffered major contract cancellations in the jet engine field (also declining) and the guided missile field, into which it had diversified during the 1950's. Its guided missile program cancellations were apparently due to technical deficiencies as well as changes in military requirements, and in 1959 a sweeping change in company management was effected. Fairchild's position among defense prime contractors continued to decline to 69th in fiscal year 1961 and 85th in 1962, although the firm was striving to obtain new missile and space work and did succeed in winning a few small contracts.[30]

It is possible that in the near future more cases in which major defense contractors are permitted to wither and possibly die will be added to the presently sparse record. Department of Defense officials have spoken of weeding out inefficient contractors,[31] and in 1962 several firms selling mainly to the armed forces were threatened with catastrophic sales declines, partly because of hesitancy in adapting to new technologies but perhaps also because of mediocre performance records. Whether the threat will become reality cannot be foretold. Certainly nothing as violent as the Navy's break with Brewster seems likely.

[30] Cf. Edward H. Kolcum, "Fairchild Seeks Larger Space Business Role," *Aviation Week & Space Technology,* November 26, 1962, p. 108; and "Fairchild Named for MDS," *Missiles and Rockets,* February 11, 1963, p. 10.

[31] Cf. "Science's Biggest Spender," *Business Week,* March 10, 1962, p. 76; and George C. Wilson, "USAF-Defense Research Conflict Aired," *Aviation Week & Space Technology,* August 13, 1962, p. 33.

In sum, the correlation between past performance and success in obtaining new weapons programs has been weak. In most source selection actions little weight has been given to past performance considerations. Only two cases could be found at the combat air weapon system and major subsystem levels in which unsatisfactory performance led rather directly to a complete loss of market position. More frequently, when reputation blemishes did count against a company in source selection competitions, the firm was able to make a comeback in other competitions, and so the pain of sales deprivation due to poor performance was only temporary.

Willingness and ability to adapt over time to major changes in weapons technology appear to have been a much more significant determinant of survival in defense contracting than good performance at any moment in time.[32]   This finding has most important incentive implications. Competitive survival in the face of a rapidly changing technology demands that contractor management give first priority not to achieving good performance in ongoing programs, but to moving into promising new fields and thereby developing company capabilities for winning programs of the future. This emphasis on long-run survival leads not only to inadequate managerial attention to current programs, but also to the excessive use of top creative technical talent on sales-generating activities and to the performance of work in-house which could be done more efficiently by specialist subcontractors.[33]

Other Limitations in the Use of Performance Criteria

Even when past performance has been accorded substantial weight in program award decisions, only certain kinds of unsatisfactory performance seem to have impaired contractors' competitive standing. Serious failures to achieve technical goals in major

[32] It is possible that these two factors could be interrelated — that the government is less willing to help firms with which it is displeased move into new fields. Our case studies provided no direct evidence on this point, although there were two cases in which "no diversification" rules coincided with service displeasure over past performance. But several other firms which had earned poor reputations were allowed to build up new capabilities at government expense. These findings suggest that no general government policy on the support of company adaptation and diversification existed.

[33] See also Peck and Scherer, pp. 586–588.

developments or to meet delivery dates in high priority efforts have had the most adverse impact on company reputations.   On the other hand, schedule slippages in low priority programs and severe cost overruns or inefficiencies appear much less damaging, for these have occurred frequently in the past with no lasting ill effects on the ability of firms to secure new contracts.   Thus, failure to come anywhere near its minimum thrust requirements was Westinghouse's fatal misstep in the J–40 program.   If experience in other programs is a guide, the Navy would have forgiven and forgotten had Westinghouse been able to meet its technical goals by incurring development contract cost overruns.   Notably, company executives listed among their mistakes the failure to expand their engineering staff quickly enough, lack of experimental parts development facilities and personnel, and insufficiency of test engines — items whose additional costs would have been reimbursed under the development contract.[34]   Similarly, had its production programs not been marred by severe schedule slippages, technical defects, and sabotage, it is unlikely that Brewster's Corsair contract would have been cancelled abruptly only because of high costs.   The subordinate role of costs is reflected in this statement by a top executive of a major defense contracting firm:

> All we need to do is stay somewhere near the middle on costs. The important factor in terms of future business is that the job done be a good one and acceptable to the procuring service.

The rare decisions to abandon contractors because of poor performance appear to have occurred mainly during times of declining demand in the weapons industry generally or in particular sectors of the industry.   For example, Brewster's elimination took place as World War II procurement began to taper off in anticipation of eventual demobilization.   Before that time, Navy officials admitted that continuing their contracts with Brewster was "not good business from any point of view," but they pointed out that the Navy's acute need for aircraft required utilization of every facility, however unsatisfactory.[35]   Likewise, Westinghouse's ill-starred

[34] House, Committee on Government Operations, *Tenth Intermediate Report, Navy Jet Engine Procurement Program* (1956), pp. 34–35.

[35] House, Committee on Naval Affairs, *Report of the Subcommittee Appointed To Investigate the Causes of Failure of Production of Brewster Aeronautical Corporation Under Its Contracts With the Navy* (1943), p. 46.

effort to regain favor as a jet engine producer coincided with the shift away from turbojet-powered aircraft and toward rocket-powered missiles and space vehicles. The threat to several firms in 1962 reflected an overcapacity situation in manned aircraft and certain other fields as much as displeasure over past performance. Thus, it may well be that the government is willing to use past performance as an elimination criterion only when redundant capacity exists. This need not be a restrictive policy, if the rapid pace of technological change continues to turn the weapons industry end-over-end every decade or so. But unless the services prove ready to help only good performers grow into new fields and to let poor performers decline with their specialties, the correlation between past performance and new program awards will remain weak.

Contrasting Experience in Commercial Practice

The government's reluctance to sever relations with weapons makers who have served it poorly stands in rather sharp contrast with the procurement practices of large private firms operating in the market sector. Our case studies of commercial product developments revealed a much greater willingness to cut off poor performers. One large manufacturing corporation reported "quite a few" cancellations of vendor relationships each year as a result of poor performance. A public utility shifted all of its considerable patronage from one plant engineering firm to another after the first had turned in an unsatisfactory job on just one assignment. A third company eliminated from its bidding lists those vendors who had not met delivery requirements in the past. Several company executives indicated that their readiness to drop vendors because of poor performance provided the strongest incentive they could offer for good performance. As one vice president remarked, "The essence of vendor relationships is, first, knowing what you're buying, and second, being able to judge performance so the supplier knows that if he isn't doing the right thing, he won't get the next job."

How can this contrast between government and industrial practice be explained? Several factors appear relevant. First, we are comparing different types of product situations. Our main interest here is the government's relationship with the suppliers of weapon systems and subsystems — complex, specialized, typically low-volume products which must be developed and produced in close cooperation with the buyer. On the other hand, most industrial procurement involves more or less standardized products, with much less intimate buyer-seller collaboration. There is reason to believe that the government and its prime contractors are more ruthless in severing relationships with standard component vendors who have performed poorly, although our case studies provided little direct evidence on this question.

Still the weapons and commercial case study findings are not completely noncomparable. For example, the public utility–engineering firm relationship was quite similar to the government's relationship with a weapons development contractor. Another commercial case study analyzed a large company's decision to end its ties with a firm which supplied a major subsystem for its product. The supplier was conducting considerable development work on that subsystem — a relationship also analogous to the weapons acquisition pattern. These two instances alone from our seven commercial case studies equal the number of total severances on grounds of poor performance which could be found for the whole weapon systems and subsystems field over a 20-year period.

A second difference concerns the implications of cancellation. When an industrial firm severs its relationship with a vendor, there are usually other buyers whose favor the vendor can seek. Even in oligopsonistic markets this tends to be true. A tail light reflector vendor abandoned, say, by General Motors can still go to Ford, Chrysler, and other auto and truck makers. Or if that fails, its capacity can be adapted to road sign, play marble, or ashtray production. But the producer of air defense guided missiles, guidance systems, or rocket engines has little prospect of selling its capacity to any buyer other than the U.S. government. Thus, while the government's decision to give no new business to a producer of weapon systems or subsystems usually means liquidation of that firm or division, no such consequence need follow when General Motors drops a supplier. It is easier to be tough in General Motors' position, when the consequences are not so harsh.

Finally, political influences deter government decisions which could put a firm out of business and create pockets of local unemployment. It was argued earlier that political pressures have relatively little direct substantive impact on particular source selection

decisions. But they undoubtedly affect high level decisions to keep
a firm in business despite unsatisfactory past performance. A poor
performer may also be sustained to preserve competition in some
field or to maintain a base of resources facilitating rapid expansion
of production in the event of military mobilization.[36] And once
the decision to keep a firm in business is made, sooner or later a
program suited to the company's resources is bound to come along.

Therefore it may be too much to expect the quick and unsympa-
thetic abandonment of poor performers in weapons acquisition,
even though this is done in commercial practice. Perhaps the most
which can be accomplished in any but the most extreme cases is
gradual reduction of a deficient contractor's market position.

Contractor Perception of the Consequences of Poor Performance

We find then from examining available historical evidence that
the correlation between the award of desirable new programs and
past performance has been fairly weak. What really matters in an
incentive system, however, is not what the performance-reward
correlation *actually is,* but what those affected *think it is.* What
the outsider sees as a weak, erratic correlation could conceivably
appear quite powerful to those whose organizations hang in the
balance.

There are indications that this is indeed so. For example, J. L.
Atwood, President of North American Aviation, Inc., stated in
congressional testimony:

> . . . our continuity in this business and our ability to get new
> work depends in considerable measure on our reputation for econ-
> omy and efficiency and secondly the very projects themselves —
> their life depends in considerable measure on economic implemen-
> tation. These incentives are very powerful to me.[37]

Along similar lines is the testimony of Robert E. Gross, late Chairman of Lockheed Aircraft:

[36] Cf. Peck and Scherer, pp. 375–379.

[37] House, Committee on Armed Services, Subcommittee for Special Investigations, *Hearings, Weapons System Management and Team System
Concept in Government Contracting* (1959), p. 75.

"What incentive do we as a company have to keep prices down?" . . . basically, if the Lockheed Co. does a bad managerial job and doesn't do its best to keep prices down, its own and its subs, we lose out in the long race. Now this is just inherent in any business, and it is just as inherent under this system as it is in any other.

. . . I must submit to you that these systems are getting to be — there seem to be fewer and fewer of them, and the competition for them is very, very severe and intense. If we miss one, we may have lost a major part of our industrial life. Consequently, this is something that I feel very strongly about. It is just there.

If you were in my position, walking the floor nights and worrying about whether or not we are going to do a good job and whether if we don't, we will lose out, you would know how I feel.[38]

The same attitude was reflected by several executives interviewed in connection with our case studies. This statement of an electronics division manager is representative:

The profit motive is insignificant. Once you're in a program, it is much more important to maintain a reputation for doing a good job.

Likewise, the vice president and general manager of a guided missile division said:

The key to getting follow-on business is to maintain a reputation for usable hardware in a reasonable time at what the government feels is a reasonable cost.

Nevertheless, the correlation between performance and program awards is far from perfect, in the perception of other defense industry executives. One aircraft company vice president said his firm's general attitude is that "If we don't do a good job in our present programs, we won't have a chance on the next go-around." But he pointed to several cases of competitors who "have done a lousy job and still been rewarded." "It's frustrating," he said, "but we still try to do a good job." Another contractor executive, discussing the inadequacy of contractor investment in research and component development, observed:

Unless there is some provision for the exceptionally well prepared contractor to profit by his excellence, you won't get invest-

[38] *Ibid.*, p. 174.

ment by companies to put themselves in a good position later. Right now the rewards go to the least prepared contractors — those who make the wildest claims.

Perhaps the strongest public assertion that past performance matters little in the competition for new programs was this speech by Simon Ramo, Vice Chairman of Thompson-Ramo-Wooldridge:

> The incentive for maximum return on investment is tied not nearly so much to performance in carrying out a major developmental project as it is to the skill shown in winning the privilege of carrying it out. . . . It is common that, as a major project reaches its crisis of activity, and before all of the problems are solved, it is necessary to commence preparation for the acquisition of another one, for a superb performance on a difficult development job is no real assurance of the award of a new one as needed for stability. . . . We cannot afford to have very many of our most creative technologists engaged in panicky promotion. . . . Competition and incentives should be working for us, not against us. . . . How can we get the smartest people out of the proposal business and back to doing a job? [39]

Thus, the perception of defense industry executives is by no means uniform. Our case study evidence supports the view of Simon Ramo that past performance has little impact on selection decisions. But how have other defense contractor executives looked at the same (admittedly complex) scene and obtained a different impression?

It could be that some defense industry officials are influenced more by fear of what might happen than by confidence in what experience shows to be the normal pattern of events. The possibility always exists that the government will begin abandoning poor performers, even though relatively few historical precedents can be found. Certainly, there were reasonable grounds for fearing such a policy change in the early 1960's, given the change in Defense Department administration and the existence of excess capacity in many sectors of the defense industry. To the extent that anxieties of this sort influence contractor behavior, the infrequent chopping off of a contractor for poor performance will have an incentive impact out of proportion to its objective significance.

The secrecy common in source selection actions could also bias

[39] Quoted in "New Incentive Contract Plan Advanced," *Aviation Week & Space Technology,* January 8, 1962, pp. 99, 100.

the perception of defense contractor executives. As a rule, source selection criteria weights and the evaluations of contractors against these criteria are not disclosed.[40] Introspection in this environment of secrecy is likely to produce polarized self-evaluations. Normally executives find it difficult to believe that the organization to which they are deeply committed is much worse than other organizations. But rejection in a source selection competition for undisclosed reasons may inspire all kinds of doubts and a conclusion that the rejection was due to past failings.[41] As a result, contractors may come to believe that the correlation between past performance and new program awards is much stronger than it actually is.

It is also possible that company officials are unable to distinguish between long-run sales declines due to demand and technology changes and those due to government dissatisfaction, viewing all weapons industry turnover as a threat which they can ward off only by good performance. Or finally, the short-run hardships connected with rejection in one or a few important source selection actions because of government displeasure may be sufficient to cause defense executives considerable concern over their company's performance.

In sum, the incentive to perform well on current programs in order to enhance the possibility of winning future programs is probably stronger than analysis of the objective historical evidence suggests. Nevertheless, it could be made even more effective if conscious efforts were exerted to correlate the award of new programs with past performance.

THE FEASIBILITY OF BASING PROGRAM AWARDS ON PAST PERFORMANCE

In 1963 the Department of Defense was preparing to establish procedures which would inject past performance considerations more positively into the selection of development contractors. To determine the feasibility of this and alternative sales-performance correlation systems, several further questions must be explored.

[40] Cf. Peck and Scherer, pp. 372–373. See also "Racing for Space Business," *Business Week,* July 14, 1962, p. 111; and the editorial by William J. Coughlin, "Toughest Customer in the World," *Missiles and Rockets,* December 17, 1962, p. 48.

[41] Another common rationalization is that the decision was influenced strongly by political considerations.

One important issue concerns the government's objectives in using past performance as a selection criterion. There can be two rather different reasons for basing program awards wholly or partly on past performance. The first has been the focus of this chapter: to create incentives for good performance by maintaining a consistent correlation between the level of firms' sales and the efficacy of their performance. But past performance might also be considered merely as a predictor of future performance, under the assumption that a firm which has performed well in some technical field in the past is likely to perform well in that field in the future. These objectives are not necessarily identical, and in some cases they may even conflict.

Although too little evidence was available at the time of writing for a confident interpretation, it would appear from early press releases and a brief interview with responsible government personnel that the new Department of Defense procedures are primarily designed to accomplish the second objective.[42] Under the plan drawn up in early 1963, essentially factual information on contractors' success in meeting program quality, time, and cost objectives is to be collected through a series of performance evaluation reports. How these reports will then be employed in source selection decisions is described in a press release:

> The complete report . . . will be available for use in evaluating bidders in subsequent competitions. For example, if companies "X" and "Y" are finalists in a subsequent competition, with proposals comparable in all respects but price, and if company "X" quotes a cost which is 20% less than company "Y," the past performance records of both companies will be withdrawn from the files and analyzed. If both companies have a consistent record of achieving contractual performance requirements, reasonably on schedule, but company "X" consistently overruns its contract cost estimates by 40% while company "Y" normally meets its cost estimates, this might provide the basis for awarding the contract to company "Y." [43]

[42] After reading a preliminary draft of this manuscript and finding its conclusions at variance with their plans, government personnel responsible for developing the new system rejected my request in February 1963 for an unclassified descriptive report.

[43] "Contractor Evaluation Comments Asked," *Aviation Week & Space Technology,* April 15, 1963, p. 32. In May 1963 there were indications that

The implication seems fairly plain that the main use of past performance records will be to forecast how actual future performance will vary from current promises.

If so, then the system may fail to do the job for which it is intended, since past performance may not be an especially good predictor of future performance. In some cases, one good job appears to follow another. But in other instances contractors have exhibited contrasting performance on successive developments — the first turned out well, the second poorly, the third well, and so on. There is reason to believe that when a firm performs poorly in one program, it often strives vigorously to strengthen its organization for subsequent programs. On the other hand, a successful job can lead to complacency or unwillingness to adopt new and better concepts made available by the advance of technology. No firm generalization is possible on the basis of existing evidence. Further research into this aspect of the Defense Department's proposed new performance rating system is needed.

Even if the new system were ineffective in achieving what appears to be its principal objective, it might at least generate strengthened incentives for good performance. Still this conclusion does not follow automatically. Performance evaluations collected for a system emphasizing the prediction of future performance may not be suitable for maintaining a consistent incentive correlation between new sales awards and past performance. This problem will be examined further in Chapters 9 and 12.

Other Conflicts of Objectives

It is virtually impossible to avoid other conflicts of objectives in applying past performance criteria to source selection decisions. As we have found, a major reason for selecting contractors on the basis of past performance is to create a pervasive incentive for good performance. In specific source selection actions, a government agency's immediate aim is typically to achieve an optimal matching of available capabilities with military needs. These objectives need not be in harmony.

What, for example, should the government do when the most

---

the plan described here had been sharply criticized and was being reformulated.

attractive design is proposed by an organization whose past performance has been poor? The typical military decision maker is inclined to let past performance be decisive only when technical considerations are roughly equal. And yet this normal reaction to the conflict between short-run objectives (obtaining the best design for the program at hand) and long-run objectives (maintaining an effective incentive system) has a most unfortunate impact upon contractor behavior. The company badly in need of a new program can always come up with a winning proposal if it assigns its best talent to proposal preparation efforts and enters one competition after another until success is achieved. But highly capable and creative scientists and engineers are a most valuable scarce resource. Assigning them to the preparation of competitive technical proposals precludes their employment in ongoing development efforts or in basic and applied research projects more likely to yield important technological advances. The result is less efficiency and progress in the conduct of actual research and development work.[44] Thus, stressing the technical factors in source selection decisions not only weakens the performance-program award correlation incentive, but also encourages nonoptimal allocation of talent. And as we have seen in Chapter 2, misleadingly optimistic time, cost, and quality promises are another undesirable result of design and technical proposal competitions.

Equally troublesome conflicts arise when the availability of technical, managerial, and physical resources is stressed as a source selection criterion. Cases of this sort are common: The firm with an outstanding record has a fairly full backlog of programs and could accept another program only by expanding its organization, perhaps with the attendant inefficiencies of breaking in new people. The firm whose performance has been mediocre, on the other hand, has managers and engineers available and eager to work. The expedient choice in this situation is the mediocre performer,

---

[44] See, for example, the speech of Dr. Simon Ramo cited earlier. See also "DOD Support for Components Promised," *Aviation Week & Space Technology,* October 1, 1962, p. 89, in which Dr. Harold Brown, Director of Defense Research and Engineering, is quoted as saying that "Too many of industry's best people are tied up in proposal making, sales talks and the like" and that "There is a great deal of wasted effort in the many proposals that come to us from industry."

which may even do a better job than the highly rated firm because of its ability to assign a higher talent allocation priority to the new project.[45] Yet such a choice invariably weakens the incentive correlation achieved by rewarding good past performance with desirable new programs. It also encourages firms to hoard surplus personnel so they will have a competitive advantage in future source selection competitions.

Again, during the late 1950's the armed services were often forced to decide between a company which had diversified into a new and growing field (e.g., electronic subsystems) by performing work in-house that could have been done more efficiently by specialist subcontractors, and a firm which pursued the most efficient subcontracting policy and consequently had little electronics capability.[46] The expedient choice is once more obvious: if electronic skills are needed, select the firm with capabilities in that field. But to do so penalizes those who perform efficiently and rewards the firm which diversifies at government expense. A perverse system of incentives is created.

Finally, there are conflicts between maintaining effective incentives for good performance and various political and socioeconomic considerations. To let an inefficient producer wither away and die is to invite pockets of local unemployment, dissatisfied voters, and angry congressmen. The need for a value judgment is plain: Do we want highly motivated, efficient contractor performance or pork-barrelling in our national defense effort? The answer cannot be provided here, although the author's bias should be evident.

The Problem of Program Weighting

Any system of basing program awards on past performance will have to solve another problem. Most major defense contractors have a number of programs under way at any given time. In some they may perform quite well, in others poorly. It is unlikely, unless the defense industry has seriously redundant capacity, that a company will be deprived of new programs because of only one moderately bad performance. How then are the good and the poor jobs to be blended together to obtain an index of over-all company performance?

[45] Peck and Scherer, pp. 374–375.
[46] For some examples, see *ibid.*, pp. 388–391.

One solution is to judge relatively autonomous units separately; i.e., the Columbus aircraft division of North American Aviation would neither benefit nor lose from the Rocketdyne engine division's record. But in many instances the smallest independent unit which can be defined will still have conducted several projects in the recent past. Programs might be weighted according to their size. But this would reinforce the contractor's incentive to allocate its top talent mainly to large programs under its control.[47] Small subcontracts from another firm's high priority program might be slighted, with unfavorable consequences for that program and the over-all defense effort.

Assuming that the program weighting problem can be solved, there would still be problems in correlating a firm's sales with its past performance. Consider, for example, a company which deserves increased sales because of excellent performance. Because of technical or intelligence breakthroughs, however, the government might have to cancel one of the largest programs in its backlog, causing the company's sales to drop. Since development programs require several years to build up to their maximum expenditure level, it would be difficult to maintain, let alone increase, the company's sales volume by the mere award of new development programs. Conversely, a company whose performance has been deficient may nonetheless have several programs in expanding expenditure phases, and reducing that firm's sales would be equally difficult. Problems of this nature will be given additional attention in Chapter 12.

Can Contractor Performance Be Measured?

An implicit assumption in the discussion thus far has been that the government can distinguish between good and not-so-good weapons program performance; that contractor performance can be measured. But is this assumption valid? If not, then the idea of correlating program awards or indeed any awards with the efficacy of performance makes little sense.

Certainly, a case can be made against the feasibility of performance measurement. Three main arguments are germane:

[47] Cf. *ibid.*, pp. 501–507.

(1) There exist no established, unvarying quantitative yardsticks which can be applied consistently to measure performance in any given program.

(2) Performance is in many respects a subjective attribute, and persons making subjective judgments of this sort are bound to be influenced by service, technical, contractor, or other biases.

(3) Performance in a weapons development program is multidimensional, involving such diverse aspects as technical performance of the end product (speed, range, accuracy, immunity to countermeasures, maneuverability, reaction time, etc.), reliability, lead time, cost, etc. Therefore, measurement on a single dimension (over-all performance) is impossible.

Objection (1) can be met on *a priori* grounds. The theoretically ideal criterion for measuring contractor performance would be the degree of success in maximizing $V-C$ (military value, measured in dollar terms, less program cost) subject to the relevant budgetary constraints and technical opportunities. But neither value nor cost functions can be quantified accurately enough, and so this approach is clearly unworkable. Likewise, performance in a weapons program cannot simply be laid out like a bolt of cloth and measured, and even if it could, the problem of finding a meaningful yardstick would remain. Therefore, an indirect approach to the problem of measurement seems necessary. The "laying out" of the performance cloth must be done implicitly by knowledgeable persons of sound judgment, and arbitrary scales of numbers rather than yardsticks with a more ready intuitive meaning must be employed for purposes of interprogram comparison. One such scale could be an ordinal ranking of programs from best to worst in terms of contractor performance.

Whether such an approach meets objections (2) and (3) is an empirical question. To test the hypothesis that unbiased and consistent ranking of over-all contractor performance is feasible, a "program evaluation experiment" was conducted. It involved 44 fairly knowledgeable officials from government, industry, and the academic community who made paired comparisons of eight recently completed weapons development programs on four attributes (state of the art advance, value to the national arsenal, government performance, and contractor performance). The detailed results are reported in the first volume of this study.[48]   In summary, the experimental results suggested that reasonably consistent ordinal measurement of over-all weapon systems development program performance by knowledgeable persons is feasible, although perfectly "accurate" measurement in the sense of obtaining on each evaluation attempt the one "true" ranking was not possible.   Intransitive or inconsistent choices — to be expected if multidimensionality of attributes precludes a unidimensional ordering — proved to be only a minor problem.[49]   Biases were quite apparent, but they could be controlled by limiting the evaluation group to persons without direct involvement in the programs evaluated and by letting biases cancel out in a balanced evaluation group.   The degree of agreement on program rankings among the experiment participants was fairly high, considering the heterogeneity of the programs and the evaluation group and the limited knowledge of some participants.

To be sure, the measurement process was not so consistent that an identical ordering of programs would occur regardless of the group doing the ranking.   However, the experimental results suggested very little likelihood that with a well-informed, balanced evaluation group serious errors would occur, such as assigning a low rank to generally superior performance or a high rank to generally inferior performance.   Perfect measurement is undoubtedly not essential for the implementation of an incentive system; a reasonably consistent correlation of rewards with performance should suffice.

The Problem of Time, Quality, and Cost Weighting

The program evaluation experiment threw light on another important problem.   There can be no doubt that weapons development program performance is multidimensional, involving many different facets of quality, time, and cost.   Yet despite this multidimensionality, intransitive choices were avoided by individual evaluators and agreement was reasonably high among the evalua-

[48] Peck and Scherer, pp. 543–580 and 668–711.

[49] A set of choices is intransitive if the decision maker indicates, for example, that A is better than B, B is better than C, and C is better than A. In the evaluation experiment, 1.2% of the completed choice sets (or triads) were intransitive.

tion group. Therefore, the persons making program evaluations must have had some fairly consistent common system of weights which they applied to the various dimensions of performance in the various programs.

Presumably, these weights should vary from program to program. For example, in high priority programs it might be expected that maximum weight would be given to the contractor's effectiveness in minimizing development time, while in other programs the greatest weight might be accorded the contractor's success in achieving state of the art advances. The program evaluation experiment was not on a sufficient scale to analyze differences in weights from program to program. This is a problem on which additional research should be conducted. It was possible, however, to detect some general patterns in the ranking of all the programs.

The question explored can be posed as follows: Which aspects or dimensions had the greatest influence in determining whether a contractor's performance was ranked high or low — the degree to which state of the art advances were made? — success in preventing schedule slippages? — success in avoiding cost overruns? — or the over-all military value of the program? By methods described in the first volume of this study, these individual dimensions were quantified in such a way that a product moment correlation analysis could be performed.[50] The results are summarized in Table 4.1.

With the exception of government performance — a relationship to be discussed later — the time slippage factors were the best single predictors of contractor performance evaluations, with r^2 of .805. The more successful a contractor was in avoiding development schedule slippages, the higher the evaluation that contractor's performance received. A trivially better prediction of contractor performance is obtained by using both time slippage factors and state of the art advance factors, with multiple R^2 of .807. The partial r^2 — .788 for time and .010 for state of the art advance — show that time clearly plays the predominant role in this correlation.

An r^2 of .513 was obtained when cost overrun factors were correlated with contractor performance. The more successful a con-

[50] Note that this means a transition from ordinal to interval measurement. See Peck and Scherer, pp. 19–23, 575–578, 684–685, and 688.

TABLE 4.1

Summary of Correlations: Contractor Performance Scaling Factors
as Dependent Variables and Selected Independent Variables

	Independent Variables	Number of Observations	r^2	R^2	Partial r^2
X_1	Time slippage factors	8	$(-).805$		
X_2	Cost overrun factors	7	$(-).513$		
X_3	State of the art advance scaling factors	8	.092		
X_4	Value to the national arsenal scaling factors	8	.358		
X_5	Government performance scaling factors	8	.862		
X_1	Time slippage factors	8		.807	$(-).788$
X_3	State of the art advance				.010
X_1	Time slippage factors	8		.811	$(-).706$
X_4	Value to national arsenal				$(-).030$
X_1	Time slippage factors	7		.738	$(-).679$
X_2	Cost overrun factors				$(-).020$
X_2	Cost overrun factors	7		.617	$(-).613$
X_3	State of the art advance				.212

NOTE: The scaling factor for a program is the total number of paired choices
in which that program was chosen divided by the total number of choices involving that program. The time slippage factor for a program is the actual development time divided by the originally estimated development time. The cost
overrun factor for a program is the actual development cost divided by the
. originally estimated development cost. Negative signs in parenthesis signify an
inverse correlation, although the squared coefficients obviously must be positive.

This table is generally similar to Table 19.10 in Peck and Scherer, p. 576.
However, some errors in the computations have been corrected and partial
correlation coefficients have been used in place of beta coefficients.

tractor was in avoiding cost overruns, the higher was the evaluation
of its performance. However, in addition to the lower r^2 there are
several reasons for believing that cost considerations were not
nearly as influential as time factors in the evaluation group's judgments. First, in a multiple correlation the partial r^2 for time is
.679, while for cost it is only .020. Second, the time slippage
factors and cost overrun factors were intercorrelated, so that if a
high r^2 were obtained with one as independent variable, a high r^2

would also be obtained with the other.[51]   Further analysis indicates that time slippages were the causal or independent variable in this time-cost relationship.[52]   Finally, with only seven usable observations, the cost overrun-contractor performance correlation coefficient was biased strongly by one extreme observation.[53]

The absence of a strong correlation between contractor performance and state of the art advance is somewhat surprising, since one would expect technical achievement to be an important dimension of over-all contractor performance.   Still all of the weapons covered in the program evaluation experiment were at least advanced enough to perform the military missions for which they were intended with reasonable effectiveness.   It is possible, therefore, that state of the art advance played the role of an important constant.[54] It should also be noted that the analysis included no variable for reliability, which undoubtedly ought to have a significant weight in over-all performance evaluations.

In sum, quantitative analysis suggests a conclusion that contractor performance on the time dimension was the most significant variable in the evaluation of over-all performance, cost and state of the art variables receiving much less weight.   This conclusion is supported by qualitative evidence.   The program with the highest contractor performance rating was characterized by outstanding success in minimizing development time, even though the job was done rather inefficiently in terms of cost.   This underscores the importance of time relative to cost.   On the other hand, the two programs with the lowest contractor performance ratings had protracted development periods (as well as severe cost overruns).

These findings, if applicable more generally, have most important incentive implications.   Let us assume that the award of new programs is based upon over-all past performance.   If, as in the program evaluation experiment, a contractor can do a cost-inefficient job and yet receive a top rating because of outstanding lead

[51] In a correlation of time slippage and cost overrun factors, r^2 was .615.

[52] Cf. Peck and Scherer, pp. 441–442.

[53] If this one observation is eliminated, r^2 falls from .513 to .037. On the other hand, the time slippage — contractor performance observations were distributed in such a way that elimination of any one or even two values would have affected the regression and correlation coefficients very little.

[54] See also Peck and Scherer, p. 574.

time reduction, the incentives provided for cost reduction will not be very strong.   Indeed, contractors may be motivated to devote more than the optimal amount of resources to lead time reduction (e.g., by pursuing too many parallel approaches and manning individual approaches too heavily).   But as we have seen, fairly strong incentives for development time minimization are usually generated by competition between substitutes and competition for budgetary support, while the incentives for cost control tend to be much weaker.   Basing program awards on over-all past performance might merely reinforce already existing incentives while adding little in the cost area, where stronger incentives are most needed.

There is one type of situation in which the system of weights observed here could have very beneficial incentive effects.   As we have seen earlier, when the retention of surplus engineers, managers, and technicians will enhance a firm's chances of winning source selection competitions emphasizing the availability of resources, budgetary pressures may incite undesirable schedule slippages instead of the work force reductions required for a trim, efficient organization.   Source selection on the basis of over-all past performance, with time factors receiving substantial weight, would alleviate this problem in two ways.[55]   First, it would generate stronger direct incentives for lead time reduction, since contractors would hurt their future sales prospects by permitting undesirable schedule delays.   And second, it would weaken the propensity of firms to hoard surplus personnel, since winning new program awards would depend more on good performance and less on the availability of large manpower pools.

Furthermore, source selection on the basis of over-all past performance would also afford at least some direct incentive for good performance on the cost dimension.   A more complete analysis of the qualitative evidence indicates that cost efficiency was not completely unimportant in the program evaluation experiment results. The programs ranked second, third, fourth, fifth, and sixth in terms

[55] Of course, it is possible that on evaluations of over-all contractor performance in low priority programs, time factors would be given less weight than the program evaluation experiment results suggest.   And it is in low priority programs that the tendency to let schedules slip in response to budgetary pressures is greatest.   Further experimentation and analysis are needed on this point.

of contractor performance involved roughly similar achievements with respect to schedule maintenance. Cost considerations were apparently decisive in determining the position of the second- and third-ranked programs, for both of these were conducted with unusual efficiency.[56] (The second-ranked program in turn involved a more substantial technical advance than the third-ranked program.) On the other hand, the programs ranked fifth and sixth were both marked by considerable inefficiency, even though they were better than the seventh- and eighth-ranked programs in terms of schedule control.

Thus, cost efficiency considerations could play an important role in determining a contractor's performance rank when time and perhaps quality considerations were roughly equal. Whether this role would be significant enough to provide effective incentives for efficiency when new programs are awarded on the basis of over-all past performance cannot be generalized from the program evaluation experiment results. The question is clearly an important one, deserving additional research.

The Intertwining of Contractor and Government Performance

Table 4.1 suggests another problem in basing program awards or indeed any kind of awards on past performance. The strongest correlation, with r^2 of .862, was between government performance and contractor performance. This result suggests that the functions of buyer and seller in weapons development programs are so complementary that responsibility for success or failure must be shared. For example, if unsound decisions are made by government agencies, the contractor is responsible for joining in them (in the case of initial program decisions) or not arguing persuasively enough against them (once the contractor is "locked into" a program). At the same time, if the contractor's decisions or performance are unsatisfactory, the buying agency is responsible for not taking corrective actions. The government's responsibility is especially dependent upon contractor performance, for successful

---

[56] The efficiency of contractors' performance is evaluated here on the basis of the definitions set forth in Chapter 1 and applied in Chapter 3, and not merely on the basis of the cost overrun factors employed in the correlations of Table 4.1. Obviously, cost overrun factors could be high because of unrealistically optimistic initial predictions as well as inefficiency.

buying agency control demands restrained noninterference when the contractor is doing well, but quick and effective intervention when the contractor's performance begins to flag.

Such an interpretation is violently unpopular among contractors. To some extent, they can argue validly that the need to maintain amicable relations with their customer precludes strong dissent against government decisions they consider incorrect. More generally, the attitude of contractors toward sharing responsibility with the government is indicated in this excerpt from an industry study group's report:

> The Cost-Plus-Fixed-Fee contract has imposed such limited penalties on the contractor for failing to perform, that the contractor has been willing to accept the blame not only for his own mistakes but for failures of performance of Government personnel in order to maintain good relationships. When the contract form is altered in such a fashion as to impose severe penalty for failure to perform, contractors will not be able or willing to accept the blame for any but their own failures, and they will be compelled to insist on accurate determination of the causes for failures in cost control, delivery, and performance.[57]

Since withholding sales in the event of poor performance would clearly be a severe penalty, the implication is that industry would be unwilling to accept joint responsibility.

There is no right or wrong answer in an argument of this sort. The answer depends upon government objectives and government-industry bargaining relationships. If the government decides that it wants stronger incentives for good performance in weapons acquisition, and if it decides that the way to achieve stronger incentives is to reward good performers with desirable programs and to keep poor performers on a starvation diet, it undoubtedly has the power to implement a reasonable plan even though contractors must share some responsibility with their customer for failures.[58] Certainly, the impersonal market forces which confront firms outside the weapons industry are no more equitable. The survival and

[57] National Security Industrial Association, Report of Task Committee 8, "New Approaches to Contracting," *Report of Cost Reduction Study* (June 15, 1962), p. 150.

[58] For a further analysis of the bargaining problems that might be faced, see Chapters 9 and 12 *infra*.

profits of companies in a market environment are influenced by consumer tastes, the course of the business cycle, the actions of competitors, tariff policies, and even international politics — factors much less within the firm's direct control than the government's weapon system program decisions, for which defense contractors provide information and advocacy.

CONCLUSION

In sum, over the past two decades the correlation between new program awards and contractor performance has been generally weak. Relatively little emphasis has been placed on past performance in source selection actions. Few firms have been deprived of new orders for any sustained period because of unsatisfactory performance in a major weapons program assignment. The occasional cases in which the government did penalize poor performers by withholding contracts have caused at least some defense industry officials to believe that new program awards depend upon good performance, but this attitude is by no means universal.

The idea of placing greater emphasis on past performance in program award decisions has many attractive features. Nevertheless, such an incentive system would not be without problems. In many source selection decisions, past performance considerations would conflict with technical and resource availability considerations, and the temptation to emphasize expediency at the expense of incentives is great. Although contractor performance can probably be evaluated with tolerable precision, the difficulty of "pinning the blame" for unsound decisions involving both the buyer and seller poses problems of contractor-government relations. It is also not certain that allocating programs on the basis of over-all past performance would generate strong incentives for cost efficiency, given the predominant influence of time and perhaps quality factors on over-all performance evaluations.

Whether the benefits of an incentive system relating program awards to past performance outweigh the costs, and whether the problems of such a system can be circumvented, are questions whose resolution must await a balanced appraisal of alternative systems.

CHAPTER 5

Competitive Bidding for Production Contracts

AT THE OUTSET of an advanced weapons program it is almost never possible to obtain true price competition. But as development gives way to quantity production and as designs become stabilized, the opportunities for price competition increase. Two major varieties are examined in this chapter: breakout for competitive bidding and second sourcing. Breakout occurs when the government invites firms other than its original prime contractor to bid directly on production items initially procured from that contractor. Competition through second sourcing occurs when contracts are awarded to one or more additional firms to produce an item concurrently with the initial producer.

BREAKOUT AND COMPETITIVE BIDDING

Competitive bidding is by long tradition the preferred method of government procurement, and even though in the late 1950's more than 80% by dollar volume of all defense contracts were negotiated rather than awarded through advertised competitive bidding, negotiated contract awards are viewed in procurement law as exceptions to the general rule favoring competitive bidding.[1] Breakout for competitive bidding, however, is a much more recent phenomenon associated with the weapon system prime contractor method of procurement. Since in this volume we are concerned mainly with the development and production of advanced weapon systems and subsystems rather than the procurement of standard equipment items, the fusion of competitive bidding with breakout will be emphasized here, although the problems we shall examine apply gen-

---

[1] 10 U.S.C. Section 2304.

erally to the competitive procurement of all technically advanced hardware.

During the 1930's and 1940's, government aircraft procurement agencies typically bought such items as bombing and navigation subsystems, instruments, radar units, electrical power supply units, ground maintenance equipment, etc., directly from specialist vendors and supplied them as government-furnished-equipment to an airframe prime contractor, which completed the job of installation. Similar procedures were followed in the procurement of tanks, ships, and other moderately complex weapons. But as the sophistication and complexity of weapon systems grew, more and more components had to be specially designed and carefully integrated into the over-all system plan. It became apparent that some single organization had to assume responsibility for this systems integration job. Government agencies frequently lacked the necessary technical personnel, and so in a number of programs the task was delegated to weapon system prime contractors. In this role the weapon system prime contractor subcontracted (and received a profit override on) components which under earlier procurement methods would have been purchased directly by a government agency.

To be sure, the transfer of procurement responsibilities to industry has not been complete even in the purest weapon system prime contractor situations. For example, Army Ordnance contracted directly for booster rockets, warheads, and fusing mechanisms even in the early developmental stages of the Nike Ajax program, a pioneering effort in weapon system prime contractor management. In the B–58 supersonic bomber program, turbojet engine development and production were under direct prime contracts. And in programs such as the Atlas ICBM utilizing special systems management groups, either in-house or on a contract basis, most of the major subsystems (e.g., guidance, rocket engines, re-entry vehicle) were procured directly by the government. In general, however, the need for skillful systems integration has led to an increased middleman's role for prime contractors.

Once a program reaches the stage of fairly stable quantity production (although many programs never do), the systems integration role loses much of its importance. During the late 1950's government agencies, led by Army Ordnance, began taking advantage of this fact, "breaking out" for direct procurement items which had initially been part of a prime contractor's subcontracting structure.

Actually, there are three somewhat different kinds of breakout, which for convenience will be called types (1), (2), and (3) here. Type (1) breakout really involves no competition at all. The government simply buys directly from the original producer items which that producer had previously supplied indirectly under subcontract to a weapon system prime contractor. The motive for this kind of breakout is mainly to eliminate the prime contractor's profit as middleman. With type (2) breakout, the government not only eliminates the prime contractor as middleman, but also secures competition on the basis of price. The original subcontractor can retain its production role only if it submits the lowest responsive bid. Type (3) breakout occurs when the government breaks out not only specific component items, but a whole system for competitive bidding. Then even the prime contractor must defend its production role against potentially lower bidders.

At least up to 1962, type (1) breakout was employed most frequently in the procurement of major original weapon system equipment items. For example, Nike Hercules was one of the first guided missile programs exposed to a concerted breakout effort. In 1958, 23% of the Army's $550 million expenditures on Nike Hercules flowed directly to contractors other than weapon system prime contractor Western Electric, mainly as a result of breakout actions.[2] Most of the important breakouts in this program involved buying directly from Douglas Aircraft Company items which Douglas had originally supplied to Western Electric on subcontracts. In addition, certain equipment trailers were also procured by the Army directly from Douglas' suppliers, thereby eliminating two tiers of middlemen's profit. In 1958 the guided missile airframe was still produced by Douglas under subcontract to Western Electric, but in 1961 it too was broken out for direct procurement. By 1961 the Army had also expanded its type (2) breakout program to include several major

[2] House, Committee on Appropriations, *Hearings, Department of Defense Appropriations for 1960,* Part 5, pp. 167–168. See also Senate, Select Committee on Small Business, *Hearings, Government Procurement — 1960* (1960), pp. 411–416.

Nike Hercules items, and in some cases the original suppliers of components had been displaced by lower bidders.

Breakout with competitive bidding [type (2)] is much more common in the procurement of weapon system replacement spare parts, on which the U.S. armed forces spend roughly $2 billion annually. During fiscal year 1962 approximately 43% of such purchases had been broken out for competition.[3]

By far the least prevalent form of breakout is type (3) — the breakout of a complete weapon system for competitive bidding. Only one postwar instance is known.[4] In 1954 the Army secured competitive bidding for the production of its Honest John rocket system, which had been developed by Douglas Aircraft Company. Most of the items originally produced by Douglas were taken over by low bidder Emerson Electric. Yet Honest John, it should be noted, was unusually well-suited for breakout. A simple unguided rocket, it posed many fewer problems of systems integration and special production know-how than the typical combat aircraft or guided missile system. Even so, the system designs were not completely stabilized at the time of breakout, and as a result the production contracts were of the cost-plus-fixed-fee type rather than the firm-fixed-price type usually associated with competitive bidding.

The Effects of Breakout and Competitive Bidding

Breakout and competitive bidding have two potential effects on the cost of weapons to the government. First, fear of losing out on future production contracts may cause the original contractor to reduce its price per unit, either by reducing cost through efficiency measures or by asking less profit. Second, even if the original producer's price is not reduced, the government may benefit by turning to another, more efficient producer whose bid is lower.

Congressional hearings abound with examples of price reductions as a result of competitive bidding, both with and without breakout. The Army claimed savings of roughly $4.2 million on 20 Pershing

[3] House, Committee on Appropriations, *Hearings, Department of Defense Appropriations for 1963,* Part 4, p. 494.

[4] Of course, contracts to produce weapons originally developed in-house by government laboratories have often been awarded after some kind of price competition.

ballistic missile transporter-erector-launcher units during 1962.[5] The price obtained through competitive breakout in this case was 74% less than the price quoted by the original contractor. Similarly, net price reductions averaging 32% were reported for 81 Nike missile parts during 1959 and 1960.[6] Of course, there is a natural bias toward presenting only the most favorable examples in congressional testimony. But according to a Department of Defense study, prices achieved through competitive bidding have averaged at least 20% lower than prices negotiated noncompetitively.[7]

When threatened with noncompetitive breakout of subcontracted items, prime contractors have also offered profit override reductions. For example, in 1958 Western Electric agreed to cut its profit on Nike Hercules missile work subcontracted to Douglas Aircraft from 6% to 3% when the Army threatened to break out the whole missile airframe for direct procurement.[8] In other segments of the Nike Hercules and Nike Zeus programs 0% profit overrides on subcontracted work were accepted in order to avert breakout actions.

Interestingly, most of the published examples of breakout and competitive bidding actions indicate that the government's benefits were secured either by forcing the original prime contractor to accept profit reductions or through price reductions obtained by switching suppliers. Seldom is any mention made of increased efficiency on the part of an original producer attempting to defend its production role from a specific breakout threat. Yet one would expect the threat of competitive bidding to generate a strong incen-

[5] House, Committee on Appropriations, *Hearings, Department of Defense Appropriations for 1963,* Part 4, p. 511.

[6] Senate, Select Committee on Small Business, *Hearings, Government Procurement — 1960,* p. 426. This document contains more than 100 pages of detailed competitive vs. noncompetitive bid tabulations. However, such comparisons must be interpreted skeptically, since the dates of the price quotations compared often differ by more than a year and since bidding quantities are often quite different.

[7] "McNamara Plans Defense Savings," *New York Times,* July 8, 1962, p. 37.

[8] Senate, Committee on Government Operations, Permanent Subcommittee on Investigations, *Hearings, Pyramiding of Profits and Costs in the Missile Procurement Program* (1962) (hereafter cited as *Hearings, Pyramiding of Profits*), p. 470.

tive for cost reduction. This problem was not explored in our case study research, and so little additional evidence is available. In one situation it was clear that the loss of a contract due to competitive bidding spurred the original producer to reorganize its operations and reduce its costs to the point where it could offer an attractive price on the next production order. But in general, our case study evidence permits no conclusion on the behavioral effects of direct competitive breakout threats.

It is also possible that breakout policies have a more indirect behavioral effect analogous to the effect of a potential new entry threat in an oligopolistic industry.[9] That is, even when no specific breakout actions have been taken in a particular program, contractors might attempt to hold their production costs to efficient levels to deter the buying agency from initiating a breakout effort. Again, our case studies did not explore this question, and so no direct evidence is available.

The Costs of Breakout and Competitive Bidding

Companies holding positions as major weapon system prime contractors have generally opposed the extensive use of breakout in their programs. This opposition can be attributed partly to a natural distaste for increased pressures on prices and profit margins. Nevertheless, there are also more persuasive arguments against breakout and competitive bidding.

One is that the savings achieved through competitive breakout do not justify the costs. In order to secure competitive bidding, detailed manufacturing drawings and specifications must be circulated. In the Nike Ajax program (the only one for which data are available) the cost of preparing this manufacturing information was on the order of $23 million.[10] This figure seems incredibly high, especially when it is recognized that the whole Nike Ajax development effort cost less than $100 million up to the time of

[9] Cf. Joe S. Bain, *Barriers to New Competition* (Cambridge: Harvard University Press, 1956), pp. 19–41.

[10] Senate, *Hearings, Pyramiding of Profits,* pp. 350–352 and 391. All of the $23 million was not spent on drawings. Also included were the cost of technical manuals and certain product improvement efforts, although it would appear that drawing costs were a significant portion of the total.

operational availability. Yet a typical guided missile system requires from 80,000 to 100,000 drawings,[11] and an average cost per drawing of $230 is somewhat easier to imagine. In the Nike Ajax program the multimillion dollar outlay was clearly a bad investment, for the drawings and specifications became available too late to be of much use, and total price reductions obtained through competitive breakout amounted to only about $4.7 million.[12] When questioned on this particular breakout effort, Army Ordnance representatives generally agreed that it had been uneconomic, adding that the main benefit was congressional approbation for their cost reduction efforts. Indeed, it was Army accounts of the Nike breakout program which led to congressional insistence that the Air Force and Navy initiate their own breakout programs during the late 1950's.

Under favorable circumstances, an extensive program of competitive breakout probably can more than repay its initial costs. For example, in 1959 Army officials estimated their cumulative savings from the Nike Hercules breakout effort at about $11.3 million, and at the time several more years of production were contemplated.[13] Still breakout programs clearly should not be initiated indiscriminately, but only when their prospective benefits outweigh the costs. In particular, extensive breakout efforts seem inadvisable for programs not expected to have substantial quantity production runs or when designs will be stabilized only late in the production run. In such cases a more economical approach would be to solicit competitive bids on only those components whose designs are stabilized and whose costs appear to be out of line. But this may be administratively infeasible. Separating out specific inefficiencies often requires more technical expertise than service agencies can bring to bear. A "shotgun" approach is therefore employed, letting potential program entrants point out through their bids which items have been inefficiently produced.

One way to reduce the costs of breakout might be to eliminate the preparation of special manufacturing drawings and specifica-

---

[11] Senate, Select Committee on Small Business, *Hearings, Government Procurement — 1960,* p. 157.

[12] House, Committee on Appropriations, *Hearings, Department of Defense Appropriations for 1960,* Part 5, p. 184.

[13] *Ibid.*

tions. Any development and design effort requires shop drawings. These, rather than drawings made especially for the government's purposes, might be used as the basis for competitive bidding. However, this alternative has been rejected by both government agencies and contractors for apparently sound reasons. The drawings prepared in the rush of a weapons development effort are often incomplete. Shortcuts may be taken, and engineers often rely upon verbal communication with production foremen to ensure that the proper manufacturing sequences and tolerances are satisfied. Contractor and government personnel alike said that it would be "unsafe" to let firms other than the original producer work from incomplete drawings of this sort. Errors might of course be avoided through wholehearted cooperation between the original producer and a new producer, but companies are seldom favorably disposed toward helping out other firms which have just beaten them out of a contract. As a result, detailed drawings and manufacturing information seem a necessary prerequisite for competitive breakout.

Even when such precautions are taken, however, minimum quality standards are not always met by new producers. For example, an item on which the Army claimed savings through breakout of $113,000 failed to meet cold weather performance requirements, and all of the units produced by the winning bidder had to be withdrawn from operational use.[14] Weapon system contractor representatives pointed to a number of similar quality problems which arose when low bidders lacked the know-how necessary to produce items broken out. To be sure, these were the exceptional cases, company officials admitted; most producers of items broken out for competition met or surpassed their specifications. But in a system or subsystem whose components are closely inter-related technically, unsatisfactory performance of any single key component can lead to an excessive rate of over-all system failure. As the materiel secretaries of the Department of Defense observed in a joint statement:

> The loss of a single B–52, and the training investment in its crew, would mean an out-of-pocket loss to the Government of over $12

[14] Senate, Select Committee on Small Business, *Hearings, Government Procurement — 1960,* p. 164.

million — but most important are the human lives lost. The loss of several planes due to unsuitable parts could cancel the full amount of savings from competitive procurement. Unfortunately, losses of equipment and personnel due to such unsatisfactory parts have, in fact, occurred. This knowledge cannot help but instill in procurement and technical personnel an appreciation of the need for utmost caution before any part capable of affecting the functioning of an airplane is released for competitive procurement.[15]

Recognizing this problem, the Army formulated a policy of breaking out only those items which were not part of a missile system's "closed loop." The "closed loop" was defined to include all components interrelated in such a way as to be critical to overall system functions. Determining what is and what is not within the "closed loop," however, has led to incessant arguments between government and contractor engineers.

Another approach to preventing quality deterioration due to breakout can be illustrated from the Nike programs. Critical component parts procured competitively for Nike Ajax and Nike Hercules were shipped through Western Electric's production plants for testing before delivery to missile bases. This obviously is an additional cost which ought to be, although typically is not, deducted from the savings credited to breakout actions.

One of the knottiest problems connected with breakout is the resolution of quality and design disputes between a weapon system prime contractor and firms producing components broken out from the prime contract. Frequently the prime contractor makes changes in system designs and insists that complementary changes be made in a component which has been broken out. But when relations between the prime contractor and the breakout contractor are poor for competitive reasons, coordination on design changes has been difficult to achieve. Component producers have objected to changing their designs, arguing that the change was unnecessary and would increase their costs. On other occasions breakout contractors disputed prime contractor allegations that a particular component did not meet specifications. Conflicts of this nature arise in every program. But prime contractor representatives insisted that such conflicts can be resolved quickly and successfully

[15] House, Committee on Appropriations, *Hearings, Department of Defense Appropriations for 1963,* Part 4, p. 560.

only if the prime contractor has direct financial control over the component producer's work; that is, only if the component producer is a subcontractor rather than a direct supplier to the government. Voluntary cooperation, they argued, tends to break down when serious conflicts arise. Government resolution of such disputes was considered unsatisfactory because it is time-consuming and because government agencies have often lacked engineers with a full appreciation of the technical questions at issue.[16]

Given the potential quality and systems integrity problems posed by breakout, some prime contractors have warned that they would be unwilling to accept over-all responsibility for a weapon system's functioning if major components were broken out.[17] As one company executive asked, "How much is it worth to the government to maintain systems responsibility with us, and how far are we willing to see government-furnished equipment used in our system and still accept systems responsibility?" It is difficult to determine to what degree such threats represent bluffs and to what extent they are genuinely intended. No cases are known in which a firm completely abdicated its prime contractor responsibilities, although on occasion firms have refused to be held responsible for the performance of specific government-furnished subsystems.

As indicated earlier, prime contractors have also reacted to breakout threats by offering to accept little or no profit override on work retained within their subcontract structures. Usually such offers involve no accounting loss to the company, since the direct costs of administering subcontracts are included in the prime contractor's reimbursable overhead. But they may involve an opportunity loss, since the managerial attention expended on subcontract direction and coordination might well be diverted to other activities yielding the firm a positive profit return. Weapons makers have nevertheless been willing to accept profitless subcontracts and perhaps opportunity losses because they feared that quality problems in components broken out for competitive bidding could degrade over-all weapon system performance, in turn damaging their reputation and impairing their ability to win future contracts.

Prime contractor officials conceded that at least up to 1960,

[16] See, for example, *Hearings, Pyramiding of Profits,* pp. 289, 372–373, and 396.

[17] *Ibid.,* pp. 293, 359.

their arguments and other actions have prevented the government from proceeding so far with competitive breakout that they would be forced to abdicate over-all system responsibility. Furthermore, assuming that government agencies continue to exclude "closed loop" items from breakout despite congressional pressures for increased competitive bidding, the trend in weapons technology is against extensive use of breakout. That is, as weapon systems become increasingly sophisticated and complex, more and more items will be included within the "closed loop." The trend is also toward shorter production runs and frequent design changes — factors which inhibit breakout. As a result, contractor executives believed that for most programs in early developmental stages during the late 1950's, the threat of extensive breakout for competitive bidding was not serious. However, one company officer stated that his organization would not enter a new program susceptible to early and extensive breakout unless the government were willing to pay a premium rate of profit on the development contract, since he would heavily discount the probability of earning profits on production contracts.

In sum, offsetting the price and cost reduction benefits of breakout and competitive bidding are a number of costs. These include the cost of preparing drawings and specifications for competitive bidding, the cost of added quality control measures, the possibility of quality deficiencies on specific components and less effective integration of over-all systems, and the potential unwillingness of firms to accept weapon system prime contractor responsibilities in extreme cases of breakout. Whether the benefits of breakout and competitive bidding outweigh the costs depends mainly upon the size of the production run expected, the relative efficiency of the initial production contractors, the complexity of the system, and the ability of government technical personnel to ensure that quality standards are maintained by new producers.

Breakout and the Military R & D Base

Another argument raised against breakout is that breaking out major weapon system components for competitive bidding impairs the ability of technically oriented firms to maintain strong research and development organizations. In case study interviews, weapon system prime contractor officials asserted that in order to perform the systems design and integration role, their firms must employ large R & D and management groups. Companies which do not perform this role have lower overhead costs and therefore can underbid the weapon system makers on production contracts. The loss of production contracts in turn makes it more difficult for weapon system contractors to keep their research and development staffs together, especially when they face a temporary shortage of R & D contracts. And maintaining the continuity of these staffs usually leads to greater efficiency in the conduct of future programs.[18]

There are two weaknesses in this argument, although both are due, not to poor logic on the part of contractors, but to faulty government policies. First, if the government in fact wishes to maintain a strong research and development base, it should look upon the R & D staff costs of its regular contractors as a fixed cost, to be reimbursed even when there is a temporary dearth of R & D work. This is seldom recognized explicitly in current policies and practice.[19]

More important, if the government expects weapon system contractors to maintain their systems design and management capabilities intact and if therefore the costs of maintaining these capabilities are properly regarded as fixed costs, they should be excluded from cost projections used in making production contract award decisions. Only incremental costs should be weighed in comparing a challenging competitive bidder against the current producer. But in fact, government bidding guidelines frequently require the allocation of research and development and other fixed overhead costs to production bid cost estimates, putting the weapon system designer at a definite but unreal disadvantage.

Of course, if the overhead costs of weapon system prime contractors are considered excessive for reasons unrelated to maintaining an essential research and development base, forcing those contractors to compete with firms whose overhead is lower is one way of motivating overhead reduction. Still there are undoubtedly

[18] For a discussion of the "maintaining the research and development base" philosophy, see Peck and Scherer, pp. 375–379.

[19] Even if it were, weapon system contractors would still *like* to achieve the higher sales and profit levels possible with a substantial production volume, but this would then be more a matter of preference than of necessity.

better methods for accomplishing this end while also assuring that production contracts are efficiently allocated on the basis of true incremental cost.

Breakout, Proprietary Rights, and Bargaining Power

Competitive breakout also raises problems which are half legal, half economic in nature. Government weapons procurement regulations include the statement that:

> It is the policy of the Department of Defense to encourage inventiveness and to provide incentives therefor by honoring the "proprietary data" resulting from private developments and hence to limit demands for data to that which is essential for Government purposes.[20]

"Proprietary data" is defined in this context as:

> . . . data providing information concerning the details of a contractor's secrets of manufacture, such as may be contained in but not limited to his manufacturing methods or processes, treatment and chemical composition of materials, plant layout and tooling, to the extent that such information is not disclosed by inspection or analysis of the product itself and to the extent that the contractor has protected such information from unrestricted use by others.[21]

Before this definition was issued, heated arguments arose over what was and what was not proprietary when government agencies demanded the manufacturing drawings and information necessary for competitive breakout. The issue reached an important test during 1954 in connection with the Army's efforts to break out Honest John rocket production from Douglas Aircraft's prime contract. Backed by other members of the aircraft industry, Douglas argued that the detailed design drawings required to manufacture Honest John were its private property. The Army argued in return that they were not, since they had been created under government contract and therefore belonged, not to Douglas, but to the government. Douglas' rebuttal emphasized that although the specific Honest John drawings were in fact done under contract, they re-

[20] *Armed Services Procurement Regulation,* 9–202.1 (a).
[21] *Armed Services Procurement Regulation,* 9–201 (b).

flected an accumulation of engineering know-how developed by Douglas over many years of both government and private work. The Army nevertheless rejected this contention and proceeded with its breakout program. The Honest John decision was considered an informal precedent for other Army breakout actions and later for the breakout programs of all three services.

Contractor representatives said during case study interviews that the implications of this decision were generally less severe for electronics companies than for aircraft makers. Manufacturing drawings for an aircraft or guided missile structural part — the forte of aircraft firms — usually provide enough information to permit almost any organization experienced in the field to manufacture that part. On the other hand, the fabrication of gyroscopes, potentiometers, and many other electronic or electro-mechanical instruments requires much specialized know-how which cannot be conveyed simply in manufacturing drawings. As a result, the ruling that detailed design drawings were government property exposed most of the aircraft industry's products to production competition on the basis of price, while many products of electronics and instrumentation firms remained protected by know-how.

Nevertheless, government agencies have also attempted to obtain the additional know-how required to secure competitive bidding on more sophisticated components. There have been many arguments over whether specific know-how was acquired directly under a government contract or whether it resulted from a contractor's privately financed work or general experience. When a contractor has won this essentially factual argument, the government has on occasion paid lump-sum indemnities to acquire trade secrets necessary for competitive bidding. No details have been made public on the frequency or magnitude of such settlements, although a government contracting attorney indicated when interviewed that the payments were sometimes quite substantial. Still the bargaining power of a firm selling its trade secrets to the government is limited by the cost of "reverse engineering" — having another firm take the detailed drawings for a component and (usually after some trial and error) independently develop the know-how necessary to manufacture it.

Bargaining position can also be an important determinant of the government's ability to secure competitive breakout even when proprietary data considerations are of little moment. In particular, when costly specialized facilities and tools are needed to produce a component, subsystem, or weapon system, the original contractor who has received such facilities is at a distinct advantage over other potential producers. Government bidding regulations have attempted to circumvent this problem by requiring those who possess special government-furnished facilities to include a rent for their use in competitive bids.[22] But this is a delusion. The fact is, a contractor with government-furnished facilities does have a *real* (although not necessarily accounting) cost advantage over less-favored firms. When rent is paid by the contractor and then reimbursed by the government, this advantage is merely concealed, not eliminated, and by requiring this accounting practice the government encourages wasteful duplication of facilities.[23]

The only true way to eliminate advantages of this sort is to transfer possession of special government-owned facilities when a new production contractor is chosen. Still for heavy equipment items this is often impractical. The most significant cases of this sort have arisen when the government has evicted one company from a completely government-owned plant and installed another firm as operator, to produce either the first operator's products or (more frequently) new products. For example, in 1957 the Sperry Gyroscope Company, which had been producing Sparrow I missiles, was removed from the Navy's Bristol, Tennessee, missile plant, and Raytheon moved in to produce its own Sparrow III missile. Similarly, the Army took steps to ensure that Douglas Aircraft Company could be evicted at will from the government-owned Nike missile production plant in Charlotte, North Carolina, although in fact no attempt to evict Douglas was subsequently made. More frequently, however, companies occupying government-owned plants pursue a strategy which minimizes the probability of this kind of breakout. By erecting its own buildings in the immediate vicinity, installing its own heavy equipment in the government's plant, and seeing to it that development and production processes are laid out in such a way as to make company and government

[22] *Armed Services Procurement Regulation,* 13–407.

[23] In some cases, the government has even paid contractors a profit markup on the rents they paid to the government and then had reimbursed! See *Hearings, Pyramiding of Profits,* pp. 482–483.

facilities highly interdependent, a firm can usually secure for itself fairly permanent tenure in a government-owned plant.

Summary

In summary, the government's ability to realize the benefits of competitive bidding on the production of weapon systems, subsystems, and components is limited by a number of conditions. These include the cost of preparing detailed drawings and specifications, the danger of reduced quality and less effective systems integration, the proprietary rights of original producers to manufacturing know-how, and the possession of immovable specialized facilities by original producers. Only when these barriers can be surmounted at an expected cost less than the prospective savings is the breakout of production for competitive bidding desirable.

SECOND SOURCING

The price competition obtained through breakout with competitive bidding is a winner-take-all type of competition. If the original producer of an item fails to submit the lowest responsive bid, it will no longer produce that item. But price competition may also be achieved through second sourcing — selecting one or more additional firms to produce a weapon system, subsystem, or component concurrently with the original contractor, which continues producing at least part of the government's requirements.

Actually, creating competitive incentives for cost reduction is only one of several reasons for establishing second production sources. During World War II and the Korean period, the primary objective was usually to achieve a rapid buildup of war materiel production. Thus, there were five production sources (including Ford Motor Company's Willow Run plant) for the B–24 bomber, four for the B–29, three for the B–17, and three for the Navy F4U–1 Corsair fighter. When the Korean conflict was at its peak, three aircraft companies were producing the Boeing B–47 bomber, and General Motors supplemented Republic Aviation's F–84 fighter production. Similarly, automobile companies were brought in as second sources to expand the production of J–47, J–48, J–57, and J–65 jet engines during the Korean emergency. When mobilization pressures have been less severe, the government has established second sources to insure that production would not be interrupted by strikes or surprise bombing attack damage and, on items such as precision gyroscopes whose fabrication is especially difficult, to obtain quality and reliability competition.

Still price competition has also been an objective in second sourcing decisions. Many variations of the second sourcing approach to providing incentives for efficiency are possible. In a number of programs, at least some cost competition has been achieved by having different plants of a single corporation produce the same weapon system or subsystem. Although conflicts of corporate sales objectives are lacking in this approach, interdivisional rivalry has apparently led in some such cases to intensified cost reduction efforts. Another method is typified by the Atomic Energy Commission's use of its government-owned Monticello plant as a "yardstick" against which to judge the costs of private uranium ore processors.[24]

Perhaps the clearest recent example of a second sourcing effort explicitly intended to generate incentives for weapon system production cost reduction is the Navy's Sidewinder program. The Sidewinder air-to-air infrared homing missile was originally developed by a team of Navy engineers at the Naval Ordnance Test Station in California. The Philco Corporation was chosen as original production contractor, but after one year General Electric was brought in as a second source. Then the division of production quantities for any upcoming year's order was based upon success in reducing costs: the more successful Philco was relative to General Electric, the larger its share of the total production order would be, and vice versa. Both companies launched drives to increase their efficiency and to simplify the product design (incidentally increasing missile reliability), and over a period of seven years the price per unit was cut to one-seventh of what it had averaged on the first lot of 300 missiles.[25] Although these cost reductions have been attributed mainly to the competition between Philco and General Electric, accumulation of production experience was undoubtedly another factor. A rough calculation suggests a progress or learning curve slope of 70%; that is, Sidewinder costs were reduced by about 24% with each doubling of the cumulative total of missiles produced by

[24] Richard A. Tybout, *Government Contracting in Atomic Energy* (Ann Arbor: University of Michigan Press, 1956), p. 38.

[25] Philip J. Klass, "Competition Slashes Sidewinder 1–A Price," *Aviation Week & Space Technology*, April 9, 1962, pp. 89–95.

each competitor.[26]   This rate of cost reduction is slightly better than the average achieved in all World War II and postwar aircraft production programs and probably a good deal higher than the typical experience in postwar guided missile programs.[27]

World War II Progress Curves Under Competition

The World War II aircraft production experience provides a much richer source of quantitative data on the effects of second sourcing competition.   Five wartime aircraft production programs — the B–17, B–24, and B–29 bomber and the P–47 and F4U–1 fighter efforts — had interfirm competition in the form of second sourcing.[28]   In all, 18 organizations (counting relatively autonomous plants of a firm as separate units) were involved.   The direct labor per airframe pound progress curve parameters for these 18 producers are compared in Table 5.1 with the class average parameters for all World War II bombers and fighters.   For the seven cases in which a producer experienced interfirm competition

[26] It is known that in November 1960, a total of 40,000 Sidewinders had been produced. *Jane's All the World's Aircraft,* 1961–1962 (London: S. Low, Marston and Co., 1961), p. 420.   It is assumed that in 1962 production reached a cumulative total of 50,000 and was distributed equally between the two competitors.   If the cost index for the first lot of 300 missiles in 1955 was 100.0, the index for 1962 would be 14.3, as indicated in the text. But the 1962 index must be adjusted for changes in factor cost levels.   The most applicable factor cost index appears to be average hourly wages in the electrical equipment and supply industry, which rose to 126.6 in 1962 from a 1955 base of 100.0.   Therefore, the adjusted 1962 Sidewinder price index is 11.3.   Given these price-quantity relationships, a linear progress curve slope of about 76% can be found.

[27] Furthermore, the argument presented by Harold Asher in *Cost-Quantity Relationships in the Airframe Industry,* R–291 (Santa Monica: The RAND Corporation, 1956), implies that at cumulative quantities as high as those attained in the Sidewinder production program, the progress curve should flatten out and tend asymptotically to a 100% slope.   If so, the Sidewinder cost reduction achievement is even more favorable than comparison with experience in relatively low-volume production programs suggests.

[28] There was brief competition between Lockheed–Burbank and Convair–Nashville on P–38 production, but since Convair delivered only 113 aircraft over a six-month period while the Lockheed P–38 production run covered five years and 9,256 aircraft, this program has been excluded.   Also omitted were programs with competition only between two or more plants of a single corporation.

Competitive Incentives

TABLE 5.1

Progress Curve Data on 5 World War II Aircraft Programs with Second Sourcing Competition

Program	Producer	Unit Numbers Included	Number of Observations	Progress Curve Slope (%)	t-ratio (Actual Slope vs. Class Average) *	Computed Unit One Intercept, as % of Class Average †	First Actual Observation, as % of Class Average
Class average — all bombers		—	—	77.2	—	100.0	—
B-17	Boeing–Seattle (total)	49–6981	54	72.0	−5.98	257.2	150.4
	Competitive period only	745–6981	35	73.7	−3.28	200.4	138.1
B-17	Douglas–Long Beach	27–3000	33	73.9	−4.26	119.6	79.2
B-17	Lockheed–Burbank	125–2750	30	70.1	−8.30	171.1	76.5
B-24	Convair–San Diego (total)	279–6435	39	77.3	+.11	83.8	85.8
	Competitive period only	811–6435	34	78.0	+.50	75.1	86.2
B-24	North American–Dallas	10– 900	14	73.2	−3.21	100.3	90.7
B-24	Ford–Willow Run	8–8238	33	69.8	−7.61	192.8	200.1
B-24 E&H	Convair–Fort Worth	93–2012	15	77.5	+.15	65.2	65.5
B-24 E&H	Douglas–Tulsa	11– 952	15	72.1	−4.10	114.5	61.8
B-29	Boeing–Wichita (total)	5–1642	31	70.4	−10.12	156.9	100.7
	Competitive period only	87–1642	22	66.7	−8.21	206.3	100.3
B-29	Boeing–Renton	8–1050	19	78.9	+1.38	58.0	57.1
B-29	Martin–Omaha	3– 531	16	77.3	+.19	54.3	57.7
B-29	Bell–Marietta	4– 597	19	74.6	−2.29	104.8	103.3

Class average — all fighters	—	—	78.7	—	100.0	—
P-47D Republic–Farmingdale (total)	8–7488	34	79.4	+1.57	115.7	156.3
Competitive period only	669–4631	15	79.0	+.19	124.5	125.2
P-47D Republic–Evansville (total)	22–5978	31	71.6	−5.67	251.2	103.3
Competitive period only	22–1904	15	78.1	−.33	131.2	103.3
P-47D Curtiss–Buffalo	15–347	13	75.4	−1.67	154.8	152.7
F4U-1 Chance–Vought (total)	333–4699	25	78.1	−.62	136.5	166.4
Competitive period only	545–4699	23	76.6	−1.98	170.0	132.7
F4U-1 Goodyear (total)	25–3939	27	73.6	−7.12	214.8	137.9
Competitive period only	25–2766	21	74.2	−5.01	203.5	137.9
F4U-1 Brewster–Long Island	5–494	9	94.5	+3.82	37.2	30.5

* $t = \dfrac{b - \text{Class average of } b\text{'s}}{\text{Standard error of } b}$.

† The class average unit one intercept for bombers is 16.0 manhours per pound and for fighters, 18.5 manhours per pound.

SOURCE: Derived from data in Army Air Forces, Air Materiel Command, *Source Book of World War II Basic Data: Airframe Industry* (Vol. I, 1952). The parameters were estimated by the least squares method, using the equation $y = ax^b$, or in linear form, $\log y = \log a + b \log x$, where y is manhours of direct labor per pound of airframe on a given lot and x is the cumulative quantity of aircraft units produced at the midpoint of that lot. The parameter b has then been converted to the conventional percentage progress curve slope. The class averages for all World War II bombers and fighters were supplied by G. H. Fisher of The RAND Corporation.

during only part of its production run, separate parameter estimates for the total production run and for the competitive period only are presented.[29]

Although it would be possible to justify using total production run parameters, let us focus on the relationship between the competitive period parameters and the class average parameters.[30] The progress curve slopes for 12 out of the 18 producers subjected to multiple sourcing competition were steeper (that is, the rate of cost reduction was greater) than the class average slopes for all U.S. bombers or fighters produced during World War II. Ten of these 12 are significantly steeper than the class averages, as evidenced by t-ratios of less than -1.95, passing a standard one-tail statistical significance test at the .05 level or higher.[31] On the

[29] The competitive period is defined as the period during which two or more firms were actually making deliveries of a given aircraft. Pre-delivery lead time is excluded.

[30] In three cases, the competitive period progress curve slopes are greater than the total production run slopes; in four cases, the total production run slopes are steeper. The average competitive period slope for all seven cases is 75.2%, compared to 74.6% for the total production run slopes. One might argue for using the total production run parameters because they have more degrees of freedom, they are less severely influenced by various short-run disturbances such as design changes, phase-out costs, and changes in accounting coverage; and the periods excluded in the competitive period estimates were affected by potential even if not actual competition. In contrast to frequent practice, no observations have been excluded from the analysis here because they seemed out of line. Only the Boeing B–17 effort at Seattle had major model changes within the production run covered, at least according to the Air Force *Source Book* notes. Two other programs (B–24, Convair–San Diego, and B–29, Bell–Marietta) had changes in accounting coverage which affected the level of unit costs.

[31] The statistical significance tests made here must be taken with more than a grain of salt, since the regressions have several undesirable properties. As we shall see in a moment, the a and b parameters appear to be linearly dependent, violating a basic property of the least squares, maximum likelihood regression model. Second, the test used here assumes no variance in the class averages, which is obviously incorrect. Also, there was evidence of autocorrelation in some of the regressions, although no definitive checks (such as the Durbin-Watson test) were made. Because of the last two problems, the test used tends to overstate the level of statistical significance. However, the use of class averages for all wartime producers, rather than for noncompetitive programs only, as a basis of comparison imparts a counter-vailing understatement of the significance level, since inclusion of the com-

other hand, for the six producers with progress curves of below-average steepness, deviations from the class averages were typically small, except for Brewster's F4U–1 Corsair production experience — a most unusual case, as we have seen in the preceding chapter.[32] The average slope for the 12 competitive bomber producers was 73.8%, compared to an average of 77.2% for all wartime bomber programs. However, the average slope for the six competitive fighters was 79.6% — less steep than the average of 78.7% for all World War II fighters. Although the results are therefore not completely uniform, there is a definite suggestion that progress curves tended to be steeper when second sourcing competition was employed than when it was not.

It does not necessarily follow that second sourcing competition spurred greater efficiency on the part of World War II aircraft producers. In his survey of the progress curve literature, Harold Asher has pointed out that the slopes of progress curves are influenced by such factors as program priority, the producer's familiarity with similar aircraft, the newness of a plant, the kind of production tooling employed, and the number of changes introduced during production.[33] He also found for a sample of 12 postwar fighters that the higher the unit number one cost intercept (as estimated by regression) was, the steeper the progress curve tended to be.[34] The wartime data analyzed here display the same relationship. For the competitive period progress curves of the 12 bomber programs, where a is the unit number one intercept value and S is the percentage slope (measured in decimal terms), the regression equation

petitive programs (with slopes generally steeper than the bomber class average) tends to reduce the class average percentage below the average which would be found for noncompetitive programs only.

[32] Cf. pp. 75–76 *supra*. Inspection also suggests that the Brewster data are not accurate representations of actual manpower inputs on early lots — a finding consistent with Navy criticisms of Brewster's accounting system, or lack of one. The Brewster regression produced by far the lowest r^2 — only .164. The next lowest — .807 — was for the Convair–San Diego competitive period. The average r^2 for all 25 regressions was .911, or .943 with the Brewster regression deleted, suggesting a rather good fit of the observations about their regression lines.

[33] Asher, *Cost-Quantity Relationships in the Airframe Industry*, pp. 41–43.

[34] *Ibid.*, pp. 76–79.

(1) $\log S = -.0202 - .0896 \log a$
                              (.0028)   (.0131)

is obtained, with r^2 of .825.[35]   Asher has interpreted this relationship as indicating that efficiency must be judged not from the slope
of a progress curve alone, but from the combination of slope *and*
unit number one intercept.[36]   That is, a program is efficient if its
parameters lie to the left of the regression line described by equation (1), while it is inefficient if its parameters lie to the right of
the line.   He suggested further that the unit number one intercept
value is a function of such variables as past experience with similar
aircraft and tooling costs.[37]

It is also possible that when actual costs on the first few units
produced are unnecessarily high due to liberal manning of initial
production operations, achieving a high rate of cost reduction subsequently is easy, while when production lines are manned austerely at the outset, cost reduction is relatively difficult and progress curve slopes are not steep.   If so, then steep progress curves
can be evidence of early inefficiency rather than sustained efficiency.   Such an explanation is consistent with the finding that programs with competition had on the average steeper progress curves
than noncompetitive programs, since the establishment of multiple
production sources in the programs covered by this analysis, and
especially in the bomber programs, was a reflection of their exceptionally high priorities.   And as we have seen in Chapter 3,
high priority programs are typically not subjected to severe budgetary pressures in their early (developmental) stages, and therefore
the early production manning of the competitive bomber programs
could have been more liberal on the average than in the lower
priority, noncompetitive programs.

Although this explanation may be partly valid, it is still not completely satisfactory.   Inspection of plotted progress curves and
analysis of the production cost elements subject to learning reveal
that progress curves do not tend toward perfect linearity on log-

[35] If one deviant observation (B–17, Boeing–Seattle) is removed, r^2 increase to .939, and the equation becomes $\log S = -.0066 - .1022 \log a$.
There is a remarkable similarity between these equations for World War II
competitive bomber programs and Asher's comparable equation for 12 postwar fighters: $\log S = .0061 - .0976 \log a$.

[36] *Ibid.,* pp. 83–86.

[37] *Ibid.,* pp. 80–83.

arithmic grids, as assumed thus far. Rather, there is reason to believe that the typical progress curve is somewhat S-shaped, first increasing in steepness and then flattening out.[38] Therefore, estimating the unit number one intercept value by linear extrapolation, as I have done here and as Asher did, could misrepresent the *actual* level of costs on early units. That this danger is quite real is suggested by comparing the last two columns of Table 5.1, which show the unit number one intercept values estimated through regression, expressed as a percentage of the unit one class averages, and the first actually observed values, expressed as a percentage of the class averages for the appropriate cumulative unit number.[39] For the 12 bomber producers, the average of the estimated unit one intercepts (competitive periods only) is 121.9% of the all-bomber unit one class average, while the average of the first observed values is only 93.0% of the relevant class average values. For the six fighter producers the estimated average is 136.9%, while the average of the first observed values is 113.7%.

At least for the bomber producers, then, efficiency tended on the average to be higher under competition in terms of *both* first observed unit costs and the rate of cost reduction. On the other hand, the fighter producers show on the average less efficiency in terms of both measures. But the fighter results may be poor indicators of competition's effects, because the Brewster situation was clearly atypical and because in the P–47 program Curtiss could hardly have been considered a serious competitor by Republic, since only 354 P–47's (out of more than 15,000 P–47's in all) were built by Curtiss. Thus, there are grounds for concluding that second sourcing competition provided perceptible incentives for efficiency during World War II.

During the Korean emergency competitive second sourcing of

[38] See *ibid.*, pp. 41–45, 102–103, and 106–109.

[39] To illustrate the derivation of actually observed percentage values, the first manhours-per-pound figure available for the B–17 bombers produced by Boeing–Seattle is 5.79, for cumulative unit number 45. The bomber class average at cumulative unit number 45 is 3.85, and so the value appearing in the last column of Table 5.1 is 100 (5.79/3.85) = 150.4%. This method tends to overestimate the percentage values, since the actual manhours-per-pound figure is for the last unit in a lot but usually covers earlier units in the same lot, generally produced at higher cost than the last unit. On the other hand, the cumulative unit number used to estimate class average manhours-per-pound represents not the last unit in its lot, but the midpoint of the lot.

airframe production was employed on a large scale only in the B–47 bomber program. Although quantitative progress curve data were not obtained, testimony of Air Force General D. H. Baker indicates that the competition spurred certain cost reductions:

> The B–47, as you know, was produced by Douglas. It is produced by Lockheed. And it is produced by Boeing. We have made studies, elaborate studies, to indicate the efficiency of each of those companies. And in one specific case we found that one of the companies . . . was quite a bit out of line and we immediately took it up with the Secretary . . . and at that time we went to this particular company and said we felt their costs were too high, what were they going to do about getting them down. They did. And since that time we have had a return, as I recall, of at least $80 million on that particular contract.[40]

Many other examples of cost reductions as the apparent result of second sourcing can be found. At the weapon system level, when the Navy established a second source for the Bullpup guided missile in 1961, substantial reductions in the original producer's costs followed.[41] At the component level, our case studies revealed, second sourcing of a complex electronic device led to a 25% decrease in the original producer's price. Company representatives admitted that the decrease was due to the added competition. In another program, second sourcing of a guidance computer transistor was followed by increases in quality and decreases in unit price. Similarly, two years after a second source was established to produce certain Air Force altimeters, the price had declined from $250 per unit to roughly $110 per unit.[42]

[40] House, Committee on Armed Services, Subcommittee for Special Investigations, *Hearings, Aircraft Production Costs and Profits* (1956), p. 2886.

[41] Cf. Hal Taylor, "Cost-Cutting Wins New Bullpup Awards," *Missiles and Rockets,* March 12, 1962, pp. 16–17, who attributes cost reductions of roughly 70% mainly to economies of large-scale production. However, Navy officials stated that cost reductions of at least 30% were due to the establishment of competition.

[42] Senate, Select Committee on Small Business, *Report, Case Problems in Government Procurement* (1960), p. 5. The exact amount of the reduction was not determinable because of design changes.

The Costs of Second Sourcing

Still second sourcing, like breakout competition, has its concomitant drawbacks. Manufacturing drawings and know-how must be conveyed by the original producer to the new second source producer, with all the costs and problems discussed in connection with competitive breakout. When learning is an important factor in production cost reduction, an original producer with considerable experience manufacturing an item (and hence far down on its progress curve) may have a decisive cost advantage over even the most highly motivated second source producer. When economies of scale are relevant, it could be uneconomical to split up an order just large enough for optimal production by one firm. Also, if production orders are too small, contractors will lose interest and assign their better supervisory personnel to larger contracts. (In this situation, however, order size is relative — an order which might become lost in a large company can be a small producer's principal contract, receiving top managerial priority.) On major production jobs, second sourcing often requires the duplication of tooling and special machinery already possessed by the original producer. And finally, second source producers have a habit of changing production tolerances and even product designs from those of the original producer. Spare parts therefore lose their interchangeability, and so complete sets of spare parts for weapons produced by each firm must be carried in inventory. This complicates the problem of field maintenance and increases logistic support costs.

For these reasons, second sourcing is clearly not appropriate in every situation. Only when production orders are expected to be sufficiently large and sustained to permit net cost savings from competition, or when other advantages such as preventing the interruption of deliveries in the event of strikes are important, is second sourcing desirable. As the Navy officer responsible for Sidewinder missile production observed:

> If it takes more than three years for dual-source procurement to begin to pay off in over-all savings to the Navy, its use is questionable. . . . If it takes more than five years to achieve a net saving, we won't touch it.[43]

[43] Klass, "Competition Slashes Sidewinder 1–A Price," *Aviation Week & Space Technology,* April 9, 1962, p. 93.

CONCLUSION

Once the design of a weapon system, subsystem, or component has been stabilized, it is frequently possible to create competitive incentives for production efficiency through competitive breakout and second sourcing. Nevertheless, there are usually costs and problems associated with securing price competition on the production of technically advanced and complex items. A high order of judgment is required to determine in any particular case whether the prospective benefits of price competition outweigh the costs.

PART II

CONTRACTUAL INCENTIVES

CHAPTER 6

The Theory and Application of Automatic Contractual Incentives

THE NEXT FIVE CHAPTERS deal with the theory and application of contractual incentives in weapons development and production. The contractual incentives approach, in its most common form, attempts to influence contractor behavior by correlating profit with performance through the determination of contract prices — a process approximating in a bargaining context what takes place automatically and impersonally in a market system of buyer-seller relationships.

There are significant problems in this adaptation of traditional market institutions to the nonmarket environment of weapons acquisition. Indeed, the role which contractual incentives should play has been one of the most controversial questions of weapons procurement policy. Unfortunately, more heat than light has been generated in perennial investigations of the subject dating back to World War I. Thus, Professor John Perry Miller observes in his leading text on the economics of contractual incentives:

> The merits of the argument that CPFF contracts are conducive to inefficiency are by no means established. In logic they seem persuasive. But there are many who have defended the contrary thesis with considerable vigor. The available evidence on the matter is not conclusive. . . . An extensive and unbiased survey . . . might shed light on the controversy as to the relative merits of CPFF and other contractual forms, a controversy which has been waged to date largely in the realm of pure speculation.[1]

[1] John Perry Miller, *Pricing of Military Procurements* (New Haven: Yale University Press, 1949), p. 132.

131

The following chapters represent an attempt to shed at least some light on questions of this nature.

The Variety of Contract Types

A fundamental variable in the contractual incentives approach is the type of contract employed. By way of introduction two more or less polar alternatives can be distinguished: the firm fixed-price (FFP) contract and the cost-plus-a-fixed-fee (CPFF) contract.

The firm fixed-price contract corresponds most directly to the contractual relationship prevailing in a market environment. With it the contractor promises to supply certain specified goods or services at a price which, after agreed upon by buyer and seller, is not subject to adjustments reflecting the seller's actual cost experience. Profit under a fixed-price contract is the residuum of price less cost, and hence is negatively correlated with cost. For every dollar of cost reduction the contractor's profit is increased a dollar, and so a clear incentive for cost reduction is provided.[2] It should be noted that this inverse correlation between profit and cost operates automatically once the fixed price has been set. Profit-performance correlations which work in this manner will therefore be called auto-correlating contractual incentives, or more simply, automatic contractual incentives.

The CPFF contract is the best known type of cost reimbursement contract. With it the buyer and seller initially agree upon a fee or profit amount related to an estimate of total costs. The cost estimate is not binding; the buyer agrees to reimburse within limits all allowable costs incurred by the contractor in executing the contract.[3] Consequently, the "price" in a CPFF relationship is almost

[2] The effect of corporate income taxes is generally ignored in this volume. Obviously, the contractor's profit after taxes is only 48% of pretax profits at current rates.

[3] Usually CPFF contracts contain cost limits which can be exceeded by the contractor only with government approval. If a cost increase necessary to meet contract specifications is not approved, the contractor is not obliged to meet the specifications. Disapproval of such cost increases is sufficiently infrequent that it can be ignored in the following analysis.

It should also be noted that certain costs — notably interest charges, certain advertising costs, charitable donations, entertainment outlays, and certain independent research costs — are not allowable for reimbursement under Section 15 of the *Armed Services Procurement Regulation*. A survey

completely flexible. The fee, however, is fixed. Barring a change in contract performance requirements, it can be neither decreased nor increased, whether costs prove to be greater or less than the initial estimate. The CPFF contract therefore provides no automatic correlation between the amount of profit and actual cost.

Given this difference between the profit-cost correlations under fixed-price and CPFF contracts, it is usually said that the contractual incentive for cost reduction is at a maximum with the firm fixed-price type and at a minimum with the CPFF type. It is also said that under firm fixed-price contracts risk is at a maximum, while under CPFF contracts it is at a minimum. In a sense this is plainly true from the contractor's point of view. Should actual costs prove to be higher than originally contemplated under a fixed-price contract, the contractor's profit amount will be reduced and the firm may even incur a loss. If, however, cost expectations are exceeded under a CPFF contract, the company will bear no loss and indeed no reduction in profit amount. Thus, the risk of possible cost increases is shifted through the CPFF contract from the seller to the buyer.

But in another sense cost reimbursement contracts also minimize risk (differently defined) for the government as buyer. Should actual costs prove to be *lower* than originally contemplated in the bargain, the savings would accrue solely to the contractor's benefit in the form of higher profits under a firm fixed-price relationship. Under a CPFF contract the contractor's profit is fixed and the government retains any savings. Relative to fixed-price contracts, therefore, CPFF contracts involve less risk of loss from the contractor's point of view and less risk of high profits from the government's point of view. It so happens, as we shall see, that minimizing the risk of loss is often just what the contractor prefers while minimizing the risk of windfall profit is what the government de-

---

of 15 aerospace firms disclosed that in 1960 nonallowable costs comprised 1.0% of government contract sales. Interest charges made up the largest single share of this figure. Stanford Research Institute, *The Industry-Government Aerospace Relationship,* prepared for the Aerospace Industries Association, Vol. I (Menlo Park: May 1963), p. 46.

"Fee" is distinguished from "profit" in contracting terminology mainly to indicate that the contractor's fee is calculated before nonallowable costs are deducted to arrive at net accounting profit. This technical distinction is largely ignored in the following chapters.

sires, and so the CPFF contract provides a mutually satisfactory relationship.[4]

The So-Called Incentive Contracts

Still, minimizing the risk of windfall profits is not the government's only objective in weapons contracting, just as minimizing the risk of loss is seldom a business enterprise's main goal. In particular, the government presumably wishes to have its weapon systems developed and produced as efficiently as possible. But the CPFF contract provides no profit amount — cost correlation, and hence (at least in a first approximation to the theory) no contractual incentive for efficiency.[5] Thus, we find a conflict between minimizing the risk of windfall profits and maximizing the incentive for efficiency. To strike a compromise between these two conflicting goals the so-called incentive contract types have been developed.

The best-known form is the fixed-price incentive (FPI) contract, under which cost savings or overruns are shared by the buyer and seller, rather than accruing entirely to the seller's benefit or loss. Initially a target cost, a target profit, and a profit-sharing formula are negotiated. Historically, profit-sharing agreements have stipulated a contractor's share of from 10% to 30% in cost overruns or underruns, although recently the use of higher sharing proportions has been encouraged.[6] If, for example, the contractor's share is 20% and actual audited costs prove to be $100,000 less than the target cost, $20,000 (20% of the underrun) is added to the contractor's target profit, the remaining $80,000 reverting to the government. Conversely, if actual costs prove to be higher than the target cost, the contractor's profit is reduced by 20% of the overrun, the government reimbursing the balance. Usually a ceiling price (historically, from 115% to 135% of the target cost) is negotiated, setting a firm limit on the amount of cost plus

[4] For a statement to this effect sanctioned as official policy, see U.S. Department of Defense, *Incentive Contracting Guide* (prepared under the direction of the Office of the Assistant Secretary of Defense, Installations and Logistics, by Harbridge House, Inc., August 1962), p. 17.

[5] It does provide a cost-profit rate correlation which may under certain conditions (to be analyzed in Chapter 7) afford an incentive for efficiency.

[6] U.S. Department of Defense, *Incentive Contracting Guide*, pp. 3, 19.

profit the government will pay in the event of a large overrun. With most FPI contracts the contractor covers 100% of any costs exceeding the ceiling price.[7] A floor may also be established, below which the contractor retains none of any further underruns.

It should be apparent that the term "incentive contract" is a misnomer, since it suggests that incentive type contracts provide something special in the way of incentives. In fact, the profit incentive under a fixed-price incentive contract is as a rule weaker than under a firm fixed-price contract, since the contractor retains only a share of cost savings as profit or forfeits only a share of cost overruns as loss, instead of the whole amount.[8] More generally, most of the major contract types (including cost-plus-fixed-fee) with which we shall be concerned in this and the next two chapters can generate some kind of automatic contractual incentive for cost reduction, and thus most might be called incentive contracts. What varies from type to type is the contractor's proportional share in overruns and underruns; that is, the strength of the profit-cost correlation.[9]

[7] This is only approximately true. With the FPI contracts negotiated during the 1950's and early 1960's, the contractor typically began absorbing 100% of overruns before actual cost equaled the ceiling price. But under certain conditions it is also possible for actual cost to *exceed* the ceiling price by a substantial margin before a 100% contractor share takes effect. In general, the lower the price ceiling and the lower the contractor's share, the sooner 100% absorption begins. Given these complications, it is often convenient to employ the concept of a cost ceiling — that is, the level of costs at which the contractor begins absorbing 100% of overruns.

[8] In algebraic terms, where π_T is the target profit amount established through negotiation, α is the contractor's sharing proportion, C_T is the target cost agreed upon in negotiation, C_A is the actual accounting cost, C_F is the floor cost, and C_C is the ceiling cost, the contractor's actual before-tax profit π will be:

$$\pi = \pi_T + \alpha(C_T - C_A) \text{ when } C_F < C_A < C_C \; ;$$
$$\pi = \pi_T + \alpha(C_T - C_F) \text{ when } C_A \leq C_F \; ; \text{ and}$$
$$\pi = \pi_T + \alpha(C_T - C_C) + (C_C - C_A) \text{ when } C_A \geq C_C \; .$$

With a firm fixed-price contract the value of α is 1.0, whereas with a so-called incentive contract α is usually less than 1.0. With a CPFF contract the value of α is 0.

[9] The term "profit-cost correlation," which is employed frequently in subsequent chapters, is apt to mislead the reader familiar with statistical

The cost-plus-incentive-fee (CPIF) contract is quite similar to the fixed-price incentive contract in its most conventional application. Just as the FPI contract was devised to reduce the risk (and incentive) below that of the firm fixed-price contract, so the CPIF contract was created to add risk and incentive to the CPFF type. Under a cost-plus-incentive-fee arrangement the contractor's profit (or fee) is not fixed, but varies according to a predetermined formula. Usually the formula stipulates that if actual audited costs are less than the negotiated target cost, the contractor's fee will be increased by some proportion of the underrun. If actual costs exceed the target cost, the contractor's fee is reduced. The CPIF and FPI contracts differ mainly in their provisions for paying cost overruns above the negotiated ceiling. With CPIF the government usually reimburses fully all costs beyond the ceiling, and therefore the contractor is guaranteed some minimum fee (or insured against exceeding some maximum loss) even if a very large overrun occurs. In contrast, as we have seen, the contractor is fully liable for all costs beyond FPI ceilings.

In some cases CPIF incentive formulas have been drawn up to correlate profit not only with cost outcomes, but also with quality and time outcomes. The first modern application of this three-dimensional incentive contract approach was in the B–58

---

methods. A strong profit-cost correlation is defined here as one in which the contractor's share in overruns and underruns is high. In a strict technical sense, this means having a high regression coefficient α in equations of the type presented in the preceding note. In technical usage a correlation coefficient (conventionally written as either ρ or r) measures the degree to which variation in one variable is related to variation in another. As long as the correlation between profit and cost is linear and automatic, it is possible to have a very low (but non-zero) value of α and hence a very weak contractual incentive, but still have the correlation coefficient attain its maximum value of 1.0. However, with contractual incentive systems which do not work automatically (e.g., redeterminable contracting), it is possible to have correlation coefficients for the profit-cost relationship of less than 1.0, and yet have fairly high values on the average for α. In this volume I use the term "consistent" as equivalent to the technical statement, "having a high correlation coefficient for the profit-cost (or some other) relationship."

Although the terms "profit-cost correlation" and "consistent" are incorrect from a strictly technical standpoint, they seem best able to convey the meanings I have in mind to readers not trained in correlation and regression theory.

supersonic strategic bomber program.[10]   The incentive provisions of the principal B–58 development contract permitted prime contractor Convair's final profit to vary from 4% to 7% of target costs, depending upon its success in meeting and surpassing negotiated technical performance, schedule maintenance, and cost control goals.   One-half of the potential profit variation was allocated to performance, one-third to schedule maintenance, and one-sixth to cost control.   More recently, increased use of multidimensional incentive contracts for development programs, with a much wider range of potential profit variation, has been advocated by Department of Defense authorities.   For example, in the Navy A2F attack aircraft program, the range of profit variation based upon various technical performance and cost control achievements was from 4% to 15% of negotiated target costs.[11]

Redeterminable Fixed-Price Contracts

The redeterminable fixed-price contract (also known as a flexible or maximum price contract) is another major variant of the firm fixed-price approach.   With it risk is reduced by deferring agreement on a firm fixed price.   There are several minor variations, but in general the redeterminable contract works as follows: At the outset, before any substantial amount of work has been performed under the contract, the buyer and seller negotiate a tentative base price (including profit) and a firm ceiling price (which in contracts not redeterminable upward is the base price).   Then, after the contractor has accumulated some experience in performing the contract (typically after 30% to 40% of expected costs have been incurred, but sometimes also at the 100% point), the parties negotiate a final firm fixed price, adjusting the original base price to reflect any changes in their cost expectations.   The contractor's expected profit margin is also redetermined in this negotiation,

[10] In 1908 the Army Signal Corps procured from the Wright Brothers a "military flying machine" under a contract which promised a schedule of bonuses for airspeed over 40 m.p.h. and flight time of more than one hour.

[11] See House, Committee on Appropriations, *Hearings, Department of Defense Appropriations for 1963,* Part 4, pp. 496–497. For a discussion of proposed applications of multidimensional incentive contracts to the space effort, see Hal Taylor, "NASA To Use More Incentive Contracts," *Missiles and Rockets,* June 18, 1962, p. 16.

presumably taking into account the efficiency, economy, and ingenuity with which the company performed prior to the redetermination point.[12]   After redetermination, any remaining work is completed under what is essentially a firm fixed-price relationship.

There is reason to question whether the redeterminable contract creates a contractual incentive for cost reduction prior to the time of redetermination.   Certainly, it is not an automatic contractual incentive, for if a contractor underruns the initial base price, there is no formula guaranteeing that its profit will be increased.   Instead, the revised profit amount is determined administratively in the redetermination proceedings.   And there has been a distinct historical tendency for profit amounts to be reduced rather than increased in redetermination when costs have been decreased. This is shown in Table 6.1, which presents data on 141 Army redeterminable fixed-price contracts with an initial negotiated value (including profit) of $475 million and 66 Navy redeterminable contracts with an initial value of $360 million.   In nearly 84% of all cases (Army and Navy combined) in which the redetermined price was less than the base price (a condition leading automatically to increased profit amounts under firm fixed-price and fixed-price incentive contracts), the contractor's profit amount was *decreased*. When overruns occurred (leading automatically to decreased profits under FFP and FPI contracts), the contractor's profit amount was *increased* 21% of the time.   The results are somewhat different if profit rate changes, rather than profit amount changes, are analyzed.   In only 36% of the underrun cases was the profit rate decreased, and in only 10% of the overrun cases was the profit rate increased.

Professor Miller noted a similar tendency during World War II for cost reductions not to be rewarded with increased profit, stating that:

> The services' great problem with the maximum-price contract is to convince the contractor that they will not set redetermined prices on an estimated cost plus conventional profit but that they will allow greater dollar profit for greater success in increasing efficiency.[13]

[12] Senate, Committee on Armed Services, Procurement Subcommittee, *Hearings, Procurement Study* (1960), p. 83.

[13] *Pricing of Military Procurements,* p. 138.

TABLE 6.1

Classification of Price and Profit Changes in the Redetermination
of 207 Army and Navy Contracts

		Contracts on which the redetermined price was greater than or equal to the base price (overruns)		Contracts on which the redetermined price was less than the base price (underruns)	
		Number	*Percent*	*Number*	*Percent*
Profit amount increased	Army	18	23.1	10	15.9
	Navy	3	12.5	2	4.8
	Combined	21	20.6	12	11.4
Profit amount the same	Army	12	15.4	4	6.4
	Navy	1	4.2	1	2.4
	Combined	13	12.7	5	4.8
Profit amount decreased	Army	48	61.5	49	77.8
	Navy	20	83.3	39	92.8
	Combined	68	66.7	88	83.8
Total	Army	78	100.0	63	100.0
	Navy	24	100.0	42	100.0
	Combined	102	100.0	105	100.0
Profit rate increased	Army	10	12.8	32	50.8
	Navy	0	0.0	10	23.8
	Combined	10	9.8	42	40.0
Profit rate the same*	Army	7	9.0	11	17.5
	Navy	3	12.5	14	33.3
	Combined	10	9.8	25	23.8
Profit rate decreased	Army	61	78.2	20	31.7
	Navy	21	87.5	18	42.8
	Combined	82	80.4	38	36.2
Total	Army	78	100.0	63	100.0
	Navy	24	100.0	42	100.0
	Combined	102	100.0	105	100.0

* Or within plus or minus .1%.

SOURCE: Office of the Assistant Secretary of Defense, Installations and Logistics. The Navy data cover all contracts redetermined during fiscal years 1958 and 1959. The Army data cover 56 Army Ordnance and 85 Army Signal Corps contracts, including most of the contracts of $100,000 or more orginal value with industrial corporations redetermined during fiscal year 1959 by those agencies. The great majority of the Army contracts were redetermined at the 100% point, and so the results shown here represent final profit outcomes. All of the Navy contracts were redetermined at the 20% to 40% point, so they do not reflect final outcomes. The technical meaning of the terms "overrun" and "underrun" is discussed in Chapters 7 and 8.

These observations suggest that government redetermination practices afford little profit incentive for cost reduction prior to redetermination, although there appears to be an incentive for avoiding cost overruns (weakened perhaps by the inconsistency of the overrun-profit reduction correlation). Nevertheless, this is not conclusive proof of ineffective incentives for efficiency under redeterminable contracts. As we shall see later, not all contract cost underruns are due to increased efficiency. The amount of profit may be reduced in redetermination despite a cost underrun when the contracting officer believes "the risk undertaken by the company was actually less than the risk (he) initially thought the company was going to undertake" [14] — in other words, when the initial base price was too generous. Profit reductions may also be negotiated when the contractor delays submitting cost data necessary for redetermination.[15] In cases of delayed redetermination and also when the parties agree in advance that the government may request a redetermination after 100% completion, the redeterminable contract tends to become more like a cost reimbursement contract than a fixed-price contract, especially when the ceiling price has been set at a relatively high level.[16] Given these complications, we must defer any conclusions about the incentive effects of redeterminable contracts until further evidence has been examined in Chapter 8.

Other Contract Types [17]

Although it is no longer in use, the cost-plus-a-percentage-of-cost contract should be mentioned. Under it the buyer agrees to re-

[14] Testimony of Army Brig. Gen. F. J. McMorrow in House, Committee on Armed Services, *Hearings Pursuant to Section 4, Public Law 86–89* (1960), p. 247.

[15] Senate, Committee on Armed Services, *Hearings, Procurement Study* (1960), p. 83.

[16] Both of these cases have been challenged as cost-plus-a-percentage-of-cost arrangements, illegal under 10 U.S.C. 2306 (a). However, the U.S. Court of Claims ruled in 1960 that a contract redeterminable after 100% completion upward to a specified ceiling and downward to an unlimited extent was legal. *National Electronic Laboratories, Inc. v. the United States*, No. 279–57, U.S. Court of Claims, decided January 20, 1960. For data on the extent of redetermination delays, see House, Committee on Appropriations, *Hearings, Department of Defense Appropriations for 1961*, Part 5, pp. 766–771.

[17] Some of the more specialized contract types such as cost-plus-no-fee,

imburse all of the contractor's allowable costs. At the outset of the contract a profit percentage to be applied to actual audited costs is negotiated. If actual costs exceed original expectations, the contractor's profit is also greater, while if actual costs are less, the contractor's profit is reduced. This contract type was employed during World War I, with criticisms that its perverse profit-cost correlation encouraged waste and profiteering. Its use was outlawed by the First War Powers Act of 1941 [18] and again by the Armed Services Procurement Act of 1948.[19]

The letter contract [20] must also be mentioned briefly, even though it is not a so-called definitive contract type. Letter contracts are issued to provide temporary contractual coverage so that urgent work can progress while a definitive contract is being negotiated. Typically they state what is to be accomplished under the contemplated contract, but contain no agreement on the price or profit to be paid. The buyer-seller relationship under a letter contract most closely resembles a cost-plus-a-percentage-of-cost arrangement in practice. As a result, reliance upon letter contracts for contractual coverage has been discouraged. Nevertheless, major weapons program activities have proceeded under letter contracts for as long as three years, usually because mutually agreeable performance specifications or profit provisions could not be negotiated. For example, on December 31, 1958, the Navy had 90 letter contracts with a total value of $1.4 billion outstanding. Thirteen of these, with a total value of $465 million, had been outstanding for more than 18 months. Although dollar value statistics are not available, on the same date the Air Force had 230 and the Army 14 letter contracts outstanding.[21]

---

cost sharing, time and materials, labor hour, and fixed-price escalation will not be considered in this volume. A more detailed discussion of the various contract types can be found in the Senate *Hearings, Procurement Study* (1960), pp. 80–92; or in the *Armed Services Procurement Regulation,* sections 3–400 through 3–409.

[18] Public Law No. 354, 77th Congress, 1st sess. (55 Stat. 838–839).

[19] 10 U.S.C. Section 2306 (a).

[20] "Letter contract" is often used synonomously with "letter of intent."

[21] House, Committee on Appropriations, *Hearings, Department of Defense Appropriations for 1960,* Part 5, pp. 19, 30–44, and 856–859. See also *ibid., Hearings, Department of Defense Appropriations for 1961,* Part 5, pp. 759–764; and House, Committee on Government Operations, *Eleventh Report, Organization and Management of Missile Programs* (1959), pp. 43–45.

EXTENT OF USE OF THE VARIOUS CONTRACT TYPES

With their many minor variations, the contract types enumerated here provide a wide array of buyer-seller relationships differing mainly in the form and strength of the profit-performance correlation. There have been pronounced variations in the extent to which each major contract type has been employed in different time periods and different government agencies.

During World War II, cost-plus-fixed-fee contracts accounted for about 45% by value of wartime supply contracts for $10 million or more and about 30% by value of all supply contracts issued by the Army (which then included the Air Force), the Navy, and the Maritime Commission.[22] Differences in the proportion of CPFF contracts employed among these three agencies were fairly small. As the war progressed, the proportion of CPFF contracts declined slightly.

As Table 6.2 shows, cost reimbursement type contracts accounted for 12.7% by value of contracts issued by the three military services in fiscal year 1951. This proportion grew steadily, reaching a peak of 42.6% in fiscal year 1960. During the same period, the use of firm fixed-price contracts fluctuated between a high of 43.9% and a low of 27.8%, with a slight declining trend. Use of the redeterminable fixed-price type contract declined from a high of 38.5% in 1952 to 4.7% in 1959, with a pronounced upsurge since then. Use of the fixed-price incentive type contract grew from 9.1% in 1951 to 25.2% in 1954, and then declined to 12.0% in fiscal year 1962.

Table 6.3 demonstrates that the Air Force has been the most active user of cost reimbursement contracts, with 55.3% by value of its purchases during fiscal year 1960 under cost type agreements. The Army ran second in that year with 35.6% and the Navy third with 29.7%. The Army used firm fixed-price contracts most extensively (52.8%) and the Air Force least extensively (20.2%). The Air Force was the principal sponsor of fixed-price incentive contracts, making 20.8% by value of its purchases under that type, while the Army used no FPI contracts at all.[23]

---

[22] U.S. War Production Board, Bureau of Program and Statistics, *Cost-Plus Contracts in the War Program* (March 8, 1945), Table I (cited in Miller, *Pricing of Military Procurements,* p. 127).

[23] These interservice differences hold true for fiscal years 1957 through

TABLE 6.2

Proportion of Military Procurement Dollars Obligated by Contract Types,
Three Services; Fiscal Years 1951–1962

	FY 1951	FY 1952	FY 1953	FY 1954	FY 1955	FY 1956	FY 1957	FY 1958	FY 1959	FY 1960	FY 1961	FY 1962
Value of procurement actions, all contract types (billions)	$21.5	$34.0	$29.3	$10.9	$13.7	$16.1	$18.0	$22.2	$22.9	$21.2	$22.9	$25.8
% of procurement actions, all contract types	100.0%	100.0%	100.0%	100.0%	100.0%	100.0%	100.0%	100.0%	100.0%	100.0%	100.0%	100.0%
All fixed-price type contracts	87.3	82.1	79.8	70.5	75.9	69.7	66.6	60.4	59.1	57.4	57.9	60.8
Firm fixed-price	43.9	29.8	31.8	38.0	39.7	36.4	35.3	27.8	32.8	31.4	31.5	38.0
Fixed-price redeterminable	33.6	38.5	21.8	5.9	12.5	9.9	8.6	7.4	4.7	6.1	10.5	7.4
Fixed-price incentive	9.1	12.0	24.0	25.2	22.9	19.2	17.8	19.2	15.3	13.6	11.2	12.0
Fixed-price escalation	0.7	1.8	2.2	1.4	0.8	4.2	4.9	6.0	6.3	6.3	4.7	3.4
All cost reimbursement type contracts	12.7	17.9	20.2	29.5	24.1	30.3	33.4	39.6	40.9	42.6	42.1	39.2
Cost plus fixed fee	8.6	13.3	16.3	23.8	19.7	24.1	29.9	33.2	34.3	36.8	36.6	32.5
Cost plus no fee	4.0	4.5	1.6	2.6	2.7	3.9	1.9	2.8	3.0	2.2	2.0	2.3
Cost plus incentive fee	—	—	2.2	2.5	1.4	1.9	1.2	3.2	3.2	3.2	3.2	4.1
Other cost reimbursement	0.1	0.1	0.1	0.6	0.3	0.4	0.4	0.4	0.4	0.4	0.3	0.3

SOURCES: House, Committee on Armed Services, Special Subcommittee on Procurement Practices of the Department of Defense, *Hearings Pursuant to Section 4, Public Law 86–89* (1960), p. 133; and Office of the Secretary of Defense, *Military Prime Contract Awards and Subcontract Payments*, July 1961–June 1962, p. 41.

Includes Army, Navy, and Air Force, but excludes Armed Services Petroleum Purchasing Agency. Beginning January 1, 1957, data for the Military Petroleum Supply Agency, successor to ASPPA, are included with the Navy figures. Includes overseas procurement except for Army actions prior to fiscal year 1958. Excludes intragovernmental procurements. Excludes procurement actions less than $10,000 except in fiscal year 1951.

TABLE 6.3

Proportion of Military Procurement Dollars Obligated,
by Service and Contract Type, Fiscal Year 1960

	Three Services	Army	Navy	Air Force
Value of procurement actions, all contract types (millions)	$21,181	$4,820	$6,826	$9,536
% of procurement actions, all contract types	100.0%	100.0%	100.0%	100.0%
All fixed-price type contracts	57.4	64.4	70.3	44.7
Firm fixed-price	31.4	52.8	31.9	20.2
Fixed-price redeterminable	6.1	10.6	6.7	3.5
Fixed-price incentive	13.6	0.0	13.1	20.8
Fixed-price escalation	6.3	1.0	18.6	0.2
All cost reimbursement type contracts	42.6	35.6	29.7	55.3
Cost-plus-fixed-fee	36.8	32.3	27.4	45.9
Cost-plus-no-fee	2.2	2.6	1.5	2.5
Cost-plus-incentive-fee	3.2	0.0	0.8	6.5
Other cost reimbursement	0.4	0.7	0.0	0.4

SOURCE: Office of the Secretary of Defense, *Military Prime Contract Awards*, July–September 1960, pp. 36–37. Includes overseas procurement, but excludes intragovernmental procurements and procurement actions less than $10,000 in value.

Data on National Aeronautics and Space Administration and Atomic Energy Commission contracting patterns show even heavier reliance upon cost reimbursement arrangements. During fiscal year 1962, 82% of NASA contracts — mostly for research and development activities — were of the CPFF type.[24] In fiscal year 1953, the only period for which data are available, approximately 88% of the AEC's obligations for construction, plant operation, materials, and research and development were made under cost reimbursement contracts.[25]

THE CHOICE OF A CONTRACT TYPE

These over-all patterns reflect changes in the weapons acquisition process over time and differences in procurement mixes. Without doubt the most important single factor influencing the choice of a contract type is the degree of uncertainty associated with cost estimates. The liberal use of cost reimbursement contracts during World War II was due to the rapidity of the mobilization effort, the inexperience of firms in producing assigned military items, and the newness of many weapons employed during the war. All of these factors created cost uncertainties and led to a preference for CPFF coverage.

The trend toward increasing use of cost reimbursement contracts during the 1950's is explained in large measure by the changing character of weapons acquisition. Research and development work is generally accompanied by significant cost uncertainties, and rightly or wrongly, cost reimbursement contracts have traditionally been chosen to cover such activities. For example, in the "major hard goods" category for fiscal year 1960, roughly 93% by dollar

---

1962, analysis of additional data shows. The fixed-price escalation contract used so extensively by the Navy (18.6% in 1960) is a variant of the firm fixed-price contract which provides for price increases contingent upon increases in labor or materials cost indices. It is employed widely for shipbuilding and petroleum supply contracts.

[24] "NASA Fiscal 1962 Procurement Doubled," *Aviation Week & Space Technology,* January 28, 1963, p. 34.

[25] Richard A. Tybout, *Government Contracting in Atomic Energy* (Ann Arbor: University of Michigan Press, 1956), p. 18. The distribution of activities by dollar value in Tybout's data is as follows: construction 43.8%; plant operation 37.5%; purchase of materials, etc., 10.7%; and research and development 7.0%.

volume of Navy research and development contracts, but only 17% of production contracts were of the cost reimbursement type.[26]   And as inspection of Table 3.1 demonstrates, research and development activities consumed a generally increasing proportion of all weapons outlays during the 1950's.[27]   A time-series analysis for fiscal years 1956 through 1962 suggests that the percentage of all military procurement obligations made under cost reimbursement contracts (Y) was an increasing linear function of the percentage of all awards going to experimental, developmental, test, and research work (X):

$$Y = 19.29 + .917X;$$
$$(.214)$$

with r^2 of .85.[28]   Thus, the growth of research and development activities in weapons acquisition appears to underlie the growing use of cost reimbursement contracts.

[26] Data supplied by the Office of Naval Materiel in connection with Department of Defense Study Project 103, June 1961. "Major hard goods" includes aircraft, missile systems, ships, weapons, ammunition, and electronics and communications equipment.

[27] Cf. p. 57 *supra*.

[28] The underlying data are found in Office of the Secretary of Defense, *Military Prime Contract Awards and Subcontract Payments,* July 1961–June 1962, pp. 24, 41. The standard error of the regression coefficient has been adjusted to compensate for autocorrelation, even though a von Neumann ratio test yielded an insignificant value of 2.03. If one deviant observation (1958) is removed, r^2 jumps to .98.

The percentage of research, development, test, and evaluation expenditures to total weapons expenditures, as computed from Table 3.1, was also correlated with the percentage of contract obligations made under cost reimbursement contracts over the 1951–1961 time period, as shown in Table 6.2. In this correlation the RDT&E data were lagged two years to approximate the lag between contractual obligations and actual expenditures. The regression equation was:

$$Y = 6.70 + 1.20X,$$
$$(.19)$$

with r^2 of .81. The standard error of the regression coefficient has not been adjusted to compensate for autocorrelation. This equation and the one in the text are not exactly comparable because of fluctuating expenditures — obligations lags and the inevitable differences in definitions of research and development. Still the similarity of the regression coefficients suggests a certain amount of stability in the R & D–contract type relationship.

In addition, the procurement mix of the armed services has shifted away from the tanks, armored personnel carriers, and conventional ordnance equipment needed for ground warfare during World War II and the Korean conflict toward more complex and sophisticated aircraft, guided missiles, and electronics equipment.[29] And as Table 6.4 suggests, the type of contractual coverage chosen is related to the complexity and sophistication of the product being procured. For example, 83.6% of all expenditures on guided missiles during fiscal year 1960 were made under cost reimbursement type contracts, while only 9.1% of combat vehicle outlays and 1.6% of clothing outlays were covered by cost reimbursement contracts. The Air Force's predominant role in the aircraft and guided missile fields explains at least in part its relatively heavy emphasis on cost reimbursement contracts, while the Army's demands for vehicles and conventional ordnance equipment undoubtedly account for its leadership in firm fixed-price contracting.

Still, analysis of the case study evidence reveals that in many contracting situations, especially in the late development and early production stages of weapons programs, there is a substantial margin of discretion in the choice of a contract type. The decision taken in any particular situation depends upon the objectives and policies of buyer and seller and their relative bargaining positions. The problem is a complex one, and here it is possible to provide only a first qualitative approximation of the factors affecting buyer and seller preferences. Closer approximations must be deferred to Chapter 8 and its appendix.

Government Preferences

From the government procurement agency's point of view, three partly conflicting objectives may be weighed: maximizing the incentive for contractor efficiency, minimizing the risk that unnecessary or excessive profits will be paid, and minimizing contract outlays. As indicated earlier, the so-called incentive contract has been one approach toward compromising these goals. And yet there have been distinct differences among the services in their use of incentive contracts for activities such as guided missile production. The Air Force, for example, has strongly endorsed the fixed

[29] Cf. Peck and Scherer, pp. 108–109.

TABLE 6.4

Proportion of Military Procurement Dollars Obligated, by Contract Type and Procurement Category, Fiscal Year 1960

Category	Total Value (millions)	Fixed Price Type (Percent)					Cost Reimbursement Type (Percent)				
		Total	Firm	Redeter-minable	In-centive	Esca-lation	Total	Fixed Fee	No Fee	In-centive	Other
All categories	$21,181	57.4	31.4	6.1	13.6	6.3	42.6	36.8	2.2	3.2	0.4
Aircraft											
Airframes	3,161	64.0	13.3	8.7	42.0	—	36.0	25.7	0.6	9.6	0.1
Engines	969	73.0	15.8	19.1	38.0	0.1	27.0	25.7	0.7	0.6	—
Other	686	86.2	68.6	6.4	11.2	—	13.8	12.4	0.1	0.5	0.8
Missile systems	5,067	16.4	4.1	0.9	11.4	—	83.6	76.2	1.8	5.5	0.1
Ships	1,030	82.1	28.0	3.7	11.9	38.5	17.9	17.6	0.3	0.0	0.0
Combat vehicles	312	90.9	29.4	61.0	0.0	0.5	9.1	8.3	0.6	0.0	0.2
Non-combat vehicles	172	94.4	80.4	14.2	0.0	-0.2	5.6	3.5	0.4	0.0	1.7
Weapons	125	71.8	48.8	20.0	2.4	0.6	28.2	26.2	0.9	0.0	1.1
Ammunition	489	37.2	25.9	7.9	2.2	1.2	62.8	61.4	1.4	-0.1	0.1
Electronics and communication equipment	3,092	53.4	31.5	11.0	10.8	0.1	46.6	42.7	1.7	1.8	0.4
Petroleum	1,096	99.9	23.2	—	0.0	76.7	0.1	0.1	0.0	0.0	0.0
Clothing, textiles, and equipage	182	98.4	98.4	—	0.0	0.0	1.6	1.4	0.2	0.0	0.0
Subsistence	533	99.7	99.0	0.6	—	0.1	0.3	0.1	0.2	0.0	0.0
Production equipment	65	43.4	42.3	-0.1	0.0	1.2	56.6	5.7	49.5	0.0	1.4
Construction	1,446	98.9	96.4	1.8	—	0.7	1.1	1.1	—	0.0	—
Services	1,757	41.3	35.9	1.8	2.6	1.0	58.7	41.8	12.7	1.7	2.5

— Less than 0.05%.

SOURCE: Office of the Secretary of Defense, Statistical Services Center, report of December 20, 1960. Includes all prime contract actions of $10,000 or more; but excludes intragovernmental purchases and most of the procurement categories with purchases of less than $100 million, as well as a miscellaneous category.

price incentive contract as ". . . one of the more fundamental means of creating an incentive to contractors to reduce costs." [30] The Army, on the other hand, scarcely used the FPI type at all up to 1962, claiming that ". . . we have not been able to find a . . . relationship in the Army procurement where we believe that the incentive-type contract would insure an advantage to the Government." [31] Instead, it emphasized the use of either CPFF or redeterminable fixed-price contracts for activities such as early guided missile production. Likewise, the Army did not share the Air Force's enthusiasm for cost-plus-incentive-fee arrangements in weapon system development work.

The arguments underlying these disparate attitudes toward incentive type contracts must be examined later. Here it suffices to note that different contractual incentive approaches were chosen by different buying agencies under substantially similar technological conditions.

Pressures from Congress and top Department of Defense leaders can also affect the relative proportions of various contract types, although perhaps less than is generally supposed. For example, the decline in cost reimbursement contractual coverage from 42.6% by value of all procurements in fiscal year 1960 to 39.2% in fiscal year 1962 may have been due in part to a strongly enunciated policy of the McNamara administration to secure the use of fixed-price type contracts whenever possible. But other factors undoubtedly played a prominent role in this trend reversal. For example, the proportion of research and development contracts to all military procurement fell from 25.6% by value in fiscal year 1960 to 22.9% in fiscal year 1962.[32] This decline of 2.7 percentage points could explain most of the 3.6 percentage point drop

[30] Statement of Air Force Assistant Secretary for Materiel Philip B. Taylor in House, Committee on Armed Services, *Hearings Pursuant to Section 4, Public Law 86–89* (1960), p. 348.

[31] Statement of Army Assistant Secretary for Materiel Courtney Johnson in *ibid.*, p. 237. Although they apparently were not very happy about it, Army negotiators began writing incentive-type contracts during fiscal year 1962, mainly because Secretary of Defense Robert McNamara and Army Assistant Secretary Paul Ignatius (the successor to Johnson) were strong advocates of their use.

[32] Office of the Secretary of Defense, *Military Prime Contract Awards and Subcontract Payments,* July 1961–June 1962, p. 24.

in cost reimbursement contracting. Similarly, purchases of aircraft, missiles, and electronic equipment fell from 60.1% of all procurement in fiscal year 1960 to 57.8% in fiscal year 1962; while purchases of automotive vehicles, ships, and conventional weapons — typically bought under fixed-price type contracts — climbed from 7.2% to 10.4%.[33]

Contractor Preferences

Obviously, the government must reach an agreement with its contractor on the type of contract to be written in any given situation. From the contractor's point of view, the choice of a contract type involves the frequently conflicting objectives of maximizing expected profit and minimizing the risk of financially unfavorable contract outcomes.

Historically, government procurement agencies have offered higher initial negotiated profit rates on those contracts in which the contractor accepts a higher share of potential cost overruns and underruns and hence (in a sense) a greater financial risk. During the late 1950's the "going rate" for CPFF contracts was 6% to 7%, for redeterminable and fixed-price incentive contracts 8% to 11%, and for firm fixed-price contracts upwards of 10%.[34] Profit rates actually realized (as opposed to initially negotiated) have followed a similar distribution by contract type, as the following Renegotiation Board data for 25 major contractors show: [35]

Type of Contract	Average Profit as % of Sales, Before Renegotiation
Firm fixed-price	18.3%
Redeterminable fixed-price	10.6%
Fixed-price incentive	8.8%
CPFF and CPIF	4.9%

Likewise, John Perry Miller found that during World War II the average realized rate of profit before renegotiation on Navy fixed-

[33] *Ibid.,* p. 22.

[34] Cf. Chapter 9 *infra.*

[35] House, Committee on Armed Services, *Hearings Pursuant to Section 4, Public Law 86–89,* p. 316. The data cover 1951–1959 sales of $25.7 billion for the 25 contractors whose total refunds under the Renegotiation Act were highest.

price type contracts was 13.6%, while the average on CPFF contracts was 4.8%.[36]

Against the expectation that on the average its profits will be higher when operating under fixed-price type production contracts, a contractor typically weighs the possibility that a contract might result in a loss if negotiated with fixed-price provisions. Its decision depends in part on the tightness of negotiated cost and profit targets, but also upon the degree of uncertainty associated with predictions of actual cost outcomes. Our case studies provided several clear examples of contractor willingness to accept lower average profit expectations to avoid risk when substantial cost uncertainties were present. Explaining his firm's insistence upon CPFF coverage for the early production work in a guided missile program, one executive remarked, "We'd much rather live with a reduction in profit and not get whipped to death on cost." A second official of that firm stated that "CPFF is a way of doing business for us." Another organization bargained strenuously with the agency procuring its guided missile system to ensure that early production work would be covered by CPFF contracts, despite the agency's stated preference for an incentive contract relationship. Company representatives explained that they would gladly accept lower CPFF profit rates in exchange for the certainty that cost overruns would be fully reimbursed if they should occur. According to Professor Miller, a major obstacle in the way of converting to fixed-price type contracts during World War II was the fact that some Air Force contractors "seemed happy with their relatively riskless contracts." [37] Similarly, Frederick Moore observed in his study of military contracting:

> The notion that businessmen willingly accept risks in order to obtain higher profits has been very commonly believed, but to find actual instances in military procurement is rather difficult. If anything, "play it safe" is the rule.[38]

But in marked contrast to these examples and general observations, some companies covered by our case studies — particularly

[36] *Pricing of Military Procurements,* p. 217.

[37] *Ibid.,* p. 130.

[38] Frederick T. Moore, *Military Procurement and Contracting: An Economic Analysis,* RM–2948–PR (Santa Monica: The RAND Corporation, 1962), p. 58.

those also operating in commercial markets which were accustomed to bearing financial risks and which had ambitious standards regarding the profitability of their defense activities — sought fixed-price type coverage on early production work involving significant uncertainties. Indeed, one firm refused to accept a major aircraft subsystem development assignment largely because the government procurement agency insisted that the production of evaluation models be covered by less profitable CPFF contracts. These apparent differences in company contract type preferences under essentially similar technological conditions suggest diverse weightings of the profit maximization and risk aversion goals.

Could the tendency of some firms to favor cost reimbursement contracts over fixed-price type contracts with a higher average profit expectation be compatible with long-run profit maximization? It might well be, if losses on a particular contract could force a firm out of business or impair its liquidity to the point that it would be unable to exploit future profit-making opportunities. But such an explanation is not consistent with the case study evidence. Most of the companies covered by case study field research and interviews were large enough and well enough diversified to withstand substantial losses on individual contracts without any serious liquidity problems. Thus, aversion to losses for their own sake, rather than for the sake of insuring corporate liquidity and survival, seems a more likely explanation for the observed risk aversion behavior.

In sum, variations in the degree of risk and uncertainty associated with particular program situations and variations in company attitudes toward profit and risk are important determinants of contract type acceptability to defense firms. However, two other factors deserve brief mention. CPFF contracts generally afford greater operating flexibility than fixed-price contracts, especially for the introduction of design changes.[39] But they also carry the disadvantage of imposing somewhat more stringent accounting and reporting requirements than do fixed-price type contracts.

[39] This difference will be explored further in Chapter 8.

CHAPTER 7

Automatic Contractual Incentives in Development Programs

CONSCIOUS EFFORTS to employ automatic contractual incentives in development programs are in many respects an innovation of the 1950's, for in earlier decades it was generally held that the uncertainties connected with research and development precluded incentives based upon price determination. Thus, John Perry Miller has written:

> At the other extreme are research and development contracts. Here there can be no adequate standards of good pricing. In such cases cost-plus-fixed-fee or maximum price contracts are probably required.[1]

As Chapter 6 brought out, most weapons research and development work has in fact been conducted under cost reimbursement type contracts. Still there has been a growing desire to provide automatic contractual incentives for good performance even in cost reimbursement situations. Recent Department of Defense emphasis on the cost-plus-incentive-fee contract, under which profit varies with the contractor's success in controlling costs and perhaps in surpassing quality and schedule goals, is the most prominent example. But the cost-plus-fixed-fee contract cannot be excluded completely from an analysis of contractual incentives. Although the amount of profit does not vary automatically with actual cost outcomes in a CPFF relationship, the rate of profit does, and in certain situations (as we shall see) this rate variation may give rise to a kind of cost reduction incentive. Furthermore, the possibility of contracting for development on a fixed-price basis

[1] *Pricing of Military Procurements* (New Haven: Yale University Press, 1949), p. 235.

153

must not be ignored, even though past practice has overwhelmingly favored the cost reimbursement approach.

The contractual incentive effects examined here will be primarily those involving tradeoff decisions and efficiency. Little attention will be given to innovative behavior. Usually the principal new concepts and devices exploited in a weapon system development effort are identified and accepted at the outset, before the development contract and its incentive provisions have been negotiated. If major innovations are fed into a development in midstream, prices and other provisions of the original contract must as a rule be forsaken and new terms negotiated. In this sense it is difficult to say that the purpose of any given development contract is to incite innovation, for if significant innovation does occur, a new contractual agreement is necessitated. Of course, many ingenious solutions may be conceived to cope with the specific problems of reducing a new concept to practice, and these do not require formal contract amendments. In this more restricted sense innovation is an important variable within a specific development contract, but normally such solutions involve relatively little fundamental insight and much routine empiricism. Therefore, this chapter will assume that ingenuity in solving the detailed problems of development is an essential aspect of development efficiency rather than an activity demanding separate, special attention.

Cost Reimbursement Contracts and Cost Overruns

One way of assessing the effects of cost reimbursement contracts is to compare their financial outcomes with those of other contract types. Our case studies revealed an overwhelming propensity for actual costs under cost reimbursement contracts to exceed originally negotiated targets by a substantial margin.[2] An Air Force study of 171 CPFF contracts with an originally negotiated value of $3.9 billion showed an average cost overrun of 18%, and a broader

[2] The so-called level of effort contracts are an exception. Under this type of contract the contractor is merely required to exert an agreed-upon level of effort, usually for a year's time. Overruns arise mainly through faulty pricing of labor and salary rates or overhead allocations, but these elements are not nearly as variable (and hence uncertain) as the amount of effort required to meet the technical objectives specified in standard CPFF contracts. Level of effort contracts have been used extensively in guided missile development.

Department of Defense study indicated that two out of every three CPFF contracts ended in overruns.[3] In contrast, as we shall discover in the next chapter, there is a general tendency toward cost underruns on fixed-price type contracts.

From such comparisons one might infer that the incentive for cost control and cost reduction is weaker under cost reimbursement contracts than under fixed-price type contracts. As a weapons industry study group concluded:

> Heavy overruns have been experienced which officials of the Department of Defense, the General Accounting Office, Congress, and Industry, believe are caused principally by the minimal working of the "Profit Motive" in CPFF contracting.

*   *   *   *   *

[3] Senate, Committee on Armed Services, Procurement Subcommittee, *Hearings, Procurement Study* (1960), p. 271; and House, Committee on Government Operations, *Hearings, Systems Development and Management,* Part 2 (1962), p. 571.

It should be noted that severe semantic problems can be encountered in using the term "overrun." Technically, "overrun" refers only to increases in cost above the negotiated target when there has been no change in the contract's qualitative and quantitative requirements. Cost increases related to changes in contract requirements are called "extra scope" rather than "overrun." But distinguishing "extra scope" from "overrun" is most difficult in practice due to the vagueness of initial contract requirements in ambitious development projects and inconsistencies in service contract administration practices.

Undoubtedly, some of what is called overrun here actually represents extra scope increases. But the true overrun tendency on CPFF contracts remains substantial, as shown by the following analysis. Extra scope cost increases are usually awarded extra profit, while cost increases recognized as true overrun are not. The average profit rate negotiated on CPFF contracts is about 6.4% of target cost (see p. 273 *infra*). The average profit rate realized by 25 large defense contractors on CPFF and CPIF contracts during the 1951–1959 period was 4.9% of sales or 5.1% of actual costs (see p. 150 *supra*). Let total non-overrun costs (target cost plus extra scope) be $100. If a 6.4% rate were applied to extra scope cost increases as well as to target costs, the resulting profit amount would be $6.40. But in fact profits turned out to be only 5.1% of actual costs. The sum $6.40 is 5.1% of what amount? The answer is $124, suggesting an overrun above non-overrun costs of about 24%. If the originally negotiated profit rate had been lower — e.g., the 5.86% rate applied on the average to CPFF airframe contracts (see p. 282 *infra*)— the overrun percentage would be 14%. The true figure undoubtedly lies between the limits of 14% and 24%.

Government contracting officers and project engineers have desired cost type contracts because they made for easy negotiation and acceptance of changes. Many contractors desired cost type contracts because of the reduced risk. Cost type contracts have therefore been used when firm Fixed-Price or other types of Fixed-Price contracts should have been used. This has resulted frequently in excessive unpredicted increases in cost, whether overruns or scope changes, and a great deal of inefficiency.[4]

Similarly, an assistant secretary of defense stated that many of the overruns experienced under CPFF contracts had been due to "sheer waste."[5]

Nevertheless, the overrun bias of CPFF contracts is not conclusive evidence of inadequate incentives for cost control. Differences in the degree of optimism in original cost estimates could also explain the tendency of cost reimbursement contracts to show less favorable financial outcomes than fixed-price type contracts. CPFF contracts have been used most frequently during the development stages of weapons programs, when to "sell" their efforts contractors commonly submit (and buying agencies encourage) unrealistically low cost estimates.[6] This practice may require accepting a low realized rate of profit on development work, but contractors have generally been willing to sacrifice initial development contract profits for the chance of earning substantial production follow-on contract profits once they are locked together with the government in a relationship analogous to bilateral monopoly.[7] With little possibility of outright loss on CPFF and most CPIF contracts, the penalties for this sort of "buying in" are small. Consequently, many cost reimbursement contracts have built-in overruns at the time they are signed — overruns which might not be avoided by even the most highly motivated performance.

It is clear that cost reimbursement (and especially CPFF) con-

[4] National Security Industrial Association, Report of Task Committee No. 8, "New Approaches to Contracting," *Report of Cost Reduction Study* (June 15, 1962), pp. 135, 138.

[5] Statement of Thomas D. Morris, Assistant Secretary of Defense, Installations and Logistics, in Senate, Committee on Government Operations, *Hearings, Pyramiding of Profits and Costs in the Missile Procurement Program* (1962), p. 897.

[6] Cf. pp. 26–29 *supra* and Peck and Scherer, pp. 411–420.

[7] Cf. p. 2 *supra* and Peck and Scherer, pp. 416–417.

tracts provide little incentive for realism at the bargaining table; at least, the incentive for accurate cost estimation is often not nearly so powerful as the competitive incentive to underestimate costs at the outset of development programs. Contracts with much higher contractor shares in overruns and underruns would encourage more accurate development cost estimation and hence permit improved budgeting. Still the willingness of contractors and government agencies to accept the risks of strong profit-cost correlations in the face of substantial development cost uncertainties is undoubtedly limited. The problem of risk aversion in negotiating contractor sharing proportions will be considered further in the next chapter.

The incidence of overruns on cost reimbursement contracts does not, however, prove the absence of incentives for cost control in the laboratory and factory once the bargain is sealed. To explore this question we must look beyond aggregate financial data to qualitative evidence on contractor behavior in specific development programs.

AUTOMATIC CONTRACTUAL INCENTIVES AND TRADEOFF DECISIONS

Let us start by examining the effects of automatic contractual incentives on time-quality-cost tradeoff decisions, temporarily ignoring the possible existence of inefficiency in development program execution.[8] Cost-plus-incentive-fee contracts operating on the cost dimension and other contracts with cost incentive provisions offer a reward in the form of additional profit for incremental cost reductions. If a contractor is operating efficiently, however, reducing current development cost requires either a more leisurely development pace (and hence later operational availability of the weapon system) or sacrifices in end-product quality (that is, technical performance and reliability).[9] Quality sacrifices, as we have

---

[8] The distinction drawn here between efficiency and tradeoffs is the one explained on pp. 3–4 *supra*.

[9] See Peck and Scherer, pp. 254–268 and 461–501. The assumption of efficiency is crucial in this statement of the relationship between time and cost. If development schedules are permitted to slip due to current cost reductions which unbalance the development effort, e.g., by the elimination of essential development activities while less productive overhead activities are not cut, the increase in development time will cause increases rather than decreases in total development cost. Cf. Peck and Scherer, pp. 265

seen in preceding chapters, tend to diminish a weapon system's production prospects relative to competing systems and to mar the reputation the contractor brings into future source selection competitions. Delays in operational availability, other things being equal, also reduce the contractor's follow-on contract expectations. A weapon system which becomes available late may see only a short production run, and one which is too late will see no production at all. Thus, there is typically a conflict in development program tradeoff decisions between the short-run accounting profits obtained by minimizing R & D contract costs and the longer-run profits attainable by securing follow-on production contracts and maintaining a reputation for high quality and timely performance.

Among his many legacies John Maynard Keynes contributed the concept of user cost, which is most helpful in the analysis of this problem.[10] User cost is defined as the expected sacrifice of future profits or benefits, discounted to present value, caused by some present economic action. It constitutes, as Keynes stated, one of the links between the present and the future. Examples cited in

---

and 441. In this case the effect of contractual incentives for cost reduction depends upon the manner in which contract goals are stated. If the contract is written to cover the full development effort or at least a segment of the effort with specific, measurable technical goals, the contractual incentive for cost reduction also provides a complementary incentive for development time control, since efficiency-reducing schedule delays will increase total contract costs and hence reduce contract profits. But when contracts are written on an annual level-of-effort basis, cost reductions under the current year's contract which lead to inefficient schedule stretchouts will cause increased costs in future years, but these costs will be negotiated (with profit added) into future contracts or amendments. Thus, to the extent that annual level-of-effort contracts encourage short-run cost reduction, they may perversely encourage both development time stretchouts and over-all program cost increases.

[10] J. M. Keynes, *The General Theory of Employment, Interest and Money* (New York: Harcourt, Brace, 1936), pp. 53 and 66–73. Naturally, the concept had been partly anticipated by earlier economists, but Keynes was responsible for naming it and giving it form. For a further analysis of the user cost concept, see Alfred C. Neal, *Industrial Concentration and Price Inflexibility* (Washington: American Council on Public Affairs, 1942), pp. 70–89; P. T. Bauer, "Notes on Cost," *Economica,* May 1945, pp. 90–97; Friedrich and Vera Lutz, *The Theory of Investment of the Firm* (Princeton: Princeton University Press, 1951), pp. 58–64; and A. D. Scott, "Notes on User Cost," *Economic Journal,* June 1953, pp. 368–384.

the standard economic literature include the sacrifice of future profits implicit in selling a stock of goods currently when prices are expected to be higher in future periods, or in using a machine today and thus reducing its useful life or building up the need for future repairs. In weapons contracting, when costs are reduced by cutting corners on quality, future sales and profits tend to be sacrificed and a user cost is incurred. Similarly, when costs are reduced by letting development schedules slip, a user cost is incurred. Other examples of how user costs arise in defense contracting will be added later. A mathematical model for the derivation of user cost under conditions of uncertainty is presented in the appendix to this chapter.

User cost is never entered into the books of account kept by defense contractors, and thus it does not affect the calculation of incentive contract profits. Yet it is a very real, even though necessarily subjectively estimated, magnitude. A defense contractor which seeks to maximize its long-run profits would be ill-advised to maximize merely the accounting profits earned in the short run of any given contract. Rather, as the appendix to this chapter demonstrates more rigorously, it would achieve its objective only by maximizing accounting profits on current contracts minus the user costs connected with contract performance.

Our case studies revealed that defense contractor executives were well aware of the future profit losses, and hence user costs, associated with quality sacrifices and schedule slippages. Furthermore, it was evident that as a rule contractor officials considered the user costs to be quite substantial. When conflicts between quality and cost or time and cost arose, time and quality were nearly always emphasized over development cost reduction. Many contractor executives asserted that when maintaining or increasing quality conflicted with reducing development cost, quality was favored whenever budgetary constraints permitted. They indicated a general willingness to sacrifice short-run contract profits in order to secure continued business and to maintain their firms' reputations for quality and timely delivery. One defense contracting organization had an explicit policy of not sacrificing quality to save costs. Our case studies included many specific examples of conscious managerial decisions to incur development cost overruns or in other ways to accept short-run profit reductions in order to add new and better weapon system features, correct known problems, improve system reliability, and generally increase quality.

The emphasis on quality maximization and time minimization is also seen in the propensity of firms to tailor their development expenditures to the availability of funds. That is, contractors ascertain how much money the government can make available in the forthcoming period and then (especially in medium and low priority programs) increase or decrease the number and level of quality-increasing and time-decreasing development activities until that sum is just fully utilized. This practice reflects the perception of contractor management that within any reasonably attainable level of budgetary support, there would still remain opportunities for accelerating the development cycle or ensuring that all attractive qualitative features are developed, and that the exploitation of these opportunities would improve their weapon's production potential.[11]

There are several possible reasons why quality maximization and lead time minimization are emphasized so consistently over development cost reduction and hence short-run contract profit maximization. First, the user costs associated with quality and time sacrifices simply *are* high. A successful technical effort can lead to follow-on development and production sales many times the value of any current development contract. The profit impact of follow-on production orders is magnified by two conditions: the application of relatively high negotiated profit rates to the fixed-price type contracts associated with production work, and the tendency for production contracts to end in underruns and hence realized profit rates higher than the negotiated rates, unlike development contracts.[12] And as we have seen in Chapters 2 and 3, quality and time of availability are crucial variables when weapon

----

[11] This raises the question considered in a different context in Chapter 2. If a weapon's production potential is enhanced by increasing quality or decreasing development time at the expense of higher development cost, is the government better or worse off? If the buying service considers a program worthwhile enough to make available a certain quantity of development funds, and if the contractor then delivers more than the service expected, the government is better off in one sense. But had the buying service known in advance what it could buy for its money, some of the funds might have provided even greater benefit (military value) if allocated to other programs, given the over-all scarcity of resources.

[12] These will be discussed further in Chapters 8 and 9.

systems and subsystems compete for military missions and budgetary support, and hence for further sales. Therefore, a firm's ability to gain future profits in the face of existing and potential competitive threats depends heavily upon its willingness to incur current development costs in enhancing quality and reducing time, even when short-run profits must be forgone in the process.

Second, given the uncertainties pervading weapons acquisition, contractor executives may tend to overestimate the user costs connected with current quality and time sacrifices. In particular, our case studies revealed a tendency of contractor officials to exaggerate the follow-on production prospects of their development programs, partly because successful development programs had generally led to large sales in the past but also because they possessed the enthusiastic optimism necessary to lead and persevere in a long and difficult technical effort.

Third, there was some evidence that contractor decision makers were anxious not only to maximize long-run corporate profits, but also to ensure organizational survival and growth for their own sake.[13] It is difficult to isolate the survival and growth goals from the long-run profit maximization objective, since even if they are distinct, they operate in tandem in the kinds of decisions examined here. Nevertheless, in case study interviews company executives often manifested a strong interest in organizational survival *per se,* partly for sentimental reasons and partly because an executive's power and prestige depend more upon the size of the organization he leads than on its profitability. In addition, the salaries of corporate executives tend to be an increasing function of sales volume, and this creates an autonomous incentive for sales growth.[14] To

[13] This is the Baumol hypothesis mentioned in Chapter 1. It is also supported by P. T. Bauer in his study of Malayan crude rubber production. "Notes on Cost," *Economica,* May 1945, pp. 90–97. Bauer found that the price of crude rubber in 1929 in what was apparently a purely competitive market was roughly twice short-run marginal cost. He attributed this to high user costs, exaggerated by the tendency of plantation managers with no ownership stake in their operations to emphasize "long life of the operating units" over profit maximization.

[14] For evidence from a survey of 642 corporations that executive compensation is an increasing function of sales volume in the airframe industry and in U.S. industry at large, see Arch Patton, "Annual Report on Executive Compensation," *Harvard Business Review,* September-October 1958, pp. 129–132. For further verification from a smaller sample, see J. W. Mc-

the extent that survival and growth are distinct goals of defense contractor executives, they reinforce the long-run profit maximization motive and increase the estimated user cost associated with current actions which will reduce future sales. Furthermore, they may lead corporate executives to apply relatively low discount rates to their estimates of possible future sales and profit sacrifices.[15]

The Suboptimization Problem

The stress on quality maximization in development programs could also follow from company management's inability to distinguish those activities which make worthwhile improvements in a weapon system from those which add little to the system's value or even degrade it through overcomplication. The goals of the individual scientists and engineers working on a weapons project often differ from the goals of corporate or divisional management. Top management may indeed wish to limit the number and level of development activities so that an optimal balance between short-run incentive profits and long-run production follow-on contract profit expectations is achieved. But strongly motivated technical personnel at the operating levels are typically more concerned with perfecting the things on which they work than with profit maximization.

Some reflections by the chief project engineer in a major weapon system development program provide insight into the attitudes of a technologist at the management level:

> What is our incentive for cranking in reliability? We've committed ourselves to build a real fighting machine, and so we have to build up to an acceptable level of reliability. This isn't for any monetary considerations, but for our corporate reputation. There's nothing that will sour your customer like selling him something that won't work. . . . I think performance incentive contracts during the initial development phases are for the birds. We've been in business for a long time. If we're going to stay in

Guire, J. S. Y. Chiu, and A. O. Elbing, "Executive Incomes, Sales, and Profits," *American Economic Review,* September 1962, pp. 753–761. The latter found that executive salaries were correlated more closely with corporate sales than with corporate profits.

[15] For a further analysis of the discount rate's relevance to user cost, see the appendix to this chapter.

business, a thing's got to be good. Giving us dollars to make our weapon go so far and be so accurate is no incentive at all to me. . . . Our main motivation is that we have dedicated people here who are interested in seeing the system go. We think — we're convinced it's a good weapon — a weapon the (service) needs. . . . It's not exactly the same as building a monument, but we're proud of it. . . . Our principal motivation for making engineering changes is that we like to get everything we can into the system.[16]

These comments manifest a concern for quality which at the same time is quite objective (the relationship of quality to program success and corporate reputation) and highly subjective (the personal satisfaction which engineers derive from building a top quality product). As one reaches further down into a development organization, the preoccupation with quality for its own sake appears to increase. For example, technical executives of one firm pointed out that their engineers were not conscious of such factors as contract type, contract lot, profit, and loss. They believed line engineers would do their best to maximize quality even under fixed-price type contracts.

To be sure, seeking technical perfection is often synonymous with long-run profit maximization. But given the existence of sharply diminishing marginal quality returns in many development situations,[17] beyond some point it usually is not, and technical personnel at operating levels are seldom in a position to see clearly, or to concede, when that point has been passed. In principle, the role of management is to prevent this sort of suboptimization from interfering with the achievement of corporate objectives. But in practice, management is typically unable to monitor in detail the thousands of time-quality-cost decisions made at operating levels during a development effort. Not only is the job too large, but the knowledge and skill required in any given technical decision are frequently so specialized that only the specialist, who may be unimpressed by such things as profit maximization, can fully appreciate the technical subtleties.[18]

Recognizing the lack of a natural interest in corporate profit

[16] Paraphrased from case study interview notes.
[17] Peck and Scherer, pp. 467–472.
[18] *Ibid.*, pp. 476–478.

maximization on the part of operating level technical personnel, many defense firms have attempted to create an interest through profit-sharing and bonus systems. However, our case study research in companies with profit-sharing plans suggested that the plans failed to alter employee behavior. The common problem was that engineers and project managers were unable to perceive any correlation between their individual performance in such activities as tradeoff decisions and the size of the bonuses they received. Rather, the amount of bonus was generally considered to be a function mainly of over-all corporate profit levels and one's position in the organization. The reaction of one project manager appears typical: "Bonuses are nice to get, but you can't interpret them back as an incentive to make our plane fly higher, faster, and so forth, at less cost."

Tradeoff Decisions Under Fixed-Price Contracts

For a variety of reasons, therefore, a strong tendency exists for quality improvement and development time reduction to be stressed over cost reduction in weapons development programs. Still the evidence on this point has come entirely from programs conducted under cost reimbursement contracts, where the profit gains from reducing costs were at best small. Would the tendency still prevail under fixed-price type contracts with much stronger profit-cost correlations?

Since none of the programs examined was covered by a fixed-price contract during development, our weapon system case studies contain no direct evidence on this question.[19] However, the case studies of commercial product developments are of value here. In its incentive implications, an in-house development effort is analogous to development contracting on a firm fixed-price basis, since in both instances the full impact of cost increases is borne by the corporation performing the actual development work.[20] The commercial product case studies showed a general propensity

[19] Evidence on the impact of fixed-price type contracts on cost-quality tradeoffs in the *production* stages will be examined in the next chapter.

[20] Of course, the division of responsibility and accountability between the development group and corporate management (especially financial management) may pose suboptimization problems similar to those encountered in weapons development.

for development cost increases to be accepted whenever the marketability, serviceability, or safety of the intended end product could be enhanced significantly. And just as in weapons acquisition, cost overruns are quite common in advanced commercial product development efforts. For example, the five commercial developments in our sample with the most ambitious technical goals had an average cost overrun of 70%.[21]

Our case studies included no examples of commercial developments carried out by contracting on a fixed-price basis. The contract awarded by the Consolidated Edison Company to Babcock & Wilcox to develop an atomic power plant was originally of the firm fixed-price type, but when severe overruns appeared early in the program, the contract was replaced by a cost-plus-no-fee relationship.[22] Considerable information has been published, however, on the results of General Electric's firm fixed-price contract to develop an atomic power plant for the Commonwealth Edison Company. Although the price was set at $45 million, GE's actual costs proved to be more than $60 million.[23] And there is no indication that GE was unconcerned with quality in its development and fabrication efforts. To illustrate, the discovery of minor flaws in certain parts led General Electric to shut down the reactor, reinspect every fuel element and control rod assembly, and make various changes, all at its own expense.[24] Any other behavior would undoubtedly have damaged GE's reputation as an atomic reactor supplier, reducing its future sales in a field in which it was anxious to be active. In other words, the marginal user costs associated with cost reduction through quality reduction exceeded the increments of current profit which could have been retained.

Thus, there is reason to believe that the use of fixed-price contracts would not greatly reduce the emphasis placed on quality in weapons development projects, although it might affect certain

[21] Cf. Peck and Scherer, pp. 433–434. This was substantially less than the 220% average for weapons programs. Obviously, the incentives for competitively optimistic cost estimation are a good deal weaker (although not entirely absent) when work is done in-house.

[22] *Ibid.*, pp. 62–63.

[23] Cf. Francis Bello, "Year One of the Peacetime Atom," *Fortune,* August 1955, pp. 112–114; and "Cost Pinch Slows Atomic Power," *Business Week,* October 12, 1957, pp. 48–50.

[24] "Shakedown Troubles," *Business Week,* December 5, 1959, pp. 27–28.

marginal tradeoff decisions with only a minor expected impact on future sales. It is probable that contractors would accept outright development contract losses, if necessary, rather than cut corners on quality and risk program termination and injury to company reputation. Whenever the long-run gains from incurring a development cost outweigh the immediate development contract profits attainable by avoiding that cost, contractual incentives for cost reduction will not be effective.

THE REDUNDANCY OF MULTIDIMENSIONAL CONTRACTUAL INCENTIVES

These findings suggest a significant limitation on the effectiveness of multidimensional incentive contracts in spurring good development program performance. The cost reduction incentive in such contracts tends, as we have seen, to be swamped by user costs when conflicts between quality and cost or time and cost arise. But in addition, the incentives provided on noncost dimensions are to a considerable degree redundant, since the desire to win follow-on development and production orders and to build a favorable company reputation form the basis of much stronger incentives for quality maximization and schedule maintenance.

This observation follows directly from the conclusion that long-run benefits are generally considered more important by contractors than the incentive profits earned in the short run of a development contract. It is supported by evidence from the one program in our case study sample covered during its development phases by a contract with incentives tied not only to cost reduction, but also to schedule maintenance and the end product's technical performance. Several members of the contractor organization and the sponsoring government agency were questioned about the effect of the contract's incentive provisions. Contractor technical and production personnel at the operating management level reported that the incentive profit correlations had little impact on their program execution behavior. All agreed that other incentives, particularly the desire to secure follow-on production orders, were vastly more important than the contractual incentive. They admitted, however, that the test vehicle used in determining the amount of the technical performance incentive payment had been "babied" more than other test vehicles. In a similar vein, the buying agency official in charge of research and development matters for that program stated that the CPIF incentive provisions had little effect on contractor performance and were not worth the additional administrative cost and effort they required.

Conflicting statements were made by other members of the organizations participating in that program. The government official primarily responsible for negotiating the CPIF contract believed that the incentive provisions worked well, even though he could cite no specific benefits. The company executive who negotiated the incentive formula expressed a general belief in incentive contracts, and although he found it difficult to identify any specific behavioral effects of the CPIF contract in question, he was convinced they existed. As one possible effect, he mentioned a cost reduction program initiated during the contract. But technical and production executives said the cost reduction drive was motivated mainly by management's desire to strengthen the firm's competitive position.

The same kinds of reactions were encountered when representatives of other organizations were asked conjecturally about the effects multidimensional incentive contracts might have if applied to development programs under their direction.[25] Technical and production executives expressed the common view that such incentives were of very little importance relative to the other (competi-

[25] It is of course unfortunate that the case study sample included only one actual application of a multidimensional incentive contract. Time and personnel limitations precluded additional field research exploiting the recent bumper crop of such contracts. Still it seems defensible to generalize from the single specific case analyzed during the late 1950's, supported by the conjectural evidence from other case studies and the logic of the user cost theory, as long as there are no significant new differences in multidimensional incentive contracting applications of the 1960's. Two recent changes — both essentially quantitative — could conceivably vitiate such generalizations. First, wider ranges of profit variation have been employed in the most recent multidimensional incentive contracts. But this should not affect the redundancy conclusion if competitive incentives on the quality and time dimensions remain powerful. A substantial amount of short-run contract profit variation on the quality dimension is just as redundant (actually, more redundant) as a little variation when adequate competitive quality incentives already exist. Second, the strength of the competitive incentives on the quality and time dimensions may have changed. This problem will be explored in the text.

tive) incentives operating in a weapons program. Only persons concerned predominately with contract negotiation and administration — highly specialized functions — seemed to believe that CPIF provisions would have any perceptible effect on contractor behavior. Given this conflict of opinion, it appears more reasonable to accept the view of the technical and production executives — those who perform and supervise the actual work of a weapons program. Just as engineers become fascinated with the products they design to the point of seeking undue perfection, contracting personnel may well overestimate the effects of the instruments they design and administer.[26]

Our case study interviews showing the preoccupation of company operating executives with follow-on sales prospects rather than current development contract profits took place mainly during 1958–1959. It might be argued that while the hope of securing sizable follow-on production contracts afforded sufficiently strong incentives for good performance on the quality and time dimensions in past years, it no longer does so.

This argument has a certain amount of historical validity. The relative size of the production follow-on sales potential in development programs has been changing over time. During the 1940's development comprised only a small proportion by dollar volume of total weapons acquisition activities, and so a dollar's worth of effort exerted in development led, on the average, to follow-on production sales of from $10 to $50. But as the performance, destructive capability, and complexity of modern weapon systems multiplied and as high obsolescence rates continued, the number of units of any given weapon system ordered for the operational military inventory has tended to decline drastically,[27] and weapons development expenditures have risen greatly relative to production outlays. In fiscal year 1953, U.S. defense research, development, test, and evaluation expenditures were roughly 12% of weapons procurement outlays. In fiscal year 1958 they were 18%, and by

[26] If this judgment is valid, then the abundant supply of generalized claims about the benefits of incentive contracting must be viewed skeptically, since the persons who have devoted the most attention to incentive contracting have been specialists in contract administration rather than development and production operations.

[27] See Peck and Scherer, p. 161.

fiscal year 1963 they had climbed to about 43% of procurement expenditures.[28]   Thus, a dollar's worth of development effort led on the average to $8 in production sales in 1953, but to little more than $2 in 1963.   Confronted with this trend, many defense firms have recognized that they are in the business of selling development for its own sake as well as for the sake of securing follow-on production contracts.[29]   Production profit expectations and their related user costs have therefore declined over time, and the incentives based upon these expectations have become weaker.

There were of course institutional lags which kept the production follow-on sales incentive stronger than it might have been.   For many executives of old-line defense firms, the transition to massive development, low production volume programs has been exceedingly difficult, and in some cases these executives have consistently over-estimated the production potential of their programs.   As veteran defense executives have slowly adapted to the new research-oriented environment of weapons acquisition and as new leaders have emerged, this essentially irrational emphasis on production prospects has undoubtedly declined.

Yet the follow-on sales motive was not nearly so weak in 1963 as mere comparisons of total development and production expenditures would imply.   The average production dollar yield of development outlays is pulled down by the relatively unsuccessful research and development efforts which led to little or no production. A successful development project can still yield several times its cost in production orders, and this possibility is what underlies the incentive to strive for success by good performance on the quality and time dimensions.   For instance, by offering an aircraft which the Navy and Air Force deemed technically and operationally superior to competing systems, the McDonnell Corporation added F4H production sales on the order of $2 billion to its initial development sales of roughly $150 million.   Several less successful competitors enjoyed much lower production sales, and in some cases none at all.

Furthermore, growing competition to secure follow-on *development* sales has at least partly offset the decline of the old production motive.   If early prototypes perform badly or if tests fall seriously

[28] Cf. Table 3.1, p. 57 *supra.*
[29] Cf. Peck and Scherer, pp. 409–410.

behind schedule, a firm is liable to find itself short of development contracts as well as production contracts. This development sales incentive is given added force by the characteristically bell-shaped expenditure pattern of weapons development projects, with spending rates building up gradually to a peak and then declining.[30] Poor performance in the early, low expenditure stages of a research and development effort can lead to program termination before the effort reaches its development sales peak, and hence to a substantial loss of profit opportunities.

Finally, despite the pessimistic assessment of actual historical program award–performance correlations rendered in Chapter 4, many contractors apparently believe that a reputation for high quality and timely delivery is important in winning future new program opportunities. To the extent that this belief is in fact held and acted upon, a less direct follow-on sales incentive for good current performance exists. The possibility of tying future sales opportunities more consistently to current performance will be examined further in later chapters.

In sum, the hope of winning future sales through good current performance remains an important determinant of contractor behavior, and therefore contractual incentive provisions relating to development time and end product quality are in most instances only a relatively weak supplement to competitive incentives.

It is nonetheless possible to identify one class of situations in which contractual incentives on the quality and time dimensions are somewhat less redundant: when follow-on development and production contracts are not expected even if the contractor performs well in development. A good example is a one-shot scientific satellite program — if the satellite is successfully injected into orbit and if its instruments function properly, the desired data will be recorded and no further shots will be required.[31] In such cases, automatic multidimensional contractual incentives may have more than a small marginal effect on contractor behavior. Even then,

---

[30] See Peck and Scherer, pp. 309–313.

[31] Thus, reliability and orbital lifetime incentives were probably used to good advantage in the Air Force's Vela Hotel radiation detection satellite contract with Space Technology Laboratories, Inc., since only five launches were contemplated, and this number could be reduced if all program objectives were satisfied before the fifth launch.

the desire to carry a favorable reputation into future source selection competitions will also spur the contractor to meet quality and time goals. And at the operating levels of contractor technical groups, the professional interest of scientists and engineers in technological achievement for its own sake creates a powerful non-administrable incentive for quality maximization. Moreover, development contracts with no follow-on potential are clearly the exception in weapons acquisition, although they may become more common in the field of space exploration. When the possibility exists of gaining substantial follow-on development and production sales contingent upon good research and development effort performance, as is more frequently the case in weapons programs, automatic contractual incentives on the quality and time dimensions merely reinforce already strong sales-oriented competitive incentives.

The redundancy of multidimensional contractual incentives is not especially undesirable in its own right. Assuming that only a certain range of profit variation can be secured in any given contract bargaining situation, however, the inclusion of profit-quality and profit-time correlations necessarily reduces the amount of profit variation which potentially could be correlated with cost dimension performance.[32] This conflict has apparently been recognized by Department of Defense policy makers:

> . . . in an initial product development contract, it generally is appropriate to negotiate a cost-plus-incentive-fee contract providing for *relatively small* increases or decreases in fee tied to the cost incentive feature, balanced by the inclusion of performance incentive provisions providing for *significant* upward or downward fee adjustment as an incentive for the contractor to meet or surpass negotiated performance targets. Conversely, in subsequent development and test contracts, it may be more appropriate to negotiate an incentive formula where the opportunity to earn additional fee is based primarily on the contractor's success in controlling costs.[33]

[32] To some extent it might be possible to increase the potential amount of cost-profit correlation on a multidimensional incentive contract by what is known as overlapping. But overlapping clearly increases the contractor's risk, and this additional risk will not be assumed gratis by the contractor.

[33] *Armed Services Procurement Regulations,* 3–405.4 (b) (italics added).

The use of multidimensional incentive contracts therefore tends to weaken incentives on the cost dimension, where a supplement to the quality and time incentives generated by competition appears most needed.

Department of Defense Policy on Multidimensional Incentive Contracts

Despite these limitations and shortcomings, greatly increased application of multidimensional incentive contracts to weapons development programs has been urged under Secretary of Defense Robert S. McNamara. The Defense Department's enthusiasm for the multidimensional approach is manifested in its official incentive contracting guide:

> Perhaps no other DOD procurement policy offers greater potential rewards than the expanded use of performance incentives in developmental contracts. Properly conceived and applied, these incentives can do more than any other factor to encourage maximum technological progress under a single contractual effort.[34]

To provide compulsions for the widespread use of multidimensional incentive contracts, the following statement of policy was issued:

> The introduction of incentives into development is of such compelling importance that, to the extent practical, firms not willing to negotiate appropriate incentive provisions may be excluded from consideration for the award of development contracts.[35]

Early government pronouncements on the use of multidimensional incentive contracts suggest a failure to recognize the existence of strong competitive incentives on the quality and time dimensions. For example, the Department of Defense incentive contracting guide appears rather clearly to declare that contractual incentives are the principal determinants of contractor behavior, and that balance among the various dimensions of performance must be achieved within the particular contract provisions:

> The reason for combining incentives is obvious. Successful performance of almost any contract consists in completing a satis-

---

[34] U.S. Department of Defense, *Incentive Contracting Guide* (prepared under the direction of the Office of Assistant Secretary of Defense, Installations and Logistics, by Harbridge House, Inc., August 1962), p. 30.

[35] *Armed Services Procurement Regulation,* 3–403 (c).

factory end item or service at a *reasonable cost* and within *certain time limits.* Since each factor is closely dependent on the others, a contract that places too heavy a premium on one risks loss of control over the other two. . . . if it becomes apparent . . . that outstanding results *cannot* be achieved in all areas, the incentive structure should compel decisions as between cost, time, and performance that are in consonance with the overall procurement objectives of the government. . . . Realization of [this] purpose . . . turns mainly on the relative weights assigned to each incentive area.[36]

A high-ranking Department of Defense official denied that the new emphasis on multidimensional incentive contracting was inspired by reasoning of this sort. He asserted that multidimensional incentive contracts offer other benefits more important than immediate short-run contractual incentive effects:

. . . there is no question but that there are frequently incentives outside the contract terms which motivate the contractor with more strength than the incentives built into the contract. It is also frequently true that the incentive factors and weights which we include in a contract are thought of differently by a contractor because of the impact of outside factors not known to the government. We concluded very early . . . that it was both impossible and unnecessary for us to try to outgame the contractor. It was, and is, our conclusion that the most important function of the technique of including performance, time and cost incentives with weights attached to each, is not in the individual contract profit motivations these apply (although . . . these can be quite effective when used right) but rather that this provides a vehicle for the government to tell the contractor precisely what it wants, the relative importance it attaches, and the standards it intends to apply in measuring whether it has gotten it.[37]

He cited several specific benefits expected from the use of multidimensional incentive contracts:

(1) The negotiation of detailed technical performance and time incentive formulas along with cost formulas would force

[36] U.S. Department of Defense, *Incentive Contracting Guide,* p. 38 (emphasis in original). This statement is qualified at p. 42 by an admission that "the contractor's tradeoff decisions may not be conditioned by fee alone." But the implications of the qualification are essentially ignored.

[37] Comment of Graeme C. Bannerman, Deputy Assistant Secretary of Defense (Procurement), on an earlier draft of this manuscript.

government agencies to formulate their development program objectives more precisely than they have in the past.

(2) The negotiation of detailed quality, time, and cost incentives would also require more disciplined commitments from contractors, mitigating tendencies toward unrealistic promises and giving the government more accurate program decision-making information.

(3) Incentive targets would be used not only to determine the amount of profits received by the contractor on a specific development contract, but also as objective bases for evaluating the contractor's performance relative to the promises it has made. These evaluations would in turn be employed to create additional incentives; e.g., the correlation of new contract awards with contractor performance.

Let us examine the second benefit first. In the past, undue optimism in contractor estimates has been an important cause of erroneous program decisions. Workable correctives are clearly needed. Nevertheless, multidimensional contractual incentive provisions are not necessary to generate incentives for realistic estimation. Because excessive optimism on the quality and time dimensions interacts with cost dimension outcomes, strong incentives on the cost dimension alone encourage realism just as effectively as more complex incentive structures. For instance, if a contractor makes unrealistically optimistic technical performance promises, one of two things will usually happen. First, the contractor may incur costs much higher than originally anticipated in order to fulfill its technical promises. Historically, this has been the principal result of unrealistic technical projections. But if the contractor operates under a development contract with strong profit-cost correlations, it would sacrifice contract profits and perhaps suffer a net loss by incurring a large overrun, and recognition of this fact should create an incentive for realism. Alternatively, the contractor might choose to deliver less technical performance than it originally promised, thereby avoiding some or all of the potential overrun. If the contractor has offered more technical performance than the government really needs and wants, both parties are better off from such a choice. But if the promised performance is important to the buying service, the contractor will probably choose to incur the overrun, since quality sacrifices would endanger the weapon's follow-on production prospects and the firm's reputation. In this more complex case, recognition that unrealistic estimates must lead either to the loss of future sales by avoiding an overrun or to the loss of short-run profits by incurring one provides an incentive for realism.

This does not mean that realism will *necessarily* follow from the use of strong automatic contractual incentives, either on the cost dimension or on all dimensions. Under the program execution and contracting philosophy evolved by the McNamara regime during the early 1960's, cost-plus-incentive-fee contracts with strong profit-performance correlations are to be used primarily in the full scale "hardware" development stages of weapons programs. Generally, hardware development is to be deferred until technical problems, military objectives, and resource requirements have been identified in detail during a program definition phase. Contractor efforts in the program definition phase are normally to be covered by CPFF contracts. With this approach, cost projections submitted by firms competing for a program definition phase role will almost certainly be optimistic. Whether the winner then estimates full-scale hardware development costs realistically following its program definition activities depends in large measure upon its competitive position. If only one firm has been chosen to perform the program definition task, it may acquire unique experience which ensures its noncompetitive selection to execute the hardware development contract. In this event, and if in addition realistic projection of costs would not endanger budgetary support of the proposed program, the firm will have little competitive incentive to underestimate future costs and a clear contractual incentive to estimate them accurately or perhaps even pessimistically. But such cases are likely to be relatively rare. As a general rule, the Department of Defense apparently intends to support at least two firms in competition through the program definition phase. And in all but high priority programs, realistic projection of future costs is apt to discourage budgetary support. Therefore, in most CPIF development contract negotiations the contractor will have strong competitive incentives to underestimate costs along with a contractual incentive to project costs realistically.

The contractor's choice in this conflict situation will depend upon the strength of the proposed contractual profit-cost correla-

tion, the intensity of the close substitute and budgetary competition, the expected probability of having development cost increases
approved as "extra scope" contract amendments with added profit,
and the expected value of follow-on production contracts once the
development effort has been completed.[38]   There is no guarantee
that this conflict will be resolved in favor of realism.   For example, despite the almost unprecedented use of a fixed-price incentive contract to cover development of the TFX fighter aircraft,
Secretary of Defense McNamara claimed that cost estimates submitted by both Boeing and General Dynamics after program definition were unrealistically optimistic.[39]   At best, the use of strong
automatic contractual incentives in development programs is likely
to incite more realism than there has been in the past, but not to
overcome competitive tendencies toward excessive optimism completely.

Thus, we see that benefit (2) is by no means unqualified, and
that to the extent it is attainable, it can be attained without going
all the way to multidimensional incentive contracting.   But this is
also true of benefits (1) and (3).   There is no reason why the
government cannot spell out its program objectives, including the
priorities it attaches to various parameters in potential tradeoff
decisions, without negotiating specific contractual profit-quality
and profit-time correlations around those objectives.   Indeed, the
purpose of the program definition effort is to accomplish exactly
that, whether or not the objectives are then written into a contract.
Similarly, there is no essential reason why the contractor's promises
must be written into contractual incentive formulas in order to be
used later as a basis for judging whether the promises were met.
They could just as well be written down and filed away until the
time for making *ex post* performance judgments arrives.[40]   Or if
formalization of contractor promises is considered important, they
could be included in the contract as performance objectives without
tying them to the contract's profit variation formula.   Despite De-

[38] Cf. also Peck and Scherer, pp. 411–420 and note 29, p. 440.

[39] "McNamara Explains TFX Award Decision" (transcript of testimony
before the Senate Permanent Investigations Subcommittee), *Aviation Week
& Space Technology,* March 25, 1963, p. 101.

[40] In Chapter 9 the desirability of making performance judgments on
this basis will be considered.

partment of Defense denials, one is led to conclude that the principal reason for the recent forced march into multidimensional incentive contracting is a desire to achieve balanced incentives on all dimensions of performance within the particular development contract provisions.   But as we have seen, this is unnecessary whenever actual and potential competition generate strong incentives on the quality and time dimensions.   And more serious, a multidimensional incentive contract which is carefully balanced internally to reflect all government objectives is likely to cause an over-all incentive imbalance, since it will generally put too little weight on the development cost dimension, where competitive incentives are most frequently lacking.

The Problems of Negotiating Multidimensional Incentive Contracts

The mere fact of building multidimensional incentive formulas into contracts also raises certain additional problems.   For the multidimensional incentive contract approach to work at all satisfactorily, valid and meaningful targets must be negotiated.   As the official Defense Department incentive contracting guide states:

> . . . advance agreement on all major issues — agreement achieved during negotiation of the contract — is more important to the success of an incentive contract than to any other type of contract now being practiced . . . analyses of requirements must be more penetrating, and statements of objectives clearer, than they have ever been in the past. . . .   It will no longer be satisfactory if both parties recognize the existence of problems in advance of contract award and nevertheless postpone their solution until work has begun.   These problems must be analyzed and resolved, and the resolutions incorporated in the contract.[41]

Obviously, the negotiations required to define contractual targets in this amount of detail will consume considerable time and manpower.   Some joint technical effort is necessary in any case for the government and its contractor to agree on program problems and objectives.   But tying specific contractual incentive provisions to time and quality targets is bound to call forth technical efforts beyond those needed for adequate program definition.   Discussing the negotiation of technical performance targets, for example, the Department of Defense incentive contracting guide notes that "the

[41] U.S. Department of Defense, *Incentive Contracting Guide,* p. 9.

upper limits will be the subject of lengthy negotiation between the government's and the contractor's technical personnel." [42] It is questionable whether the best use of government and contractor technical talent is in the negotiation of contract provisions, as opposed to actual research and development work.

More importantly, the multidimensional incentive contract approach appears to assume better predictive ability and foresight than circumstances often warrant. As indicated earlier, current Department of Defense policies call for the application of multidimensional incentive contracts only to full-scale hardware development efforts, after a program definition phase has been completed. Although the need for exceptions in cases of special urgency has been recognized, as a rule programs are not to be allowed out of the program definition phase until promising solutions to all major technical problems have been identified.[43] This is in general a sensible policy, and it will undoubtedly limit the excesses which have characterized past weapons programs. Yet unless an extraordinarily conservative bias is to be introduced into weapons programs, many technical uncertainties will remain at the outset of full-scale hardware development contracts.[44] And even if tech-

[42] *Ibid.,* p. 35. Similarly, Assistant Secretary of Defense Thomas D. Morris told a congressional committee that the expanded use of contractual performance incentives was being retarded by "the inexperience of our negotiators and . . . the need for much closer collaboration between technical and procurement personnel in defining performance objectives." "DOD Plans More Equitable Contracting," *Missiles and Rockets,* June 3, 1963, p. 18.

[43] See "A Definition of Program Definition," *Missiles and Rockets,* March 25, 1963, p. 45, quoting Dr. Harold Brown, Director of Defense Research and Engineering.

[44] It is clear that the McNamara administration has injected greater conservatism into the planning of full-scale hardware development programs. I am unable, however, to determine how far the pendulum has swung away from past practice. Therefore, to estimate the uncertainty which would remain under a conservative development policy, I must refer to our commercial project case studies as an extreme. These were generally conducted much more conservatively than the weapons developments, and yet significant uncertainties often remained at the start of full-scale hardware development. For five of the most advanced commercial projects, actual development time averaged 40% greater than original predictions, and actual costs 70% greater than original predictions. Cf. Peck and Scherer, pp. 290–298 and 433.

nical performance targets are valid in the sense that they can be attained with virtual certainty within the stated time and cost constraints through vigorous contractor effort, subsequent technical or strategic events may destroy their military validity. At least in recent years, technical objectives and major design parameters in some of the best-planned programs have been altered significantly in midstream as technological progress made new subsystem and component possibilities available or as intelligence agencies and military planners modified their assessments of the hostile threat. Midstream changes in objectives and designs can be very desirable, and although the converse is also frequently true, there is no reason to expect that such changes will be eliminated in future programs.

But development contracts with highly detailed technical performance, time, and cost targets are apt to inhibit adaptation to changes in the technical and strategic environment. It is worthwhile to quote the Department of Defense incentive contracting guide at some length on this point:

> . . . a successful incentive arrangement demands that the need for supplemental agreements be minimized. A too-heavy incidence of changes, modifications, and misunderstandings during contract performance will severely damage the effectiveness of the incentive provisions and, in addition, impose a heavy administrative burden on both the government and the contractor. Thus the contract must leave no doubt in the mind of either party as to precisely what is required and what steps will be taken to meet the requirement. And this can be accomplished only if the business and technical aspects of the procurement are carefully and completely planned in advance.[45]

*   *   *   *   *

> . . . it is not easy to derive a multiple incentive matrix wherein the most profitable tradeoff decision for the contractor will *always* be coincident with the decision that DOD would prefer. In fact, as conditions change during contract performance, the interrelation between the incentive elements may also change; and a relative weighting pattern that was suitable when the contract was awarded may be less satisfactory at a later time.[46]

*   *   *   *   *

[45] U.S. Department of Defense, *Incentive Contracting Guide,* p. 9.
[46] *Ibid.,* p. 43.

One of the most difficult problems in the administration of contracts that contain incentive provisions is negotiating equitable adjustments in the contract price (target cost and target fee) and/or delivery schedule that result from contract changes. Changes are troublesome enough under contracts that do not contain incentive provisions, when only the price or fee and delivery schedule are at issue; the problem is compounded under the simplest type of cost incentive arrangement, when the effects of the change not only on target costs and fee, but also on maximum and minimum fees, the sharing formula, and the confidence range must be determined. . . . Introduction of a second incentive — for example, delivery — complicates the process of adjudicating the change. Completing the triangle, a change in performance incentives is perhaps the most complex, and, in combination with the other parameters, poses grave problems.[47]

Given the technical and strategic uncertainties which characterize advanced weapons development, attempts to plan completely in advance all business and technical aspects of a program appear unrealistic and misguided. And if detailed plans are nevertheless negotiated into contracts, inevitable changes in the strategic and technical environment will either lead to "grave problems" and "a heavy administrative burden," as admitted by the proponents of multidimensional incentive contracting, or it will discourage program goal modifications which would be accepted if judged only on their technical and strategic merits. In short, widespread use of multidimensional incentive contracts is likely to cause undesirable inflexibility in the conduct of weapons development programs.

Automatic Contractual Incentives and Efficiency

Thus far it has been assumed for expositional clarity that development cost could be reduced only by sacrificing quality or reducing the rate of development progress. But quality and/or time sacrifices are not always necessary. Often there is ample opportunity for making pure efficiency gains by eliminating unnecessary technical activities, reducing overhead costs, improving engineering and production manpower productivity, implementing more economic buy vs. make decisions, and so forth. What effects do automatic contractual incentives have in these areas?

[47] *Ibid.,* pp. 48, 49.

Here only a partial analysis of the efficiency question will be attempted, since in many respects the problems of securing efficiency in development are analogous to those connected with gaining production efficiency. Therefore, several questions will be deferred to the following chapter. Still a few points following from the analysis already presented can be discussed at once.

Limits on Contractual Incentives for Efficiency

As we have seen, competitive optimism at the outset of development programs often leads to the underestimation of costs, and when these biased estimates are accepted as cost targets, to contracts with built-in overruns. This initial handicap can eliminate or reduce considerably the possibility of gaining incentive profits through cost reduction under cost-plus-incentive-fee contracts, since usually a cost ceiling is negotiated above which the contractor's cost-correlated profit can be reduced no further, no matter how great the resulting overrun is. Development activities in two of the programs in our case study sample were covered by contracts with cost reduction incentive provisions. In both cases contractor officials recognized from the moment the contracts were signed that they had little or no chance of earning any incentive profit on the cost dimension.

Thus, the operation of CPIF incentives for cost reduction can be frustrated unless cost targets are realistic or unless high cost ceilings and a wide potential range of profit variation are negotiated. But the first of these conditions is often hard to meet. The government negotiator may be instructed that "target cost should represent that figure at which there is equal probability of either a cost underrun or overrun." [48] However, since he seldom has any good basis for judging the validity of cost estimates in an ambitious development program, he will instead strive for the lowest cost target acceptable to the contractor, and if the contractor is willing to oblige with a very low target for competitive reasons, the government man is not likely to insist upon an upward adjustment. Indeed, he would be accused of falling down on the job or perhaps even graft if he encouraged the contractor to raise its target estimate.

[48] *Ibid.*, p. 12.

Increasing the range of cost outcomes over which profit can vary will increase the probability that at least some incremental incentive profit can be gained through cost reductions considered feasible by the contractor. But for any given potential range of profit variation in an incentive contract, increasing the range of costs over which the profit-cost correlation operates necessarily decreases the contractor's share in overruns and underruns, and hence the strength of the contractual incentive.

To illustrate, assume that realized profits can vary between $2 million and $12 million to correlate with the actual cost outcome of a development contract whose target cost is $100 million. If the cost incentive range is ±$20 million about target cost, each dollar of cost reduction within the incentive range will yield 25 cents in incentive profit. But if costs are badly underestimated, the contractor may find it impossible to cut actual costs below the ceiling of $120 million. Therefore it will receive only its minimum profit of $2 million, and any cost reductions it does achieve above the $120 million ceiling will bring no incremental reward. If the cost incentive range is extended to ±$50 million, the contractor may find it possible to operate within the incentive range, but then each dollar of cost reduction is rewarded with only 10 cents in incremental profit.

The only unambiguous way of strengthening automatic contractual incentives for development efficiency in such situations is to increase the amount of potential profit variation. Recently the Department of Defense has made worthwhile strides in the direction of greater development contract profit variability, although as we have seen, its policy of encouraging multidimensional incentive contracting simultaneously restricts the amount of profit variation correlated with cost outcomes. As the next chapter will bring out, risk aversion characteristics of both contractors and the government also limit the range of potential profit variation.

There is another more fundamental limitation on the effectiveness of contractual incentives for cost reduction in development programs. Reducing development costs on a specific contract in order to gain incentive profits can reduce long-run company profits, even when adverse quality-cost and time-cost tradeoffs are unnecessary. One such case is pointed out in the Department of Defense incentive contracting guide:

Basically, the problem arises when the potential contractor will be operating at less than 100 percent capacity during performance of the incentive contract. In this situation, if the contribution to fixed overhead for every dollar of cost reduction is greater than the amount by which fee is reduced, the contractor will be strongly motivated to maximize rather than minimize his costs. Obviously, situations of this kind can be avoided only through astute and skillful negotiation of maximum and minimum fees and by a desire on the part of both sides to incorporate meaningful incentives into the contract.[49]

Since undercapacity operation is quite common in the rapidly changing defense industry, the problem indicated here is an important one — too important to be dismissed with homilies about skillful negotiation and the desire to incorporate meaningful incentives. If a contractor has overhead costs it considers fixed, it will certainly attempt to have them reimbursed under current incentive contracts if no other opportunities for reimbursement exist, even though its incentive profits will be reduced (by much less than a dollar) for every dollar of overhead covered in this way.

The need to cover current overhead costs is only a part of the difficulty, however. Pruning costs to efficient levels also involves user costs, given the fact that service decision makers place considerable emphasis on the availability of human and physical resources in source selection competitions. [50] By hoarding engineers, technicians, skilled production workers, and administrative personnel not required on current contracts but useful for winning and executing future contracts, a firm avoids the user costs of possible future sales losses. Performing work "in house" which could be done more efficiently by specialist vendors is another means of avoiding the user costs associated with layoffs and of building up new capabilities for future business.[51] Engaging in technical tasks and buying equipment essentially unrelated to an ongoing development effort also enhances an organization's ability to compete in new fields for profitable future contracts.[52] In such instances, user costs associated with cost reduction often can outweigh the short-run

[49] *Ibid.*, p. 14.
[50] Cf. pp. 69–72 and 90–91 *supra*.
[51] Cf. Peck and Scherer, pp. 388–394.
[52] *Ibid.*, pp. 498–501.

incentive profits attainable thereby. If so, the efficiency-increasing measures will be rejected.

The analysis here is also relevant to a problem raised in Chapter 3: contractors' willingness under budgetary pressures to accept schedule slippages which might be avoided by increases in efficiency.[53] The reason for this behavior should now be apparent: the user costs associated with efficiency-increasing measures such as personnel layoffs must exceed the user costs connected with cost reductions accomplished by letting development schedules slip. Furthermore, setting up contractual incentives explicitly related to schedule maintenance in addition to the usual cost incentives will normally do little to avert the problem. If a development schedule stretchout is not accompanied by the reduction of costs to new efficient levels, total cost to contract completion will increase along with time to completion.[54] Under a multidimensional incentive contract the contractor then forfeits incremental profit on both the time and cost dimensions. The cost and time effects work in tandem. Therefore, it makes little difference whether the potential amount of profit variation is correlated only with cost, only with time, or split between the two dimensions. The contractor loses the relevant incentive profits in any event. And if a contractor nevertheless accepts such inefficiency-connected schedule slippages, the net user costs it avoids thereby must exceed its combined time and cost incentive profit losses. The only way to solve this problem is to attack it at its source: the tendency for work force cutbacks and other short-run efficiency measures to hurt a firm's chances in future source selection competitions. There are no simple solutions to this dilemma, although some possibilities for improvement will be studied in Chapter 12.

Opportunity Cost and CPFF Incentives for Efficiency

An interesting converse exists to the user cost problems considered thus far. When a firm finds itself with a surplus of engineers, technicians, production workers, and administrative personnel, it is usually because business has fallen off and the company has been unable to obtain enough new contracts to absorb its capabilities. Firms in such a position, with too few opportunities for

---

[53] Cf. p. 61 *supra.*
[54] Cf. note 9, pp. 157–158 *supra.*

employing available resources, are said to have low opportunity cost.[55] Persistence of this condition is associated especially with declining areas of technology, as in the manned aricraft and turbojet engine sectors of the defense industry during the late 1950's. On the other hand, companies in new and expanding fields of technology are apt to have more opportunities for program participation than they can assimilate, given either natural limits on the rate at which organizations can grow or artificial constraints such as a policy decision not to exceed a certain size or rate of growth. Such firms are said to have high opportunity cost. Many defense electronics firms and aircraft company guided missile divisions had high opportunity cost during the 1950's, although by 1960 there was evidence of a decline for some participants in these fields.

Under conditions of high opportunity cost, firms have a kind of automatic contractual incentive for efficiency even when operating with cost-plus-fixed-fee contracts. Although the amount of profit received under the CPFF contract does not vary with cost outcomes, the rate of profit does. And when opportunity cost is high, realizing low profit rates on CPFF development contracts because of inefficiency reduces long-run company-wide profit, since long-run profits could be increased by putting the inefficiently used resources to work on other contracts. That is, if a firm with high opportunity cost uses fewer scientists, engineers, project managers, and skilled production workers on one development contract, it can employ those persons to obtain and execute other development contracts which yield additional profit in their own right, as well as increasing production follow-on contract profit expectations.

The evidence from our case studies and published sources indicates that defense contractors are well aware that inefficiency with high opportunity cost reduces potential profits, even under CPFF contracts. As an executive of a firm troubled by overruns on earlier development contracts remarked:

[55] The terms "user cost" and "opportunity cost" are sometimes used interchangeably in economic analysis. They are kept distinct here because I employ them to explain directly opposite behavioral phenomena. User cost is the loss of future profits due to cost reduction on current contracts; while opportunity cost is the loss of profits due to using resources inefficiently, or in essence, *not* reducing costs on current contracts.

Why do we want to avoid overruns now? Well, why are we looking for capable engineers? Because we're short on good people like _____ and _____ in our laboratories. There are lots of other contracts we could win and hold, if we could reduce the number of good people we're using on our present contracts.

Similarly, a Boeing executive testified concerning his company's motivation for minimizing costs under CPFF contracts:

Let's assume that we take on an R & D job for $1 million. One million dollars is our estimated cost, and to that is added a fee.

Now the incentive is for us to do that job on time and for $1 million or less, because if it costs us $2 million we tie up our scarce scientific and technical people and high-priced research and development facilities for the basic fee. That is the incentive, sir.[56]

To explore the role of opportunity cost further, it was possible with reasonably high confidence to classify 10 of the 12 major development programs covered by our case studies as either "efficient" or "inefficient." In this classification an attempt was made to equalize such factors as over-all technical difficulty and urgency, considering only what the development effort might have cost if work forces were no larger than necessary, specialized work was judiciously subcontracted, marginal technical tasks were avoided, prompt decisions were made to cut off unpromising development approaches, and so on. Obviously, efficiency is not a two-valued attribute, but in 10 cases the differences were clear enough to draw a dichotomy.

The results of this classification, using Roman numerals to denote the various programs, are summarized in Table 7.1. Four of the developments could be classified as efficient. In all four, the principal contractors had high opportunity cost. In Programs I and II, the contractors were diversified corporations which had limited by policy decision the size of their military research and development staffs. They had many more opportunities for using their technical personnel on both commercial and military projects than they could handle. In efficient Program III, the principal

---

[56] Testimony of Clyde Skeen, Assistant General Manager of the Systems Management Office, Boeing Airplane Company, in the House, Committee on Armed Services, *Hearings, Weapons System Management and Team System Concept in Government Contracting* (1959), p. 232.

TABLE 7.1

The Relationship Between Opportunity Cost and Efficiency
in 10 Weapon System Development Programs

	Efficient Developments	*Inefficient Developments*
High opportunity cost	Program I Program II Program III Program IV	Program V
Low opportunity cost	None	Program VI Program VII Program VIII
Opportunity cost indeterminate	None	Program IX Program X

contractor operated in a rapidly expanding field of military technology and was anxious to get into new projects, but had a policy constraint on the size of its development group. In Program IV, the principal contractor was also in a mushrooming field of technology. The firm was expanding to embrace new opportunities, but its rate of growth was limited by fairly high recruiting standards and because facilities shortages (essentially, lack of desk and bench space) prevented it from hiring as many technical and administrative people as its project managers desired. As a result, company officials were quite conscious of their inability to win and man attractive new programs.

Six of the 10 programs were classified as inefficient. For various reasons it was not possible to estimate the degree of opportunity cost in Programs IX and X.[57] One development — Program V — was executed inefficiently even though the principal contractor had

[57] In Program IX the development organization was so fragmented that it was impossible to determine who was mainly responsible for the inefficiencies. Our research was not sufficient to estimate the degree of opportunity cost in Program X. At least early in the program, the contractor had on hand a sizable staff with nothing to do but Program X. Later it would appear that this situation changed, although it is not clear how much it changed. Still many of the inefficiencies in this program were clearly due more to unrealistic planning and lack of technical competence than to low opportunity cost.

high opportunity cost. The most prominent inefficiencies in this program were related to overly rapid organizational growth: personnel recruiting was on a mass basis with only limited selectivity, organization of work was poor because informal relationships had not yet developed, and hundreds of new employees were not sure what they were supposed to be doing. In Programs VI, VII, and VIII, inefficiency coincided with unquestionably low opportunity cost. Each of the three programs was for its principal contractor the only major development activity utilizing available company skills during most of its development period. In two of the three programs, the contractors' production backlogs were declining rapidly due to the phase-out of production on earlier weapon systems. With no alternative opportunities for employing their resources, the contractors in these three programs assigned most of their surplus personnel and facilities to their sole remaining development effort, and as a result development costs were inefficiently high.

Thus, we find a fairly strong correlation between opportunity cost and efficiency in development programs.[58] In a sense, therefore, the fixity of the CPFF profit amount provides a contractual incentive for efficiency. When a firm has high opportunity cost, short-run efficiency-increasing measures which maximize the rate of profit under a CPFF contract also tend to maximize the long-run company-wide amount of profit. Still the crucial variable here is the existence of high opportunity cost, not the choice of a contract type. Even if an illegal cost-plus-percentage-of-cost development contract were employed, a firm with high opportunity cost would probably have a net incentive for efficiency. By transferring surplus resources to other development efforts, it could not only match the profit markup received through inefficient resource use, but also generate incremental production opportunities which add to total company profits.[59]

[58] This contrasts with the finding in Chapter 3 that differences in priority among the 10 programs did not explain differences in efficiency, despite an *a priori* expectation that they would. Cf. p. 55 *supra*.

[59] For a discussion of this "multiplier effect" in the use of development resources, see Peck and Scherer, pp. 406–407.

CONCLUSION

The analysis in this chapter suggests a conclusion that contractual incentives can have only limited effectiveness during the development stages of a weapons program. Contract provisions which correlate development profit with quality and schedule outcomes tend to be redundant, since there exist more powerful sales-oriented competitive incentives for good performance on these dimensions. Contract provisions which correlate profit with cost reduction are often overwhelmed by user costs reflecting the long-run profit maximization advantages of incurring development costs. When a contractor possesses attractive alternative opportunities for employing its resources, however, long-run profit maximization considerations may work in tandem with short-run contract profit maximization to spur efficiency.

More generally, it cannot be assumed that defense contractors maximize accounting profits in the short run of any single development contract. Instead, a contractor interested in its long-run profitability will tend to maximize something like the following expression:

$$\pi_{LR} = \pi_A - U_{qual} - U_{time} - U_{org} + O_{pp};$$

where π_{LR} is long-run profit, π_A is accounting profit earned in the short run of a given contract, U_{qual} is the user cost associated with cost reductions which decrease quality, U_{time} is the user cost associated with cost reductions which increase development time, U_{org} is the user cost associated with cost reductions which weaken the organization and impair its ability to win future source selection competitions, and O_{pp} is the opportunity cost connected with foregoing alternative profit-making opportunities through inefficient resource use. More frequently than not in the defense industry, the value of O_{pp} is small because firms find themselves in declining fields of technology, while the value of the several user costs tends to increase rapidly as costs are reduced. When these relationships prevail, the ability of contractual incentives to spur cost reduction will be severely limited.

Even the use of fixed-price type contracts to cover development programs would probably lead to only marginal changes in time-quality-cost tradeoff decisions, although greater efforts to achieve efficiency and more accurate estimation of costs might be encouraged. The last two effects are closely related, for as we shall see in the next chapter, incentives for efficiency are strongest under fixed-price type contracts when cost targets are tight. But the government's ability to negotiate tight cost targets depends upon its bargaining power. And whether fixed-price type contracts could be used at all for development work depends upon the willingness of contractors and government agencies to accept the concomitant risks. These bargaining power and risk-acceptance variables will be examined further in the following chapter.

CHAPTER 8

Automatic Contractual Incentives in Production Programs

As a weapons program progresses into its production stages, the use of fixed-price type contracts becomes increasingly acceptable to both buyer and seller. Quality-cost tradeoffs become more constrained. With specifications defining in detail the product to be exchanged, the government can assure that the contractor delivers what was promised and the contractor can ensure that it will be asked to deliver no more than what was promised. Equally important, the accumulation of experience on prior production activities provides a basis for projecting future costs with greater confidence.

To be sure, cost uncertainties are far from completely eliminated, especially when development and early production take place concurrently, as is customary in the more urgently conducted programs. Thousands of changes may be fed into production designs as prototype tests and operating experience pinpoint deficiencies. Usually it is difficult to estimate the direct cost of such changes with any assurance, and the introduction of numerous changes may also affect over-all production costs by disrupting the smooth flow of production and causing delivery schedules to slip. Also uncertain is the rate of unit cost reduction facilitated by accumulated production experience; that is, the slope of the relevant progress or learning curve.

As a result, the whole spectrum of contract types — from CPFF to firm fixed-price — sees use in weapon system and subsystem production, depending upon such factors as the degree of uncertainty and the willingness of contractors and government to accept pricing risks. In this chapter we shall be concerned mainly with the incentive effects of fixed-price type contracts on production activities.

191

TABLE 8.1

Cost Outcomes of 699 Weapons Procurement Contracts

Sample	Total Negotiated Cost (millions)	Dollar-Weighted Mean[a] Overrun (Underrun)	Unweighted Mean of V_i [b] Overrun (Underrun)	Standard Deviation of V_i	Significance Level at Which Hypothesis That True Mean of $V_i \geq 0$ Is Rejected
(1) 171 Air Force CPFF contracts	$3,900	17.9	n.a.	n.a.	n.a.
(2) 161 Air Force and Navy fixed-price incentive contracts	3,960	2.2	(1.72)	10.11	2%
(3) 47 Air Force fixed-price incentive contracts with initially firm targets	1,289	(1.7)	(5.66)	10.01	1%
(4) 47 Navy fixed-price incentive contracts	2,535	(2.7)	(2.05)	10.18	10%
(5) 51 Air Force fixed-price incentive contracts with delayed firm targets	4,806	(2.8)	(2.70)	6.33	1%
(6) 66 Navy redeterminable fixed-price contracts	360[c]	(5.8)	(5.18)	9.87	1%
(7) 156 Army redeterminable fixed-price contracts	475[c]	(1.9)	(.42)	11.81	35%

[a] Total overrun or underrun, divided by total negotiated cost, multiplied by 100.

[b] $$\frac{\sum V_i}{n} = 100 \left[\frac{\sum_{i=1}^{n}\left(\frac{C_i}{T_i} - 1\right)}{n} \right]$$

[c] Negotiated total price (cost plus profit).

SOURCES: Unpublished compilations of the Office of the Assistant Secretary of Defense, Installations and Logistics; Senate, Committee on Armed Services, Procurement Subcommittee, *Hearings, Procurement Study* (1960), pp. 222, 223, 271; House, Committee on Armed Services, *Hearings Pursuant to Section 4, Public Law 86–89* (1960), pp. 607–611, 614.

Sample (2) includes all Air Force and Navy FPI contracts settled between July 1959 and December 1961; samples (3) and (5) all Air Force FPI contracts settled between January 1957 and June 1959; sample (4) all Navy aircraft and guided missile FPI contracts settled between January 1957 and December 1959; and sample (6) all Navy redeterminable fixed-price contracts over $1 million in value redetermined during fiscal years 1958 and 1959. Sample (7) covers most contracts of $100,000 or more original value with industrial corporations redetermined during fiscal year 1959 by Army Ordnance and the Army Signal Corps. When major contract lots were costed and priced separately, they were counted as separate contracts in sample (7). All of the contracts in sample (6) were finally redetermined at points from 20% to 40% of completion, so the results shown here do not reflect final outcomes. All but 19 of the 156 contracts in sample (7) were redetermined at 100% of completion, so the results shown here largely reflect final outcomes.

For samples (3), (4), (5), and (6) the target prices were adjusted to include changes in contract scope, and so any indicated overruns were overruns in the strictly technical sense. Cf. note 3, p. 155 *supra*. It is not known whether similar adjustments were made for samples (1), (2), and (7).

The fixed-price incentive contracts cover aircraft and guided missile system and major subsystem production work almost exclusively. The redeterminable fixed-price contracts cover radar and communications system work and combat vehicle (e.g., tank) production as well as some aircraft and guided missile production.

THE FINANCIAL OUTCOMES OF FIXED-PRICE TYPE CONTRACTS

Aggregative evidence on an extensive sample of fixed-price type contracts (Table 8.1) reveals financial outcomes quite different from the typical outcomes of cost reimbursement contracts. There is a strong propensity for CPFF contracts to overrun their negotiated cost targets — by an average of 17.9% for the group of 171 Air Force contracts included in Table 8.1. In contrast, the six groups of fixed-price type contracts covered by Table 8.1 show an almost perfectly consistent tendency to underrun target costs or base prices, whether the financial outcomes are measured in terms of total dollar results or by averaging the percentage variations of actual costs from target costs on individual contracts.[1] The average dollar-weighted underrun for all 528 fixed-price type contracts was 1.25%, while the average of all percentage variations indicates an underrun of 2.25%.

The Distribution of Individual Cost Outcomes

Although the net tendency is toward underruns in fixed-price type contract outcomes, there is considerable variation both above and below the average. This is shown in Figures 8.1 through 8.6, which present frequency distributions of the percentage variation V_i of the ith contract's actual cost (or redetermined price) from its adjusted target cost (or base price).[2] Two properties of these distributions are of special interest.

First, visual inspection suggests that the distributions resemble the familiar bell-shaped normal curve. The results of Chi-square goodness-of-fit tests, summarized in Table 8.2, confirm that only for the two distributions of redeterminable contract outcomes can we reject with high confidence null hypotheses that the process generating the percentage variations V_i was normal.[3] The non-

---

[1] The sole dollar-weighted average overrun, shown for sample (2), was due to overruns of 21% or more on four especially large contracts.

[2] The percentage variations were computed by the formula:

$$V_i = 100 \left(\frac{C_i}{T_i} - 1 \right),$$

where C_i is actual cost (or redetermined price) and T_i is adjusted target cost (or base price).

[3] The presumed normality of the fixed-price incentive contract outcome distributions might be explained by the central limit theorem. The percentage

TABLE 8.2

Summary of Tests for Normality on Six Distributions
of Fixed-Price Type Contract Outcomes

Sample	Value of Chi-square	Degrees of Free-dom*	Probability of Obtaining That Value of Chi-square or Greater When Parent Process Is Normal
161 FPI contracts	6.36	8	.65
47 Air Force FPI contracts	2.69	4	.65
47 Navy FPI contracts	5.21	4	.30
51 Air Force FPI contracts	5.75	4	.25
66 Navy FPR contracts	13.99	4	.01
157 Army FPR contracts	18.55	7	.01

* In every case, the number of degrees of freedom is two less than the number of groups used to allow for sample estimation of two parameters, the mean and standard deviation.

normality of the redeterminable contract distributions may be due to the use of price outcome data rather than cost outcomes as a basis for measurement. That is, in many cases redeterminable contract prices were constrained by firm ceilings and therefore increased less than actual costs, and so the left hand (overrun) tails of the redeterminable contract distributions are skewed to the right, especially in the zero to plus 4.9% range.

Second, the samples yielded a surprisingly consistent tendency toward standard deviations on the order of 10 percentage points, as shown in Table 8.1. The one exception was the group of 47 Air Force fixed-price incentive contracts with delayed firm targets, whose standard deviation was 6.33 percentage points. This one

variation V_i of actual cost from target cost on the ith contract is the mean of the percentage variations v_{ij} of actual cost from estimated cost on $j = 1, \ldots, m$ individual contract tasks, weighted by the task dollar values ω_{ij}. Let $z_{ij} = \omega_{ij}v_{ij}$. If the process of making individual task estimates is subject to random errors such that each z_{ij} has almost any distribution and a variance σ_{ij}^2, the distribution of the mean of m z_{ij}'s will tend toward normality as long as m is fairly large but finite, $\sqrt{\sum_{j=1}^{m} \sigma_{ij}^2} \to \infty$ as $m \to \infty$, and no one σ_{ij}^2 is large relative to $\sqrt{\sum_{j=1}^{m} \sigma_{ij}^2}$. For a proof see M. G. Kendall, *The Advanced Theory of Statistics*, Vol. I (London: Lippincott, 1943), pp. 180–182. The last condition seems most apt to be violated in practice, since certain task cost predictions may have especially large variances. But no definitive evidence is available on this point.

FIGURE 8.1

Distribution of Cost Outcomes on 161 Air Force and Navy Fixed-Price
Incentive Contracts Settled Between July 1959 and December 1961

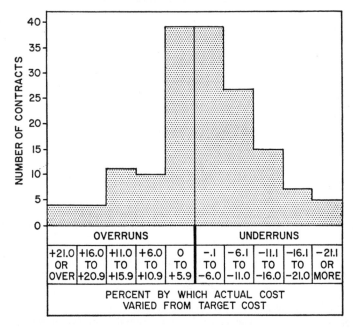

deviant result is undoubtedly explained by the fact that target prices
were not established until some cost experience had been accumulated on these contracts, and therefore some of the cost un-
knowns had been eliminated.

These findings provide insight into the average degree of uncertainty associated with production situations in which fixed-price
incentive and redeterminable fixed-price contracts have been employed. It is well known that when a random error generating
process is normal, as the contract target cost negotiation process
appears to be, roughly 95% of all outcomes will fall within two
standard deviations of the process mean. Taking a standard deviation of 10 percentage points and the average underrun for all
fixed-price type contracts of 2.25%, this implies a range of actual
costs between 77.75 and 117.75% of target costs 95% of the
time.

FIGURE 8.2

Distribution of Cost Outcomes on 47 Air Force Fixed-Price
Incentive Contracts With Initially Firm Targets Settled
Between January 1957 and June 1959

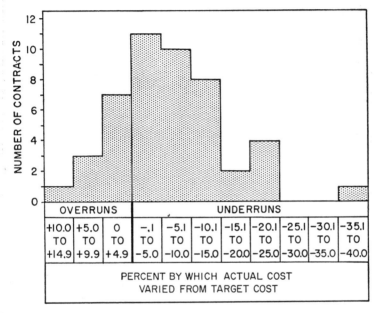

If firm fixed-price contracts with an initially negotiated profit of
10% of target costs were used under these circumstances, assuming no change in contractor behavior, roughly 11% of all contracts
would result in net losses to the contractor, and on about 4% of all
contracts losses of 5% or more would be incurred. On the other
hand, in approximately 22% of the cases the contractor's profit
would be 20% or more. We have therefore a rough indication
of the firm fixed-price contract pricing risk in advanced weapon
system and subsystem production situations. Whether contractors
and government agencies should and would accept such risks must
be considered later. In point of fact, as the data on aircraft, guided
missile, and combat vehicle prime contracts in Table 6.4 suggest,[4]
weapons production situations with the degree of uncertainty implied here have generally been covered not by firm fixed-price con-

[4] Cf. p. 148 *supra.*

FIGURE 8.3

Distribution of Cost Outcomes on 47 Navy Fixed-Price Incentive
Contracts Settled Between January 1957 and December 1959

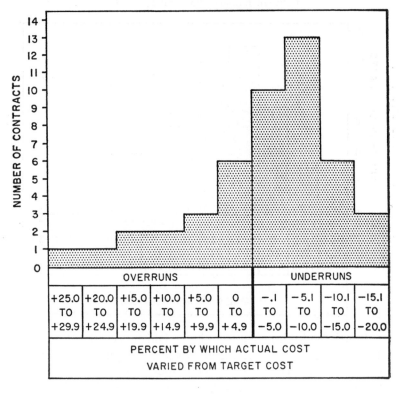

tracts, but by fixed-price incentive or redeterminable contracts with
less risk of loss and high profits.

The Reasons for a Net Underrun Tendency: Some Hypotheses

Given these findings about the distribution of contract cost outcomes, we can analyze the net tendency toward underruns somewhat more rigorously.   Three alternative hypotheses can be proposed to explain the bias toward underruns:

(1) The tendency shown by the fixed-price type contract samples is a statistical accident, due to random deviations in the process
generating negotiated cost targets and actual cost outcomes.

FIGURE 8.4

Distribution of Cost Outcomes on 51 Air Force Fixed-Price
Incentive Contracts With Delayed Firm Targets Settled
Between January 1957 and June 1959

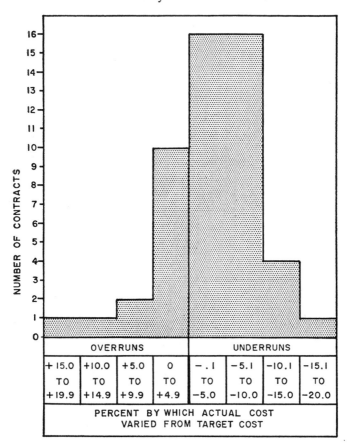

(2) There was a pessimistic bias in the negotiation of target costs for the fixed-price type contracts. That is, target costs tended to be set at levels higher than true cost expectations, assuming some constant level of production efficiency.

(3) The distribution of cost outcomes shifted after targets were set due to the incentive effects of the fixed-price type contracts. That is, contractors were motivated to higher efficiency and more effective cost control than the negotiation process contemplated.

FIGURE 8.5

Distribution of Price Outcomes on 156 Army Redeterminable Fixed-
Price Contracts Redetermined During Fiscal Year 1959

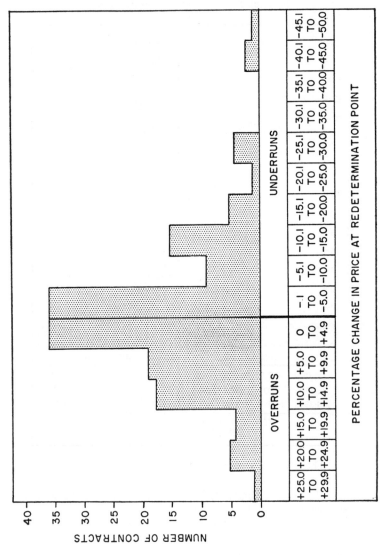

FIGURE 8.6

Distribution of Price Outcomes on 66 Navy Flexible and Maximum
Fixed-Price Contracts Redetermined During Fiscal Years
1958 and 1959

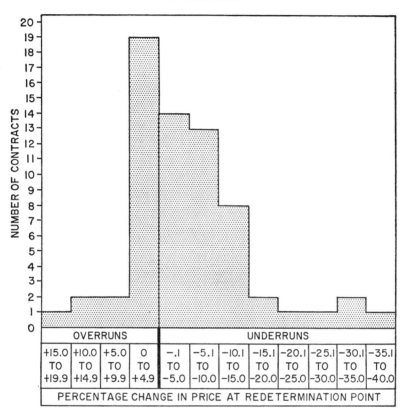

Hypothesis (1) can be rejected immediately. As shown in
the last column of Table 8.1, a null hypothesis that the true process average percentage variation of actual costs from target costs
was greater than or equal to zero (that is, on the overrun side) was
rejected in three cases at the 1% level, in one case at the 2% level,
in one case at the 10% level, and in one case at the 35% level.
Taken together, these results strongly indicate that the net underrun
tendency shown by the six samples of fixed-price type contracts is
genuine, rather than a statistical accident.

This leaves hypotheses (2) and (3) — one emphasizing behavior at the bargaining table, the other behavior in the actual conduct of production activities. We shall be concerned with these alternatives in much of the present chapter.

Quantitative Evidence on the Alternative Hypotheses

Further analysis of the available quantitative evidence sheds some light on the relative importance of bargaining and incentives for efficiency. Visual examination suggests that on the underrun (right hand) side, the distributions of redeterminable contract outcomes in Figures 8.5 and 8.6 are generally similar to the distributions of fixed-price incentive contract outcomes in Figures 8.1 through 8.4. If anything, there is a slightly greater tendency for large underruns to appear on redeterminable contracts. Yet as we have seen in Chapter 6, the usual government practice in redetermination actions is to reduce profits when costs have been reduced, and as a result redeterminable contracts provide at best a weak, inconsistent profit amount incentive for underruns.[5] In contrast, the profit amount increases automatically when actual costs underrun cost targets on fixed-price incentive contracts. Thus, even though in principle they provided weaker incentives for underruns, the redeterminable contracts produced underrun distributions comparable to those of the fixed-price incentive contracts.

Obviously, we cannot examine only the underrun side of the distributions. When the complete distribution of outcomes is taken into account, we find that the 156 Army redeterminable contracts had the smallest average underrun (measured as the mean of the V_i) — only .42%.[6] But this result is due largely to the fact that relatively more Army redeterminable contracts resulted in overruns, rather than to the weakness of incentives on those contracts which did yield underruns. As the following summary shows, the Army

[5] Cf. pp. 138–140 *supra*.

[6] Note that the mean underrun figures are not strictly comparable between contract types, since the redeterminable contract outcomes are measured in terms of prices and the FPI outcomes in terms of costs. As indicated earlier, the existence of redeterminable price ceilings tends to skew the overrun tail of the redeterminable outcome distributions to the right, and therefore *cost* underrun tendencies of the redeterminable samples are overstated by an unknown degree.

redeterminable contracts had the largest proportion of overruns among the six samples:

Contract sample	Proportion of all contracts overrunning	Mean of V_i
47 Air Force FPI	23.4%	-5.66
51 Air Force FPI	27.4	-2.70
47 Navy FPI	31.9	-2.05
66 Navy redeterminable	36.4	-5.18
161 Air Force & Navy FPI	42.1	-1.72
156 Army redeterminable	53.2	$-.42$

This apparently unfavorable tendency of the Army redeterminable contracts cannot, however, be attributed simply to ineffective incentives for cost control. On many of the contracts tight price ceilings had been negotiated, and overruns which impinged upon these ceilings reduced contractor profits on a dollar-for-dollar basis. In at least 40 of the 83 overrun cases covered by the Army sample, the redetermined price equaled the ceiling price. In 29 of these situations the contractor ended up with zero profit or a net loss, and in five additional cases the contractor's profit was less than 3%. Similarly, in 17 of the 24 Navy redeterminable contract overrun cases the ceiling price was reached, and in six of these cases the contractor's profit margin was completely wiped out by cost overruns.[7] In contrast, on only two of the 145 fixed-price incentive contracts covered by Figures 8.2, 8.3, and 8.4 did costs rise to the point where further overruns reduced contractors' profits dollar-for-dollar; on all of the other contracts in these groups which overran, profits were reduced by no more than 10 to 30 cents per dollar of overrun.[8] Only one of these 145 contracts resulted in a loss.

In short, the redeterminable contracts showed a higher incidence of overruns than the fixed-price incentive contracts, even though the redeterminable contracts provided generally stronger incentives for avoiding overruns than the FPI contracts. Among the con-

[7] Note that none of these Navy results reflect final contract outcomes, since redetermination took place between the 20% and 40% completion points. However, for all but one of the Army contracts on which the redetermined price equaled the ceiling price, redetermination had occurred at the 100% point, and so the losses indicated here were final outcomes.

[8] Individual contract data were not available for the sample of 161 Air Force and Navy FPI contracts.

tracts which ended in underruns, the distribution of redeterminable outcomes was comparable to the distribution of fixed-price incentive outcomes, even though the FPI contracts provided more consistent incentives for cost reduction on the underrun side.

These findings are wholly at variance with the incentive effect hypothesis. They strongly suggest that differences in the degree of optimism or pessimism negotiated into original cost targets had more influence on actual cost outcomes than differences in contractual incentives.

THE CRUCIAL ROLE OF BARGAINING

We need not, however, rely only on quantitative evidence. Our case studies and published sources afford numerous qualitative insights into the factors which determine the effects of contractual incentives on production activities. Let us begin by examining the question of bargaining in cost target negotiation.

The buyer's goals in contract bargaining are often threefold: to minimize the contract's expected dollar cost, to create incentives for efficient contractor performance, and to avoid the risk that unnecessary or excessive profits will be realized. All three are served by negotiating tight cost targets and prices. The contractor may seek to maximize expected profits and to avoid the risk of outright financial loss. While these goals are often dissonant in other matters, in cost target negotiations both are served by securing loose, pessimistic targets. On the other hand, the contractor's desire to maintain and extend its role as producer may impose a countervailing pressure to keep cost estimates tight when competition is keen.

Thus, there is a conflict of objectives at the bargaining table: the government buying agency wishes to negotiate tight cost or price targets, while the contractor wants to negotiate loose targets, to the extent that its ability to secure follow-on orders is not endangered. How this conflict is resolved depends primarily upon the relative bargaining power of the two parties and to a lesser degree upon the bargaining strategies and tactics employed.

Knowledge of Costs

Probably the most important element of bargaining power in contract cost negotiations is knowledge of costs. It is almost a truism that the contractor customarily has the upper hand in this regard. As a General Accounting Office report on 14 alleged overpricing cases observed:

> Unrealistically high estimates have been a serious problem where proper recognition has not been given by both of the contracting parties to pertinent costs and other data available at the time of the price negotiations. The buyer's lack of knowledge and adequate consideration of the latest cost data available to the vendor in establishing prices is the most important weakness observed in cases covered by this report.[9]

The position of the government procurement agency is reflected in this statement by an Air Force general:

> As you know, we have been placing a substantial amount of reliance on representations made to us during negotiations by contractors' negotiators in establishing contract prices. I am sure you will agree with me that it is to our mutual benefit to strengthen our negotiating relationship to the point where we can continue to rely on such contractors' representations.[10]

The basic reason for this reliance upon contractor representations is the lack of familiarity on the part of buying agency personnel with the detailed technological considerations underlying cost estimates. To be sure, government negotiators and auditors do not simply accept contractor proposals at face value. But our case studies revealed repeatedly that most of the cost analysis performed by government agencies centered on such consolidated magnitudes as profit rates, overhead rates, progress curve slopes, and labor wage rates. When more detailed analyses were performed, they typically involved minor items such as advertising and entertainment costs and bonuses, whose payment might not be allowed under the *Armed Services Procurement Regulation,* or items like travel costs, which might be subjected to official criticism. In addition, calculations were checked for clerical errors.

[9] Comptroller General of the United States, *Report, Examination of the Pricing of Selected Department of the Air Force Contracts and Subcontracts* (May 1959), p. 12.

[10] Letter to various industry associations from Gen. E. W. Rawlings, Commander, Air Materiel Command, January 6, 1959; cited in House, Committee on Armed Services, *Hearings, Weapons System Management and Team System Concept in Government Contracting* (1959), p. 368.

But usually overlooked or considered on only a very superficial basis in contract cost analyses were more fundamental questions, such as: "Is the contractor performing unnecessary development and production operations?" "Is the level of manpower on specific operations reasonable?" "Could some other process or design or component or material meet the requirements more economically?" While covering many large negotiations, our case study research turned up only one trifling example (involving costs of roughly $1 million) in which a really penetrating job of cost analysis was done by the buying agency, and government representatives admitted that this example was quite atypical. For the most part, government negotiators, auditors, and cost analysts lacked the technical competence required to make sound judgments on the basic determinants of contract cost.

Service personnel interviewed in connection with our case studies frankly acknowledged their lack of "a good feel" for the validity of contractor cost estimates. Even when technically competent persons were asked to participate in the cost analysis process (an exceptional happening), they seldom had enough time to delve into detailed questions. For example, personnel in one buying agency which brought its in-house technical staff to bear on major negotiations claimed that they were "good" at detecting cost estimates two to five times higher than the optimum because of hidden inefficiencies or overly elaborate designs. But determining whether an item ought to cost $70,000 instead of $100,000 took more time and concern over costs than they possessed.

Nor is the problem unique to government agencies. Prime contractors also found it difficult to discern whether price and cost estimates submitted by their subcontractors were reasonably tight, especially when the subcontracted items lay outside their regular lines of specialization. For example, an executive of one especially competent defense contracting organization said that in pricing matters, it was "necessary to place a large amount of reliance on the integrity of the subcontractor's management."

Recognizing their inability to tell whether contractor cost estimates are reasonable, government procurement agencies have established a variety of training programs for cost analysts and negotiators. For instance, in 1962 the Air Force sponsored a five-week course on cost estimating techniques, conducted largely by

RAND Corporation specialists.[11] That such efforts will lead to improvements seems a virtual certainty. But technique is at best an inferior substitute for thorough technical understanding. When service cost analysts lack the basic technical expertise required to understand in detail what contractors are doing, they will seldom be able to identify the most important kinds of cost reduction opportunities. And if past experience of the few agencies using technically competent personnel to review cost estimates is any guide, even those who emerge from the training courses with greatly enhanced abilities will lack the time to do a thorough job of cost analysis on even the high dollar value items of major production contracts. At best, they will be able to determine consistently when contractor cost estimates contain inefficiencies on the order of 30% or more.

Deficient Accounting Systems

Another explanation commonly offered by the services for their inability to differentiate between loose and tight estimates is the inadequacy of the historical cost data generated by contractor accounting systems. This was a problem during World War II, Professor Miller reported:

> The services found and OPA has since confirmed that many firms, in fact most firms in terms of number, do not have accounting systems which permit the accurate estimate of unit costs on a product or item basis. If firms cannot tell what it has cost to produce their customary items in the past, how much more difficult it is to estimate future costs! [12]

Despite almost continual efforts by the services to obtain improvements, the problem remained in 1958 and 1959, our case studies disclosed. The accounting systems of many contractors permitted reasonably accurate determination only of total actual contract costs, but not the actual cost of particular development and production operations or individual subassembly or subsystem lots

[11] See William H. Gregory, "USAF Drive Begins to Improve Forecasts," *Aviation Week & Space Technology,* June 4, 1962, pp. 76 ff. See also House, Committee on Armed Services, Subcommittee for Special Investigations, *Hearings, Overpricing of Government Contracts* (1961), p. 29.

[12] John Perry Miller, *Pricing of Military Procurements* (New Haven: Yale University Press, 1949), p. 134.

within the total contract effort. In several instances it was impossible even to ascertain the actual costs of complete weapon system production lots when several lots were covered by a single contract. For example, in one program the unit costs reported by the prime contractor for several different lots of guided missiles were identical to the penny, even though the missiles within these lots were quite dissimilar due to major engineering changes. Faced with similar deficiencies in another program, the government negotiator exclaimed, "We have piles of cost documents, but none of them tells us what we need to know in making projections." In a third program, company executives who had been hired away from more cost-oriented (nondefense) industries deplored the lack of cost accumulation efforts by their new employer.

Even the figures on such composite magnitudes as overhead may be inaccurate or misleading. For instance, recognizing that overhead rates were commonly subjected to interfirm comparisons by government cost analysts, many companies have actively attempted to charge to direct labor the wages of personnel who normally would be assigned to overhead categories.[13]

Frequently, when asked by the government to develop accounting systems which provide the information needed to make cost projections, contractors have balked, arguing that their systems already followed "accepted accounting practices."[14] But this response typically evades the problem. Much of accounting theory and practice is oriented toward presenting a fair and consistent *ex post* statement of a corporation's operating results and financial position, not toward providing the data needed for *ex ante* managerial decisions and projections. Indeed, so-called managerial accounting is a relatively new development in the accounting discipline. It is therefore quite possible for a system to conform to "accepted accounting practices" without generating a scrap of information relevant to future unit cost projections.

The reluctance of contractors to adapt their accounting systems has undoubtedly been motivated partly by a desire to prevent gov-

[13] Cf. Peck and Scherer, p. 518.

[14] See, for example, the exchange of correspondence relating to proposed paragraph 7–109.2, *Armed Services Procurement Regulation,* in Aerospace Industries Association, Industry Planning Service Memorandum, IP Proc & Fin 60–98, June 6, 1960.

ernment agencies from getting the kinds of data needed to negotiate tighter contract prices. Yet this is not the only reason. Although the question cannot be explored here, there may be truth in the contractor argument that, given the complexity of weapons development and production operations, the cost of collecting data detailed enough to be useful in cost projections exceeds the value of the additional precision attainable. In any event, the principal point to be made here is that government cost analysts typically have not had such data.

Furthermore, even the best historical accounting data will not tell the government analyst some of the most important things he must know to distinguish loose cost projections from tight ones. For instance, historical unit cost data disclose only what items have cost, not what they should have cost, and if early production operations were conducted inefficiently, the application of standard progress curves to project future costs will underestimate the possibilities for cost reduction and perhaps perpetuate the inefficiency.[15] Similarly, historical costs are no substitute for technical understanding in determining whether items can be produced more economically if they are redesigned or if different production processes are employed.

Contingency Factors

To some extent, whether contractor cost estimates are tight or loose depends upon the degree to which contingency factors have been built in. According to one Air Force procurement official, buying agency personnel can isolate these contingencies, as the following exchange in Congressional hearings suggests:

> MR. VINSON. . . . any man making an estimate is going to be sure he is on the safe side in making the estimate. That is commonsense.
>
> GENERAL DAVIS. And we can recognize those contingencies. We are just as good at pricing as he is.[16]

---

[15] Cf. Peck and Scherer, pp. 510–511. See also Harold Asher, *Cost-Quantity Relationships in the Airframe Industry*, R–291 (Santa Monica: The RAND Corporation, July 1956), pp. 83–86.

[16] House, Committee on Armed Services, *Hearings Pursuant to Section 4, Public Law 86–89* (1960), p. 373. Maj. Gen. W. A. Davis was director of procurement and production, Air Materiel Command, at the time.

Still there are many ways of burying contingencies in cost estimates, and the weight of evidence indicates that government negotiating personnel are able to recognize only the more obvious
factors. As another Air Force official stated:

> In far too many instances for it to be coincidental, target prices
> in incentive contracts have been too high, and excessive underruns
> have resulted. In some cases, such over-pricing has amounted to
> as much as 15%–20%.[17]

These underruns, he continued, resulted from contractors' use of

> . . . low quantity prices when high quantities would be pur-
> chased; from using other than current experience; from anticipat-
> ing such things as increased labor costs, increased engineering costs,
> or increased material costs; from anticipating design changes when
> in fact no such changes were in the offing.[18]

Perhaps even more important, it is especially difficult for government negotiators to detect overly liberal estimates of the number of men and machine hours required to perform complex, specialized production and assembly operations. As the chief of a
government guided missile procurement office observed, the contractor bidding on a fixed-price type contract is bound to come
up with an initially high price estimate, and the government negotiator, with less basis for judging costs, is in no position to say
the firm's estimators are wrong.

Thus, in preparing their negotiation estimates contractors generally strive to cover all costs they expect and/or desire to incur,
along with an allowance for uncertain contingencies. When government negotiators and cost analysts have an inferior understanding of the underlying technology, the target negotiated for any
particular contract need not and usually will not reflect that level
of costs which would be incurred if contractor operations were
conducted efficiently. It follows that one cannot assume that a
firm has performed efficiently simply because it has avoided cost
underruns and perhaps achieved a substantial underrun. Rather,
the tightness or looseness of cost targets must also be ascertained.

[17] From a speech by Lt. Gen. M. E. Bradley, Deputy Chief of Staff for
Materiel, cited in "Gen. Bradley Urges Correction of Costly Procurement
Mistakes," *Aviation Week & Space Technology,* November 7, 1960, p. 33.
[18] *Ibid.*

Analogous Problems in the Soviet Union

This problem is by no means limited to the U.S. weapons acquisition process. The Soviet Union has faced almost the same difficulty. The Russians also use a kind of automatic contractual incentives system to spur good performance in weapons and other production. When actual costs turn out to be less than planned costs, the production organization realizes what the Soviets, following good capitalistic tradition, call unplanned profit. Unplanned profits are desirable from the production plant's point of view because a small share of the realized profits goes into the so-called director's fund, to be used for management and worker bonuses, improvements in worker housing and recreation facilities, the construction of plant improvements, paid vacations to resorts, and so forth.[19] They are also encouraged by the central government, for at least in principle, high profits reflect high production efficiency. As a Russian text on aircraft production stated:

> The more profitable the enterprises of the defense industry are, the smaller will be the expenditures of human, material, and financial resources . . . and the more funds the State will be able to shift to other branches of industry for the direct satisfaction of the material and cultural needs of the workers of the socialist society. Profitable operation of the defense enterprises is therefore of enormous significance for the development of our production.[20]

[19] The Liberman proposals considered but set aside by the Communist Party Central Committee in 1962 essentially called for increasing the share of unplanned profits retained by plants. See E. G. Liberman, "Planning Production and Standards of Long-Term Operation," *Voprosy ekonomiki,* 1962, No. 8, translated in *Problems of Economics,* December 1962, pp. 16–22. See also "Soviet May Adopt Profit Incentive To Spur Output," *New York Times,* October 14, 1962, p. 1.

[20] V. I. Tikhomirov, *Organizatsiya I Planirovaniye Samoletostroitel' nogo Predpriyatiya (Organization and Planning of an Aircraft Construction Enterprise)* (Moscow: 1957; translated by the U.S. Air Force Technical Documents Liaison Office), p. 665 of the translated version. Similarly, no less an authority than Nikita S. Khrushchev stated at the Communist Party Central Committee meeting of November 19, 1962, that ". . . if we take an individual enterprise . . . the question of profit is of great importance as an economic index of its operating efficiency." Cited in "Khrushchev Hits Soviet Industry Planning," *Aviation Week & Space Technology,* January 21, 1963, p. 107.

With only minor changes in wording, this quotation could pass for an American defense industry brief arguing for the repeal of renegotiation!

But in Russia as in the United States, profits can be gained by padding original cost estimates as well as by increasing efficiency. To quote the Soviet text further:

> The 19th Congress of the Party [held in 1952] condemned the antistate practice of planning the production cost of the output, in which certain economic leaders limited by their narrow departmentalized interests and to the detriment of the State interests, artificially build up "reserves" in their plans for the production cost of their output by raising their standards of consumption of raw material and other materials, and, without justification, thus increase the planned labor cost of the finished product.[21]

The Soviets have found no easy solutions to the problem of target cost padding in both defense and nondefense production. For almost inevitably, plant managers are in a better position than outsiders to discern the tightness or looseness of cost projections. As Professor Alexander Gerschenkron, referring to "a fundamental peculiarity of the Soviet industrial system — that is, the well-built-in discrepancy between plan and reality," wrote:

> The stream of paper reports that flow from the plants to the central authorities may belittle the majesty of the Volga River, but it provides no assurance of real insight into the conditions within the individual plant. The fundamental ignorance of the central authorities restricts their ability to enforce their will. Obversely, it is knowledge of the manager that assures for him his area of freedom.[22]

Again, substitute "Potomac" for "Volga" and one would never know that this was written about Russian industry rather than American weapons acquisition.

Indeed, the inclusion of deeply concealed contingency factors is likely whenever one organizational entity (whether it be a socialist central planning office, a government contracting office, cor-

---

[21] Tikhomirov, p. 665.

[22] "Industrial Enterprise in Soviet Russia," *The Corporation in Modern Society,* ed. E. S. Mason (Cambridge: Harvard University Press, 1959), pp. 292–293.

porate headquarters, or a plant production scheduling unit) must make resources available to an operating entity on the basis of the latter's superior knowledge of costs.

The Government's Bargaining Power

Yet knowledge of costs is by no means the only weapon useful in a contract negotiating session. In particular, the government need not worry about detailed cost data if it can obtain at will a comparable product for less money — if, for example, there is intense competition from close substitutes or from would-be producers of the item in question. Then the government may have the upper hand in terms of bargaining power. But as we have observed in Chapter 2, often the substitutes available for a weapon system or subsystem are not close enough to put strong pressure on contractor cost estimates. And as Chapter 5 revealed, the government's ability to threaten the breakout of production work for competitive bidding is limited by the danger of degrading systems integrity and quality, the cost of obtaining and disseminating detailed manufacturing information, and the need for retooling and relearning when new producers are established.

Variations in bargaining power of this nature could explain in large measure the striking dissimilarities observed earlier between fixed-price incentive and redeterminable fixed-price contract outcomes. As we have seen, there was only one outright loss in a sample of 145 Air Force and Navy fixed-price incentive contracts, while more than 25 losses were recorded in a sample of 156 Army redeterminable fixed-price contracts. One difference between the two samples stands out immediately: the average negotiated value of the FPI contracts was $60 million, while the average value of the 156 redeterminable contracts was only $3 million.[23] All but one of the redeterminable contracts ending in losses were under $5 million in value, and all but five were under $1 million. We might hypothesize that contract size *per se* was the crucial factor. Firms could have been more careful in estimating and negotiating cost targets and they may have paid more attention to cost control when the stakes were high. But this is an unlikely explanation, since many of the small contracts ending in losses were held by small firms, and for them the stakes were clearly high in a relative

[23] See Table 8.1.

sense.[24]   Rather, it would appear that differences in contract size coincided with differences in the type of product being procured, and that the bargaining relationship in turn varied with product type.   The large FPI contracts were almost entirely for aircraft

[24] It is also possible that large firms are more proficient at cost estimation and cost control than small weapons vendors, or that large size confers a bargaining advantage in dealing with the monopsonistic government. Since our weapons program case studies examined only the role of relatively large firms, they provided no evidence on this point.

Another possibility is implied by Frederick T. Moore in *Military Procurement and Contracting: An Economic Analysis,* RM–2948–PR (Santa Monica: The RAND Corporation, 1962), pp. 47–48.   Moore observes that in a sample of fixed price incentive contracts which apparently overlaps the samples analyzed in Figures 8.2, 8.3, and 8.4, proportionately large overruns and underruns occurred mainly on the small contracts.

This suggests that the standard deviation of cost outcome percentage variations decreases as contract size increases.   Such an explanation would be consistent with the hypothesis formulated in note 3 *supra* that the percentage variation V_i of the ith contract's cost outcome is the mean of the dollar-weighted variations z_{ij} on $j = 1, \ldots, m$ individual tasks. If so, and if the standard deviation σ_{ij} of z_{ij} were constant for all j, then the standard deviation of V_i would equal $\sigma_{ij}/\sqrt{m}$.   If then larger contracts had more tasks, m would be larger and the contracts should have smaller cost outcome standard deviations.   The assumption of a constant σ_{ij} for all j is of course only an approximation, but the general tendency should also hold for more complex cases.

However, I was unable to find any consistent indication that the standard deviation of cost outcome percentage variations in fact decreases as contract size increases.   For example, inspection of Table 8.1 shows that the samples of Army and Navy redeterminable contracts, with low average dollar values per contract, had standard deviations roughly equal to those in the samples of fixed-price incentive contracts, with relatively high average dollar values per contract.   Still this is not a conclusive comparison, since the standard deviations of the redeterminable contract samples are constrained by the use of price outcomes (subject to firm negotiated ceilings) instead of cost outcomes.   A further analysis was performed on the samples of 47 Navy fixed-price incentive contracts and 47 Air Force fixed-price incentive contracts with initially firm targets.   In the Navy sample, 20 contracts with adjusted target costs of over $50 million had a standard deviation of 10.01, while for 24 contracts with target costs in the $10–50 million range the standard deviation was 9.16.   In the Air Force sample, the standard deviation for five contracts with target costs over $50 million was 7.05, and for eight contracts in the $10–50 million range was 4.79. There is an abrupt increase (significantly different at the 5% level from the complete-sample standard deviation in an F-ratio test) to 14.56 for 14 contracts in the $2–10 million range.   But then, for 20 contracts below $2 million in value, the standard deviation drops again to 7.91.

and guided missile systems or their principal subsystems, which seldom have technical substitutes close enough to permit direct cost comparisons. On the other hand, the small redeterminable contracts ending in losses mainly covered the production of electronic components, minor electronic subsystems, standard ordnance items, and (in one case) small trucks. Typically the armed services have a wider range of alternatives in procuring these items, and the degree of substitutability between alternative products is higher. Changes from one "black box" full of standard electronic components to a different firm's black box can be made with relative ease. In such situations the government buying agency can base its demands for tight cost targets on interproduct comparisons rather than cost analysis. Similarly, the government negotiator may exploit his bargaining power by demanding low price or cost ceilings. To the extent that close substitutes are found in much greater abundance at the component and minor subsystem level, the incidence of contract losses should be greater at that level than in large weapon system and subsystem procurement situations.[25]

Even when a weapon system has no close substitutes, however, the government may benefit in cost target negotiations from budgetary competition. As we have seen in Chapter 3, there was a gradual intensification of budgetary competition during the late 1950's as new resources poured into the defense industry while the level of defense spending grew only slowly. This trend was accompanied by an apparent tightening of contract cost target negotiations. Actual costs turned out to be lower than target cost in

[25] This hypothesis could explain a related phenomenon. In 1962 the Renegotiation Board reported that 1,034 firms recorded losses on their most recent fiscal year's defense sales. Although the data do not permit an exact breakdown, the average sales per company in the group including firms which sustained losses was $4.4 million, while the average for firms whose profit rates were high enough to merit detailed consideration by the Renegotiation Board was $38.3 million. Cf. U.S. Renegotiation Board, *Seventh Annual Report: 1962,* pp. 6–7.

However, an explanation along lines suggested by the preceding note might also be possible: the variability of profits for small firms may be greater than for large firms. Some evidence of such a tendency is found in Peck and Scherer, pp. 211–214. For analogous evidence with respect to company growth rates, see Stephen Hymer and Peter Pashigian, "Firm Size and Rate of Growth," *Journal of Political Economy,* December 1962, pp. 556–569. The whole question of firm size, contract size, and the variability of profit outcomes deserves further research.

some 64.6% of all Air Force and Navy incentive-type contracts settled between fiscal years 1954 and 1958. In the fiscal year 1959–1961 period the proportion of underruns fell to 51.0%.[26] This suggests that contractors became more willing to accept tight negotiated cost targets as they faced increasingly severe budgetary competition. It will be interesting to see whether the proportion of underruns turns upward again for contracts settled in 1964 and 1965, reflecting the upsurge in defense and space spending during 1962 and 1963. Such a reversal would be clear support for the hypothesis that budgetary competition has a significant general impact on the tightness of cost targets.

There are two main ways in which the government gains from bargaining power in contract price negotiations. The more important benefit is probably realized even before negotiations begin. If a contractor must face competition from close substitutes, budgetary competition, or the threat of breakout, it may bring into the negotiations a target cost estimate much tighter than it would have submitted under milder competitive pressures. Second, the government may exploit its bargaining power in actual negotiating sessions to secure reductions in the contractor's original cost estimate.

The sequence of moves which generally occurs in contract cost target negotiations has been characterized by Hitch and McKean as follows:

> Too often, at present, the process takes on the following pattern. The contractor prepares his estimate of the target cost, anticipating that the military service will "ruthlessly" bargain for a (familiar) percentage adjustment downward. As expected, the military service does hold out firmly for that adjustment. But analytical assistance during this process is so meager that the military bargainers have little feeling for the reasonableness of any of the estimates.[27]

Similarly, an industry group observed:

[26] Testimony of Assistant Secretary of Defense Thomas D. Morris in Senate, Committee on Government Operations, Permanent Subcommittee on Investigations, *Hearings, Pyramiding of Profits and Costs in the Missile Procurement Program* (1962), p. 898.

[27] C. J. Hitch and R. N. McKean, *The Economics of Defense in the Nuclear Age* (Cambridge: Harvard University Press, 1960), p. 232.

> The Contracting Officer is sure that the contractor has buried at least a 10% contingency in his proposal and feels impelled to get this contingency out by any method, fair or foul. On the other hand, the contractor knows that the Contracting Officer is substantially under a firm directive that he must reduce the contractor's proposal by at least 10%. The obvious reaction on the part of the contractor is to put this contingency in the initial proposal so the Contracting Officer can take it out and make the record of the negotiation look good.[28]

Contractor representatives interviewed in connection with our case studies manifested a common expectation that government negotiators would insist upon cost target reductions at the bargaining table. For instance, discussing an upcoming negotiation, one contractor official said that he expected the government negotiator to try to cut his firm's estimate and observed, "We'll sure come in higher on our proposal than the final negotiated price."

Nevertheless, the government negotiator may be able to win larger-than-normal price concessions when he has especially strong bargaining power. The existence of vigorous close substitute competition or the threat of breakout can of course strengthen his hand. In addition, he may pursue certain bargaining tactics to good advantage. For example, he may be able to win concessions by playing a waiting game when the contractor has low opportunity cost — when it must start work on the contract being negotiated or lay off employees. This tactic is especially effective when the weapon system being procured is not needed urgently. The government negotiator may also apply financial pressures by letting work proceed on a letter contract basis, providing only 70% progress payments on costs incurred and requiring the contractor to finance the balance until it agrees to concessions. This, however, can work both ways — he could find himself forced to yield if the contractor holds out successfully. In any event, by exerting whatever bargaining power he happens to possess, the government negotiator frequently is able to obtain target cost reductions essentially unrelated to specific cost expectations. Thus, the negotiation of cost targets is seldom a completely one-sided affair.

---

[28] National Security Industrial Association, Report of Task Committee 8, "New Approaches to Contracting," *Report of Cost Reduction Study* (June 15, 1962), p. 144.

Supporting this conclusion, our case studies suggested that although government demands for cost target cuts could be expected with certainty, the vigor and tenacity of those demands could not always be anticipated. Rather, there was considerable evidence that in some instances contractors believed that the buying agency was driving an unusually tough bargain, while in other negotiations they were satisfied that comfortably large numbers were being written into target cost clauses. In other words, the "percentage adjustment downward" described by Hitch and McKean was not always a familiar one.

Tightness of Cost Targets and the Choice of a Contract Type

The course taken by bargaining over cost targets also influences the choice of a contract type. Although there are additional differences in price or cost ceiling and floor provisions, a key variable distinguishing the most important contract types (with the exception of redeterminable contracts) is the proportion by which the contractor shares in cost overruns and underruns. Firm fixed-price contracts have a 100% contractor share; CPFF contracts a zero percentage share; and FPI and CPIF contracts an intermediate proportion. What contract type — or in essence, sharing proportion — should be negotiated, given some cost target? A mathematical and numerical analysis of the sharing proportion choice problem is presented in the appendix to this chapter. Here the more subtle analytical points will be skipped over to explore the influence of buyer and seller goals on the choice of a sharing proportion.

Let us begin by assuming that the contractor seeks to maximize the certain or expected value of its long-run profits, given some negotiated cost target and taking into account the existence of user costs. Then if the cost target has been loosely negotiated so that the contractor is confident of a cost underrun,[29] the firm should, except in one special case, insist upon firm fixed-price coverage, retaining

[29] One complication requiring mathematical analysis is the fact that when user costs are recognized, a contract's cost outcome depends upon the choice of sharing provisions. Thus, it is not sufficient to say that the contractor expects an underrun, given only the negotiated cost target. The sharing proportion, which is being determined here, must also be determined.

a 100% share of the expected cost underrun.[30]   Any lower sharing proportion would reduce the contractor's profit by letting the government recoup part of the underrun.   It can also be demonstrated that if actual costs are expected exactly to equal target cost, firm fixed-price coverage will always be optimal.   If, on the other hand, the cost target has been tightly negotiated so that a substantial overrun is anticipated, the firm will generally maximize its profits by demanding CPFF contractual coverage, insuring that its fixed fee remains unimpaired while the government reimburses 100% of the expected overrun.   If only a modest overrun is expected, the optimum is more difficult to specify on *a priori* grounds, since the reduction in profit due to absorbing a high share of the overrun could be offset by the negotiated profit rate premium usually awarded to contractors accepting the risk of a high sharing proportion.[31]   The appendix to this chapter shows that under certain special conditions, contractors may prefer shares intermediate between zero and 100% when small overruns are anticipated.

The government's sharing proportion preferences also depend upon its objectives.   As a first approximation, let us assume that the government wishes to minimize the contract's total monetary cost — e.g., actual cost incurred by the contractor plus profit paid to the contractor.   Then once the cost target is set, if the government negotiator expects a sizable overrun, he should demand firm fixed-price coverage, letting the contractor absorb 100% of the overrun.   If, on the other hand, an underrun is anticipated, the government negotiator should strive for a sharing formula which permits the buying agency to recapture a substantial proportion of the underrun.   One's first impulse might be to propose CPFF coverage, letting the government retain the whole underrun.   But the appendix shows that when user costs exist, this is optimal only in certain cases.   Cost-plus-incentive-fee or fixed-price incentive contracts with a contractor share higher than the zero rate of CPFF

[30] The exception arises when high profits due to a substantial underrun are undesirable or cannot be retained for various reasons to be discussed later.   Although the evidence is not conclusive, such cases appear to include a fairly small proportion of all weapon system and subsystem production contracts.

[31] As Chapter 9 will bring out, negotiated profit rates average from about 6.4% on CPFF contracts to roughly 11.5% on firm fixed-price contracts.

contracts should incite some incremental cost reduction, increasing the magnitude of the shared underrun. The government negotiator must therefore strike an optimal balance between motivating a larger underrun and decreasing the government's share of that underrun. Frequently the contractor sharing proportion which minimizes the government's monetary outlay when a cost underrun is expected will lie somewhere between the zero percentage rate of CPFF contracts and the 100% rate of firm fixed-price contracts. An intermediate share will also tend to be optimal for the government when actual costs are expected exactly to equal the target cost in a situation involving user costs.

More generally, the tighter the negotiated cost target is, the higher the contractor sharing proportion desired by the government. But the tighter the negotiated cost target is, the lower the sharing proportion a profit maximizing contractor wants. Thus, under the assumptions made up to this point, there is a definite asymmetry between buyer and seller preferences in the negotiation of sharing proportions. How is this conflict resolved?

One possible answer is that a mutually acceptable compromise is reached through bargaining. Our case studies revealed a good deal of vigorous bargaining over sharing proportions. Yet further analysis points to bargaining positions inconsistent with what has been predicted. As we have seen earlier, there was a significant underrun propensity in four samples of fixed-price incentive weapons production contracts, including a total of 306 contracts.[32] This evidence, plus recognition that firm fixed-price contracts bear higher negotiated profit rates than fixed-price incentive contracts, would lead us to expect profit maximizing firms to have preferred a firm fixed-price relationship for many if not most of the production efforts covered. That is, except in special cases the companies should have preferred FFP coverage on all contracts with an expected underrun, which (barring a pessimistic bias in expectations) should have included the majority of all the contracts. Or if because of technological uncertainty they could not discern in advance which contracts would underrun but expected an average

---

[32] The two samples of redeterminable contracts also showed an underrun bias. They have been excluded from the analysis here because they have a profit-cost correlation mechanism different from that of firm fixed-price and fixed-price incentive contracts.

underrun bias, the expected value of their profits would presumably have been maximized by choosing FFP coverage in every instance. Nevertheless, not one of the 306 contracts was of the firm fixed-price type. This distinct tendency toward the use of contracts which did not maximize contractors' profits could have resulted from successful government efforts to minimize its monetary costs in the face of loosely negotiated cost targets. But our case studies indicated that it was the contractors, not the government, who typically fought for weak sharing proportions. Such behavior would be expected when cost targets were negotiated so tightly as to make substantial overruns likely, but it occurred far too frequently and consistently to be explained on that basis alone. Conversely, government negotiators were customarily in the position of demanding a high contractor share in overruns and (more likely) underruns. Bargaining behavior predictions assuming outlay minimization by the government and profit maximization by contractors are controverted, and therefore it is necessary to challenge the assumptions.

Uncertainty clearly has an important influence on contractor goals and behavior in the choice of sharing provisions. As Chapter 6 has shown, some contractors explicitly accepted reduced average profit expectations through the use of CPFF contracts in order to insure against the uncertain possibility of occasional losses.[33] The contract preference tendencies observed here suggest that contractors are also willing to sacrifice the high profit expectations associated with firm fixed-price coverage for the greater safety of FPI contracts with relatively weak sharing proportions. Thus, the evidence supports a conclusion that contractors frequently do not maximize their profits at the bargaining table. Instead, they strike a compromise between profit maximization and risk aversion.

The assumption that the government seeks to minimize total contract outlays (cost plus profit) in negotiations is also open to question. Our case studies afforded some evidence of contract outlay minimization efforts, although contradictory behavior was also observed. Government contracting regulations offer ambiguous guidance on this crucial point, with some prescriptions supporting a kind of Thomistic *justum pretium,* some the minimization of

---

[33] Cf. pp. 151–152 *supra.*

cost alone, and some the minimization of cost plus profit. The following passages are representative:

> The proper selection of an appropriate type of contract is of primary importance in obtaining fair and reasonable prices.[34]

> * * * * *

> The objective is to negotiate a contract type and price that includes reasonable contractor risk and provides the contractor with the greatest incentive for efficient and economical performance.[35]

> * * * * *

> While the public interest requires that excessive profits be avoided, the contracting officer should not become so preoccupied with particular elements of a contractor's estimate of cost and profit that the most important consideration, the total price itself, is distorted or diminished in its significance. Government procurement is concerned primarily with the reasonableness of the price which the Government ultimately pays, and only secondarily with the eventual cost and profit to the contractor.[36]

Given these ambiguities, it is important to decide what the government's objective in contract negotiations should be, since when user costs exist, minimization of contract cost plus profit is seldom compatible with cost minimization or efficiency maximization in underrun situations. The incompatibility lies in the profit payment. When contract cost targets have an underrun bias, firm fixed-price contracting should lead to lower costs, but higher profits and a higher total contract outlay (cost plus profit) than the use of fixed-price incentive contracts with a contractor share of less than 100%. Is the government better or worse off with firm fixed-price in this case?

The answer depends in part on the real or opportunity cost to government of the higher profit payment. What does a contractor do with the incremental profits it gains by operating under firm fixed-price rather than fixed-price incentive contracts? Plainly, 52% usually returns to the Federal Treasury through corporate profits taxes. This share has no direct opportunity cost to the

[34] *Armed Services Procurement Regulation,* 3–801.1 (a).
[35] *Ibid.,* 3–803 (a).
[36] *Ibid.,* 3–806 (b).

government.[37]   A significant proportion of the remaining incremental after-tax profits will undoubtedly be distributed as dividends. The share of these dividend payments not returning to the government through personal income taxation is generally spent or invested in a multitude of ways not directly related to government needs and/or the public welfare, and so it has a clear opportunity cost. That is, dividends represent a diversion of government purchasing power from desired to neutral or undesired ends.[38]   Finally, some incremental after-tax profits are plowed back into additional company-sponsored research and development (which reduces the firm's tax obligations when the expenditures occur) and into new capital equipment and facilities.   If company reinvestment of profits in R & D and facilities is a direct substitute for equivalent government investment, such profits have zero opportunity cost to the government.   But if the profits are invested in projects the government would not choose to support, they can have a positive opportunity cost.   In sum, the opportunity cost to government of an incremental dollar paid to contractors as an incentive for increased efficiency is clearly not one dollar, but it is also not zero.   Although precise *a priori* determination is impossible, the average is probably closer to zero than to a dollar.   This suggests that government negotiators should generally be more interested in maximizing efficiency (minimizing contract costs) than in minimizing cost plus profit.

[37] However, it should be recognized that a contractor must consider the tax rate in deciding how far to push its cost reduction efforts.   If user costs are the principal barrier to cost reduction, an increase in the corporate profits tax rate will not impair incentives for cost reduction, since future after-tax profit rate expectations will be reduced commensurately, and therefore the slope of the user cost function will be decreased.   But if, as I shall argue later, cost reduction is also impeded by a disutility function, an increase in the profits tax rate will definitely reduce the contractor's incentive for reducing costs.   Ideally, a formal analysis should include $(1 -$ the profits tax rate) as a multiplier before α and $P(t)$ in the appendices to Chapters 7 and 8.

[38] The analysis might be pursued further into the effects of these outlays on the level of national income and employment, since maintaining full employment is a government objective.   Generally, one would expect dividend payments to have a smaller multiplier effect on employment than direct government purchases of labor and materials, since they would tend to flow to persons with lower marginal propensities to consume.   However, the problem is much too complex for any simple generalizations.

Because the government is a virtual monopsonist in an absolutely large sector of the U.S. economy, we must probe further into the aggregative effects of efficiency maximization as opposed to contract outlay minimization. Efficiency gains due to stronger contractual incentives imply the displacement or nonuse of some factors of production — engineers, production workers, clerks, raw materials, etc. — and hence a decrease in the weapons industry's demand for those factors. If the supply of, say, production engineers remains constant, wages should fall or (more realistically) the rate of increase in production engineers' wages should taper off.[39] The government therefore benefits by having to transfer less real purchasing power from taxpayers in the aggregate to factors used more efficiently in the weapons industry.

The higher profits realized by contractors when fixed-price contracts are negotiated despite an underrun bias will also have broader long-run effects. They will attract new entry into the weapons industry, creating increased competition which in turn, as we have seen, will lead to tighter contract cost targets and perhaps complete elimination of the underrun bias.

Finally, the government benefits in another dynamic way from efficiency maximization in the negotiation of current production contract provisions. As a rule weapons production contracts are written to cover some single fiscal year's deliveries. Cost minimization on, e.g., 1963's production contract may require the government to accept a firm fixed-price contract allowing the contractor to realize substantial profits, and the government's total 1963 contract outlay (cost plus profit) might not be minimized in this way. But when contracts for further production of the weapon system or subsystem are negotiated, the new cost targets are commonly established by projecting (through such devices as the learning curve) the cost experience of past and ongoing contracts. If costs are minimized on the 1963 production contract, the government will have the lowest possible base from which to project 1964's target cost. The end result will be tighter cost targets in 1964 and subse-

---

[39] Of course, there could also be a tendency for factors to flow out of the weapons industry to more remunerative alternative employment opportunities. However, due to specialization of skills many weapons industry employees would find it impossible to shift to jobs outside the weapons industry at salaries at all comparable to their present salaries.

quent years, and hence lower future government outlays on cost plus profit.[40]

Thus, the analysis up to this point implies that the government can benefit from attempting to maximize incentives for efficiency in sharing proportion negotiations, even when an underrun bias is present so that contract outlays will not be minimized.[41] Government officials apparently recognize this in a general way, for as a matter of broad public policy the use of firm fixed-price contracts in production programs is urged. But at the operating levels the desire to negotiate high contractor sharing proportions is far from universal. Many government contracting agencies and personnel are also risk averters. Just as contractors often seek to avoid the risk of loss, government contracting officers commonly wish to minimize the risk of especially profitable contract outcomes which might reflect unfavorably on their negotiating ability. Although they usually press harder than contractors for strong profit-cost correlations, government negotiators are frequently unwilling to go all the way to a firm fixed-price relationship when a sizable cost underrun is possible. Fixed-price incentive contracts offer a satisfactory compromise between risk aversion and other objectives for both contractors and government negotiators, and therefore they are used much more extensively than firm fixed-price contracts to cover the production of major advanced weapon systems and subsystems.

Further Evidence on the Negotiation of Sharing Provisions

For expositional reasons a discrete two-stage negotiation process has been assumed thus far: a cost target is decided upon, and then buyer and seller attempt to compromise on sharing formulas which best serve their diverse objectives. But the problem is more complex, since sharing formulas, cost targets, and other contract provisions are generally negotiated simultaneously. Changes on one dimension of the negotiation can induce further changes on another. If the government were to insist that all weapons production con-

---

[40] Obviously, the contractor takes this fact into account in estimating the user costs of cost reduction. I will have more to say about this problem in the next chapter.

[41] Some crucial qualifications related to the diminishing marginal utility of contract profits will be added later.

tracts have strong profit-cost correlations, contractors would surely attempt to reduce their risk of loss by holding out for high cost targets. For example, in several negotiations covered by our case studies, contractors reacted to service demands for fixed-price incentive coverage by submitting clearly pessimistic target cost estimates and standing firm against reductions. Recognizing the possibility of windfall profits, government negotiators backed off and suggested CPFF coverage. The contractors were then willing to revise their cost estimates downward. Similarly, complex and sensitive bargaining often occurs over specific provisions of a fixed-price incentive relationship. For instance, in one program the prime contractor agreed to a 4% across-the-board reduction in target cost and a decrease in the negotiated profit rate from 10.0% to 8.5% on the condition that its share of cost overruns be only 5%, instead of the 25% rate originally demanded by the government negotiator.[42] In other cases bargaining centered on the cost ceiling, above which the contractor generally absorbs overruns on a dollar-for-dollar basis.[43]

As we have observed, from the standpoint of both profit maximization and risk aversion contractors generally prefer higher sharing proportions when cost targets are loose than when they are tight. Conversely, government negotiators generally prefer higher sharing proportions, the tighter the cost target. Quantitative analysis employing the sample of 47 Navy fixed-price incentive contracts covered by Figure 8.3 suggests (although not unambiguously) that negotiation outcomes tend to satisfy contractor preferences better than buyer preferences. The sample was divided into two groups — 23 contracts with relatively low contractor shares of

[42] Note that a profit maximizing contractor would have been indifferent between these two contracts if it expected a certain overrun of 8.5%. Since it preferred the agreement with 5% sharing, the contractor must either have expected an overrun larger than 8.5%, or it was averting risks. If the contractor was not averting risks, and if the cost target could have been held at its original level, the government negotiator should have demanded a firm fixed-price contract!

With data of this sort on many negotiations along with data on actual contract outcomes, it should be possible to quantify a risk aversion function for contractors. The data might be found in existing government contract files.

[43] Cf. note 7, p. 135 *supra*.

overruns and underruns (5% to 15%) and 21 contracts with relatively high shares (20% to 30%).[44] The low-share contracts had a smaller average underrun (0.90%) than the high-share contracts (3.57%).[45] A regression of contractor sharing proportions Y_{1i} (measured in percentage terms) on the percentage variations V_i of actual costs from target costs showed that the greater the observed bias toward underruns was, the higher the contractor's share tended to be:

$$Y_1 = 19.44 - .296V.$$
$$(.122)$$

An r^2 of .117 indicates, however, that only a small part of the sharing proportion variance is explained by this tendency. Another regression, of the ratio Y_{2i} of ceiling prices to target costs (measured in percentage terms) on V_i, showed that the weaker the observed underrun bias was, the higher the price ceiling tended to be:

$$Y_2 = 124.36 + .198V;$$
$$(.059)$$

with r^2 of .200.

One interpretation of these results is that success in bargaining runs in favor of contractors. When contractors believe that cost targets will be tight (that is, when there is an overrun bias) they bargain successfully for low sharing proportions and high price ceilings, while when loose targets (i.e., an underrun bias) are expected, they accept a high share of overruns and (more likely) underruns and relatively low price ceilings. Or when relatively high sharing proportions are agreed upon in advance of cost negotiations, contractors hold out for pessimistic cost targets. On the other hand, the causality could conceivably run in another direction — high shares and low ceilings could provide stronger incentives for cost control and cost reduction, and hence lead to larger underruns. Both explanations may be valid, but the qualitative evidence from our case studies lends greater support to the first (bargaining) hypothesis.

[44] Three contracts had more complex sharing arrangements and had to be excluded from the analysis.

[45] The difference between means is significant at the 20% level.

The data on 47 fixed-price incentive contracts also point to another variable affecting the choice of sharing provisions. The standard deviation of cost outcome percentage variations (V_i) for the 23 contracts with low contractor shares was 12.53, compared to only 7.74 for the 21 contracts with high shares.[46] Since the standard deviation is a measure of uncertainty, it would appear that when the *ex ante* uncertainties associated with a contract were relatively great, relatively low sharing proportions tended to be chosen.[47] This finding is consistent with the hypothesis that both government agencies and contractors avert risks in the choice of sharing proportions.

Another contractor reaction to tight or risky target cost situations has been to delay agreement on pricing provisions. For instance, when in one program the weapon system prime contractor accepted a firm fixed-price contract with a price it considered quite tight, it insisted that its major subcontractors also convert to fixed-price contracts with equally tight prices. Four out of nine principal subcontractors objected strongly, and so work had to proceed for a considerable time on letter contracts until at last fixed-price incentive contracts (instead of the firm fixed-price relationship requested by the prime contractor) were agreed upon. In other cases firms delayed agreement on a final target price until they could accumulate additional production experience and reduce cost uncertainties.

Still another strategy chosen by firms squeezed into a close bargain is to compensate for the tight contract price by negotiating loose prices on the inevitable contract amendments covering design changes.[48] Referring to this practice, an executive of one defense contracting organization observed, "You can write up changes any

[46] This difference is significant at the 3% level, using a variance ratio (F) test.

[47] Again, the causality could run in another direction to some extent. If the marginal utility of profit is assumed to be constant, we would expect the strength of incentives to have no impact on the standard deviation of cost outcomes. But if, as I shall argue later, profit has diminishing marginal utility, the standard deviation of cost outcomes should decrease with increases in the strength of profit-cost correlations and hence in the potential variability of profit outcomes.

[48] Cf. Peck and Scherer, p. 417.

way you want." [49]   Our case studies provided two examples in which this approach was pursued successfully on fixed-price type production contracts.   Similarly, making up for initially optimistic CPFF cost estimates through the negotiation of change agreements with additional profit was fairly commonplace on development contracts.   Nevertheless, when buying agency representatives assumed a tough and wary attitude in negotiating contract amendments, as they sometimes did, this strategy proved less effective as a means of salvaging profit margins.

THE IMPORTANCE OF TIGHT COST TARGETS

Despite the availability of evasive bargaining tactics such as these, government negotiators were occasionally successful in obtaining cost targets which contractors considered quite tight and contract provisions (e.g., firm fixed-price or fixed-price incentive with a high contractor share and low ceiling) in which contractors perceived considerable risk.   Was contractor behavior under these contracts any different from the behavior observed under loosely negotiated contracts?

Much of the literature on contractual incentives suggests that behavior does vary with the tightness of cost targets.   For instance, a War Department policy statement issued in 1942 asserted that:

> Under war conditions administrative control is necessary to keep prices close enough to costs to exert pressure on them.[50]

John Perry Miller's analysis of World War II profit margins led to a conclusion that "the cushion of safety under which many contractors operated was large" and that "Clearly many contracts were not priced so closely that they could be called 'incentive' prices." [51]   Richard A. Tybout has argued that incentives for effi-

---

[49] The same problem exists in nonweapons sectors.   As the president of a commercial firm which procured considerable complex equipment said, "It doesn't do much good to sharpen your pencil and get too excited about the periods or decimal places.   The contractor can collect his fee under a good many different names if you squeeze him too hard."

[50] Cited from an October 1942 memorandum by John Perry Miller in *Pricing of Military Procurements,* p. 95.

[51] *Ibid.,* p. 220.

ciency may be ineffective under fixed-price contracts when substantial cost contingencies are included in prices:

> . . . Each contractor, if he has to bear the risk of an enterprise like nuclear fission, will make charges for risk-bearing. . . . To saddle a contractor with uncertainties in these circumstances may be to pay in the fixed price a large share for unpredictable contingencies. Under conditions of extreme uncertainty, the contingency element may be great enough to completely overshadow the addition to the profit share that the contractor could make through increased efficiency in operations, with the result that incentives are of no real importance.[52]

An Air Force general stated that:

> A drive to reduce costs in a cushion situation . . . naturally is less compulsive than one in which the estimate is known to be tight.[53]

The Reward and Pressure Theories

That the tightness of cost targets on firm fixed-price and fixed-price incentive contracts should affect contractor behavior is an interesting and perhaps surprising assertion. Under a firm fixed-price contract, every dollar of cost reduction increases the contractor's profits (or reduces its losses) by one dollar, regardless of whether the price has been set loosely or tightly. The profit-cost correlation persists, whether the contractor is trying to increase its profit margin from 15% to 20% or to reduce its losses from 10% to 5%. Likewise, within ceilings and floors which in practice are rarely penetrated, every dollar of cost reduction under a fixed-price incentive contract increases the contractor's profit by some constant proportion of a dollar. Since the monetary incentive for incremental cost reduction is constant, why should the level at which targets have been set make a behavioral difference?

[52] *Government Contracting in Atomic Energy* (Ann Arbor: University of Michigan Press, 1956), p. 9. The order of the sentences has been altered to clarify the context. See also pp. 158–159 of the same work for an elaboration.

[53] Speech of Maj. Gen. W. T. Thurman, "Use of the Profit Motive in Present Defense Procurement Practices," in National Security Industrial Association, *Addresses Delivered at the NSIA Joint Industry—Defense Department Symposium on the Profit Motive and Cost Reduction* (June 15 and 16, 1961), p. 31.

There are several possible answers to this question. We shall explore them in time, but for a first approximation, let us focus on the phenomenon of risk aversion. As we have seen, contractors display definite signs of risk aversion in the choice of overrun-underrun sharing proportions. A similar propensity appears to affect actual contract performance once cost targets and sharing provisions have been negotiated. For corporate executives, there is something especially repugnant about financial losses. A $1 million loss is disliked and feared not only because it entails, e.g., $2 million less profit than a $1 million net profit, but also because it is a loss *per se*. One reason for this aversion to losses is undoubtedly the fact that losses are a symptom of managerial failure. Executives responsible for losing money on a particular contract are liable also to forfeit their opportunities for promotion and perhaps even their jobs.

Assuming that a valid psychological and economic distinction can be drawn between the profit maximization goal and the risk aversion goal, we may differentiate conceptually between the two principal *modus operandi* of contractual incentives. The term "reward theory" is used to describe the correlation between increments of profit and decrements of cost at the margin of a contract. The reward theory of operation implicitly underlies all automatic contractual incentives. The term "pressure theory" is used to describe situations in which the profit-performance correlation is expected to occur in such a range as to pose a serious possibility of financial loss. Obviously, a fixed-price contract always provides a contractual incentive under the reward theory, but it may provide an incentive under the pressure theory only if a tight price is established.

The pressure theory must be elaborated further. We have found the distribution of actual cost outcomes from cost targets, with standard deviation of roughly ten percentage points, to be a manifestation of the uncertainty present in weapons production contract pricing. This uncertainty need not be exclusively of the technological species. Deviations of actual costs from cost targets could be due to the vagaries of the bargaining (target-setting) process and to the random incidence of incentive effects as well as to the vagaries of nature. If *no* uncertainties of a strictly technological sort were experienced by producers, then once the cost target and profit correlation provisions of a contract were established, a contractor would know with certainty whether, at some assumed level of efficiency, the end result would be a net profit or loss.[54] But usually technological uncertainties do exist, and so the level of cost to be incurred at any given level of efficiency is perceived not as a single value, but as a distribution of possible values. As a result, the relationship between negotiated target costs and expected actual costs may be such that the contractor foresees a *possibility* of loss, but recognizes that the *probability* of loss can be reduced by increasing efficiency. This situation is illustrated by Figures 8.7a and 8.7b. Assuming in Figure 8.7a a 70% level of efficiency (at which its operations are currently running), contractor management perceives a prior subjective probability distribution of possible profit outcomes which includes (as the shaded area under the curve) a substantial probability of loss.[55] However, by achieving 80% efficiency (Figure 8.7b) the distribution can be shifted so that the probability of loss is reduced to a tolerable level and the average profit expectation (the mean of the distribution) is also greater. The higher the perceived probability of loss at some current level of efficiency, the stronger the pressure theory incentive for increased efficiency will be.

An illustration of this concept can be drawn from one of our case studies. After negotiation of a large fixed-price incentive contract, the operating management of a defense firm expected on a "best guess" basis that actual costs would run 3% less than target costs.[56] Yet members of the management team were still worried about what they considered to be a substantial possibility that costs might rise above their expectations so much that losses would actually be incurred. In other words, even though the mean profit expectation was greater than the target profit (as in Figure 8.7b),

[54] It is conceivable (although not likely) that contractors know the level of costs to be incurred at any given level of efficiency with certainty, while government negotiators, because of their inferior knowledge of costs, can visualize only a broad probability distribution of cost outcomes.

[55] These distributions assume firm fixed-price contracts (100% sharing) with a standard deviation of cost outcomes of roughly 10 percentage points.

[56] It is worth pointing out that in this case the expected value of the contractor's profits would have been maximized with firm fixed-price contractual coverage. But in fact, the firm showed a strong preference for CPFF coverage in negotiations.

FIGURE 8.7a

Seventy Percent Efficiency

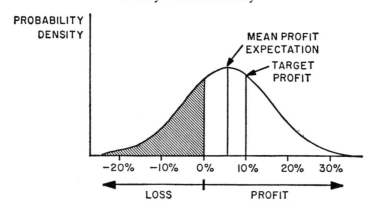

FIGURE 8.7b

Eighty Percent Efficiency

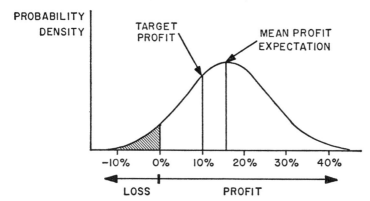

management believed that the left tail of the distribution extended well into the loss sector.

This probabilistic conception of the problem suggests several incentive implications. The tighter the cost target negotiated, the stronger the pressure theory incentive for cost reduction will be, other things being equal. Likewise, the less the negotiated target profit, the more slender the contractor's margin of protection against losses is for any given degree of uncertainty, and therefore the stronger the pressure theory incentive will be.   But as we have seen, *ex ante* uncertainty (that is, the expected standard deviation of possible cost outcomes) varies from one contract situation to another.   And normally, given some negotiated cost target and profit target, the greater the expected standard deviation of possible cost outcomes, the higher the total probability of loss and hence the stronger the pressure theory incentive will be.[57]   Finally, the probability of loss with any given combination of target cost, target profit, and uncertainty depends upon the contractor's share of overruns and underruns.   The strength of the pressure theory incentive for cost reduction is therefore an increasing function of three variables — cost target tightness, the contractor's sharing proportion, and uncertainty — and a decreasing function of the negotiated target profit margin.[58]   On the other hand, ignoring certain complications to be introduced later, the reward theory incentive's strength is a function only of the contractor's overrun-underrun share, remaining constant over variations in target cost, target profit, and uncertainty.[59]

Evidence from the Case Studies

The case study evidence on this question indicates that contractual incentives under the pressure theory have more powerful behavioral effects than incentives under the reward theory alone. In only one program was a firm fixed-price contract negotiated at the weapon system prime contract level with a price the contractor considered really tight.   In this case, the government had an unusually strong bargaining position because of special competitive

[57] This relationship will be reversed if the mean profit expectation falls in the loss sector.

[58] There are undoubtedly complex interactions among these variables. For example, by offering a higher negotiated profit margin (and thereby decreasing the pressure theory incentive) the government may be able to induce contractors to accept a higher sharing proportion (thus increasing the pressure theory incentive).   Further empirical research on contractor risk aversion propensities is needed in order to determine an optimal schedule for increasing the negotiated profit rate as the sharing proportion is increased.

[59] For an implicit statement of these relationships, see Miller, *Pricing of Military Procurements,* pp. 220–221.

circumstances, and it was able to persuade the company to accept a contract with a substantial element of risk. Personnel at several levels of the contractor organization showed exceptional concern over this contract and its cost-profit implications. The company was plainly attempting to control the costs of its subcontractors more vigorously. Buying agency representatives observed that the firm was changing its behavior — tightening up on its engineers and production supervisors, applying more cost controls, and in general trying to reduce the risk of loss. Contractor personnel conceded that the contract had altered their thinking, and that particularly in the engineering field, cost reduction efforts were being intensified.

The program described here was the only one in which firm fixed-price contractual coverage was employed for relatively early weapon system production. With 100% contractor absorption of overruns and underruns, the reward theory incentive was unusually strong. But the possibility of loss was clearly of paramount concern to contractor management. An overrun of roughly 10% could wipe out the company's entire profit, and since a very tight price had been established, this was considered a strong possibility. By way of comparison, had the production effort been covered by a typical fixed-price incentive contract with 25% sharing and a 125% price ceiling, an overrun of 25% could have accumulated before losses would be incurred.

In none of the other programs covered by our case studies was a bargain struck with as much pressure on the prime contractor as this one, and in none of the other programs did the concern for cost reduction in terms of immediate profit and loss implications appear as intense. To be sure, certain fixed-price incentive contracts with cost targets and ceilings considered especially tight by contractors appeared to have at least some impact on contractor behavior. Perhaps the most pronounced effects were observed when a fixed-price incentive contract was negotiated with a target cost some 20% lower than the contractor's CPFF proposal estimate. According to service personnel, contractor cost control practices improved considerably on that contract. But in other situations involving fairly tight fixed-price incentive contracts, there was a perceptible qualitative difference in the attitudes of contractor executives and technologists. Company representatives typically indicated in these cases that other factors, such as competitive and budgetary pressures, had more influence on their cost reduction efforts than the desire to gain profits or avoid losses on current contracts. Only in the program with early use of a tightly negotiated firm fixed-price contract did contractual incentive considerations appear to be of greater concern than competitive factors.

In sum, our case study evidence suggests that automatic contractual incentives had a relatively weak impact on contractor behavior when prices were negotiated so loosely or sharing proportions were so low that only reward theory incentives were operative. This conclusion is consistent with the apparently widespread belief of others studying the contractual incentives problem that tight targets are needed for strong incentives. Yet as we have seen, only when the government has an especially strong bargaining position can it obtain in one contract all the elements of the pressure theory — a tight cost target, a narrow negotiated profit margin, a high contractor share of cost variations, and considerable uncertainty of cost outcomes. More frequently, weapon system and major subsystem contractors are able to secure either loose cost targets or weak sharing provisions when they face substantial cost uncertainties. As a result, the possibilities for applying really strong contractual incentives in advanced weapons production appear severely limited.

CONTRACTUAL INCENTIVES AND QUALITY TRADEOFFS

This finding that only relatively weak contractual incentives can be achieved in many weapons production situations still does not permit a complete assessment of the effects of automatic contractual incentives. To proceed further, we must examine the areas in which incentive effects can be realized.

One way of reducing costs is to make cost-quality tradeoffs. Particularly when specifications are not spelled out in detail or when the end product surpasses its specifications in various respects, contractors conceivably could gain incentive profits by sacrificing increments of quality. This need be no unmixed evil, if uneconomic qualitative features have been built into the original weapon system design.[60] But usually it is difficult to simplify overly elaborate designs during the production phases of a weapons program, and

[60] Cf. Peck and Scherer, pp. 472–485.

so the quality sacrifices made to reduce production costs may fall in areas where they degrade over-all weapon system effectiveness rather than enhance it. Government representatives indicated that any tendency for contractors to sacrifice quality and especially reliability in production would be undesirable. Indeed, one service official flatly asserted that fixed-price type contracts encourage firms to make uneconomic reliability tradeoffs.

An area in which this problem could be explored in some detail through our case studies was the introduction of engineering changes which improved a weapon's performance or reliability. In general, the use of fixed-price type contracts appeared to inhibit contractor willingness to make changes. For instance, company executives responsible for the program with an especially tight firm fixed-price production contract stated shortly after negotiations were completed that they would be more careful in approving the introduction of engineering changes at both the prime and subcontract levels. The price on their contract would of course be increased to cover the cost of approved engineering changes (along with an additional profit margin). But the introduction of many changes could delay production and increase over-all costs, and this factor could seldom be included in change cost estimates, they believed. (The buying agency was displaying an unusually tough attitude toward contract amendment negotiations at the time.) Under the firm fixed-price relationship they were therefore less willing to accept the risk of incorporating major changes. Still company representatives declared that because of the premium they placed on their firm's reputation for quality they would not permit any serious sacrifices of actual or potential product quality. Furthermore, they pointed out, the engineering orientation of their company ensured that technical performance and reliability would be highly valued for their own sake by those who made change decisions, as well as for the sake of maintaining company reputation and hence ability to win new business. These predictions were borne out by actual results. A government official observed after the contract was completed that the weapon system turned out somewhat unexpectedly to be one of the most reliable weapons in the service's operational inventory — more reliable than competing weapons produced under fixed-price incentive contracts. Thus, the strong pressures for cost reduction and cost control in this high risk contractual relationship apparently led for the most part only to very minor, marginal quality sacrifices.

Under fixed-price incentive contracts, with less powerful profit-cost correlations and hence less risk, there was also evidence that the introduction of engineering changes was inhibited somewhat. According to contractor personnel, changes were discouraged in these cases not so much by fear of losses as by the administrative burden connected with obtaining the approvals required before additional cost and profit could be awarded.[61]   Under CPFF contracts, it is standard practice for contractors to introduce changes with nothing more than informal approval from local plant representatives of the government procurement agency.   When this procedure is followed the additional costs are reimbursed, but additional profit is foregone.   For instance, under CPFF contracts one firm typically introduced changes without resorting to formal authorization procedures if the change did not increase contract costs by more than $1,000.   Other firms appeared to have higher limits.   But if a $1,000 change were introduced informally under a fixed-price incentive contract with 25% sharing, the additional cost would not be authorized, and the contractor's profit would be reduced by $250.   Under these circumstances defense producers have typically been unwilling to introduce a change unless it has been processed through formal authorization channels (involving a delay of from six weeks to more than a half year), and in many cases they have even declined to do this because of the red tape and administrative bother.   To illustrate, in one missile program a certain resistor sometimes caused excessive guidance system oscillations, reducing the missile's reliability slightly.   However, the problem was not considered serious enough by contractor management to go through all the bother of processing an engineering change proposal.

In situations such as this, the quality increment involved was rather minor.   Whether the totality of these small decisions has a significant impact on over-all weapon system quality could not be determined through our case studies.   Certainly, the unreliability of seemingly unimportant components has been responsible for many spectacular missile and aircraft failures.[62]   But when major

[61] *Ibid.*, pp. 465–467 and 537.
[62] *Ibid.*, pp. 43–44 and 467–468.

questions of weapon system quality arose, contractors clearly tended even under fixed-price type contracts to sacrifice cost (and short-run profit) in order to maintain the military effectiveness of their products and protect company reputation. To the extent that longer-run considerations of this sort are emphasized over short-run contract accounting profit maximization, contractual incentives are unlikely to incite cost reductions at the expense of quality.

CONTRACTUAL INCENTIVES AND EFFICIENCY

Usually, more feasible opportunities are available for reducing weapons production costs by increasing efficiency than by cutting corners on quality. By reducing costs through efficiency measures under a firm fixed-price or fixed-price incentive contract, the contractor can increase its accounting profit. Yet connected with the task of cost reduction may be user costs and disutilities which must be set off against the additional profits.

The user cost problem has already been discussed in Chapter 7. Briefly, since the award of new programs is often based upon the availability of human and physical resources, reductions in engineering, production, and administrative staffs, and the shutdown of unneeded plants may lead to future sales and profit losses. These future profit sacrifice expectations are reflected by user costs. The user costs associated with production efficiency-increasing measures are probably a good deal less than those connected with development cost reduction, since the availability of production resources is usually given less weight than development resource availability in source selection decisions. In addition, inefficiency in production is more apt to endanger a program's competitive position than inefficiency in development, and so production cost reductions might actually decrease rather than increase user costs in certain circumstances.[63] Still to the extent that particular cost reduction measures give rise to positive increments of user cost, the user costs must be deducted from relevant incentive profit increments by a firm which seeks to maximize its long-run profits.

But the cost reduction problem is even more complex. In particular, few executives enjoy laying off surplus personnel. If there were more hatchet men in industry, there would be less head wagging and tongue clucking when one is hired. The difficulty of im-

[63] Cf. pp. 35–36 and 62–63 *supra*.

plementing personnel reductions was brought out clearly by one of our case studies. The chief operating executive of a defense firm reached the conclusion that his organization was badly overstaffed and that the company's competitive position was suffering as a result. (At the time the firm was operating almost entirely under CPFF contractual coverage, and so fixed-price incentives did not enter into the decision.) Nevertheless, he found department heads unwilling to initiate their own staff reductions. He was forced to call supervisors into his office and order them to let a certain percentage of their staffs go. This was an exceptional example, and the executive was an unusually forceful person, our case studies suggested. More frequently, there appeared to be a general tendency for firms to let overstaffing conditions continue until some crisis (like the loss of a major ongoing program) made it absolutely necessary to enforce reductions.

This sort of barrier to efficiency in weapons development and production efforts has deep organizational roots. Operating level supervisors are often motivated strongly to behave in a way inconsistent with corporate profit maximization. For instance, a project engineer or production foreman can as a rule commit no worse error in terms of job security and promotion opportunities than to have work incomplete when a deadline arrives. Consequently, he is naturally inclined to err on the conservative side, building up and maintaining his work group well beyond the level required to conduct assignments efficiently and maximize corporate profits. This propensity is reinforced by the desire of supervisors to build an "empire," by their reluctance to impose upon fellow engineers and workers the hardships which layoffs inevitably cause, and by their fear that agreeing to layoffs will give higher management good reason to suspect past laxity. For all these reasons operating level supervisors almost invariably resist staff reduction demands from above. Top company executives are therefore confronted with a dilemma. They may well desire to increase corporate profits. But they also wish to maintain amicable relations with their operating level supervisors and to limit the social dislocations caused by large-scale layoffs. Furthermore, top managers seldom possess the detailed knowledge required to be certain that complex and technically advanced design, testing, and assembly operations are really overstaffed or to judge how far staff reductions can be carried without endangering schedules and quality. Unable to present an incontrovertible case for layoffs on efficiency grounds, and unless severe economic pressures afford an independent justification, top managers frequently choose to let suspected overstaffing conditions persist rather than undertake the unpleasant chore of forcing subordinates' unwilling compliance in work force reductions.[64]

As a result, the contingencies buried deep in contract cost estimates, such as liberal production and engineering manpower projections, have a way of turning into cost. It usually takes more, and sometimes much more, pressure than the profit-cost correlations at the margin of a loosely negotiated fixed-price incentive or even firm fixed-price contract to spur managers into ferreting out and correcting overstaffing conditions. In such cases the "cushion" between contract price and the contractor's expectation of an efficient cost level may show up not as profit, but as cost.

The fundamental difficulty is that when contracts are negotiated in such a way that the perceived risk of loss is small, cost reduction through efficiency measures is not a matter of necessity, but of managerial discretion. This discretionary aspect is an important limitation on the effectiveness of automatic contractual incentives for efficiency. When corporate executives weigh the desirability of incentive profits against the unpleasant aspects of cost reduction before making a choice, they are essentially maximizing some complex utility function and not maximizing profits, as the theory of incentive contracting commonly assumes.[65] In this case con-

---

[64] As Gerhard Colm, Research Director of the National Planning Association, observed, "Despite what may be a prevailing view to the contrary, business as a whole is too softhearted to engage in mass firings unless it is forced into it." "Behind the Growth of the Economy," *Business Week,* June 1, 1963, p. 26.

[65] Many economists have come to accept the proposition that firms often do not maximize profits in any conventional sense. See, for example, William Fellner, *Competition Among the Few* (New York: Knopf, 1949), pp. 142–174; Carl Kaysen, "The Social Significance of the Modern Corporation," *American Economic Review,* May 1957, pp. 311–319; Joel Dean, *Managerial Economics* (Englewood Cliffs: Prentice-Hall, 1951), pp. 28–39; C. F. Carter and B. R. Williams, *Investment in Innovation* (London: Oxford, 1958), pp. 38–53; Julius Margolis, "The Analysis of the Firm: Rationalism, Conventionalism, and Behaviorism," *Journal of Business,* July 1958, pp. 187–199; and Robert N. Anthony, "The Trouble With Profit

tractual incentives spur efficiency increases if and only if, in the judgment of management, the utility of short-run contract profit increments net of user costs exceeds the disutility associated with particular cost reduction efforts.

There are certainly situations in which this condition is satisfied, as indicated in earlier observations on behavior under tightly negotiated firm fixed-price and fixed-price incentive contracts. Even under loosely negotiated contracts some incentive effect upon efficiency must be realized. It would appear, for example, that managers associate less disutility with *cost control* than with *cost reduction*. But our case study research indicated that very many cost reduction opportunities go unexploited in weapons programs because profit increments at the margin of the contracts (fixed-price incentive and loosely priced firm fixed-price) which normally can be negotiated are overwhelmed by disutilities and user costs. Thus, although the automatic contractual incentives in common use have at least some influence on contractor behavior, only if much stronger incentives can be applied will significant increases in the efficiency of weapons development and production be realized. The opportunities for establishing a stronger system of incentives will be considered in subsequent chapters.

DIMINISHING MARGINAL UTILITY OF PROFIT

The assertion that some cost reduction efforts are less acceptable to managers than others implies that the opportunities for cost reduction can be ranked in such a way that the most acceptable are exploited first, and so on down to the most disagreeable. In other words a function $\mathfrak{D}(\Delta C)$ can be constructed showing the total disutility of cost reduction increasing at an increasing rate — cost reduction has increasing marginal disutility. If then we assume that firms maximize some complex utility function measurable (at least theoretically) in terms of utiles, it is possible to illustrate graphically the empirical finding that many cost reduction opportunities go unexploited. The simplest case is shown in Figure 8.8a. Profit is a linear function $\pi(\Delta C)$ of cost reduction and it is

Maximization," *Harvard Business Review,* November–December 1960, pp. 126–134. For a spirited defense of the profit maximization assumption, see Fritz Machlup, "Marginal Analysis and Empirical Research," *American Economic Review,* September 1946, pp. 519–554.

assumed to have constant marginal utility. Therefore the utility of profit is a linear function $\psi[\pi(\Delta C)]$ of cost reduction. It is also assumed that no user costs are incurred. Then at OA, the marginal utility of profit equals the marginal disutility of reducing costs further, net utility is maximized, and no further cost reduction opportunities are exploited. If, as in Figure 8.8b, user costs $U(\Delta C)$ are incurred as a result of cost reduction, the firm will maximize $\psi[\pi(\Delta C) - (U\Delta C)] - \mathfrak{D}(\Delta C)$, and fewer cost reduction opportunities will be exploited. Finally, if profit should have diminishing marginal utility, as illustrated in Figure 8.8c, still fewer cost reduction opportunities will be exploited. The equilibrium point is OD, compared to the equilibrium OA for constant marginal utility of profit with no user costs and OB for constant marginal utility of profit with positive user costs.[66]

Our case studies provided evidence that profit on weapons production contracts in fact has diminishing marginal utility to company executives. In part, this is implicit in the earlier conclusion that contractual incentives under the pressure theory are stronger than incentives under only the reward theory, for if the pressure theory is valid, increments of profit (or decrements of loss) must have greater utility when a firm is operating or threatened with operating at a loss than when a contract promises to yield high profits. In the simplest interpretation of this case, the firm has one inflection (at the zero profit level) in its profit utility function.[67] When uncertainty and hence a continuously variable risk of loss are taken into account, a concave curvilinear profit utility function of the sort shown in Figure 8.8c could exist.

A firm's profit utility function may also be inflected due to aspiration levels beyond which, presumably, profits have little or no marginal utility.[68] One firm covered by our case study research had an explicitly defined profit objective in terms of profit per

[66] Of course, one might conceive diminishing marginal utility of profit cases in which, in the region of bankruptcy-inducing losses, increments of profit might have more utility than in the linear case. In extreme situations, the equilibrium could lie to the right of the linear utility equilibrium.

[67] For an analogous finding with respect to risk-bearing on financial investments, see Peck and Scherer, p. 540.

[68] Cf. Herbert A. Simon, "Theories of Decision-Making in Economics and Behavioral Science," *American Economic Review*, June 1959, pp. 262–265.

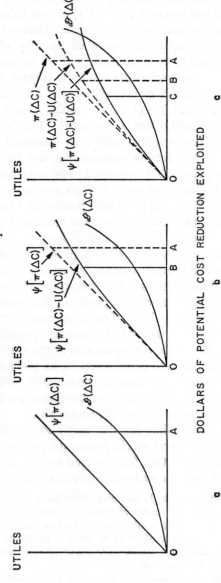

FIGURE 8.8

Illustrations of Cost Reduction Equilibria

share of common stock, but the goal had never been attained, so the aspiration level was not an operational constraint. Executives of other companies also expressed dissatisfaction with their current profits and a desire to earn higher profits — although as we have seen, they were frequently unwilling to pay the price in terms of layoffs and other efficiency measures required to secure short-run contract profit increases. It must be noted, however, that our case study interviews were conducted during a period of generally declining weapons industry profits — a time when, according to aspiration level theory, firms would naturally tend to be dissatisfied with their profits. The case study evidence is therefore too limited to permit any conclusive generalizations on the existence and effects of aspiration levels.

Nevertheless, the case studies revealed another rather different constraint on contract profit aspirations with most important implications. Executives of several firms said it was unwise to earn and retain more than about 10% or 12% profit on any single incentive type contract. Some companies even made it a regular practice to refund voluntarily any profits realized above some such level, although they were legally entitled to retain them.

There are excellent reasons for avoiding or refunding profits higher than roughly 12%. One is related to the political milieu in which weapons contracting takes place. In recent years the General Accounting Office has been particularly alert to contract situations in which negotiated costs were underrun significantly and high profits were retained by the contractor. Such contracts are audited in detail, and many of the audits have provided at least some grounds for suspecting that the original cost targets were negotiated too loosely.[69] It is seldom possible in such cases to show deliberate intent, but the reaction of Congress has unfailingly been to suspect cost padding in order to obtain windfall profits, or more bluntly, profiteering.[70]

[69] See, for example, Cabell Phillips, "Accounting Office Is Watchdog Over Spending," *New York Times,* July 8, 1962, p. 42, who reveals that between 1957 and 1962 the GAO reported 73 cases of overpricing involving a total of $66 million in alleged excess profits. See also House, Committee on Armed Services, Subcommittee for Special Investigations, *Hearings, Overpricing of Government Contracts* (1961), pp. 2–11.

[70] In 1962 Congress passed a bill requiring that defense contractors certify the accuracy, completeness, and currency of data submitted for

In interviews, company officials repeatedly manifested a strong desire to avoid the unfavorable publicity which accompanies GAO and congressional investigations of high contract profits. They noted that such investigations typically injure a firm's reputation and could affect the company's ability to obtain further government contracts. For example, officials of several defense firms mentioned the investigation of General Motors' 18% profits on two lots of F–84F aircraft, indicating their belief that the dispute and investigation were partly responsible for GM's rapid decline as a defense prime contractor.[71] That retention of high profits can lead to sales losses is also suggested by the testimony of a Navy official:

> If in a particular instance there is what might be classified as a recalcitrant, this information is furnished to higher authority and appropriate action is taken. I can say in one particular instance a very strong letter was written by the Under Secretary of the Navy to a substantial company indicating that unless they corrected their methods we would have to stop doing business with them. He was that severe.[72]

Avoiding high profits on defense contracts is also good customer relations in a more immediate sense. When a contract yields high

contract price negotiations and providing for refunds whenever cost underruns were determined to be the result of inaccurate, incomplete, or noncurrent pricing data. 10 U.S.C. Section 2360. An earlier version of the bill would have required that a contractor be deprived of any profit "resulting from causes other than those which the contractor can clearly and completely demonstrate are due to his skill, efficiency, or ingenuity in the performance of such contract." H. R. 12,572, 86th Congress. See also *Armed Services Procurement Regulation,* 7–104.29.

[71] Cf. House, Committee on Armed Services, *Hearings, Study of Air Force Contract AF 33 (038) 18503; General Motors Corp.—Buick-Oldsmobile-Pontiac Assembly Division* (1957), pp. 2555–2925; and *Hearings, Overpricing of Government Contracts* (1961), p. 35. GM subsequently refunded $9 million of $17 million alleged excessive profits, reducing its realized profit rate to roughly 14% of costs. Further adjustments were made by the Renegotiation Board. GM fell from first in the list of defense prime contractors during fiscal years 1951–1953 to 21st in fiscal years 1958–1960.

[72] Statement of M. E. Jones, Assistant Director, Procurement Division, Office of Naval Materiel, in House, Committee on Armed Services, Subcommittee for Special Investigations, *Hearings, Overpricing of Government Contracts* (1961), p. 56.

profits due to large underruns, government negotiators are likely to feel that the contractor has taken advantage of them. The result typically is tighter, more cynical government bargaining in subsequent negotiations. Recognizing this, contractor officials stated that it is poor practice to make a "killing" on any one contract. "They know — and they'll get it back in the long run," one executive admonished.

Indeed, perhaps the best way to maximize profits in defense contracting is to appear disinterested in maximizing profits. One firm did precisely that, quickly refunding any profits over the originally negotiated rate whenever underruns developed. Government negotiators thought of the company as "not out to make a killing" and, knowing that underruns would be refunded, tended to accept the company's cost estimates at face value without insisting upon downward adjustments. As a result, the company seldom experienced the pressure of tight cost targets and ceilings, and so it was able to accept fixed-price type contracts (with a 9% or 10% profit rate) when contractors with which the buying agency bargained more vigorously chose to rely upon CPFF coverage (with a 6% or 7% profit rate). The effectiveness of this strategy was clearly perceived by company officials, who explained that if their firm were to retain windfall profits, the government would make up for it through closer negotiation.

In any event, awareness that windfall profit suspicions could injure their relations with the government has led most contractors to refund questionable profit increments either as soon as they are realized, or at least as soon as a General Accounting Office investigation intimates that original cost estimates were unnecessarily high. Between 1951 and 1961, defense contractors made voluntary price reductions and profit refunds totaling more than $1 billion.[73] Of $66 million in profits alleged to have been unearned by GAO reports between 1957 and 1962, some $47 million were refunded.[74]

Furthermore, when an ample cushion exists between price and expected costs, it is often preferable to incur additional costs rather than exceed some "politically tolerable" net profit rate, executives

[73] U.S. Renegotiation Board, *Sixth Annual Report: 1961,* p. 10. This figure excludes refunds and price reductions made in redetermination and renegotiation actions.

[74] Cabell Phillips, "Accounting Office Is Watchdog Over Spending."

of two companies said in case study interviews. This practice of absorbing cushions in the form of cost rather than profit could explain the slight tendency visible in Figures 8.1 through 8.4 for the distributions of underruns on fixed-price incentive contracts to be somewhat truncated, relative to the distributions of redeterminable contract underruns (Figures 8.5 and 8.6). Under fixed-price incentive contracts with significant contractor sharing proportions, large underruns lead automatically to high realized profit rates and potentially unfavorable customer relations, while under redeterminable contracts any profits considered excessive will be recaptured in the redetermination action. Therefore, one might expect firms to have fewer qualms about permitting large underruns on redeterminable contracts.

The same phenomenon is suggested more vividly by Figure 8.9, which shows the distribution of realized profits as a percentage of actual costs on the 47 Navy fixed-price incentive contracts whose

FIGURE 8.9

Profit Rates Realized as a Percentage of Actual Cost
on 47 Navy Aircraft and Guided Missile
Fixed-Price Incentive Contracts

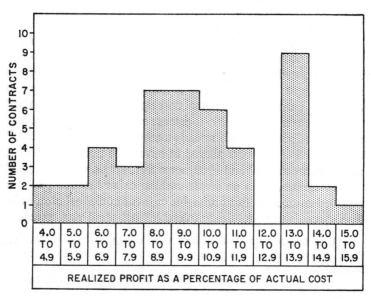

cost outcomes were presented in Figure 8.3. There is a pronounced mode in the 13.0%–13.9% range which appears only barely explicable by the (perhaps random) absence of any outcomes in the 12.0%–12.9% range.[75] No comparable bimodal tendency was found for the two samples of redeterminable contracts covered by Figures 8.5 and 8.6 and for a large sample of cost reimbursement contracts — the only other recent samples on which profit outcome data were available.[76] The unique 13% mode for the FPI contract sample is clearly consistent with a profit cushion absorption hypothesis. That is, when firms anticipated a potential underrun leading to realized profit rates higher than 13% of actual costs, they may have begun absorbing the margin in the form of additional cost. An alternative (but not necessarily conflicting) hypothesis is suggested in the mathematical appendix to this chapter: when firms anticipated a substantial underrun, they may have chosen a sharing proportion just sufficient to yield a "safe" expected profit rate of roughly 13%.

Nevertheless, further analysis of the Navy FPI sample profit outcomes warns us not to attach excessive weight to this result. When realized profits on the 47 Navy contracts are plotted as a percentage of target cost instead of actual cost, as in Figure 8.10, the bimodal tendency observed in Figure 8.9 vanishes.[77] This permutation has

[75] A Chi-square test for normality of the distribution was rather inconclusive. Chi-square was 8.03, with five degrees of freedom. With this result, a null hypothesis that the distribution was generated by a normal process would be rejected at the 20% level. However, such a test is quite sensitive to changes in grouping when the data are distributed as in Figure 8.9. To err in favor of accepting the null hypothesis, I grouped the 11.0–11.9 and 12.0–12.9 outcomes together. Similarly, the right tail of the distribution from 13.0 upward was combined into a single group.

[76] For a description of the cost reimbursement contract sample, see Figure 9.1 *infra*. The distributions of actual profit outcomes for these three samples can be found in U.S. Department of Defense, Report of Project No. 103, June 26, 1961. A distribution of profit outcomes on Navy fixed-price type contracts during World War II was also neither truncated nor bimodal, although a rather different institutional situation prevailed then. See Miller, *Pricing of Military Procurements,* p. 218.

[77] The choice of a measurement base affects the profit outcome distributions so markedly because of differences in the sharing proportion from contract to contract. Either a modest underrun with a high sharing proportion or a large underrun with a low sharing proportion may lead to the same moderately high realized profit percentage, when actual cost is taken

FIGURE 8.10

Profit Rates Realized as a Percentage of Target Cost
on 47 Navy Aicraft and Guided Missile
Fixed-Price Incentive Contracts

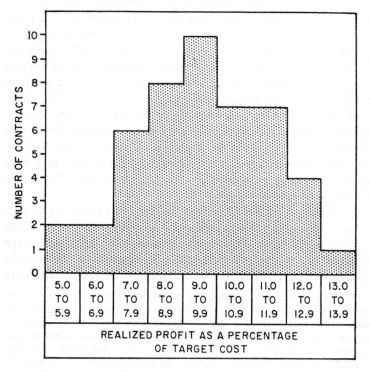

two possible interpretations. First, the bimodal tendency of Figure 8.9 could have been a statistical fluke. Or second, firms may have viewed the undesirability of realizing high profit rates measured against actual costs as an important constraint upon their behavior, while they attached no such importance to profit as a percentage of target cost. Unfortunately, our case studies provided

---

as the base. But when target cost is used as the base, the large underrun low sharing proportion profit rate will be deflated considerably due to the higher denominator.

The crucial role of sharing proportion variations in the results observed lends some support to the constrained profit maximization hypothesis advanced in the appendix to this chapter.

no information on this crucial point.[78] Yet evidence from other sources suggests that profit as a percentage of actual costs is the dominant concept in government contracting circles. Military service statistical summaries of contract outcomes almost invariably measured realized profits as a percentage of actual cost and not as a percentage of target cost. Similarly, when percentages were calculated at all, General Accounting Office reports typically analyzed contract profit outcomes against actual costs rather than target cost. If in fact profit as a percentage of actual cost is the dominant concept, the pronounced mode in the 13.0%–13.9% range of Figure 8.9 may be more than a statistical accident. Although no positive conclusion is possible, the observed bimodal tendency is at least consistent with case study interviews revealing contractors' reluctance to exceed some "politically tolerable" profit margin.

We find therefore an institutional limit on the rate of profit which can safely be earned on any single incentive-type contract. Beyond some rate on the order of 10% to 14%, additional profit can be a discommodity, injuring customer relations and inviting more cynical future negotiations. In other words, the mere fact of realizing high contract profits is a source of substantial user costs. This, combined with previous findings, indicates that adjusted incentive contract profits (that is, actual accounting profits less user cost) yield diminishing marginal utility to defense contractors. In the loss sector, increments of profit (or decrements of loss) have very high utility. In the zero to roughly 12% range, profit increments yield intermediate utility. Beyond 12% or 13%, the net utility realized from contract profit increments is trifling or perhaps even negative.

This conclusion has two significant implications. First, contractual incentives for cost reduction are much stronger in the loss and low profit range than in the high profit range. When high profits are anticipated, the incentives may even work in favor of incurring additional costs rather than avoiding them. This suggests the second implication: one effect of automatic contractual incentives may be to tighten the distribution of actual cost outcomes (e.g., to reduce the standard deviation of cost outcome percentage variations) relative to the distribution which would prevail

---

[78] It is especially unfortunate that the case study interviews did not determine whether company executives were referring to profit as a percentage of actual or target cost when they spoke of the safe 10% to 12% range.

without such incentives.[79]   On contracts with tight cost targets threatening high overruns and low profits, the incentive for cost reduction can be relatively strong, spurring the contractor to increase efficiency and shift its actual cost outcome toward the right (underrun) side.   But on contracts whose cost targets are loose enough to permit large underruns and high profits, the incentive for an efficiency (rightward) shift will at best be weak, and there may be an incentive to incur unplanned costs, shifting the actual cost outcome to the left.

THE IMPACT OF RENEGOTIATION

Another potential constraint on profit realizations is the group of profit limitation and renegotiation laws covering defense contracting.   The Vinson-Trammell Act provisions applicable to aircraft production require that contractors refund any profit exceeding 12% of the price of all contracts completed during a taxable year.[80]   However, contractors covered by the Renegotiation Act are exempted from Vinson-Trammell Act coverage, and therefore we shall focus on the impact of renegotiation here.[81]

The compulsion for, enactment of, and administration of the various excess profit laws have a long and stormy history.[82]   Renegotiation in particular, enacted originally in 1942 and periodically revised and extended since then, has been a subject of almost continual controversy.[83]   As Professor Miller has observed:

[79] Cf. note 47, p. 228 *supra*.

[80] 10 U.S.C. Section 2382.   Procurements of scientific equipment for communications, target detection, navigation, and fire control are exempted if designated for exemption by the appropriate service secretary.   For naval vessels, the profit limitation is 10%.   10 U.S.C. Section 7300.   The Vinson-Trammell Act was originally passed in 1934 (48 *Stat.* 505, Section 3) and has been amended periodically.

[81] All firms whose defense and space sales exceed $1 million in a given year are subjected to renegotiation.

[82] For a most interesting history dating back to the French and Indian War, see Richards C. Osborn, "Background and Evolution of the Renegotiation Concept," *Procurement and Profit Renegotiation,* ed. J. Fred Weston (San Francisco: Wadsworth, 1960), pp. 13–42.   A 20th Century legislative history is found in J. P. Miller, *Pricing of Military Procurements,* pp. 162–174 and 236–239.

[83] The currently applicable statute is the Renegotiation Act of 1951, as extended and amended, 50 U.S.C. Appendix Sections 1211–1233.

The net effect of renegotiation upon procurement is perhaps more hotly debated than any other aspect of the procurement policies pursued during World War II.[84]

In more recent years the debate has subsided little. Indeed, there is an extensive literature on renegotiation, and here no attempt will be made to cover in detail issues already fully explored by other authors.[85] Rather, in this section I shall merely define the basic issue of renegotiation's impact upon automatic contractual incentives, summarize the principal positions found in the literature, and add the insights provided by our case studies.

The principal objective of renegotiation is to eliminate excessive profits on defense contracts.[86] The administrative mechanism for accomplishing this objective is after-the-fact review of contractors' defense activities on an annual total (as opposed to contract-by-contract) basis to determine if profits have been excessive. Obviously, the interpretation given the word "excessive" is of crucial importance. On this point the Renegotiation Act provides several general criteria:

In determining excessive profits favorable recognition must be given to the efficiency of the contractor or subcontractor, with particular regard to attainment of quantity and quality production, reduction of costs, and economy in use of materials, facilities, and manpower; and in addition, there shall be taken into consideration the following factors:

(1) Reasonableness of costs and profits, with particular regard to volume of production, normal earnings, and comparison of war and peacetime products;

(2) The net worth, with particular regard to the amount and source of public and private capital employed;

(3) Extent of risk assumed, including the risk incident to reasonable pricing policies;

(4) Nature and extent of contribution to the defense effort, including inventive and developmental contribution and cooperation

[84] *Ibid.,* p. 179.

[85] See, for example, Miller, *Pricing of Military Procurements;* the collection of papers in Weston (ed.) *Procurement and Profit Renegotiation;* and the periodic hearings on renegotiation of the House Committee on Ways and Means and the Senate Committee on Finance, which have responsibility for initiating extensions of the act.

[86] 50 U.S.C. Appendix Section 1211.

with the Government and other contractors in supplying technical assistance;

(5) Character of business, including source and nature of materials, complexity of manufacturing technique, character and extent of subcontracting, and rate of turnover;

(6) Such other factors the consideration of which the public interest and fair and equitable dealing may require, which factors shall be published in the regulations of the Board from time to time as adopted.[87]

In brief, the Renegotiation Board presumably considers efficiency, reasonableness, financial structure, risk, contribution to the defense effort, and character of the contractor's business in ruling on profits.

Renegotiation and Incentives for Efficiency

The principal objective of automatic contractual incentives is to encourage cost control and cost reduction, assuming that optimal time-quality-cost tradeoffs are also secured. This purpose is paralleled in the Renegotiation Board's efficiency criterion. However, there are two situations in which renegotiation might impair incentives for efficiency:

(1) When the efficiency criterion is administered ineptly in renegotiation; that is, if good performance is not consistently rewarded with relatively high allowed profits and poor performance penalized by relatively low allowed profits.

(2) When the several criteria unrelated to efficiency swamp the efficiency criterion, limiting the extent to which profit can vary to correlate with efficiency variations.

Professor Miller's analysis of the World War II experience indicates that for both of these reasons renegotiation did not provide a positive incentive for efficiency, and may in fact have impaired the working of other incentives:

The theory of renegotiation was that allowable profits should be determined in such a way as to reward the contractor who in the light of all circumstances controlled his costs well and sought to use labor and materials efficiently. For greater efficiency the contractor was to receive greater reward in dollar terms. It has been widely alleged, however, that renegotiation far from rewarding

87 50 U.S.C. Appendix Section 1213 (e).

efficiency placed a premium on the incurring of high costs. It has been pointed out that renegotiators were often not in a position to distinguish effectively between an efficient and an inefficient firm because of the absence of adequate tests of relative efficiency. Moreover, it is quite widely believed that the range of allowable profits in terms of which the boards operated was too narrow to allow for significant variations in rewards. There is a general belief that once the pattern of allowable profits had been established, a contractor could expect about the same rate of profit on costs in subsequent years that he had been allowed in his initial renegotiation. Consequently it was argued that far from being rewarded for efforts at cost reduction the contractor had a positive incentive not to reduce his costs any more than necessary.[88]

He concluded that:

. . . it is extremely difficult to negotiate contracts with appropriate incentives to efficient production so long as there is in the background a scheme for recouping excessive profits such as renegotiation. This difficulty remains and becomes intensified in peacetime when patriotic motives for efficiency are inevitably weaker. The extension of renegotiation to peacetime operations threatens to weaken the incentives to efficient production. . .[89]

More recently, the defense industry has presented a united front for repeal or at least amendment of the Renegotiation Act, arguing that it nullifies the incentive effects of fixed-price type contracts.[90] Industry briefs alleged that renegotiation has often eliminated all or most of the incentive profits realized by weapons makers.[91] From this an Aircraft (now Aerospace) Industries Association statement concluded:

This treatment by the Renegotiation Board removes the contractor's incentive to strive for the very cost reductions for which the procuring agency provided the incentive. Thus, the now obso-

[88] *Pricing of Military Procurements,* pp. 181–182.

[89] *Ibid.,* p. 238.

[90] It is curious that the attack on renegotiation of the late 1950's and early 1960's has emphasized the impact on fixed-price incentive contracts even though, as we have seen in Chapter 6, such contracts provide weaker profit-cost correlations than firm fixed-price contracts.

[91] House, Committee on Ways and Means, *Hearings, Extension of the Renegotiation Act* (1958), pp. 79–80.

lete Renegotiation Act acts as a dead hand on the incentive to reduce costs.[92]

A Machinery and Allied Products Institute brief argued:

> The fact is that the mere existence of the renegotiation process is a built-in drag on, and a disincentive to, increased efficiency in defense production. Faced with the certainty that profits beyond some point, the determination of which surpasseth all understanding, will be extracted from him in the laborious, painful, and costly process of renegotiation, a defense contractor has no substantial incentive to strive for superior performance. Indeed, he may reasonably feel that special efforts which result in reduced costs and increased profits will do little more than increase the refund to the Government.[93]

Another industry group, recommending that the Renegotiation Act be amended to exclude incentive-type contracts, stated:

> The uncertainty of renegotiation must be eliminated before defense contractors can appropriately accept and effectively use the incentive philosophy. At the present time many defense contractors are not interested in accepting an incentive-type contract. The Defense establishment has in most cases the power under the present economic and cold-war status to force the incentive-type contract upon its vendors. This, however, does not accomplish the objective. Cost reductions do not come easy. They are not, as some have said, just windfalls. They are the result of hard work, concentrated planning and the exploitation of ingenuity. Many defense contractors might not go to this trouble, whether they have an incentive-type contract or not, if there is any question as to whether they can retain the results of their efforts.[94]

Perhaps the most ardent critic of renegotiation during the late 1950's has been William M. Allen, President of the Boeing Company, who stated in one of his many appearances before a congressional committee:

> Now when we get an incentive contract we go to our supervisors, and we say we have this contract, this is the target. Here is

[92] *Ibid.,* p. 81.

[93] *Ibid.,* p. 130.

[94] National Security Industrial Association, Report of Task Group 8, "New Approaches to Contracting," *Report of Cost Reduction Study* (June 15, 1962), p. 168.

an opportunity to save the Government money and to make some for ourselves in additional earnings. . . . We have an incentive plan in our company which is shared in by all supervisors. This last year 8,000 supervisors shared in it. Now, when I say that to my people, and I have had this experience, I have had a foreman raise his hand and say, "But having done this what about those boys that second-guess us."

There is not any answer to that. That is an example of how to kill incentive in industry and in defense industry. The Renegotiation Act is not being administered in accordance with its intention. No one, certainly I do not, want to earn earnings beyond what are reasonable and proper. But this matter of incentive is all important, and I only cite it as an example. We must have it. We must have that incentive. We must preserve competition. That is the American way. And it is not being done.[95]

The former chairman of the Renegotiation Board responded to these industry criticisms as follows:

It may sometimes happen that a determination of excessive profits by the Board either approximates or exceeds the amount of the contractor's incentive profits. Apparently the (Aircraft Industries) association believes it useful, as a forensic expedient, to charge that in any such cases the Board has taken away the entire amount of the contractor's incentive profits. This is a snare and a delusion. Incentive profits as such are not eliminated. The Board does not, and indeed could not consistently with the act, isolate profits resulting from the operation of contract incentive provisions and consider such profits separately and apart from the target profits realized on such contracts. The Board's determination is based upon an evaluation of the contractor's entire profits under incentive contracts during the fiscal year, not just the profits realized under the incentive formula, and upon a review of profits from all other renegotiable business performed by the contractor under other types of contracts. Indeed, in more than one case, excessive profits realized under incentive-type contracts have been offset in the Board's determination by deficient profits realized in other segments of the contractor's business. One must not be misled by any numerical similarity between incentive profits and excessive profits; if it exists, it is purely coincidental.[96]

[95] Senate, Committee on Armed Services, *Hearings, Inquiry Into Satellite and Missile Programs* (1958), pp. 1262–1263.

[96] Statement of Thomas Coggeshall in House, Committee on Ways and Means, *Hearings, Extension of the Renegotiation Act* (1958), p. 167.

The Incremental Nature of Incentive Profits

Nevertheless, the industry spokesmen appear to have the sounder case, at least in terms of the reward theory of automatic contractual incentives. Whether or not the specific profits eliminated in renegotiation were so-called incentive profits is essentially irrelevant. The evidence available on renegotiation actions of the 1950's suggests strongly that more weight was placed on criteria such as over-all reasonableness of profits and return on investment than on the efficiency criterion; the efficiency criterion tended to be swamped by other considerations. The amount of profit variation permitted in renegotiation to reflect efficiency differences was at best small, and the emphasis placed upon criteria other than efficiency tended to place a rough ceiling on company profits. To a contractor, incentive profits are incremental profits, since they are contingent upon reducing actual costs once contract pricing provisions have been negotiated. They need not be secured, and they will not be secured unless discretionary cost reduction efforts are deemed worthwhile. When contractor management in fact believes that any incremental profits beyond a certain total amount or rate cannot be retained after renegotiation, those profits will have little lure, and there will be little or no automatic contractual incentive for the incremental cost reductions potentially associated with them.

This notion may be illustrated by a hypothetical example. Let us assume that on the basis of net worth, volume of sales, character of sales, past precedents, and other considerations, the Renegotiation Board believes that Alpha Company profits on the order of $10 million are reasonable. Efficiency is also considered by the Board, but it is given less weight than the combination of other factors, so that a variation of $2 million to reflect efficiency will be permitted. That is, profits of $11 million will be allowed if the firm performs very efficiently, while profits of $9 million will be allowed in the event of poor performance. Assume further that in a given year, Alpha Company has contracts which will yield total profits of $11 million if target costs are just met and $13 million if a 10% average underrun is achieved.[97] Even if it attains a suf-

[97] These figures are chosen to reflect the average experience with renegotiation in fiscal years 1956 through 1960, when refunds ran between

ficiently high level of efficiency to achieve the 10% underrun, Alpha can expect to retain none of the $2 million in incremental incentive profits, and so those profits must have zero utility to the company. Obviously, incremental profits for even larger underruns would also have no net value to Alpha. At best, the firm can expect to receive more favorable consideration in the Renegotiation Board's determination of where in the $9 million–$11 million range its profits should lie.

Of course, recognition by contractors that they must be efficient to gain favorable treatment in renegotiation could create an incentive for efficiency partly offsetting the automatic contractual incentives eliminated through renegotiation. But the effectiveness of this substitute incentive depends upon the Renegotiation Board's ability to convince contractors that it can make valid efficiency judgments — a problem to be considered further in a moment.

In a recent key decision on the reasonability of refunds required by the Renegotiation Board, the U.S. Tax Court handed down a dictum which suggests a failure to understand that automatic contractual incentives operate on an incremental basis:

> Simple arithmetic demonstrates that the 8 percent profit factor [on total costs] is of more importance dollarwise than the 20 percent factor [on underruns and overruns] until cost underruns approach 40 percent at which point the two factors take on equal weight. It is only at this point, which we think is unrealistic, where real incentive to produce at low cost begins to exist under such contracts.[98]

In other words, the court argued that only when the amount of profit obtained through the contractor's 20% share of underruns became as large absolutely as the original target profit (8% of

---

13% and 16% of renegotiable profits for those firms which paid any refunds at all. Thus, a 15% refund on profits of $13 million would leave the company with slightly more than $11 million — a profit level considered by the Renegotiation Board to be proper for efficient operations in this example. The incentive profit figures assume operation under fixed-price incentive contracts (17% contractor sharing) with a target cost of roughly $120 million and a target profit rate of about 9.2%.

[98] *In the Matter of Boeing Airplane Company,* 37 U.S. Tax Court Reports 613, 649 (January 10, 1962). Appeals to clarify the decision on this point were denied.

target cost) did incentives for efficiency take effect. But such reasoning, emphasizing the *absolute amount* of profit awarded in the target and incentive categories, completely overlooks the basic reward theory of automatic contractual incentives: continuous correlation of *increments* of profit with *increments* of cost reduction.

Cost Padding and Inefficiency

Still the possibility remains that underruns yielding so-called incentive profits may actually be due to the negotiation of pessimistic cost targets instead of increased efficiency, and in this respect the Renegotiation Board's actions are at least partially vindicated by good intentions, if not good theory. The Board has tried to distinguish between profits gained at the bargaining table and profits gained through efficiency measures. In 1958 it amended its regulations to include the following profit determination criterion:

> 1. The Board will take into consideration the extent to which any differences between estimated costs (target costs) and actual costs are the result of the efficiency of the contractor.
> 2. The contractor may furnish, or the Board may require the contractor to furnish:
>   a. A breakdown of the estimated costs;
>   b. A corresponding breakdown of its actual costs; and
>   c. The reasons for any variances between such breakdowns with particular reference to whether such variances are attributable to the performance of the contractor or to other causes.[99]

There are, however, two problems in implementing this regulation. First, underruns may be caused not only by efficiency or deliberate cost padding, but also by good luck on cost factors which at the outset of a production effort could be predicted only within a range of uncertainty. As we have seen, on fixed-price incentive contracts actual cost outcomes have tended to be normally distributed around the mean outcome, with standard deviation of roughly 10 percentage points. The Renegotiation Board is clearly justified in recouping profits gained due to a persistent underrun bias in the mean outcome. But outcomes which *by chance* are more favorable than the mean will also give rise to incentive profits not jus-

---

[99] U.S. Renegotiation Board, *Regulations,* 1460.9.

tifiable on strict efficiency grounds, and such profits are subject to recapture by the Renegotiation Board. On the other hand, outcomes which by chance prove less favorable than the mean bring about profit reductions which, unless favorable and unfavorable outcomes cancel out within a single fiscal year, will simply be ignored in renegotiation, pulling down the contractor's long-run average profit rate. For the Renegotiation Board to recoup profits gained purely by chance, but to ignore low-profit outcomes due to chance, is plainly inequitable. But more important, such a practice is likely to discourage the acceptance of contracts with strong profit-cost correlations. By consistently accepting high sharing proportions a contractor has much to lose and little to gain if random overruns lead to low profits or losses while random underruns yield profits which tend to be recouped.[100]

Second, it is questionable whether the Renegotiation Board is able to make discerning efficiency judgments. Appointments to the headquarters board, which rules on the most important cases, are made on a political basis. Board members sometimes have no prior experience with the weapons acquisition process and as a rule no technical competence.[101] Although normally the specific considerations underlying Renegotiation Board determinations are not released, it was possible to learn the Board's evaluation of prime contractor performance in one program covered by our program evaluation experiment.[102] The Board considered the principal contractor's performance in that program as a favorable factor, deserving of enhanced profits. And yet the program re-

---

[100] Deviations from targets due to technological uncertainty have been emphasized here because the equities are clear-cut. However, as the mathematical appendix to this chapter shows, recouping profits gained through the contractor's good luck at the bargaining table may also discourage the acceptance of high sharing proportions. And if bargaining advantage in the target-setting process is randomly distributed in the long run, one might argue that it is inequitable to recoup any profits but those gained through an *average* underrun bias.

[101] The backgrounds of the first four Kennedy Administration appointees are as follows: Herschel C. Loveless was former governor of Iowa. Thomas D'Alesandro, Jr., was former mayor of Baltimore. William M. Burkhalter was a lawyer specializing in government contract law and securities law. Jack Beaty was associated with a food and drug brokerage firm since 1942.

[102] Cf. Chapter 4 *supra*.

ceived the lowest contractor performance ranking of the eight programs in our evaluation sample. Even modest familiarity with the program in question would have revealed that it was inefficiently conducted. Likewise, the Board's efficiency judgments in renegotiating North American Aviation profits for 1953 and 1954 were sharply criticized by the U.S. Tax Court in an appellate decision:

> Respondent [the Board] argues that in the performance of most of its major contracts petitioner was inefficient in its operations; that the quality of its products was deficient; that it failed to reduce costs and was not economical in the use of materials, facilities, and manpower.
>
> The evidence of record is overwhelmingly to the contrary. It shows that in each of these categories petitioner was at or near the top of the aircraft industry.

*   *   *   *   *

> [the] deputy director of procurement and production of the Air Force . . . testified that "North American's efficiency, both as to cost to produce and initial technical design far surpassed any other manufacturer."

*   *   *   *   *

> Respondent contends that the airplanes built by petitioner, particularly Models F–86D and F–86F, which were produced in large quantities, the F–100, and some of the other Air Force and Navy models, were of inferior quality. The evidence as a whole refutes this contention. . . . All of these airplanes admittedly fell short of perfection — and all of the witnesses agreed that no perfect airplane has ever been built — but they were the best of their types produced up to that time.[103]

Although this is meager evidence, it certainly raises doubts about the Board's ability to make "efficiency" evaluations.

Apparently this deficiency has been recognized by the Board. In 1961 and 1962 arrangements were worked out to build up data on contractor efficiency in procurement agency contract files and to provide the Board with "more precise and discriminating reports than . . . heretofore furnished" for use in evaluating contractor

---

[103] *In the Matter of North American Aviation, Inc.,* 39 T. C. No. 19 (October 25, 1962).

performance.[104]   When conflicting opinions or self-serving procurement agency briefs are presented, however, the Board will probably be in no position to make sound independent judgments.

Case Study Evidence on Renegotiation's Effects

Thus far the question of renegotiation's impact on contractual incentives has been examined mainly on the basis of published statements and theoretical considerations. The evidence provided by our case histories contrasts sharply with what the declarations of industry spokesmen imply.

During the course of our 12 weapons program case studies many contractor representatives were questioned as to why particular technical decisions were made or not made, how certain contractual arrangements influenced their behavior, what factors incited or impeded specific cost reduction efforts, and so on.   In this essentially nondirective interviewing, the subject of renegotiation was simply never broached by contractor personnel as a factor relevant in specific decisions or actions.   To be sure, a few interviewees (notably those in top management positions concerned with financial matters) spontaneously raised general objections to renegotiation, including the objection that it reduced the incentive for cost control and cost reduction.   Yet in no instance was a direct link established between renegotiation and any particular operating action or inaction, even when company representatives were pressed to support their generalizations with specific examples.   In short, our case study research suggested that the existence of renegotiation was not a significant consideration in weapons program operations and decisions.

There are at least two possible explanations for this somewhat surprising finding.   First, the field interviews for our case studies were conducted during 1958 and 1959, a period of declining weapons industry profits.[105]   As Table 8.3 shows, the average profit rate

[104] U.S. Renegotiation Board, *Release No. 3–62,* April 17, 1962. Paragraph 1–319 was added to the *Armed Services Procurement Regulation,* requiring government contracting officers to maintain detailed files on performance in each contract for use by the Renegotiation Board.

[105] Reasons for this decline included the increasing use of cost reimbursement contracts, with consequently lower negotiated and realized profit rates; increased contractor absorption of research, proposal preparation, and

TABLE 8.3

Sales, Profit, and Refund Statistics of Renegotiation: 1956–1962

| Fiscal Year | All Firms Filing Renegotiation Reports | | | Firms Required to Make Refunds | | | |
	Renegotiable Sales (millions)	Renegotiable Profits (millions)	Profit Rate	Renegotiable Sales (millions)	Original Profit Rate	Total Refunds (millions)	Allowed Profit Rate
1956	$29,838	$1,897	6.4%	$7,854	12.1%	$153	10.2%
1957	28,657	1,638	5.7	8,661	10.9	151	9.1
1958	27,100	1,310	4.8	6,796	11.1	113	9.4
1959	26,578	1,118	4.2	4,279	10.4	61	9.0
1960	28,853	1,156	4.0	4,583	8.8	53	7.6
1961	25,084	909	3.6	1,554	8.6	17	7.5
1962	29,262	916	3.1	n.a.	n.a.	8	n.a.

SOURCE: Annual Reports of the Renegotiation Board. All profit data are before taxes.

on all renegotiable sales of defense contractors fell from 6.4% before taxes in fiscal year 1956 — the first year for which comprehensive data are available — to 4.8% in 1958 and 4.2% in 1959. Table 8.3 also manifests a steady decline in the volume of sales subjected to excessive profit determinations and in the amount of profits declared to be excessive. Since there is a lag of approximately three years between the time when profits are accrued and the time when they are renegotiated, the refunds demanded in fiscal years 1961 and 1962 should be associated with earnings reported in 1958 and 1959. Total refunds during 1961 and 1962 amounted to only 1% of all renegotiable profits realized by contractors during 1958 and 1959.

These results suggest that contractors had little reason to expect the loss of incremental incentive profits as a result of renegotiation. Yet this explanation is not altogether consistent with the fact that, during the same period, industry spokesmen were publicly arguing most vigorously that renegotiation eliminated incentive profits and hence weakened incentives for cost reduction. It may well be that industry briefs were influenced more by emotion and memories of the post-Korean defense profits boom than by sober analysis of the weapons industry's actual position during the late 1950's.

Second, it is possible that renegotiation captured mainly profits of low utility with only a minor influence on contractor behavior. As Table 8.3 shows, companies required to make refunds through renegotiation were still allowed to retain average before-tax profit margins ranging from 10.2% of sales in 1956 to 7.5% in 1961. Incremental profits above these allowable margins may have had rather low utility to contractors. If so, all that renegotiation did was weaken already feeble contractual incentives for cost reduction. Such an explanation is consistent with the findings of earlier sections.

In sum, it would appear that renegotiation had fairly little net impact upon contractor behavior in recent weapons development and production programs. Even if statutory renegotiation did not exist, many (although undoubtedly not all) defense contractors would probably consider it disadvantageous to accrue and retain

---

other costs; and the negotiation of generally tighter cost targets due to increasing competition. Cf. pp. 142, 150, and 215–216 *supra*. See also Peck and Scherer, pp. 208–209.

large profits on fixed-price type contracts. Repealing the Renegotiation Act could eliminate the quasi-illegality of windfall profits, but it could not eradicate the suspicions that high profits were obtained not through increased efficiency, but by taking advantage of government negotiators at the bargaining table. Most firms intending to remain active in defense contracting are likely to view the potential injury that these suspicions could inflict upon their government relations as more serious than the loss of incremental profits through renegotiation. In such cases the effect of renegotiation in weakening contractual incentives is clearly redundant and of secondary importance.

AUTOMATIC CONTRACTUAL INCENTIVES FOR STABILIZED PRODUCTION

We have learned that the behavioral effects of automatic contractual incentives depend significantly upon the strength of the profit-cost correlations employed and the tightness of cost targets. Firm fixed-price relationships, with their dollar-for-dollar correlation between cost avoidance and profit, have a more potent incentive effect than overrun- and underrun-sharing fixed-price incentive and cost-plus-incentive-fee contracts, which in turn have a stronger effect than CPFF contracts, other things being equal. Tightly negotiated contracts which confront the contractor with a substantial risk of financial loss tend to be more effective than loosely negotiated contracts, other things being equal.

The ability of government representatives to negotiate strong profit-cost correlations and tight cost targets depends in turn partly upon the degree of production cost uncertainty. Cost uncertainties decline as production becomes more stabilized; that is, as the introduction of engineering changes subsides and as the contractor accumulates experience producing its assigned items.

As costs become less uncertain, contractors generally grow more receptive toward firm fixed-price contracts. At the same time, the government's relative bargaining power tends to increase. The accumulation of historical cost data decreases the disparity between contractor and government knowledge of costs, and opportunities for cost analysis increase.[106] Furthermore, as we have seen in

---

[106] However, as stressed repeatedly, the really important opportunities for cost reduction lie not so much in the examination of historical cost data

Chapter 5, once the rate of engineering change introduction falls off (although many advanced weapon system and subsystem programs never really reach this stage), the government may be able to threaten or actually to initiate breakout for competitive bidding to put additional pressure on prices. In general, therefore, as weapons production stabilizes, the opportunities for implementing stronger automatic contractual incentives expand.

Even in the later stages of weapon system and subsystem production programs, however, there are limits on the effectiveness of contractual incentives. First, unless the government negotiator's bargaining power or skill is great, conversion to firm fixed-price contracts will not coincide with tightly negotiated prices, for contractors will resist the change if they perceive a substantial pricing risk. Second, contractors will often find it disadvantageous to

FIGURE 8.11

Cost Reduction Equilibria Under Firm Fixed-Price
and Fixed-Price Incentive Contracts

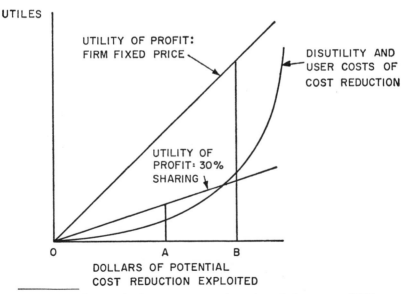

as in improving production processes and product designs — possibilities whose recognition typically requires more technical competence than government cost analysts possess.

achieve substantial underruns and hence high profits because of the possible repercussions on their relations with the government. Finally, even the dollar-for-dollar profit-cost correlations of firm fixed-price contracts could be insufficient to incite certain kinds of cost reduction, especially when holding on to presently unneeded personnel, "making" items in-house which should be subcontracted to more efficient specialist vendors, and so on, can enhance a firm's future competitive position. Yet the margin at which cost reductions are rejected undoubtedly shifts to a higher level of efficiency when stronger profit-cost correlations are enforced. This is illustrated in Figure 8.11, which assumes linear utility of profit on a firm fixed-price contract (100% sharing) and a fixed-price incentive contract (30% sharing). The firm fixed-price equilibrium *OB* is clearly more efficient than the fixed-price incentive equilibrium *OA*.

CONCLUSION

The analysis in this chapter suggests a general conclusion that the automatic contractual incentives normally attainable in advanced weapon system and subsystem production programs are of limited effectiveness.

There are several reasons why this is so. Most are related to the fact that firms usually do not maximize accounting profits in a strict sense during the short run of a single contract. We have seen, first, that short-run accounting profit sacrifices are often accepted in order to secure enhanced long-run profits. By incurring costs and thereby foregoing incentive profits, a firm can improve follow-on production prospects, build its reputation for quality, and maintain a work force in being to capture and execute future programs. Second, reducing costs is difficult and unpleasant, and therefore has disutility to contractor managers. This disutility offsets and often exceeds the utility afforded by short-run incentive profit increments. Third, firms are more strongly incited to efficiency-increasing measures by the risk of loss than by the possibility of earning profit increments at fairly high levels of profitability. But given their inferior knowledge of cost factors and the lack of directly comparable substitute products, it is seldom possible for government personnel to negotiate weapon system and subsystem production contract cost targets and other provisions which confront the contractor with a significant risk of loss. Fourth, earning large profits on any single contract arouses suspicions of cost padding and profiteering, encouraging more cynical future negotiations and perhaps damaging corporate reputation. Finally, when over-all company profits are relatively high, renegotiation tends to absorb the incremental profits gained through cost reduction.

It is sometimes argued that even though uncertainties in the process of cost target negotiation lead to a wide distribution of overruns and underruns, a system of automatic contractual incentives can be presumed effective in the aggregate as long as the mean of actual outcomes roughly equals the mean of target outcomes. This view has been used, for example, to support the application of firm fixed-price contracts to production situations involving substantial uncertainties. Historical evidence shows that in fact mean actual outcomes have not departed greatly from mean target outcomes: the mean percentage underrun for the 528 fixed-price type contracts analyzed in this chapter was only 2.25%. Yet such a view ignores several important problems. In particular, it overlooks the relationship between the diminishing marginal utility of contract profits and contractor behavior.

On contracts with strong profit-cost correlations and tight targets, posing a significant risk of loss, fairly robust incentives for cost control and cost reduction exist. But when targets are loose and the contractor perceives little risk of loss and a high probability of ample profits, the incremental profits attainable through cost reduction usually have low utility, and the incentive for cost reduction is weak. Unless the government is able in the future to bargain more potently than it has in the past, contracts with strong profit-cost correlations and tight targets are likely to comprise but a small minority of all contracts.

If, in the absence of enhanced bargaining power, the government attempts to increase the strength of contractual incentives by demanding contracts with higher contractor sharing proportions, contractors will react by insisting upon more pessimistic cost targets. And when contracts are negotiated with large cushions, those cushions will tend to turn into cost rather than additional profits. As a result, a pronounced underrun bias — the presumed indicator of unsatisfactory incentive system operation — will not in fact materialize.

More generally, there are two basic weaknesses in a "law of averages" approach to an automatic contractual incentives system: (1) Although below-average profits do offset above-average profits in a statistical sense, contractors tend to choose negotiation strategies and make operating decisions in terms of particular, not aggregate, contract profit implications; and (2) above-average contract profit expectations do not have the same behavioral effects as below-average profit expectations.

For all these reasons a system of automatic contractual incentives leaves much to be desired as a means of motivating efficiency in advanced weapons production and development. Still such a system undoubtedly stimulates at least some cost control efforts, and when strong profit-cost correlations and tight cost targets can be achieved simultaneously, a fairly effective incentive for efficiency may be created. The automatic contractual incentives approach may well be the best we can do in a very imperfect and uncertain world. Whether or not this is true must be decided in the balanced appraisal of alternative incentive systems beginning in Chapter 11.

CHAPTER 9

Variations in Negotiated Profit Rates as an Incentive Approach

ANOTHER WAY OF PROVIDING profit incentives for good performance is the correlation of negotiated profit rates with past performance. The basic idea is simple — indeed, so simple that it is commonly overlooked in discussions of contractual incentives. If a firm's performance has been superior on past work, higher-than-average negotiated profit rates would be applied to contracts for future work. If its performance has been deficient, lower-than-average profit rates would be applied to new contracts.

Since these profit-performance correlations would be effected after conscious, deliberate evaluation of past performance, the approach comes much closer to being an administered incentive system than those systems which operate automatically once correlation formulas and target profits and prices have been established. Consequently, if effective incentives are to be created, one further condition is essential: the system must be administered consistently, so that contractors actually expect their future profit rates to be relatively high if their current performance is good or relatively low if their current performance is poor. If this expectation is lacking, there will be no special reason (at least in terms of the particular system) for contractors to prefer performing well.

ACTUAL PROFIT RATE VARIATIONS AND THEIR CAUSES

Thus, for a negotiated profit rate incentive system to function, two main conditions must be met: (1) there must be variations in negotiated profit rates; and (2) the profit rate variations must be significantly and consistently related to variations in contractor performance. Let us begin by determining whether these conditions have been satisfied during the 1950's.

The first condition is readily fulfilled. If all contracts are considered together, a fairly high variability of negotiated profit rates — from 0% on cost-plus-no-fee contracts to as much as 15% — can be found. If exceptional situations such as those conducive to no-fee relationships are disregarded, the lower limit tends toward 4%.[1]

What are the reasons for this variability in the 4% through 15% range? Prior to a substantial revision scheduled to appear after this volume went to press, the *Armed Services Procurement Regulation* listed a number of factors which government negotiators had to weigh in negotiating contract profit rates.[2] These can be paraphrased as follows:

a. Degree of risk. The less pricing risk assumed by the contractor, the greater the number of contingencies provided for, and the less firm the commitment to performance specifications, the lower should be the profit.

b. Nature of the work to be performed. The more complex, difficult, or unusual the work to be performed, the higher should be the profit.

c. Extent of government assistance. The more assistance contributed by the government in terms of facilities, financing, etc., the less should be the profit.

d. Extent of the contractor's investment. The more the contractor's investment in a contract (both equity and borrowed capital), the greater should be the profit.

e. Character of contractor's business. Recognition must be given to the type of business normally carried on by the contractor, the complexity of manufacturing techniques, the rate of capital turnover, and the effect of the procurement on the contractor's business.

f. Contractor's performance. ". . . the contractor's past and present performance should be evaluated in such areas as quality of product, quality control, scrap and spoilage, efficiency in cost control (including need for and reasonableness of cost incurred), meeting delivery schedules, timely compliance with contractual provisions, creative ability in product development (giving con-

[1] As Table 6.2 shows, cost-plus-no-fee contracts amounted to 2.3% of military procurement by dollar volume in fiscal year 1962.

[2] *Armed Services Procurement Regulation,* 1960 edition, 3–808.2. The revision institutes the so-called weighted guideline approach to profit determination, which essentially is a more formalized, mechanistic method of implementing the factors summarized here. Cf. note 15 *infra.*

sideration to commercial potential of product), engineering (including inventive, design simplification, and development contributions), management of subcontract programs, and any unsual services furnished by the contractor. Where a contractor has consistently achieved excellent results in the foregoing areas in comparison with other contractors in similar circumstances, such performance merits a proportionately greater opportunity for profit or fee. Conversely, a poor record in this regard should be reflected. . . ."

g. Subcontracting. To the extent that the prime contractor has less responsibility and risk on subcontracted work, profit should be lower than on in-house work. However, to the extent that subcontracting provides a better product, lower cost, aids small business, etc., the profit rate on subcontracted work may be increased.

h. Unrealistic estimates. If there is evidence that the contractor typically submits unrealistically high cost estimates, a lower profit rate should be considered.

Clearly, contractor performance has been only one of several criteria influencing the variability of negotiated profit rates. We must therefore attempt to isolate the relative importance of each major criterion.

Pricing Risk

Without doubt the most important single reason for variations in negotiated profit rates has been presumed pricing risk. It is generally believed that cost-plus-fixed-fee contracts impose the least pricing risk on contractors and firm fixed-price contracts the most, other contract types requiring intermediate degrees of contractor risk assumption.[3] The greater the presumed risk, the higher the negotiated profit rate, as the following averages estimated from a variety of service data show:

Contract Type	Average Negotiated Profit as a Percentage of Target Cost
Cost-plus-fixed-fee	6.4%
Cost-plus-incentive-fee	7.0
Fixed-price incentive	8.6
Redeterminable fixed-price	9.6
Firm fixed-price	11.5

[3] But as we have seen in Chapter 8, risk depends not only on the strength of the profit-cost correlation provisions, but also on the uncertainty of cost outcomes and the tightness of cost targets.

Within specific contract type categories there is some variation in negotiated profit rates, but the range of variation is typically narrow, as the frequency distributions in Figures 9.1 through 9.4 illustrate. A 2% range of variation includes 78% by dollar volume of the Air Force CPFF and CPIF contracts (Figure 9.1), 92% by number of the Navy fixed-price incentive contracts (Figure 9.2), 76% by number of the Navy redeterminable fixed-price contracts (Figure 9.3), and 54% by number of the Army redeterminable fixed-price contracts (Figure 9.4). A 3% range includes 91%, 98%, 87%, and 66% respectively of the contracts in these samples.

Some of the variation within contract type categories is also explained by differences in pricing risk. For example, of the 47 fixed-price incentive contracts covered by Figure 9.2, the two with the lowest profit rates (7.3% and 7.5%) had low sharing proportions (each 10%) and high price ceilings (30% and 35% above target cost). Thus, they were relatively low risk relationships. The two contracts with the highest profit rates (each 10.0%) were for guided missile production, while all but one of the other 45 contracts covered manned aircraft production — a more traditional field, presumably involving less uncertainty than guided missile work. Similarly, government procurement agencies generally pay higher profits on contracts with early redetermination points than on those with late redetermination and hence less risk to the contractor. To illustrate, all of the 63 Navy contracts represented by Figure 9.3 were finally redeterminable at 20% to 40% of completion, after which they became firm fixed-price instruments. The average negotiated profit rate for this group was 10.4% of target costs. On the other hand, most of the 156 Army contracts covered by Figure 9.4 were redeterminable at 100% completion. Presumably these involved less pricing risk, and their average negotiated profit rate was 9.1% — 1.3 points less than the Navy redeterminable contracts.

We should also expect pricing risk, and hence the negotiated profit rate, to vary inversely with the ratio of redeterminable contract ceiling price to base price. However, a correlation of these magnitudes for the 156 Army redeterminable contracts yielded an insignificant r^2 of .005.

FIGURE 9.1

Originally Negotiated Profit Rates on CPFF and CPIF Contracts
Held by 22 Major Air Force Contractors and 38 Small
Business Concerns in 1957 and 1958

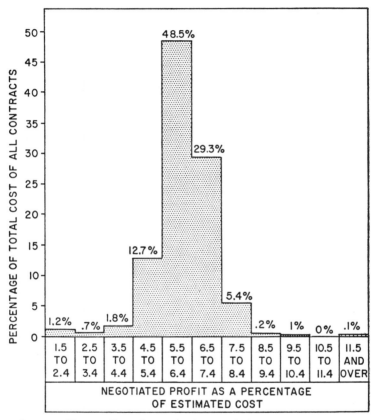

Source: House, Committee on Appropriations, *Hearings, Department of Defense Appropriations for 1960,* Part 5, p. 577; from an Air
Force study covering approximately 1,500 contracts with a total value
of roughly $7 billion.

Contractor Investment

One important role of profit is to regulate the flow of capital
investment into and out of industries. In this sense the relevant
profit concept is not rate of return on sales, but rate of return on

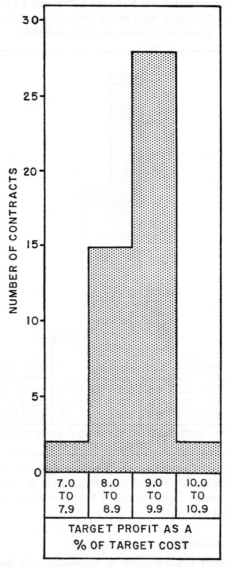

FIGURE 9.2

Originally Negotiated Profit Rates on 47 Navy Aircraft
and Guided Missile Fixed-Price Incentive Contracts

Source: Navy data supplied by the Office of the Assistant Secretary
of Defense, Installations and Logistics. Cost outcomes of these contracts are shown in Figure 8.3.

FIGURE 9.3

Originally Negotiated Profit Rates on 63 Navy Redeterminable
Fixed-Price Contracts With Domestic Firms

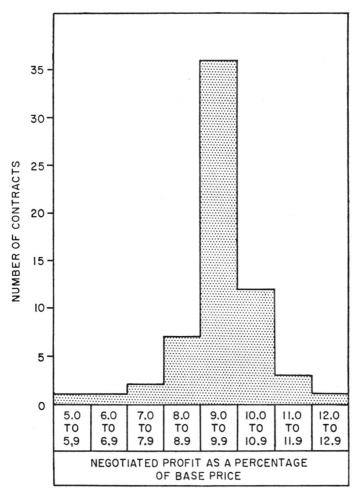

Source: Navy data supplied by the Office of the Assistant Secretary
of Defense, Installations and Logistics. This sample is the same as
that used to show cost outcomes in Figure 8.6, except that here three
contracts with foreign firms have been deleted.

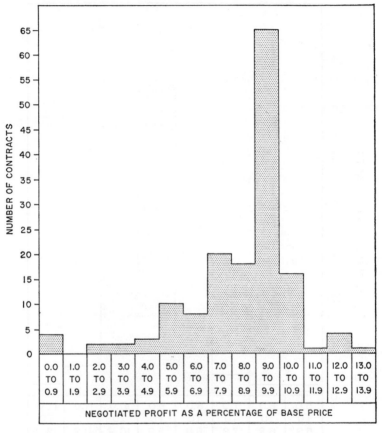

FIGURE 9.4

Originally Negotiated Profit Rates on 156 Army Ordnance
and Signal Corps Redeterminable Fixed-Price Contracts

Source: Army Ordnance and Signal Corps data supplied by the
Office of the Assistant Secretary of Defense, Installations and Logistics.
Cost outcomes of these contracts are shown in Figure 8.5.

some measure of invested capital.[4]   If the rate of return on invested
capital is higher than the marginal cost of capital, an industry will
tend to attract new capital investment.   If the opposite is true,
there will be little or no new investment, and when capital already

[4] Cf. note 13, p. 11 *supra*.

invested has attractive alternative uses, there will be net disinvestment. To the extent that the government wishes to encourage private investment by contractors, it must pay higher profit rates on sales involving substantial contractor investment than on sales involving relatively little private investment.

This need is recognized at least generally in government procurement regulations and practice. Profit rates tend to be higher for contractors who furnish their own plant and equipment than for firms using government-furnished facilities. The range of variation to reflect such differences is on the order of one percentage point, our case studies revealed. Similarly, profit rates are typically adjusted to reflect the amount of work-in-process financing provided by contractors. For example, when Department of Defense policy was altered in 1957 to allow only 80% progress payments instead of the 100% rate previously in effect, the profit rates of contractors who assumed the 20% financing burden were increased to compensate for additional interest costs.[5] In one apparently typical program this change added seven-tenths of a percentage point to the contractor's profit rate.

Thus, adjustments are made to reflect differences in capital investment requirements. Whether the adjustments have been sufficient to encourage the optimal amount of contractor investment cannot be determined here. Certainly, many difficult questions are encountered in establishing the relative desirability of contractor vs. government investment, in relating investment requirements to specific contracts, and in setting profit rates just sufficient on the average to attract the desired amount of investment. The problem of enunciating general contract profit rate policies is complicated by the existence of considerable excess capacity in many sectors of the defense industry while demand for investment in the newer fields runs high. The research underlying this study was not focused on these questions, which clearly deserve further attention.[6]

[5] The change from 100% to 80% progress payments was initiated by Department of Defense Directive 7800.6 of November 1, 1957. After this policy was criticized by the General Accounting Office on grounds that the government could borrow the required funds at lower interest costs than contractors, a return to 100% progress payments was ordered on March 15, 1961.

[6] The government-sponsored Logistics Management Institute conducted a study of defense contract profit policies with special emphasis on the in-

Extent of Subcontracting

Although the *Armed Services Procurement Regulation* stated that "it is not possible to define precisely the exact profit or fee treatment to be accorded each [subcontracting] situation," [7] as a rule contractors have received a lower profit rate on subcontracted work than on work performed in-house. For example, the profit structure on Western Electric's Nike Hercules production prime contracts during 1959 was as follows:

> Western Electric's contract provides for a 10-percent profit on "inhouse" work on NIKE–HERCULES. Western Electric receives either a 6- or 3-percent profit on that part of the NIKE–HERCULES system subcontracted to Douglas. The 6-percent profit is received for items manufactured by Douglas, but furnished to Western Electric for further manufacturing operations. The 3-percent profit is received on items furnished directly by Douglas to the Government. In both instances Western retains responsibility for the system, however, the lower fee does reflect Western Electric's reduced engineering responsibility. The Western Electric profit rate on items furnished by some 5,000 subcontractors, other than Douglas, varies between 3 and 10 percent. The particular rate in each instance will depend on the size of the subcontract and whether the item is a component or subassembly furnished direct to Western Electric or delivered directly to the Government, and the extent of assistance, engineering, etc. furnished by Western to the subcontractor.[8]

This differential treatment of subcontracted work causes average profit rates on contracts with a high proportion of subcontracting to be lower than profit rates on contracts of the same type with

---

vestment problem. However, the report it issued in early 1963 is rather disappointing, since the most fundamental problems were sidestepped to concentrate on essentially procedural matters. For example, the report notes repeatedly that there is a superabundance of firms competing for defense dollars, but it does not attempt to determine how negotiated profit rates can be adjusted to secure the optimal inflow and outflow of resources. Cf. Logistics Management Institute, *Study of Profit or Fee Policy* (Project 5B1, undated), pp. 52–59 and 86.

[7] *Armed Services Procurement Regulation,* 1960 edition, 3–808.2 (h).

[8] House, Committee on Appropriations, *Hearings, Department of Defense Appropriations for 1960,* Part 5, p. 169.

relatively little subcontracting. Differences in the amount and kind of subcontracting can account for as much as two percentage points in profit rate variation.

It should be noted that even though the structure of profit rates for subcontracted Nike Hercules components during 1959 was fairly typical of government practice, the Nike effort was singled out by a subcommittee of the Senate Government Operations Committee as an example of "profit pyramiding." [9]   The so-called McClellan Committee alleged that prime contractor Western Electric received unjustifiably high profits on its Nike subcontracts and that subcontractor Douglas likewise commanded unjustifiably high profits on its third tier subcontracts. Two special circumstances drew attention to the Nike program's profit structure. First, an unusually high proportion of Western Electric's Nike production contract receipts — 75% by cost — went into subcontracts and purchase orders.[10]   By way of comparison, the average subcontracting proportion for major weapons contractors during the late 1950's ran between 49% and 58%.[11]   Second, in its early years the Nike subcontract profit structure was not as elaborately differentiated as in 1959, and on many subcontracted items which brought a 3% profit in 1959, the override had been 6% or higher.[12] Both of these conditions arose largely because the Nike program was in many respects the first and perhaps the most extensive application of the weapon system prime contractor management approach to weapons development. As a result, there were no clear profit structure precedents when the first Nike production contracts were negotiated under the pressure of Korean conflict and Soviet atomic bomb threat urgency during the early 1950's.

It is likely that the profit rates applied to subcontracted work early in the Nike program were higher than they needed to be, since subsequent reductions were accepted by the principal contractors with no ill effects on program execution. Nevertheless, a policy of paying little or no profit override on subcontracted work

[9] Senate, Committee on Government Operations, Permanent Subcommittee on Investigations, *Hearings, Pyramiding of Profits and Costs in the Missile Procurement Program* (1962), pp. 1–545.

[10] *Ibid.,* p. 416.

[11] Peck and Scherer, pp. 624–625.

[12] After 1959 even lower profit overrides — in some cases 0% — were negotiated on Nike production contracts. Cf. pp. 104–106 *supra.*

would clearly be unsound, since it would undoubtedly aggravate the undesirable tendency of prime contractors to perform work in-house which can be done more efficiently by specialist vendors.[13] Furthermore, at least some profit override must be offered if the government wants capable firms to accept responsibility as weapon system managers. The magnitude of this override should vary from case to case, with relative bargaining power playing a more important role than rigid policy precedents.

Contractor Bargaining Power

Contractor bargaining power also affects profit rate negotiations in a more general way. Historically, aircraft companies have tended to receive lower profit rates than firms in such industries as electrical equipment, electronics, and chemicals. This is suggested in part by the following breakdown of negotiated profit rates from the sample of Air Force CPFF and CPIF contracts covered by Figure 9.1:

Procurement Category	*Dollar-Weighted Average Profit Rate (Percentage of Cost)*
Electronics	6.91%
Research and development	6.49
Missiles	6.49
Engines	6.36
Airframes	5.86
Average for all categories	6.19%

Profit rates averaged about one percentage point higher on electronics work than on airframe work. This difference is partly due to the tendency of electronics firms to have a higher investment in company-owned facilities than aircraft manufacturers. But it is also explained by the greater bargaining power of electrical equipment and electronics firms, which have more alternative commercial opportunities for employing their resources than aircraft companies. Our case studies revealed that for a given program and a given proportion of government facilities financing, electronics firms averaged from one-fourth to one-half percentage point more negotiated profit on CPFF contracts than aircraft manufacturers.

Obviously, bargaining power varies not only from industry to in-

[13] Cf. Peck and Scherer, pp. 386–394.

dustry, but also from company to company within an industry. For instance, three of the four Navy redeterminable fixed-price contracts with the highest profit rates (11% to 13%) shown in Figure 9.3 were held by a single firm which had many nondefense resource employment opportunities and which is known to bargain especially vigorously over its defense contract profit rates. Our case studies disclosed that the same firm customarily obtained CPFF profit rates more than a half percentage point higher than the average rate in its own industry.

Special bargaining situations may lead to even wider variations from the average. For example, while the "going rate" for ballistic missile "hardware" contractors was 6% to 7%, the Air Force initially awarded the Ramo-Wooldridge Corporation, its systems engineering contractor, a 14.3% fee. This was done primarily because Ramo-Wooldridge agreed not to produce "hardware" in the programs it coordinated, thereby foregoing an opportunity for sales growth and increased profits.[14] On the other hand, firms anxious for competitive reasons to obtain work in certain fields have sometimes accepted no-fee contracts or CPFF contracts with unusually low profit rates.

The Nature of the Work Performed

Negotiated profit rates also vary with the nature of the particular work being performed. Profits for research and development contracts have generally run about 1% higher than the rates awarded on CPFF production contracts. Some government procurement

[14] Cf. House, Committee on Government Operations, *Eleventh Report, Organization and Management of Missile Programs* (1959), pp. 45–46 and 87–88. "Bargaining" is perhaps not quite the appropriate word in this case, since Ramo-Wooldridge allowed the Air Force to set its profit rate unilaterally. However, under the circumstances this may have been the most effective bargaining strategy possible. As the above House report observed (p. 88), "In letting the Air Force set the fee without company bargaining, it appears to the subcommittee that the company made a virtue out of the necessities of the moment." It should be noted that the 14.3% rate was set before the Air Force had any basis other than work on a study contract for evaluating the new Ramo-Wooldridge organization's past performance. Later the profit rate was reduced to 10% to make it more compatible with profits awarded on other Air Force contracts, and still later a not-for-profit organization (the Aerospace Corporation) was founded to take over the systems engineering role formerly held by Ramo-Wooldridge.

agencies have gone even further in this respect, applying different percentage rates for different kinds of activity to arrive at the over-all rate they will attempt to negotiate on any given contract. For instance, to establish a negotiation target on one contract, government contracting personnel applied a 10% rate to research and development engineering labor, 9% to production engineering labor, 7% to factory labor, 5% to engineering materials, 3% to travel costs, etc.[15]

Interservice Profit Rate Differences

There appear to be slight differences in the average profit rates negotiated by the various armed services on similar contract types covering similar work. In particular, Air Force rates have tended to run about one-half a percentage point lower than Army and Navy rates on CPFF contracts and (for the Navy only) fixed-price incentive contracts.[16] Why this differential existed is not known. One possible explanation is that the Air Force has relied more heavily on private industry to meet its weapons needs over the years and has developed program management policies more to industry's liking. To offset these Air Force attractions, it may have been necessary for the Army and Navy to offer slightly higher profit rates.

Past Contractor Performance

Finally, we have the factor in which we are primarily interested here: variations in negotiated profit rates to reflect differences in contractor performance. Evidence from our case studies and else-

---

[15] In 1963 the Logistics Management Institute recommended a similar "weighted guideline" approach as the first step in determining negotiated target profits. *Study of Profit or Fee Policy*, p. 77. Underlying the choice of suggested rates were such considerations as required investment and opportunity cost.

[16] Frederick T. Moore found a somewhat different pattern of interservice differentials on CPFF contracts: the Air Force average was 6.8%, the Army average 6.7%, and the Navy average 7.4%. *Military Procurement and Contracting: An Economic Analysis*, RM–2948–PR (Santa Monica: The RAND Corporation, 1962), pp. 29–31. Moore also observed that CPFF profit rates varied inversely with contract size. This tendency might be due to a higher proportion of subcontracting on the larger contracts. Or it might be necessary to offer premium negotiated profit rates to get large firms to accept small contracts.

where indicates that there has been little if any variation in profit rates to correlate with past performance. Profit rate differences were invariably explained as the result of the first six factors discussed here rather than performance differentials. In nearly all the programs covered by our case studies, no serious attempt was made to effect profit-performance correlations. The government official responsible for contract negotiations in one major program did have discretion for adjusting profit rates to reflect performance by rounding after the decimal, once investment, type of work, and other criteria had been weighed. Thus, he might adjust a CPFF fee rate of 6.78% obtained by preliminary analysis downward to 6.5% if the contractor's performance had been poor or upward to 7.0% to reward good past performance. However, the adjustments he actually made in such cases were motivated not by the objective of rewarding good and penalizing poor performance, but by the need to make the negotiated rate conform to the "going rate."

More generally, our case studies disclosed that once a profit rate was established for a certain type of contracting situation, it was most difficult to make any changes. In only one program was there evidence that the government negotiator actively attempted to reduce a profit rate because of what he considered inefficient past contractor performance. The attempt was unsuccessful. Reflecting upon his experience, the negotiator said:

> If you start looking at efficiency, people will look at you like you've got two heads. They'll say, "We've already established the fee."

These observations were confirmed by contractor personnel, who perceived no real correlation between performance and profit rates and who considered profit rates essentially fixed against either upward or downward adjustments once they were established. Similarly, an Air Force group which studied the negotiation of profit rates on cost reimbursement contracts stated:

> We have learned, from interviews with principal Air Force contract negotiators, that patterns established by repetitive negotiations over the years with the same contractor or with contractors in the same industry pretty well fix the levels of fees we pay. Fees tend to group in a range between 4% and 8% of estimated costs.

There are variations in this cluster of fees that can be explained by differences between the military services, buying offices, or types of products but the shifts are relatively slight. We tried, in the interviews, to find out the principal factors in establishing fees but the conclusion was that most interviewees were influenced most strongly by the concept of the "going rate." [17]

We may conclude that during the 1950's there was little or no variation in negotiated profit rates to reflect differences in contractor performance, and that the variation shown in Figures 9.1 through 9.4 was due almost entirely to nonperformance factors. Thus, during the 1950's a negotiated profit rate incentive system did not exist.

THE FEASIBILITY OF A NEGOTIATED PROFIT RATE INCENTIVE SYSTEM

This conclusion is supported by the Logistics Management Institute's study of negotiated profit policies, which found that "the potential of profit as an incentive for contractor performance has only been minimally realized." [18]   The Institute's report recommended that negotiated target profit rates be adjusted upward by as much as two percentage points to reflect superior performance and downward by as much as two points in cases of unsatisfactory performance.[19]   In mid-1963, Department of Defense implementation of the recommendation appeared likely.   Here some of the more fundamental problems connected with maintaining a system of negotiated profit rate incentives will be analyzed.

Consistent Performance Evaluations

As indicated earlier, one prerequisite for a negotiated profit rate incentive system is sufficient consistency in the profit-performance correlations that contractors actually expect good performance to be rewarded and poor performance to be penalized.   Is it possible to measure performance consistently enough to meet this condition?

[17] House, Committee on Appropriations, *Hearings, Department of Defense Appropriations for 1960,* Part 5, p. 575.

[18] *Study of Profit or Fee Policy,* p. 1.   At p. 2 the report observes that "presently the most important consideration of procurement personnel in establishing target profit is the historically established profit or fee percentage allowed the individual contractor."   See also pp. 36–38, 44, and 49.

[19] *Ibid.,* p. 78.

Our case studies revealed that government contract negotiators responsible for major programs were seldom in a position to make well-founded performance evaluations. In some instances negotiators attempted to judge efficiency on the basis of such misleading indicators as comparative overhead rates and learning curves.[20]   In other cases they detected real inefficiencies in contractor operations, but were unable to assess their relative significance. For example, the negotiator mentioned earlier who unsuccessfully sought a downward profit rate adjustment due to inefficiency appeared to have diagnosed certain contractor deficiencies correctly. But our case study research made it possible to compare that program with other programs having generally similar technical goals and problems. Analysis on that basis showed the contractor's *relative* efficiency to be fairly high.

This type of problem arises mainly because the government contract negotiator's world is too circumscribed. Usually a negotiator is assigned on a continuing basis to only one or two major programs, and this prevents him from becoming familiar with contractor performance in other programs. In addition, negotiators typically lack the technical knowledge required to make discerning performance judgments.[21]

Nevertheless, the results of the program evaluation experiment described in Chapter 4 indicate that meaningful comparative performance judgments can be made through ranking when the judges have access to relevant information on a larger group of programs and the competence needed to evaluate that information.[22]   It therefore appears possible to obtain the performance measurements needed to administer a consistent correlation between negotiated profit rates and contractor performance.

In 1963 a procedure which for the first time would generate explicit evaluations of contractor performance in development programs was established by the Department of Defense. The evalua-

[20] Cf. pp. 208–209 *supra.*

[21] On the basis of interviews with government negotiators, the Logistics Management Institute report observed that "in the field of advanced research, the procurement personnel felt that it was impossible to compare one contractor's performance against another when they couldn't even evaluate what was successful performance." *Study of Profit or Fee Policy,* pp. 37–38.

[22] Cf. pp. 93–101 *supra.* For a more complete analysis of the results, see Peck and Scherer, pp. 543–580 and 668–711.

tions provided by this system will apparently be used as a basis for varying negotiated profit rates, as well as in the selection of contractors for new programs. However, certain questions must be raised concerning the new system's ability to yield valid performance judgments.

According to mid-1963 plans, primary responsibility for preparing contractor performance evaluation reports in any given development program will be assigned to the government official responsible for managing and directing that program. But when more than a purely mechanistic report is required, a government program manager can scarcely be objective in his evaluations. His judgments are apt to be colored by the emotional experiences he has had in directing the program. And since he shares responsibility for contractor actions by approving contractor decisions and intervening (or choosing not to intervene) in program problems, a poor evaluation of contractor performance by the program manager usually implies a condemnation of his own performance.[23] Thus, program managers will be defending their personal records when they make performance evaluations — a situation hardly conducive to unbiased judgments.

Furthermore, a government program manager is in much the same position as the contract negotiator described earlier: engrossed as he is in the problems of a single program, he is likely to lack perspective, being unable to determine whether his contractor's performance is relatively good or relatively poor compared to the work of other contractors. It is therefore unlikely that performance evaluations will be comparable across program lines. Indeed, the Defense Department's new evaluation system is explicitly designed to avoid comparative performance judgments.[24] And yet comparability is essential if one contractor is to be awarded a higher profit rate than another on differential performance grounds.

Although there was no evidence of serious efforts to solve the comparability problem, Department of Defense officials responsible for the new evaluation system have shown definite concern for the

[23] Cf. pp. 99–101 *supra*.

[24] Cf. "Contractor Evaluation Comments Asked," *Aviation Week & Space Technology*, April 15, 1963, p. 32. This and brief informal conversations with government representatives were the only sources of information on the evaluation system available at the time of writing.

objectivity problem.   Apparently, the subjective judgments of government program managers are to be only a minor part of contractor performance evaluations.   Primary emphasis will be placed on "factual" measures of performance — in particular, on the degree to which the contractor meets or surpasses contractual quality, time, and cost targets.   But this approach in turn poses its own set of dilemmas.   There is nothing in the contract negotiation process that assures the validity of negotiated targets.   In fact, there are many aspects of the process which encourage a definite bias toward invalid targets, especially on the cost dimension.   It follows that variances of actual program outcomes from original targets are not necessarily valid indicators of how well the contractor has actually performed.   For example, a contractor may exceed its electronic subsystem reliability target because it held out for pessimistic goals in target negotiations or because some firm operating outside the contractor's sphere of managerial control developed a much more reliable standard component, as well as because of outstanding in-house technical efforts.   Similarly, a contractor may achieve a substantial cost underrun because it was fortunate enough to enjoy a noncompetitive position during cost target negotiations, and therefore was able to make ample provision for meeting the costs of its inefficiently large engineering staff.   Or more likely, the contractor may show a large overrun because of truly unpredictable technical difficulties or because competition at the time of contract negotiations virtually compelled an unrealistically low cost estimate.   As we have seen in Chapters 7 and 8, the incidence and magnitude of overruns and underruns appear to be explained more by differences in the degree of optimism or pessimism negotiated into contract cost targets than by variations in contractor efficiency.

Department of Defense leaders recognize this, but they apparently do not regard it as a deficiency.   On the contrary, published statements suggest that a paramount government objective in establishing the new performance evaluation system was to combat the historical tendency toward excessive optimism in development program outcome predictions.[25]   This is an undeniably important

---

[25] *Ibid.* A fascinating story probably underlies the development of this policy. Some day historians may be able to dig it out. It would appear that early in his administration, Secretary of Defense McNamara was

goal, and penalizing contractors for excessive optimism will create desirable corrective incentives. Still honesty in the sales presentation room and at the bargaining table should not be the government's only objective in weapons development programs. Good performance once the bargain is sealed is also important. Basing negotiated profit rate differentials on a comparison of actual outcomes against original targets will not necessarily ensure a consistent correlation between profit awards and actual performance in the laboratory and factory. And unless that correlation is consistent, a negotiated profit rate incentive system will not succeed in creating strong incentives for good performance.

To penetrate beyond the superficial precision of contract target vs. actual outcome comparisons and make valid performance evaluations requires judgment, including judgment on essentially subjective factors. If this responsibility is entrusted to the managers of specific programs, problems of bias and interprogram comparability are unavoidable. The only likely solution appears to be a more or less centralized group of experienced and technically competent judges removed from direct responsibility for particular programs, rendering comparative performance evaluations on the basis of detailed program execution studies. This need seems to have been perceived at least in part by the Department of Defense, since its evaluation system plans call for a central evaluation group to review the judgments of program managers. The central group will also conduct an independent field investigation at the end of each major development program. In Chapter 12 the centralized evaluation approach will be considered at greater length.

The Multidimensionality of Performance

Another fundamental problem has already been analyzed in Chapter 4, and therefore needs only brief mention here. Performance in a weapons program, and especially in a weapons development program, is multidimensional, involving many different facets of quality, time, and cost. Often these dimensions come into conflict, and so in judging over-all contractor performance, weights

---

"mousetrapped" into certain major decisions by deliberately optimistic cost estimates. He is evidently not the kind of person who takes mousetrapping lightly, and by late 1962 his speeches began to reflect a persistent insistence upon improved cost estimates.

must be assigned to evaluations of performance on the various individual dimensions.

Chapter 4 presented evidence that development time and perhaps quality considerations are weighted much more heavily than cost in evaluations of over-all contractor performance.[26] Consequently, the incentive for cost reduction and efficiency created by correlating negotiated profit rates with over-all performance would be weak relative to incentives generated on the time and quality dimensions. But competitive incentives already exert fairly strong pressures for good performance on the quality and time dimensions. Basing profit rates on over-all performance might merely reinforce already adequate incentives while adding relatively little on the cost dimension, where stronger incentives are most needed.

There are two possible reactions to this problem. First, while time and perhaps quality did receive higher weights in experimental program performance evaluations, cost considerations became decisive when time and quality were roughly equal. This suggests that correlating negotiated profit rates with over-all contractor performance would add at least some incentive for efficiency, even though it would not create really potent cost dimension incentives. A slight improvement is preferable to none at all, if the cost is not too high.

Second, it is possible that negotiated profit rates could be correlated not with over-all contractor performance, but with performance on the cost dimension alone. This would permit the full profit rate correlation to reflect efficiency variations rather than being dissipated on time and quality variations. A balanced system can be visualized in which competitive incentives are related to over-all performance, with the greatest weight on time and quality, while contractual incentives (negotiated profit rate variations as well as automatic contractual incentives) would be focused largely

[26] It is worth noting that the quantitative correlations in Chapter 4 involved indices relating actual development time and cost to predicted time and cost. As I have just emphasized, these indices are not necessarily valid measures of the efficacy of contractor performance on the individual dimensions. Their use is defensible only on grounds that no better quantitative data could be obtained in a very limited study. Cf. Peck and Scherer, p. 670. A much richer statistical study of the multidimensionality problem is badly needed. To the best of my knowledge, the Department of Defense has not concerned itself with this central problem.

on the cost dimension. In fact, until multidimensional incentive contracting came into vogue the existing system of incentives in weapons acquisition approximated this division of emphasis, except for the absence of a correlation between negotiated profit rates and efficiency. What is lacking is balance, not recognition that effective incentives are needed on all performance dimensions.

This second proposal raises the question whether contractor efficiency can be measured consistently. While the evidence on this point is meager, it seems reasonable to infer that satisfactory efficiency judgments could be made by a competent group with access to the relevant data. As indicated in Chapter 7, it was possible with fairly high confidence to draw a dichotomy between development programs in our case study sample which were conducted efficiently and those executed inefficiently.[27] And there are grounds for believing that more discriminating judgments can be made. Certainly, efficiency is a less complex attribute than over-all performance. Since the program evaluation experiment indicated that consistent ordinal rankings of over-all contractor performance and of state-of-the-art-advance (a dimension of over-all performance) were feasible under favorable conditions, judgments on the efficiency dimension should be feasible too. In any event, the experiment demonstrated that questions of this nature are well suited to rigorous testing. Additional research should be conducted before a final conclusion is drawn on the feasibility of measuring contractors' relative efficiency.

It is also necessary to consider the kinds of contract sequences on which negotiated profit rate–performance correlations might be implemented. There are many possible approaches. One would be to correlate the rate of profit awarded on development contracts with performance on prior (and not necessarily related) development efforts, and the rate of profit on production contracts with efficiency on prior production efforts. However, to the extent that contractors consider production profits more important than development profits, the incentives for efficient development program performance provided by such a sequence would be weak.

Another approach would be to correlate the rate of profit applied to production contracts with the efficacy of performance on related prior development contracts. If over-all performance in develop-

[27] Cf. pp. 186–188 *supra*.

ment were the criterion, this approach would be somewhat redundant, since weapons makers commonly view production follow-on contracts *per se* (or more accurately, the profits they provide) as the principal reward for good over-all performance in a development effort. The redundancy problem could be avoided by correlating production contract profit rates with development efficiency only, rather than with over-all development performance. In this case good performance on the time and quality dimensions of development would be required to win follow-on production orders, while good performance on the efficiency dimension would be required to make those production contracts profitable. Presently, a contractor can incur excessive development costs and yet not be penalized by a loss of production orders or reduced profits on those orders. This approach appears promising as a means of achieving better balance among incentives on the various dimensions of development program performance. However, basing production contract profit rates on *development efficiency* could conceivably detract from incentives for *production efficiency*. By way of compensation, strengthened automatic incentives on production contracts might be required, or some of the negotiated profit rate variation might be reserved to correlate with production efficiency.

Performance Correlations vs. Other Reasons for Profit Rate Variation

As we have seen, there are many reasons why negotiated profit rates have varied in the past. Performance correlations have not been important among them, and yet profit rates have ranged from zero to 15% for the aggregate of all contracts, and over several percentage points within any specific contract type category. Barring fairly fundamental changes in weapons contracting, any variations in negotiated profit rates to correlate with past performance would have to be superimposed on the variations reflecting other factors.

It is possible that nonperformance variations could swamp the performance-correlated variations, rendering the latter relatively unimportant. But this would not happen if contractors perceived that, given the type of contract, the type of work, the balance of government and private facilities investment, the amount of subcontracting, and other relevant factors, profit rates would in fact vary significantly to reflect the efficacy of their performance. A reward theory incentive would at least be provided by this incremental variation, even though the administered analogue to a pressure theory incentive might not exist when nonperformance factors dictated relatively high negotiated rates. To illustrate, the increment in negotiated profit rate attainable by choosing firm fixed-price rather than CPFF contractual coverage might exceed the increment attainable by performing well rather than poorly. But for any given type of contractual coverage, a company could enhance its negotiated profit rate by performing well.

It is also possible that the variability of contract profit rates for nonperformance reasons could be reduced by a new approach to contracting, to be considered in Chapter 12.

The Extent of Performance-Correlated Variations and Contractor Behavior

A crucial element in the kind of incentive system contemplated here would be the extent to which negotiated profit rates vary to reflect differences in contractor performance. The variations must be large enough to "matter" to contractors if they are to alter their behavior in appropriate directions. As the two preceding chapters have suggested, modest profit variations have often been insufficient to spur desired behavioral changes. If significant increases in weapons development and production efficiency are to be achieved, strong compulsions are required to offset the user costs and managerial inertia blocking vigorous cost reduction efforts.

Our case studies revealed that contractors frequently attached considerable importance to relatively small variations in negotiated profit rates. Many firms bargained strenuously over two- or three-tenths of a profit rate percentage point. In two programs the principal contractors made substantial concessions in their target cost estimates on initial production contracts (in one case CPFF, in the other CPIF), accepting lower expected profit *amounts* on the particular contracts so that government negotiators would agree to higher profit *rates*.[28] Underlying this emphasis on profit rates was the belief of contractors that once a higher rate was negotiated, it would serve as a precedent in future negotiations. In one case con-

---

[28] For a similar finding see Logistics Management Institute, *Study of Profit or Fee Policy*, p. 41.

tractor management also considered the negotiated profit rate to be important because it reflected their firm's status relative to other firms engaged in similar work.

When negotiated profit rates are based significantly on precedent, it is assumed that once a new rate is established it will endure for a long time, and therefore that a small change in the profit rate can make a large difference in the long-run amount of profit. The longer a change in profit rate is expected to last, the more important it will be to the contractor. But under the kind of incentive system contemplated here, negotiated profit rates would be based much less on past precedent and much more on past contractor performance. As a result, rate adjustments would be made more frequently — perhaps as frequently as once a year — to reflect changes in the contractor's performance record. It follows that a given change (say, one percentage point) in the negotiated profit rate would be of much less moment to contractors under such a system than it would be in the institutional environment of 1963. To matter as much to the contractor, a negotiated profit rate change would have to be larger to compensate for the decrease in its expected longevity. Just how great the variability of negotiated profit rates must be to accomplish a given effect on contractor behavior depends upon the expected duration of the incentive correlation.

If profit rates were adjusted annually to correlate with contractor production efficiency, then as a first approximation, the behavioral effects of the negotiated rate variations would be analogous to the effects produced by *realized* rate variations under one-year production contracts with automatic profit-cost incentive provisions. In the sample of 47 Navy fixed-price incentive contracts covered by Figure 8.9, realized profit rates varied between 4.2% and 15.3% of actual costs, with a mean of 10.0%. The standard deviation of realized rates from their mean was 2.8 percentage points.[29] And yet as Chapter 8 found, this amount of cost-correlated realized profit variation in the short run of a fixed-price incentive contract was generally insufficient to motivate vigorous cost reduction efforts.

[29] Of course, this figure is affected by variations in originally negotiated profit rates as well as by variations due to the automatic profit-cost correlations. The standard deviation of the deviations of realized profit rates from originally negotiated profit rates was 2.5 percentage points.

Greater efficiency-correlated variability of negotiated profit rates would hardly be practical. Could we therefore expect a negotiated profit rate incentive system with annual adjustments to have a significant impact on contractor efficiency? On initial analysis, a negative answer is indicated.

There is, however, one flaw in this analogy. Under the automatic profit-cost incentive correlation provisions of a fixed-price type contract, the rewards for cost reduction are strictly limited to the short run of the particular contract. Achieving cost reductions during 1963 brings a reward in the form of enhanced profits under the incentive contract covering 1963's production. But as we have seen in Chapter 8, cost targets for the 1964 contract will be extrapolated from the level of efficiency reached in 1963. To gain further incentive profits in 1964, the contractor must make further cost reductions. Assuming that the purely technical difficulty, user costs, and disutilities associated with cost reduction increase at an increasing rate, each year's cost reduction efforts make it harder to earn incentive profits in the next year.[30] The rewards for cost reduction under a system of automatic contractual incentives tend to be noncumulative. In contrast, if a contractor achieves a high level of relative efficiency during 1963 and merely maintains that level (adjusted, of course, for secular cost trends and cumulative learning) its negotiated profit rate would remain at a high level. A negotiated profit rate incentive system therefore affords cumulative rewards or penalties. Consequently, if the range of profit rate variation under systems of negotiated profit rate and automatic contractual incentives were the same, the negotiated profit rate system would produce stronger behavioral effects.

Of course, the strength of the incentives created in this way would depend not only on the range of profit rate variation, but also on the shape of the distribution of variations. The distribution might be normal, rectangular, or take virtually any other shape. To illustrate, assume that the range of negotiated profit rate variation for all but the most exceptional cases (e.g., 5% of all contracts) will be 6 percentage points. If a normal distribution were chosen, 68% of all contracts would be negotiated with profit rates

---

[30] Similarly, it is easier to gain incentive profits starting from an initially inefficient situation than it is when early production operations are conducted efficiently. See pp. 124–125 *supra*.

within 1.5 percentage points of the base or mean rate. Roughly 14% of all contracts would have rates between 1.5 and 3.0 points above the base (rewarding high efficiency) and 14% would have rates between 1.5 and 3.0 points below the base (penalizing inefficiency). On the other hand, if a rectangular distribution were chosen, 24% of the rates would fall in the +1.5 to +3.0 range and 24% in the −1.5 to −3.0 range.

The results of the program evaluation experiment suggest, although very inconclusively, that the distribution of over-all contractor performance evaluations more nearly approximates the normal than the rectangular distribution.[31] That is, average performance tends to occur more frequently than either clearly superior or clearly inferior performance. If this is also true of performance on the efficiency dimension, a rectangular distribution of negotiated profit rates would tend to over-reward better-than-average producers and over-penalize poorer-than-average producers. While a rectangular distribution might therefore provide stronger incentives than a normal distribution, it would also be somewhat inequitable, especially when the process of measuring efficiency is subject to error.[32] This problem will be considered further in Chapter 12.

The discussion thus far has implicitly assumed that efficiency-correlated negotiated profit rate variations would be used as a substitute for realized profit rate variations due to automatic profit-cost correlations under incentive contracts. This is by no means essential; it would also be possible to combine both systems. Thus, the target profit negotiated for an incentive-type contract would vary to reflect the contractor's past performance. Then the actually realized profit would vary further, increasing above the target profit if cost underruns were achieved or falling below if cost overruns appear. In general, we should expect this double system of variation to provide stronger incentives than either of the individual systems used alone. However, complex and not always favorable in-

---

[31] A cumulative frequency distribution of contractor performance scaling factors was plotted on normal probability paper. The plot of points obtained suggested a single-humped distribution slightly skewed toward the better-than-average performance side. However, eight observations are too few to construct an unambiguous distribution or to apply a Chi-square goodness-of-fit test meaningfully.

[32] Cf. Peck and Scherer, pp. 579–580.

teractions would probably occur. For example, if excellent past performance merited a high negotiated profit rate, the probability of outright losses due to serious overruns might be quite small, and so automatic pressure theory incentives would be inoperative. The contractor might even be so satisfied with its target profit rate that no effort to achieve underruns would be exerted. On the other hand, if poor past performance warranted a low negotiated profit rate, the probability of loss would be enhanced and unusually strong pressure theory incentives would come into play.

Bargaining and Entry-Exit Considerations

One additional set of potential problems must be mentioned. In practice it might prove difficult to administer a wide range of performance-correlated variation in negotiated profit rates. There is a legal constraint on upward variation: government procurement laws prohibit negotiated profit rates higher than 15% of target cost on CPFF research and development contracts and 10% on most other CPFF contracts.[33]

Even thornier problems might arise at the lower end of the profit rate spectrum. The government could probably flex its bargaining muscles and impose profit rates of zero or 3% on, say, aircraft companies which have performed poorly and whose only alternative to defense contracting is to go out of business. But it would have a more difficult time attempting to negotiate low profit rates with companies possessing alternative commercial opportunities for employing their resources. Bargaining situations could develop in which the government would either have to back off in its attempts to enforce a performance–profit rate correlation or drive the contractor out of defense work.[34] Of course, if a contractor's performance has been so poor that it deserves only a very low rate

---

[33] 10 U.S.C. Section 2306 (d). Lower limits of 10% and 7% respectively, to be exceeded only with the authorization of a service secretary, are set forth in the *Armed Services Procurement Regulation,* 3–405.5 (c) (2).

[34] It is also possible that a policy of awarding high profit rates to good performers would draw especially efficient new resources into the defense industry, compensating for the loss of poor performers. But because the technical and managerial resources required for weapons development tend to be highly specialized, many years might be required before a significant amount of new entry could be realized in this way.

of profit over an extended period, perhaps it *ought* to be driven out of the defense industry.   Yet there are more direct ways of doing this — notably, by not awarding the firm new contracts.   Furthermore, during periods of general defense mobilization or rapid growth in particular sectors of technology, the government is generally reluctant to lose experienced contractors, even when their past performance has been deficient.   Bargaining problems of this sort could limit the government's ability to effect a strong correlation between negotiated profit rates and contractor performance.

Conclusion

In summary, the implementation of an incentive system which correlated negotiated profit rates with contractor performance would pose many complex problems.   It would be necessary to develop methods of evaluating performance more consistent and objective than those presently in existence.   Achieving the proper balance of incentives for efficiency, lead time reduction, and quality maximization in both development and production activities would require a deft administrative touch.   The range of performance-correlated profit rate variation might be constrained by causes of variation unrelated to performance, by procurement laws, and by the exigencies of bargaining.

Nevertheless, such a system offers certain inherent advantages over a system of automatic contractual incentives.   Because of its cumulative features, the negotiated profit rate approach can generate stronger incentives for efficiency than the automatic approach with any given amount of profit rate variation.   Moreover, profit variations would be correlated clearly and definitely with contractor performance variations, not with variations in the relationship between actual outcomes and initial targets whose validity at the time of negotiation is uncertain at least to the buyer, if not also to the seller.   The attractions of a negotiated profit rate incentive system are at least sufficient to warrant further consideration in terms of public policy.   This will be done in Chapters 12 and 13.

CHAPTER 10

Other Contractual Incentives

THE PAST FOUR CHAPTERS have dealt with the principal systems of incentives operating through contract profit variations. There are, however, several other incentive approaches involving contract profits which merit less extensive analysis. These will be considered in the present chapter.

PAYING NO PROFIT ON DEVELOPMENT CONTRACTS

One approach is to pay little or no profit on development contracts, requiring contractors which do both development and production work to come up with products useful in the government's operational weapons inventory before they receive any substantial profit returns.[1] In this way an incentive to satisfy the government's qualitative demands quickly is generated.

This system is a normal feature of development efforts in a market environment, for a company receives no profit and indeed no reimbursement of costs on its commercial development projects until they yield successful marketable results. Incentives of this sort have also operated to some extent in weapons acquisition. To be sure, most weapon system and subsystem development contracts have provided both cost reimbursement and a profit. But historically, weapons contractors have viewed the profits attainable on production follow-on contracts as the most important reward of their development efforts — more important than development profits *per se*. The dominant role of production profit expectations before and during World War II is stressed by Robert Schlaifer in his analysis of aircraft engine development:

> Since profits on quantity production are the only real incentive for private industry, and development payments are at best only a

[1] Obviously, this approach could not be employed with firms that specialize in research and development work only.

form of assistance, not a genuine incentive, it is even more important for government to hold out the most vivid possible prospects
of profits than it is to make its development contracts attractive
as such.[2]

As we have seen in Chapter 7, although the growing research and
development orientation of weapons acquisition has reduced the
relative strength of production follow-on sales expectations, the lure
of production profits remains an important (but no longer all-
important) determinant of contractor behavior.[3] To the extent that
contractors are still driven by a desire to gain the potentially greater
profits of production contracts, a policy of paying little or no profit
on development contracts would reinforce the production motive.
To the extent that changes in the nature of weapons acquisition
have weakened the production motive, paying little or no profit on
development work would help restore it to its former vigor.

Effects on Contractor Behavior

Presumably such a policy would generate strengthened incentives
for contractors to get on with their development efforts as quickly
as possible so that weapon systems and subsystems useful in the
operational inventory can be produced. The most obvious incentive effect therefore would be a tendency toward reduced development time. This is a desirable result, as long as quality and cost
outcomes are not adversely affected. In practice, however, complex and not necessarily beneficial time-cost-quality tradeoffs might
be incited.

Efforts to reduce development time might, for instance, take the
form of running tasks concurrently rather than sequentially, manning tasks at higher levels, and pursuing additional technical approaches to hedge against uncertainty — all contributing to development cost increases.[4] But these time-reducing efforts would be
constrained by budgetary limitations, especially in low and medium
priority programs. And in high priority programs, sacrificing cost
to reduce development time usually represents an optimal strategy.[5]

[2] Robert Schlaifer, *Development of Aircraft Engines* (Boston: Division
of Research, Harvard Business School, 1950), p. 65. See also pp. 9, 41, 64,
and 83.

[3] Cf. pp. 168–170 *supra*.

[4] Cf. Peck and Scherer, pp. 257–266.

[5] *Ibid.*, pp. 280–281.

Stronger incentives for development time reduction might on the other hand work to *reduce* development costs. When schedule slippages are avoided because of a greater sense of urgency, a better balancing of development tasks, and more rapid decision making, and when averting schedule delays permits fuller utilization of overhead resources, true efficiency gains may be realized.

Schedule slippages are also accepted in order to exploit recognized possibilities for improving weapon system performance and reliability before starting production for the operational inventory. To the extent that such improvements are of little military value, incentives for time reduction which discouraged midstream changes in technical objectives would be beneficial. Often, however, decisions to accept schedule slippages and cost overruns are highly rational — e.g., when a weapon system is not urgently needed and when improvements might postpone the weapon's obsolescence date.[6] If paying little or no profit on development contracts led contractors to resist these quality-increasing changes, the net effect might be undesirable. But nonoptimal quality sacrifices by contractors would be prevented when government decision makers can recognize and insist upon desirable improvement efforts. In addition, competition among close substitutes and competition for budgetary support afford a countervailing incentive for contractors to seek high technical performance and reliability. When quality sacrifices reduce a weapon's military value and endanger its production prospects, it is usually sound tactics to suppress one's desire for early production profits to insure that *some* production profits will eventually be attained.

Paying little or no profit on development contracts could also affect weapon system quality (and particularly technical performance) in a more fundamental way. Defense contractors might become more conservative in their feasibility studies and new system proposals, emphasizing those concepts which can be developed quickly to provide the minimum acceptable advance over existing capabilities and avoiding those concepts which require many years of costly development before reaching the production stage. The ability of weapons makers to attempt large steps without worrying too much about the immediate profit implications may be one reason why technological advance has generally been more dramatic in

6 *Ibid.,* pp. 474–475.

the weapons field than in nondefense fields. This difference is illustrated, for instance, by the propensity of aircraft companies to display much more technical conservatism in company-financed airliner developments than in government-financed weapons programs. Still as long as the government continues to reimburse at least the costs of weapons development, it is probable that competition will provide fairly potent incentives for shunning overly conservative development approaches.

Indeed, a major cause of program failures and severe development cost overruns and time slippages during the 1950's and early 1960's has been the establishment of excessively ambitious technical goals, mainly in response to competitive pressures. It may well be that the goal-setting process in weapon systems development (to be clearly distinguished from applied research and component development) needs an over-all correction in the direction of greater conservatism. This, however, is an issue on which knowledgeable persons disagree, and the debate cannot be resolved here.[7] Perhaps the simplest expedient is to recognize that both optimistic and conservative technical biases have their place depending, among other things, on the urgency of the relevant military requirements. If then there is a place for ambitious, long-time-span weapons developments, it is important not to discourage all such contractor efforts.

It is unlikely that a shortage of new advanced weapon system ideas and concepts would arise under a no-profit-on-development policy, since these ideas emerge from a great many sources other than contractors, and their appearance is virtually inevitable as long as progress is made in basic scientific and technological fields.[8] But ideas do not lead automatically to development program decisions. If, despite the pressures of competition, contractor advocacy of farsighted new programs were to decline, the timely inception of ambitious programs would depend upon the military services' willingness to embrace attractive new concepts in the absence of persuasion. In the past the services have had only a fair

[7] For a comparison of two leading viewpoints (those of Dr. Harold Brown, Director of Defense Research and Engineering, and Gen. Bernard A. Schriever, commander of the Air Force Systems Command), see George C. Wilson, "USAF-Defense Research Conflict Aired," *Aviation Week & Space Technology,* August 13, 1962, pp. 32–34.

[8] Cf. Peck and Scherer, pp. 236–237.

record of independent receptiveness to new ideas, although there is evidence of improvement in recent years.

Once service requirements were defined, the effect of a no-profit-on-development policy would depend significantly on contractor attitudes toward entering ambitious long-range programs. Contractors would no doubt prefer developments with good, early production potential, just as they presently do when profit *is* awarded on development contracts. But if past experience is a valid guide, there will be too few conservative programs to employ all the defense industry's technical resources, and so contractors will be compelled to accept the more ambitious assignments despite a preference for those which promise quicker production profits.

Alternatively, the most capable contractor organizations might take advantage of their high opportunity cost and hence strong bargaining power by choosing the most desirable programs — those with early production potential. However, the greatest need for the superior technical capabilities of such firms probably lies in the more ambitious programs, while organizations of mediocre capability would be better-suited for tackling the more routine problems — presumably, those involving a shorter development span. In this sense a no-profit-on-development policy could generate incentives which direct resources away from rather than toward optimal fields of utilization. But since weapons makers generally considered production potential more important than development profits during the 1950's, we might expect to find historical evidence of a propensity for superior technical resources to gravitate into quick-payoff projects. Our case studies gave no substantial indication of such a tendency, possibly because persons and organizations with superior technical abilities preferred for reasons of professional specialization and interest to undertake the more challenging projects. Only one instance was found in which a highly capable development organization clearly attempted to focus its efforts on projects with strong short-run production potential despite government requests that it work on more farsighted projects. Government officials objected to the company's plans, and after considerable negotiation the resource allocation conflict was settled by a compromise.

Effects on Entry and Exit

It is doubtful that a policy of paying little or no profit on development contracts would encourage a wholesale migration of technical resources out of weapons work, since the alternative to defense development contracts for most firms would be commercial projects which provide neither profits nor reimbursement of costs. Many defense contracting organizations are also fairly rigidly confined to defense work by virtue of resource specialization. Still to prevent the exit of technical resources it would probably be necessary to increase the level of production profits so that the over-all defense contracting profit expectations of firms with alternative resource employment opportunities would not fall.

Even though average profit expectations remained constant, a no-profit-on-development policy might increase weapons contracting risks and hence stimulate the exit of resources. Historically, only about one-third of all advanced weapon system development projects have led directly to production for the operational inventory.[9] Some companies, particularly those able to handle only one or a very few projects simultaneously, might consider the risk that production contracts will not materialize too great and seek less risky uses for their technical talent. A special hardship could be worked on small businesses. Yet the risks of commercial product development efforts for both small and large firms would usually be even greater than those of weapons development, especially if an appreciable migration of technical resources out of weapons work were to increase commercial competition. For instance, commercial airliner development proved unprofitable to most of the participants during the late 1950's partly because the efforts of many aircraft firms to diversify away from weapons contracting led to excessive competition. It is more likely that, instead of leaving the

[9] Dr. C. C. Furnas, former Assistant Secretary of Defense for Research and Development, stated that only one out of every three military aircraft projects into which the U.S. armed forces have seriously entered has led to production. Senate, Committee on Appropriations, *Hearings, Department of Defense Appropriations for 1957*, p. 243. In a sample of 99 aircraft and guided missile programs, 47% of the programs saw production, although this figure is biased on the high side because some projects which were cancelled at an early stage were not included in the sample. Peck and Scherer, pp. 645–667.

weapons field, companies would attempt to avoid defense contracts which engross a high proportion of their resources, striving for a diversified menu of development projects to insure that at least some will lead into production.

Conclusion

In sum, a policy of paying little or no profit on development contracts would yield benefits mixed with certain drawbacks. Potential benefits include strengthened incentives for rapid development of weapon systems and subsystems into operationally useful configurations, for more efficient use of technical resources, and for the avoidance of overly optimistic and elaborate technical approaches. The chief problem is the possibility that contractors would make undesirable quality sacrifices, either by choosing unduly conservative technical approaches or by resisting product improvements which delay the start of production. However, this disadvantage would be minimized when the government can independently specify appropriate quality objectives and maintain vigorous technical competition among contractors. Another problem might be the exit of resources from defense contracting, but adverse effects of this sort could be avoided by increasing the level of production contract profits.

SOME SPECIAL CONTRACTUAL INCENTIVES

Certain other contractual means of creating incentives for desirable performance deserve brief attention. These include termination for default, the enforcement of penalties for specification noncompliance, the assessment of liquidated damages, and performance bond requirements.

When a contractor negligently fails to fulfill contract performance or delivery requirements, the contract can be terminated for default by the government. Although the exact contractor liability in such cases depends upon the factual circumstances, in general the contractor is paid for any work completed successfully, is not paid for incomplete work, and (except in certain cost reimbursement situations) is liable to the government for the additional cost of having incomplete work finished by another firm.[10] Thus, a contractor

[10] Cf. *Armed Services Procurement Regulation,* Sections 8–407 and 8–602, covering termination of cost reimbursement and fixed-price type contracts respectively.

can expect to incur losses on defaulted contracts, and this expectation serves as an incentive to avoid default. In practice, however, government procurement agencies resort to termination for default only on relatively small contracts and when contractor performance has been flagrantly unsatisfactory. For example, in fiscal year 1957 the U.S. Navy terminated for default only 221 contracts with a total face value of $8 million, and hence an average value per contract of $36,000. In fiscal year 1958 it terminated for default 228 contracts with a total value of $3 million and an average value of $13,000. In contrast, the Navy terminated for convenience of the government 819 contracts worth $459 million during 1957 and 748 contracts worth $249 million during 1958, with an average value per contract for the two years of $450,000.[11] Reviewing similar evidence, a House of Representatives committee concluded that:

> Apparently the default clauses of the armed services procurement regulations are a "dead letter" so far as large aircraft contracts of the Navy are concerned. . . . the leniency manifested toward the large corporate contractor is often lacking in respect to the small contractor, who is more readily considered as expendable by the military services.[12]

A less drastic penalty available when contractors fail to comply with contract specifications is the negotiation of a profit reduction on the specific contract. Still this is done infrequently in connection with development and advanced production work. For instance, the government negotiator in one program covered by our case studies had to bargain for a considerable period of time before securing a small but in his opinion precedent-setting profit reduction on one of many specification waivers. In another rather small development project, some 200 deviations from original contract specifications were approved by the government, but the contractor was still paid the full agreed-upon profit for its efforts. When specification noncompliance occurs on cost reimbursement contracts, the government often requires the contractor to remedy any correctable deficiencies without additional profit, although additional costs are reimbursed. This procedure may also be followed on

[11] House, Committee on Appropriations, *Hearings, Department of Defense Appropriations for 1960,* Part 5, pp. 19–20.

[12] House, Committee on Government Operations, *Tenth Intermediate Report, Navy Jet Aircraft Procurement Program* (1956), pp. 20–21.

fixed-price type contracts, in which case the contractor's realized profit is reduced to the extent that cost increases are absorbed. But on both cost reimbursement and fixed-price type contracts, when specification waivers are authorized by the government, the contractor's profit is usually not reduced.[13]

Occasionally government procurement agencies have insisted that liquidated damages clauses be inserted in contracts, especially for fixed-price construction contracts. Such clauses provide a specific dollar penalty for each day by which deliveries fall behind scheduled dates.[14] An unusual example of their application to advanced weapons work occurred in connection with the Minuteman ICBM program, when the Army Corps of Engineers Missile Construction Office proposed to penalize Minuteman base construction contractors $2,000 for each day of completion date slippage on each launcher or control facility.[15] But perhaps partly because of the liquidated damages requirement, the lowest firm fixed-price bid received was 55% higher than government estimates of what the work should have cost.[16] As a result, new bids were solicited on the basis of cost reimbursement and fixed-price incentive relationships, and apparently the liquidated damages provisions were eliminated.

A final possibility is to require contractors to post a performance bond guaranteeing contract completion. Performance bonds are commonly demanded in connection with military construction contracts, but are used very infrequently on nonconstruction con-

[13] There is some evidence that the British government has been tougher on its contractors in this respect. For example, in the Seaslug guided missile program a profit reduction of more than $100,000 was negotiated because of unsatisfactory progress by the contractor. Cf. "British Missile Costs Soar," *Missiles and Rockets,* March 28, 1960, p. 41.

[14] Section 1–310 of the *Armed Services Procurement Regulation* states in part that: "Liquidated damages provisions normally will not be utilized but may be used where both (i) the time of delivery or performance is such an important factor in the award of the contract that the Government may reasonably expect to suffer damages if the delivery or performance is delinquent, and (ii), the extent or amount of such damages would be difficult or impossible of ascertainment or proof."

[15] Cf. "Missile Site Builders Face Slippage Fines," *Aviation Week & Space Technology,* November 7, 1960, p. 71.

[16] Cf. House, Committee on Appropriations, *Report No. 51, Air Force Intercontinental Ballistic Missile Construction Program* (1961), p. 2.

tracts.[17]   Our case studies revealed only one instance of their application to development or production work.   In that case, a subcontractor which had experienced financial difficulties was required at the prime contractor's initiative to post a performance bond.

In general, termination for default, liquidated damages provisions, and performance bond requirements appear poorly suited for sizable advanced weapons development and production contracts. On the other hand, negotiating profit reductions for specification noncompliance seems feasible.   Yet a general policy of reducing profits for specification waivers on CPFF contracts might encourage contractors to incur undesirable overruns to comply with marginal specifications, thereby building uneconomic quality increments into weapons hardware.   Profits probably should be reduced only when specifications have not been met because of faulty workmanship, incompetence, or obvious competitive optimism in agreeing to unrealistic specifications, but not when it is decided on the basis of accrued technical experience that the cost of meeting particular specifications would exceed the value of the quality increment involved.   Clearly, implementing such a policy would require a high degree of judgment on the part of government procurement agency personnel.

[17] *Armed Services Procurement Regulation,* Section 10–103.

PART III

INCENTIVES AND GOVERNMENT POLICY

CHAPTER 11

Existing Incentive Systems: Summary and Balanced Appraisal

THERE IS NO DEARTH of incentives affecting contractor performance in advanced weapons development and production programs. To be sure, government agencies have failed to exploit all the possibilities, and the administration of certain incentive systems has been deficient. But despite popular notions to the contrary, even in cost-plus-fixed-fee situations the behavior of defense contractors is conditioned and modified by a number of relatively powerful incentives.

Only the most important examples from previous chapters need be recalled here. Contractors must in many situations perform well or lose sales to firms offering substitute weapon systems and subsystems. When competition from close substitutes is lacking, a contractor must nevertheless strive to hold its program's position in the national defense budget — a position easily lost if quality deteriorates, deliveries fall behind schedule, or costs rise to exceed expected military value. The firm's reputation and perhaps its ability to win future program opportunities depend upon the efficacy of its performance in ongoing programs. When confronted with more program opportunities than it can assimilate, a company maximizes long-run profits by utilizing key managerial and technical resources efficiently, even under a CPFF contract. And the desire of contractor personnel to accomplish significant technological advances and to contribute usefully to the national defense effort also affects performance, although incentives of this sort cannot be administered by the government.

Moreover, our case study research provided considerable evidence that most contractor executives, project managers, and other

313

responsible employees are strongly motivated in many respects — that they are really trying hard to do an acceptable job under difficult circumstances. It is appropriate therefore to inquire: is the over-all system of incentives in weapons acquisition as good as we can reasonably expect? In other words, are defense contractors performing about as well as they can be expected to perform, given human frailty and the inherent uncertainty and complexity of weapons acquisition?

The "givens" in this question must be emphasized. We clearly cannot hope for perfection in weapons acquisition. Mistakes are inevitable as long as the responses of nature and potential enemies to our development efforts cannot be predicted with certainty. Perhaps as important, deficient judgment and incompetence are unavoidable sources of error and inefficiency. Not every game can be played by the first team; many programs must be executed by managers, scientists, and engineers whose judgment and competence are either unproved or recognizably inferior. Motivation is a very imperfect substitute for competence. At best, an incentive system can deal with human weaknesses by impelling firms to train and develop inexperienced personnel and to withdraw responsibility from those who fail repeatedly. But changes of this nature cannot be accomplished overnight. It is naive to expect dramatic improvements in the human element of weapons acquisition, as former Secretary of Defense Charles E. Wilson correctly observed:

> Really I am frank to say that I do not know how to get almost 4 million people to be suddenly smarter and accomplish more. Realistically, we just have to take what we have and keep working and trying to do it better all the time, but that rate of improvement with over 4 million people is pretty slow — any more than you can ask the contractors to suddenly get more efficiency in their plants and reduce their price 5 percent. I do not know how to do that.[1]

If improvements in contractor performance are to be achieved, it will have to be through alterations in the "system," not the people — that is, through changes in the systems of controls and incentives applied to weapons acquisition.

The analysis in this volume indicates that, in general, contractors

[1] Senate, Committee on Appropriations, *Hearings, Department of Defense Appropriations for 1958,* p. 35.

have been well motivated to strive for high technical performance and reliability and to control development schedules. To be sure, there have been quality deficiencies and schedule slippages which were both undesirable and unnecessary in many weapons programs. But these can seldom be traced directly to inadequate incentives on the quality and time dimensions. Rather, they have been caused largely by errors, inadequate technical competence, or complex tradeoffs related to the inability or unwillingness of firms to utilize human and physical resources efficiently. Problems due to error and incompetence probably cannot be attacked very fruitfully through the incentives approach. It is on the efficiency dimension that the greatest opportunities for improvement exist. Costs — and especially development costs — have been higher than they needed to be in all too many programs. And a substantial portion of the cost efficiency problem is related to the system of incentives prevailing in weapons acquisition.

COMPETITIVE INCENTIVES AND EFFICIENCY

One fundamental difficulty is that the most pervasive varieties of competition in weapons acquisition generate powerful incentives for quality maximization and development time minimization, but relatively little pressure for cost minimization. In fact, competition frequently motivates inefficiency.

As Chapter 2 has shown, quality differentials and (to a lesser degree) time of availability tend to be decisive in competitions between close substitute weapons, while development cost differentials are crucial only in uncommon borderline cases. Although too little experience has been accumulated for a conclusive judgment, this scheme of relative importance seems to hold true even under the new regimen of cost awareness imposed by Secretary of Defense Robert S. McNamara. Contractors are therefore pressed to enhance quality and reduce development time, accepting higher production and especially development costs whenever a possible advantage over competing weapons can be gained. Incentives of this sort operate even when no immediate close substitute programs are being supported, for contractors recognize that high quality and timely delivery are required to withstand future challenges from potentially more advanced substitute weapons.

Again, time and quality appear to receive more weight than cost in evaluations of past contractor performance. To the extent that past performance is considered when the government selects contractors for new programs, an incentive to favor time and quality over cost is created. But in most source selection actions, reputation for past performance has not been a major criterion of choice. Instead, technical proposals and the availability of suitable technical, managerial, and physical resources have been stressed. From this emphasis follow some of the most serious conflicts between efficiency and competitive survival.

The best known problem is the diversion of top technical talent from the actual work of research and development into sales efforts — feasibility and design studies and the preparation of technical proposals. These activities cannot of course be condemned out of hand. Contractor engineers and scientists are most receptive to new ideas during competitive technical studies, when commitment to a particular approach is at a minimum and the pressure to try new concepts is strong. And the government profits by being able to choose from a variety of alternative technical possibilities, with a high probability that at least one will meet its needs. Some competition at the concept and idea stage would be essential in any system of weapons acquisition.

Offsetting these benefits are competitive excesses producing an end result which, in balanced appraisal, appears undesirable. Technical competitions often attract many more entrants than the minimum number required to stimulate innovation and give the government an adequate array of technical alternatives. When there are too many competitors in this sense, scarce creative technical talent is wasted. The struggle to win also encourages firms to make unrealistically optimistic technical projections, and if a new development program is built upon these misleading promises, all sorts of time, quality, and cost problems inevitably follow. Third, the amount of technical effort firms devote to their proposals tends somewhat paradoxically to be both excessive and inadequate. It is excessive because in order to make their sales brochures more attractive to government decision makers, companies refine and elaborate their designs far beyond what is needed to satisfy the government's need for basic alternatives. It is inadequate because in numerous instances the uncertainties associated with proposed new concepts preclude confident choice of the optimal technical approach. Further experimental work on actual hardware — seldom a part of the competitive efforts considered here — is necessary before these uncertainties can be resolved. For all these reasons competition for new program opportunities on the basis of technical proposals leads to nonoptimal allocation of technical resources.

The armed services have recognized this problem and tried to curtail the excesses of technical proposal competitions. In recent years they have sought to de-emphasize technical proposals, placing growing emphasis on the technical, managerial, and productive capabilities of potential contractors as a basis for new program awards. But while this is a sound approach in some respects, it interacts with other factors to magnify the undesirable effects of interfirm competition.

The chief complicating factor is technological change. During the past quarter century military technology has advanced at a furious pace, and although extrapolation from the past is hazardous, there is no particular reason to predict less technological change in coming decades. The process of change has made old skills and industrial capabilities obsolete while creating demands for new and different skills. The result has been the decline of weapons suppliers which failed to adapt and the relative growth of companies which embraced new technologies. Forty-one firms included among the Department of Defense's top 100 prime contractors during the Korean conflict failed to appear for reasons other than mergers in the list for 1958–1960.[2] In Chapter 4 we found that the principal reason for their disappearance was changes in demand related to changes in military technology.

This rapid turnover — roughly twice as rapid as in U.S. industry generally [3] — underlies what has been called "the insecurity of national security contractors." [4] Defense contractor executives are extremely conscious of the insecurity of their market positions. And most have learned the lesson of recent history well: to survive the onslaught of technological change, their organizations must move into new specialties and develop new capabilities.

How this process of adaptation has taken place is of primary interest. Sometimes established defense producers moved into new

[2] Cf. p. 74 *supra*. See also Peck and Scherer, pp. 127–128 and 599–620.

[3] *Ibid.*, p. 127.

[4] *Ibid.*, pp. 586–590.

fields by acquiring small companies through mergers or by forming small new divisions. The new organizations were then nurtured into relative maturity. But in numerous other instances the shift into new fields has been accomplished by transforming already mature organizations. Two kinds of implicit government support have eased these transformations. First, contractors have discreetly, and often without government approval, grafted onto current programs technical activities with little relevance to the immediate development problem, but with much relevance to their plans for the future. Second, companies have developed and produced in-house items which could be handled more efficiently by outside specialists, thereby building up experience, skills, and physical capabilities which would permit them eventually to compete openly with the specialists. In both cases, firms aggrandized their capabilities for future projects at the expense of efficient performance on current projects. And in both cases — extremely common during the 1950's — the costs were fully paid by the government, usually with profit added.

Nor does the process end there. Some of the capabilities created in this way have been redundant. For instance, the diversification of airframe and other old-line defense firms into such fields as automatic checkout equipment and guidance subsystem production contributed to the growth of excess capacity in specialized defense electronics organizations and in the defense industry at large. The resulting overcapacity, combined with excess capacity caused by other forces, intensifies the insecurity of national security contractors, breeding several additional problems. For one, firms with excess capacity and declining sales are reluctant to release surplus trained personnel, since availability of a skilled and experienced work force is almost a prerequisite and certainly an advantage in the competition for new programs. This hoarding constitutes inefficient utilization of defense resources. Second, overmanned technical groups make work for themselves through "goldplating" — building unnecessary complication into weapon system designs, with concomitant increases in cost and perhaps decreases in reliability.[5] Third, to utilize their surplus resources contractors also indulge in misleadingly optimistic bidding for new contracts, and this

[5] Cf. pp. 162–164 *supra*. See also Peck and Scherer, pp. 473–478 and 496–501.

in turn is a partial cause of erroneous program decisions by the government.

Of course, not all the capacity created by implicit diversification under development contracts has been redundant. And the need for adapting old organizations to new technologies can scarcely be denied — even though the expansion of existing specialists and vigorous new organizations might be a more satisfactory way of meeting government demands in new and growing fields.[6] As Joseph Schumpeter has written:

> . . . there is certainly no point in trying to conserve obsolescent industries indefinitely; but there is point in trying to avoid their coming down with a crash and in attempting to turn a rout, which may become a center of cumulative depressive effects, into orderly retreat. Correspondingly there is, in the case of industries that have sown their wild oats but are still gaining and not losing ground, such a thing as orderly advance.[7]

His perception that progress requires a certain amount of short-run inefficiency is also relevant to the weapons acquisition problem:

> A system — any system, economic or other — that at *every* given point of time fully utilizes its possibilities to the best advantage may yet in the long run be inferior to a system that does so at *no* given point of time, because the latter's failure to do so may be a condition for the level or speed of long-run performance.[8]

But on the whole, the pell-mell adaptation and diversification typical of the late 1950's appear to have been unnecessarily costly in terms of current program outcomes. At the very least, decisions to sacrifice efficiency for the development of future capabilities ought to be made explicitly by the government as buyer of weapons, rather

---

[6] Rapid organizational growth also has its costs in terms of inefficiency, while established defense producers have the advantages of seasoned management, experience in quantity production, and well-developed internal personal relationships. But a small, growing firm with high opportunity cost is more likely to choose a novel, uncomplicated technical approach than a firm with many idle engineers, and often simplicity of design leads to both reduced costs and increased reliability.

[7] J. A. Schumpeter, *Capitalism, Socialism, and Democracy* (3rd ed.; New York: Harper, 1950), p. 90.

[8] *Ibid.*, p. 83.

than through contractor subterfuge in buy vs. make decisions and technical approach choices.

In any event, it is clear that competition among close substitute weapons and competition for new program awards on the basis of reputation have as a rule generated strong incentives for contractor emphasis on quality and time, but only weak incentives on the cost dimension. Competition for new program awards on the basis of technical proposals and company capabilities has produced incentives for nonoptimal allocation of technical talent and inefficient program execution.

Competition for budgetary support should at least in principle afford an offsetting incentive for efficiency. If costs get out of hand, a program may be dropped to support efforts yielding more military value per dollar of cost. But in practice this system of incentives functions very imperfectly. High priority programs are seldom threatened with termination because of excessive costs, and so the budgetary incentive for efficiency is weak. And in the development stages of low priority programs contractors are often able to survive budgetary competition by revealing cost overruns only gradually, after considerable momentum has been gained and cancellation has become difficult. Contractors may also react to budgetary pressures by accepting undesirable time and perhaps quality sacrifices rather than weeding out those inefficiencies which insure the receipt of future new contracts. Under certain conditions budgetary competition can furnish incentives for efficiency during the production phases of low priority programs, but these incentives may be emasculated by low unit price elasticities of demand.

CONTRACTUAL INCENTIVES AND EFFICIENCY

Thus, the burden of stimulating efficiency in weapons development and production programs has fallen in large measure on various types of contractual incentives. As Chapter 9 brought out, up to 1963 the government had not effectively implemented a system of contractual incentives based upon correlating negotiated profit rates with past performance. Instead, the emphasis has been on automatic contractual incentives — correlating under a pre-arranged formula the amount of contract profit realized with the contractor's success in surpassing (or failing to surpass) negotiated performance targets, usually on the cost dimension.

A conventional assumption of the automatic contractual incentives approach is that contractors tend to maximize accounting profits in the short run of an individual contract. But the analysis in Chapters 7 and 8 has demonstrated that this assumption is at best a weak one. Deviations from strict short-run maximization greatly limit the effectiveness of automatic contractual incentives. Increments of short-run contract profit obtained through cost reduction under incentive contracts do not represent pure, unmixed gain to the contractor. To be sure, they have utility, although at high profit levels the marginal utility of incentive profits is frequently slight or even negative. But against the utility of these incentive profits contractors must weigh the many user costs and disutilities connected with cost reduction.

For instance, by incurring costs and foregoing incentive profits a firm can increase the quality of its weapon system or decrease development time, thereby increasing the expected value of follow-on production sales and profits and enhancing its competitive reputation for good performance. Similarly, by incurring costs the contractor can maintain and build up its technical and production capabilities to capture future programs.

Choices of this nature reflect a conflict between short-run accounting profit maximization (reducing costs to acquire contract profit increments) and long-run profit maximization (incurring costs to ensure that sales volume, and the accompanying profits, will be maintained and increased in the future). The accumulation of theoretical and empirical knowledge in economics strongly suggests that if firms tend to maximize any kind of profits at all, it is the long-run variety. Observation of weapons contractor behavior confirms the long-run viewpoint's dominance. Moreover, in the vast majority of conflict situations, contractor expectations were such that future gains tended to outweigh offsetting current gains. The reason for this emphasis, however, was not simply that contractors believe the value of future profits which might otherwise be sacrificed, discounted to the present at a rate considered appropriate, generally exceeds the value of particular short-run incentive contract profits. Rather, there appear to be important nonprofit goals which reinforce the long-run profit maximization objective. In particular, most company executives place a very high value on organizational survival for its own sake, as well as for the sake of maintaining profit-earning opportunities. Similarly, sales growth is an autonomous goal, since the power, prestige, and salaries of a firm's executives is an increasing function of sales volume.[9] Thus, long-run profit maximization, survival, and sales growth are complementary and mutually reinforcing organizational goals. When conflicts arise, the combined long-run competitive benefits associated with incurring costs tend to swamp the value of short-run incentive contract profits.

Even when cost reductions can be accomplished without sacrificing long-run competitive benefits, the job of cost reduction remains a difficult and unpleasant one. Overcoming the disutilities of cost reduction often requires compulsions much stronger than those supplied by the incentive contracts typically employed in advanced weapons work.

Given, therefore, all of the user costs and disutilities connected with cost reduction in weapons programs, the equilibrium amount of cost reduction incited by all but the strongest automatic contractual profit-cost correlations has historically been rather small. And because weapon system and major subsystem contractors generally have a bargaining advantage in contract negotiations due to their superior knowledge of costs and the imperfection of close substitute competition, the incidence of really strong automatic contractual incentives (e.g., contracts with tight cost targets, high sharing proportions, and substantial uncertainty) has been low.

Government officials (and economists too) have on the whole been slow to recognize these limitations in the automatic contractual incentives approach. In fact, many persons with experience in government contracting offices will be surprised by the assertion that contractors do not maximize contract profits. They have witnessed contractors fighting long and hard in negotiations for higher profit rates and cost targets, and therefore they infer that contract profits are being maximized. The perception is fairly accurate,[10] but the inference is not. There is nothing inconsistent in the statement that contractors attempt to maximize contract profits *at the bargaining*

---

[9] Cf. pp. 161–162 *supra*.

[10] However, we have seen in Chapters 6 and 8 that frequently firms are willing to sacrifice average profit expectations for security against loss in the choice of contract types — an example of nonmaximization of contract profits at the bargaining table.

table but do not do so *in the laboratory and factory.* Fundamentally different types of behavior are involved.

The fact that contractors may try to maximize contract profits at the bargaining table does, of course, raise other problems. There is a tendency, limited only by the pressures of typically indirect and imperfect competition, for contractors to use their superior knowledge of costs by setting cost targets at generously high levels — in other words, to pad their costs. The proclivity is so natural that it plagues not only U.S. defense contracting, but also the Russian weapons acquisition process. So-called incentive profits may therefore owe their existence to superior bargaining instead of superior efficiency. Or they may be due to plain good luck on the outcome of certain costs or other parameters which could be predicted in advance only within a range of uncertainty, rather than to any specific actions taken by the contractor. (In this latter case, bad luck and hence profit reductions are equally likely.) The analysis in Chapters 7 and 8 indicates that variations in the cost target negotiating process were a much more important determinant of contract underruns and overruns — and hence the level of incentive profits realized — than variations in efficiency.

The ability of contractors to win (or lose) incentive profits at the bargaining table as well as in the laboratory or factory is an inherent defect of the automatic contractual incentives approach. The problem is intensified in several ways by the impact which suspicions of cost padding and profiteering have on government-contractor relations. First, fear that contractors are out to exploit their relative ignorance of costs imbues many government officials with a cynical, hostile attitude which ill serves the spirit of close collaboration required in weapons programs. Second, the growth of direct government controls over contractor operations has been prompted at least in part by a general conviction among long-term government officials that automatic contractual incentives cannot be relied upon to spur efficiency rather than cost padding.[11]   Third,

---

[11] The desire to ferret out cost padding lay behind substantial increases in service contract proposal pre-audit activities, involving the creation of several hundred new auditing jobs, during the late 1950's. See House, Committee on Armed Services, Subcommittee for Special Investigations, *Hearings, Overpricing of Government Contracts* (1961), pp. 28–29 and 57. For a further discussion of the growth of direct controls, see Chapter 14 *infra.*

Congress has demanded statutory guards against cost padding and profiteering which limit the possibility of retaining substantial incentive contract profits and hence reduce their motivational effectiveness. These safeguards may also impair contractors' willingness to accept high-risk contracts. Finally, recognition that a large underrun could provoke charges of profiteering induces contractors to absorb price cushions in the form of cost rather than profit.

This last aspect of the automatic contractual incentives problem has also not been fully assimilated into the thinking of government leaders. The standard assumption of veteran congressmen and Department of Defense employees is that when contractors submit padded target cost estimates, they do so to gain windfall profits. Contractors deny the truth of this assertion, and for the most part their denials are probably justified. The really serious problem of cost padding is not the negotiation of cushions which will be exploited in the form of windfall profit, but of those which will be taken in the form of cost. Even when it estimates costs as realistically and accurately as possible, a contractor will try to ensure that it can live in the style to which it is accustomed. An analogy is appropriate. The son of a wealthy family working out his college budget is in all probability going to plan on steaks, shrimp cocktails, and sports cars; not spaghetti, beans, and bus transportation. And when his budget is approved, he is not apt to adopt a spaghetti and beans diet, adding the difference between budgeted and actual expenditures to his savings account. So it is with Uncle Sam's favorite nephews. The cost reduction problem is not a problem of high profits, for in recent years defense contract profits have on the average been quite modest, but a problem of excessive costs.

Inefficiencies of this sort will not be eliminated merely through the application of "cost control procedures" and "management tools," as proposed by an industry group.[12] Rather, strong pressures — indeed, compulsions — for cost reduction are essential. The automatic contractual incentives applied to most advanced weapon system and major subsystem development and production efforts have not been powerful enough to compel the elimination of

[12] National Security Industrial Association, *Report of Cost Reduction Study* (June 15, 1962), pp. 11, 169, 170, and 172.

inefficiencies which companies were reluctant to eliminate. They have not been able to offset the inherent tendencies toward inefficiency propagated by weapons makers' competition for survival in an environment of rapid technological change. Nor is it likely, given the strategic role which contractors play in drawing up cost estimates and negotiating profit-cost correlation provisions, that the automatic contractual incentives approach can be greatly strengthened.

THE BALANCE PROBLEM IN MULTIDIMENSIONAL INCENTIVE CONTRACTING

In recent years there has been a growing awareness that something was seriously wrong with the incentive systems employed for advanced weapons development. Many changes have been initiated, especially since Robert S. McNamara took office as Secretary of Defense. Although it is doubtful whether adequate attention has been given to certain fundamental problems, most of the new incentive policies — e.g., the establishment of a contractor performance evaluation system, the injection of past performance criteria into source selection decisions, and the variation of negotiated profit rates to reflect past performance — are at least aimed in the right direction. However, one major new policy could make matters worse rather than better. That is the emphasis on multidimensional incentive contracting for weapon systems and subsystems development.

The basic problem in the multidimensional incentive contract approach is one of balance. Even before multidimensional incentive contracting came into vogue, there was an over-all imbalance of incentives in weapons development. We have found that mainly because of the competitive milieu of weapons acquisition and the quest for technical perfection by engineers and scientists, incentives for quality maximization and development time control have in general been quite strong, but that incentives for development cost efficiency have been deficient. If this assessment is correct, then where strengthened incentives are most needed is on the development cost dimension. But while adding essentially redundant incentives on the quality and time dimensions, the multidimensional incentives approach necessarily reduces the amount of profit variation which might otherwise be correlated with cost outcome variations.[13]   A multidimensional incentive contract with internally balanced incentives on all dimensions of program performance therefore preserves and perhaps aggravates the over-all incentive imbalance by failing to supply the strongest possible incentives for cost efficiency.[14]

In ambitious weapons development programs the multidimensional incentive contract approach also makes excessive demands upon the ability of government and contractor personnel to predict strategic needs and technological possibilities and problems. Given the existence of substantial uncertainties, the validity of negotiated quality, time, and cost targets will continually be suspect. Detailed, rigid performance incentive formulas will almost certainly cause either inflexibility in reacting to inevitable changes in the strategic and technological environment or a ponderous administrative burden in the negotiation of contract amendments.

Thus, the recent Department of Defense policy compelling extensive use of multidimensional incentive contracts must be found wanting. A reversal of the trend toward contractual quality and time incentives appears warranted. But because of the other automatic contractual incentives approach limitations summarized in this chapter, a really satisfactory solution to the incentives problem could not be achieved even if the full variability of development contract profits were correlated with cost dimension outcomes. Something new — a means of creating incentives for good over-all performance and cost efficiency which avoids the inherent flaws of existing systems — is much to be desired.

[13] As Chapter 7 brought out, time dimension contractual incentives are also redundant because a schedule slippage typically leads to increased program costs, and under a cost incentive contract with specific technical objectives the resultant cost overrun would reduce the contractor's profits.

[14] The limitations of this conclusion must be made perfectly clear. *If* competitive incentives were well balanced, then balanced contractual incentives would be in order. But the analysis in Chapters 2 through 4 suggests strongly that competitive incentives are generally much stronger on the quality and time dimensions than on the cost dimension. To reject the conclusion drawn here, one must show that competitive incentives are optimally balanced.

CHAPTER 12

After-the-Fact Evaluation: A New Incentive Approach

THIS CHAPTER EXPLORES a relatively new incentive approach — after-the-fact evaluation — which attempts to cope with the environment of uncertainty and change, the need for flexibility, and the other problems which characterize advanced weapons development and production programs. No claim is made to originality in suggesting the central idea, which during the past few years has attracted the attention of numerous government officials and others concerned with the weapons acquisition process.[1] However, the

[1] Let me stress that I make no claim to priority in "inventing" the concept examined here. But in fairness, it should be noted that the present proposal was neither copied from nor inspired by after-the-fact evaluation systems set in motion by the Department of Defense in 1962 and 1963. Many persons within and outside of government appear to have been thinking along such lines in 1960. At that time the possible desirability of an after-the-fact evaluation incentive system was recognized by Gerald Siegel (then a member of the Harvard Weapons Acquisition Research Project) and me as a result of our case study field research. This chapter closely follows a memorandum I prepared for the research project group and a few "outsiders" in February 1961. Later Paul W. Cherington and I co-authored a watered-down version for the Secretary of Defense, issued as the report of Department of Defense Project No. 103 on June 26, 1961. It is doubtful whether there is any close link between the Project 103 report and the subsequent Defense Department actions. Rather, the commissioning of the report apparently reflected the independent interest of certain DOD officials in some sort of after-the-fact evaluation scheme. The report itself was not well-received within the defense establishment, and subsequent plans have developed along lines quite different from those suggested.

I did not participate in the 1962 and 1963 deliberations, nor was I (despite my specific request in February 1963) given access to an official report describing the new Department of Defense evaluation system. Access to the report would have been most helpful in making revisions to this volume.

For published discussions of the proposed Department of Defense and

327

approach outlined here departs in several important respects from after-the-fact evaluation systems thus far implemented on a limited experimental basis by the Department of Defense and the National Aeronautics and Space Administration. Therefore *de novo* implementation will be assumed, and no effort will be made to integrate the concepts proposed here with complementary or alternative concepts and procedures accepted or being studied by government agencies during 1963.

The open-ended analytical attitude of Parts I and II is largely abandoned in this and the following chapter to concentrate on articulating and in some instances advocating definite policy measures. There are two main reasons for this shift. First, the universe of potential policy variants is virtually infinite. For succinctness the discussion must be limited to one or at most a few specific alternatives which appear most interesting and/or promising. Even though preference for a single alternative is often implied in concrete proposals, many detailed deviations from the fundamental approach proffered here might usefully be considered. Second, the incentive approach explored in this chapter represents a substantial departure from past practices and traditions. Recognizing that any new proposal can all too easily be drowned in a sea of well- and not-so-well-meaning objections, the present chapter assumes the role of friend in court for after-the-fact evaluation, attempting to bring out its most promising features and to examine critically common objections to the system. Chapter 15, on the other hand, offers an assessment of the proposal's over-all merit which strives to be as balanced and objective as human frailty permits.

EVALUATING CONTRACTOR PERFORMANCE

The basic operating principle of an after-the-fact evaluation incentive system is as follows: Contractor performance in each pro-

National Aeronautics and Space Administration evaluation systems, see Katherine Johnsen, "NASA Sole Judge in New Incentive Plan," *Aviation Week & Space Technology,* June 25, 1962, pp. 28–29; William H. Gregory, "DOD, NASA Study Common System for Rating Company Performance," *Aviation Week & Space Technology,* February 4, 1963, p. 95; Hal Taylor, "System Will Rate Contractors," *Missiles and Rockets,* February 11, 1963, p. 14; and "Contractor Evaluation Comments Asked," *Aviation Week & Space Technology,* April 15, 1963, p. 32.

gram covered by the system would be measured or evaluated retrospectively. On the basis of these evaluations, those contractors which have performed well would be rewarded with relatively high profits and/or increased opportunities for sales growth, while those contractors which have performed poorly would be penalized by relatively low profits or losses and reduced opportunities for sales growth.

The most important prerequisite for such a system is an effective, consistent method of measuring performance after-the-fact. As we have seen in Chapters 4 and 9, measuring performance poses very difficult problems.[2] For instance, the concept of performance appropriate to an incentive system is one which indicates how well a contractor has performed, not in some absolute sense, but how well it performed relative to the strategic needs and technological possibilities and relative to what a well-motivated, efficient organization could do. There are no established quantitative yardsticks which provide readings of this sort. Furthermore, performance in a weapons development program is a complex multidimensional attribute. Some system of weights must be applied to combine measurements on the various dimensions into an over-all performance value. These weights would necessarily vary from program to program, reflecting objective and subjective judgments of what was important to the government. No method is known to the author of solving all these problems through some kind of mechanistic measurement process. Rather, it appears necessary to obtain evaluations of contractor performance from knowledgeable persons of sound judgment.

There are two basic organizational alternatives for accomplishing this end. One is to have performance judgments made by the government official directly responsible for the program being evaluated. This decentralized approach clearly satisfies the knowledgeability criterion best — by virtue of day-to-day experience the judges would have detailed familiarity with their programs' problems and accomplishments. But there are strong grounds for questioning whether the "sound judgment" criterion could be met. As Chapter 9 pointed out, serious problems of bias and lack of comparability between program evaluations are likely to arise when performance judgments are made by persons deeply involved in

[2] Cf. pp. 92–101 and 286–292 *supra*.

the programs.[3]   The alternative to this decentralized approach is to rely for evaluations upon a more or less centralized group of competent individuals who have no direct involvement in any particular program.   Problems of bias and noncomparability are minimized (although not completely eliminated) in this way. Through steps to be outlined later, the evaluators could presumably gain sufficient knowledge to make well-informed performance judgments.   Since it offers promise of meeting requisite standards of knowledgeability at a higher level of objectivity and interprogram comparability, the centralized performance evaluation approach appears preferable to the decentralized approach.

As the cornerstone of its after-the-fact evaluation incentive system, the government would therefore establish a central organization to evaluate periodically and systematically the performance of the principal contractors executing large advanced weapon system and major subsystem development and production programs. This organization might be called the Program Evaluation Board.

Although other workable methods might be devised, the specific performance measurement method best suited to application for an incentive system appears to be an ordinal ranking from best to worst of all principal contractors' performance in all programs conducted during a given period, either generally or in specific classes (e.g., over-all aerospace systems, propulsion subsystems, guidance and communication subsystems, etc.).   The Program Evaluation Board members would make better-or-worse comparisons of each contractor's performance in each program with the performance of each other contractor during the relevant period to obtain an over-all performance ranking.   As new programs reached the point at which performance evaluations became appropriate, they would be added to the list of programs among which comparisons were made, while older programs would be dropped from the list.

Ranking is, in a very loose sense, a means of measuring the unmeasurable.   It has a long tradition of use in economics to handle otherwise intractable measurement problems.   The ranking method has been tested and shown to have considerable promise in the program evaluation experiment described briefly in Chapter 4 of

[3] Cf. p. 288 *supra*.   See also Peck and Scherer, pp. 562–568.

this volume and at length in the first volume of this study.[4]   It has several attractive advantages over other possible evaluation methods.   First, it is a relativistic approach — it explicitly demands interprogram comparisons, thus permitting relatively good performance to be singled out for relatively high rewards and relatively poor performance for relatively low rewards.   Second, the method can be extended in various ways to provide not only a simple ordinal ranking of programs, but also a measure of the degree of performance difference between programs (that is, an interval measure).[5]   This interval scale would be most useful in establishing an appropriate distribution of rewards and penalties for all programs covered.   Finally, the ranking approach makes it possible to measure the consistency (or in technical terms, transitivity) of individual judges and the degree of agreement among various judges in their evaluations, so that problems of multidimensionality and bias can be identified.[6]   The last two measures would permit a continuing check on how well the performance evaluation process is working.

Once the Program Evaluation Board completes any particular contractor's program performance ranking, that ranking would be used to determine the amount of profit to be given the contractor.[7] It would also be considered in awarding new contracts to the firm. Because each of these incentive applications has several possible variations and involves a number of special problems, a more detailed analysis of each is desirable.

[4] Cf. pp. 93–101 *supra* and Peck and Scherer, pp. 543–580 and 668–711.

[5] Cf. Peck and Scherer, pp. 684–685 and 688.

[6] *Ibid.,* pp. 543–580.

[7] It is possible that a given program might be included in several different rankings as a benchmark for evaluating performance in other programs, even though its profits would be determined in only one ranking.   To illustrate, all programs completed during the past three years might be included in each ranking.   If Program Alpha were evaluated for the first time immediately after its completion for the purpose of determining the contractor's profit, it would be compared with all programs completed in the previous three years.   As time went on Program Alpha would remain on the list for comparative (but not profit determination) purposes until, three years after its completion, Alpha would be dropped from the list.   Obviously, many other ways of securing a large enough sample to achieve sensitive comparisons can be conceived.

THE USE OF AFTER-THE-FACT EVALUATION IN PROFIT DETERMINATION

Since the difficulty of setting valid cost, quality, and time targets in advance of performance is greatest during the research and development phases of weapons programs, the most obvious application of after-the-fact evaluation would be to determine development contract profit awards. A system along the following lines is proposed: The contractor's development and prototype production activities would be covered by some kind of profitless term contract. Costs would be reimbursed fully as they were incurred, as in current practice. When the program reached some predetermined point — e.g., six months after the completion of initial operational units — the contractor's performance up to that point would be evaluated and given a position in the Program Evaluation Board's rank list of programs. A lump sum profit payment would then be related to the contractor's performance rank: the higher the rank (that is, the better the contractor's performance relative to other contractors), the greater the amount or rate of profit would be.

Alternatively, each contractor's performance might be evaluated every year or two during the course of a development effort.[8] Profit awards would then be made more frequently, covering only partial segments of any given development program. However, it is doubtful whether midprogram performance evaluations could be made with sufficient consistency and validity to serve as a satisfactory basis for incentive awards. Most development efforts experience valleys of pessimism as difficult unanticipated technical problems arise, along with peaks of optimism when tests prove unexpectedly successful.[9] Midprogram performance evaluations could hardly avoid being influenced by these transient events, even though they may be poor indicators of what really matters: ultimate

[8] Under the proposed new Department of Defense performance evaluation system, evaluations are to be made every six months. "Contractor Evaluation Comments Asked," *Aviation Week & Space Technology,* April 15, 1963, p. 32.

[9] See, for example, S. W. Herwald, "Appraising the Effects of the Technological State of the Art on the Corporate Future," in *Technological Planning on the Corporate Level,* ed. James R. Bright (Boston: Division of Research, Harvard Business School, 1962), pp. 62–65.

program success or failure. Similarly, the timing of tangible results varies widely from program to program. In some developments impressive results are obtained at an early point, while in
other programs — e.g., when the first complete integration of subsystems occurs relatively late in the game — there is little
substantial basis for early performance judgments.[10] Indeed, a
system of incentives based upon segmented performance evaluations might encourage short-sighted technical approaches which
look good at any moment in time, but lead to inefficiency and nonoptimal outcomes over the full development span. Therefore,
although the feasibility of segmented performance evaluations deserves further exploration, initial applications of after-the-fact
evaluation should correlate profit awards with contractor performance in complete development programs.[11]

Historically, development lead time in U.S. advanced weapons
programs has averaged between 8 and 11 years.[12] Even though
contractor technical activities seldom reach an intensive level until

[10] A good illustration of this point is had by comparing the Nike Ajax
and Sparrow III development programs, which involved quite different
sequences of results, partly because of different technical and strategic problems and partly because the contractors held different development philoso-
phies. Only after six years of development was a test of the complete Nike
Ajax system conducted, convincing skeptics that the system would in fact
work. Two years later the first operational Nike Ajax units were deployed.
I would venture to say that performance evaluations made during the early
years of the Nike Ajax program would have differed substantially from
those made after the first successful demonstration. On the other hand,
the first successful test of a Sparrow III missile was accomplished less than
three years after the start of development, although nearly five more years
of development effort followed before the system became operational.

[11] This conclusion raises two related questions. First, how would programs which were terminated before their completion be evaluated? The
problem of obtaining good evaluations would clearly be more difficult.
Whether the program was terminated because of failures on the contractor's
part or because of changes in national strategy or enemy capabilities would
undoubtedly be an important factor. Second, how would product improvement efforts be evaluated after a weapon system became operational? A
development program is seldom really completed when the first operational
units are delivered, and often improvement effort expenditures have been
larger than original development outlays. In such cases a separate evaluation might be made of contractor performance during the product improvement program, although other solutions might also be evolved.

[12] Peck and Scherer, pp. 53–54.

relatively late in the development cycle, it might be argued that firms would be forced to wait too long for the first profit returns on their efforts. But under a profit-award-after-evaluation system the contractor would still be better off than firms which develop new products for the commercial market, for the latter receive neither profits nor reimbursement of costs until their development efforts yield a successful end product.[13] Forcing contractors to wait until a militarily useful product emerges from development could provide a desirable incentive for development time reduction, although as we have seen in Chapter 10, other complex and not necessarily beneficial effects might also appear. Should the financial burden of waiting several years for development profits prove too great for the majority of hardware development contractors, a token fee — sufficient only to cover minimum interest charges and other costs not reimbursed directly — might be added to reimbursed costs.

Over-All Performance vs. Efficiency

It is natural to suppose that the profit awards made under an after-the-fact evaluation system of incentives would be related to over-all contractor performance. In certain situations this would no doubt be optimal. But in advocating a general correlation of development contract profits with over-all performance, one risks making the assumption criticized in Chapters 7 and 11: that within a single incentive approach balanced incentives must be offered on all dimensions of performance. When competition supplies strong incentives for quality maximization and development time minimization but not for development cost minimization, a better over-all incentive balance would be achieved by emphasizing efficiency as the basis for development contract profit correlations.

The program evaluation experiment results analyzed in Chapter

[13] The ratio of production to development outlays is often so much higher in commercial product lines that some weapons makers might insist they should be compared only with firms such as Arthur D. Little, which sells development for its own sake. But in programs whose specific purpose is to create operationally useful military hardware, the concept of selling development for its own sake is inappropriate. An alternative profit award arrangement would of course be necessary for projects with little or no follow-on production potential, as well as more generally for firms which sell only development efforts and do not engage in production.

4 suggest that variations in cost outcomes affect evaluations of over-all contractor performance only when time and quality considerations are roughly equal. Basing profit awards on an evaluation of over-all performance might therefore provide rather weak, in-consistent incentives for cost efficiency. An inefficient develop-ment job could still win a high over-all performance rank and hence high profits.[14] To be sure, such a system would afford somewhat stronger incentives for efficiency than cost-plus-fixed-fee contracts and perhaps also multidimensional cost-plus-incentive-fee contracts stressing profit-quality and profit-time correlations. But it cer-tainly would not create the strongest possible incentives for develop-ment efficiency.

Therefore, an alternative system is proposed for programs whose purpose is to develop operationally useful military hardware: basing the profit payment not on the contractor's over-all performance rank, but on its rank when evaluated only in terms of development efficiency. Competitive incentives would then be relied upon to motivate good performance on the quality and time dimensions, while contractual (profit) incentives are focused on the cost dimen-sion. The soundness of this approach hinges, of course, on the feasibility of rendering development efficiency judgments through after-the-fact evaluation. On this question there is little evidence. As indicated in Chapter 9, *a priori* reasoning suggests that valid efficiency rankings could be made by a competent Program Evalua-tion Board, but the problem should be subjected to further study and empirical testing.[15]

The Distribution of Profit Awards

The strength of the incentives created by an after-the-fact evalua-tion system would also depend upon the range and form of the distribution of profit awards. Awards might range from 15% of costs (corresponding to the statutory maximum on cost reimburse-ment contracts) down to 0% or even net losses.[16] For reasons

[14] Cf. pp. 97–98 *supra*.

[15] Cf. p. 292 *supra*.

[16] The statutory maximum applies to *estimated* costs. To avoid bargain-ing problems it would probably be preferable to relate the after-the-fact evaluation award rate to *actual* costs, although this could lead to other prob-lems noted in the next paragraph.

discussed in Chapter 9, the distribution should be approximately normal; that is, profit rates near the average would be awarded more frequently than profit rates near 0% or 15%.[17] The average rate would be set at a level sufficient to maintain the desired quantity and quality of technical resources in weapons development work. The average rate might also be adjusted to reflect the average efficiency of weapons developers; that is, if the median contractor in the Program Evaluation Board's rank list were relatively efficient in some (difficult to measure) absolute sense, the average profit rate would be set at a level somewhat higher than if the median firm had been relatively inefficient.[18]

Actually, it may be preferable to relate the distribution of profit rates to some base such as contractor investment or stockholder's equity instead of cost. When a cost base is employed, even though the *rates* applied vary directly with efficiency, a contractor might still be able to increase its profit *amount* by incurring high development costs. An asset base would be less troublesome in this regard, although inefficient investment in facilities might then be encouraged. In fact, there is undoubtedly no perfect solution to the problem of finding an appropriate base for profit awards in non-market situations, as public utility theorists have long recognized.[19]

Using contractor investment as a base for profit awards does, however, offer another more clear-cut advantage. Varying the profit rate to reflect differences in investment and subcontracting would no longer be necessary, and the full range of profit rate variation could be allocated to efficiency correlations.[20] As we have seen in Chapter 9, when a cost base is used, rate adjustments reflecting investment are essential for profit effectively to govern the

[17] Cf. pp. 296–297 *supra*.

[18] A further refinement would be to adjust the range of profit rates to reflect the degree of agreement achieved by Program Evaluation Board members in their rankings. If most firms performed with roughly equal efficiency, we should expect rather low agreement among Board members, while if there were marked efficiency differences, agreement would tend to be high. See Peck and Scherer, pp. 557–560 and 693. The lower the agreement among Board members, the less profits would vary.

[19] See D. Philip Locklin, *Economics of Transportation* (Chicago: Business Publications, Inc., 1935), pp. 355–370 and 394–398.

[20] Variations in profit rates to reflect differences in financial risk would also be unnecessary, since pricing risks would not vary from contract to contract under an after-the-fact evaluation system.

flow of investment into and out of weapons work.[21]   If an investment base were employed for profit awards, the *average* rate could be adjusted to perform this allocative role, while the *distribution* of rates around the average would perform the role of motivating efficiency.[22]

Application to Production Contract Profit Determination

The system outlined up to this point implies that after development contract profits were related to the Program Evaluation Board's development efficiency rankings, conventional automatic contractual incentives would then be relied upon to motivate production efficiency.   Nevertheless, as we have seen in Chapters 8 and 9, the automatic contractual incentives approach also has inherent problems when applied to advanced weapons production situations. The rewards for cost reduction under automatic contractual incentives are noncumulative, and so-called incentive profits can be gained through superior bargaining over cost targets as well as through superior efficiency.   Both of these problems could be minimized, even if not eliminated, by employing an after-the-fact evaluation approach to production contract profit determination. Each contractor's production efficiency would be evaluated annually, and the rate of profit awarded would be correlated with the relative level of efficiency achieved.   Under this system contractors would not be rewarded merely because the negotiation of loose cost targets made underruns easy to attain, nor would they be penalized because the government struck an unusually hard bargain in cost target negotiations.   Similarly, if a firm cut its costs to the bone at the start of a production program and then merely maintained that relative level of efficiency, it would continue to receive a high production efficiency ranking, realizing high profits on every production contract rather than on the first contract only, as under the automatic approach.[23]

---

[21] Cf. pp. 275–279 *supra*.

[22] Profit rates might also have to be adjusted somewhat in individual cases to reflect differences in bargaining power, if companies with many commercial opportunities for employing their technical resources balk at accepting development contracts on the same terms as firms with low opportunity cost.   Or alternatively, such firms might be paid a somewhat higher token fee.

[23] Cf. p. 296 *supra*.

Thus, after-the-fact evaluation offers potential advantages even in advanced weapons production programs, when costs cannot be estimated in advance (at least by government analysts) with high confidence. However, the case for determining production profits through after-the-fact evaluation is not nearly as compelling as for development. And bringing an after-the-fact evaluation system covering development profits alone to the stage where it runs smoothly will require concerted analytical and administrative efforts, and this task deserves priority. Despite their shortcomings, therefore, retention of automatic contractual incentives to spur production efficiency would undoubtedly be judicious until extension of after-the-fact evaluation is clearly feasible.

Exemption from Renegotiation

An after-the-fact evaluation approach to profit determination virtually eliminates the possibility of windfall profits. But since the Renegotiation Board considers over-all corporate profits on an annual basis and uses criteria of reasonableness broader than those the Program Evaluation Board would apply, the determinations of the two agencies could conceivably conflict. In years when especially large awards were received by a contractor, the Renegotiation Board might be tempted to seek unusually large refunds. Even though Renegotiation Board officials may claim their decisions were predicated on a consideration of over-all profits rather than the specific payment, determinations of this sort could emasculate the Program Evaluation Board's profit-performance correlations. To prevent this, profits earned as a result of after-the-fact performance evaluations should be explicitly exempted from renegotiation.

Summary

In sum, it is proposed that a Program Evaluation Board be established to evaluate contractor efficiency in the major weapon system and subsystem development programs of the three armed services.[24] Profit awards would be correlated with contractors' relative development efficiency, as evaluated by the Board. The

[24] Obviously, after-the-fact evaluation could also be applied to good advantage in the advanced development programs of the National Aeronautics and Space Administration and the Atomic Energy Commission.

higher a contractor's efficiency rank, the higher the profit return (as a percentage of either actual cost or some investment base) that contractor would receive. At first automatic contractual incentives would be relied upon to generate profit incentives for production efficiency, although eventually the after-the-fact evaluation approach might be extended to cover technically advanced production work too.

THE USE OF AFTER-THE-FACT EVALUATION IN SALES DETERMINATION

An after-the-fact evaluation system can also be employed to create incentives by correlating contractors' sales with their performance. The basic concept is quite simple: defense contractors which perform relatively well will be awarded desirable new programs and permitted to grow in sales volume, while contractors which perform relatively poorly will be deprived of new program awards and hence sales volume, perhaps to the point of disappearance.

There are many possible ways of achieving the required sales-performance correlation. For each of the alternatives, assuming that profits are related to contractor efficiency through after-the-fact evaluation and/or automatic contractual incentives, the best balance of incentives would probably be attained by making *overall* contractor performance evaluations the basis of sales awards. Then to survive and grow, a firm would have to perform relatively well over-all, with typical emphasis on the quality and time dimensions of performance. As in the existing system of incentives, it would still be possible to survive despite cost-inefficient program execution. But in order to make its survival profitable, a firm would also have to perform relatively well on the cost dimension.

Performance Evaluations as a Basis for Source Selection

One means of correlating sales with performance is to make the Program Evaluation Board's rankings of over-all contractor performance a mandatory factor in source selection decisions. For instance, a Department of Defense regulation could be issued requiring that in source selection actions using quantitative criterion point lists, some specified minimum percentage of the criterion points be allocated to past performance. The full potential variability of this category should then be exploited; that is, the competitor with the best performance rank should receive the maximum number of performance points, while the competitor with the lowest performance rank should receive no performance points.[25]

Such a policy would afford stronger incentives for good over-all performance than current source selection practices, in which little weight is assigned to past performance considerations.[26] Still the four-way conflict among past performance, attractiveness of technical proposals, availability of appropriate technical and managerial resources, and political and socioeconomic objectives as selection criteria would remain. Past performance could certainly not be the only source selection criterion, for if it were, the firm with the best performance record in a field would capture every new contract in that field. This could lead not only to short-run inefficiencies as the dominant firm's capabilities became overloaded (while other firms' resources went underutilized), but also in the long run to the reduction or elimination of competition.[27] On the other hand, if too little weight were assigned to performance differences, contractors might still find it worthwhile to divert their best technical talent from research and development activities to sales proposal preparation, to hoard surplus personnel, and to take other actions which enhance their future competitive prospects while detracting from current program execution efficiency. Clearly, a delicate balance must be struck in determining how much weight past performance variations ought to receive in source selection decisions.[28]

A sound special solution to the criterion-weighting problem has been suggested by Simon Ramo, Vice Chairman of Thompson-

[25] Cf. p. 69 *supra.*

[26] Cf. pp. 69–73 *supra.*

[27] The long-run result is by no means self-evident. The long-run dynamics of the system proposed here pose fascinating questions, but in the present state of knowledge little more than speculation is possible. If the outstanding firms remain outstanding, there would be a long-run tendency toward increasing concentration and decreasing competition. But if the firms outstanding at some point in time became complacent due to their high rewards or less efficient because of inability to assimilate their growth, while poorer performers were spurred to greater efforts by the desire to increase their low rewards, the level of concentration could remain essentially constant or perhaps even decrease.

[28] See also Peck and Scherer, pp. 361–385.

Ramo-Wooldridge, Inc.[29]   Heavy emphasis would be placed on past performance and relevant technical capabilities in choosing contractors for projects considered "extremely speculative" — those in which the uncertainties associated with design and technical approach proposals are especially great.   When more modest state of the art advances are sought, relatively more weight could be allotted to the attractiveness of technical concepts and designs.

A Level-of-Effort Incentive System [30]

An alternative incentive system utilizing after-the-fact evaluation avoids these criterion-weighting problems more completely while striking at the heart of the competitive incentive problems highlighted in Chapter 11.   The basic idea is as follows: At regular intervals, each major weapon system and subsystem contractor's in-house sales or value added for a coming period would be projected on the basis of its over-all performance in recent programs.[31] Firms with especially good performance records would be scheduled to grow at rates as high as 10% or even more per year.   Firms with especially poor performance records would be scheduled to decline at similar rates.   Firms with average performance records would be scheduled for constant, slightly increasing, or slightly decreasing value added levels, depending on whether total defense expenditures in the relevant sector are constant, increasing, or declining.   In short, a company's future level of effort would be correlated with its over-all past performance.

This incentive approach is appropriate mainly for firms or autonomous divisions which specialize in weapon system and major subsystem development and production.   Component vendors, material suppliers, and other firms or divisions not primarily engaged in systems work would be excluded.   Planned government expenditures on weapons research, development, and production

[29] Cf. "New Incentive Contract Plan Advanced," *Aviation Week & Space Technology,* January 8, 1962, p. 103.

[30] I am indebted to David Novick for discussions which helped inspire the approach outlined here.

[31] In a strict technical sense, the definitions employed here are not completely consistent.   Value added and in-house sales differ from level of effort by the contractor's profit margin.   These inconsistencies are tolerated to avoid outlining the proposed system in excessively rigid and tedious detail.

would be broken down periodically into two principal parts: the amount to be divided among organizations covered by the performance-correlated level of effort system, and the amount to be allocated to all other defense suppliers.[32]   In making this allocation decision government planners might consider not only the over-all size of the defense budget, the amount of capacity possessed by weapon system and subsystem producers, and the demands for that capacity, but also the desired volume of defense work to be channeled to small business entities and other firms excluded from the level of effort incentive system.   Firms in the excluded category would compete for sales volume in much the same way as they have in the past.

Given a high-level decision on the over-all level of effort to be expended by major weapon system and subsystem producers, the shares of particular firms in that total (and hence their scheduled rates of in-house sales growth or decline) would depend upon their past performance records.   Once a firm's level of effort has been projected for a coming period, the organization would be loaded with work until the scheduled rate of growth or decline is achieved. This would be done in several ways.

First, new program awards would be related partly to past performance, as suggested above.   When a firm with an excellent performance record needs a new program to achieve its projected increase in value added, it would be selected over companies not in that position, as long as its technical approach and specialized capabilities are not significantly inferior to those of other competitors.   Similarly, a firm whose performance record is poor would be deprived of new program awards until its scheduled rate of decline is attained.

This method alone could not assure the matching of actual with projected in-house sales levels.   The size and timing characteristics of weapons program awards complicate any efforts to enforce a smooth correlation between sales and performance.   Assume, for example, that the Omega Corporation is scheduled, on the basis of good past performance, to grow 15% over a two-year period.   But

---

[32] A finer breakdown by product categories might also be made for the level of effort incentive system group.   However, if the subdivision were too fine it would be difficult for firms with good performance records in declining fields to achieve sales growth by diversifying into new fields.

what if, because potential enemies are found to have a new defensive system, the program in Omega's backlog with the largest immediate sales growth potential becomes obsolete and must be cancelled? Since new development programs typically begin at low expenditure levels and build up only slowly to an expenditure peak, several new programs might be needed to fill the immediate gap, while a few years hence, when the rate of spending in those programs accelerates, Omega might be forced to grow at an excessive rate. Again, what if Omega's largest program suddenly takes on unanticipated strategic significance and must be expanded drastically, implying two-year company growth of 30%? Cancelling other programs or withholding initially small new program awards might also be unacceptable methods of holding the company's growth to the 15% level planned. At best, increasing or withholding new program awards would permit only a very rough matching of actual with warranted levels of effort.

One way of securing a more exact matching is to supplement new program award variations with variations in subcontract awards. Firms which are in the position of growing faster than their past performance merited would be required to do an unusually large amount of subcontracting, favoring firms with appropriate capabilities which otherwise would grow more slowly than the warranted rate. To be sure, this approach would pose coordination and facilities transfer problems. But past experience indicates that these would not be insuperable, since major subcontracting decisions have often been employed to balance out defense industry work load disparities. For example, the establishment of Douglas and Lockheed as second source producers of the B–47 bomber was influenced in part by the Air Force's desire to limit prime contractor Boeing's rate of growth relative to other industry members. The principal innovation in the approach recommended here is the emphasis on consistent value added-performance correlations as a reason for subcontracting.

When a development group in a company scheduled for growth finds itself with insufficient work, subcontracts from other firms are one way of filling the gap until new program awards can have their effect. But the armed services might also utilize this temporary excess capacity by commissioning feasibility studies and other special studies of problems in which they are interested. Similarly, the company might be encouraged to work at government expense on projects (suggested either by the government or company planners) which will facilitate its transition into promising new fields of technology. On the other hand, if a firm is scheduled to decline because of inferior past performance, its opportunities to build up capabilities in new fields at government expense would be restricted.

Thus, every reasonable effort would be exerted to maintain a consistent incentive correlation between major system and sub-system contractors' in-house sales levels and their performance. This level of effort approach offers more, however, than simply strengthened competitive incentives. It in effect says to a firm, "If you perform well on current programs, you need not worry about your market share five years hence. You will be given the neces-sary opportunities for survival and growth, contingent only on sustained good performance." It therefore would modulate the insecurity problems discussed in Chapter 11. Defense contractors would no longer find it essential to divert their best technical talent from actual R & D work to one sales proposal preparation effort after another; they would not have to sneak superfluous technical tasks into development programs in order to build new capabilities; they would not need to hoard surplus engineers by overmanning development efforts. In fact, activities of this nature, by degrading performance in ongoing programs, would hurt their future sales expectations rather than help them.

Moreover, the performance-correlated level of effort approach could bring about a new philosophy of national defense resource allocation. Guaranteed a certain rate of market share growth (or decline) contingent only on how well they perform, firms would no longer have to ask themselves, "How heavily must we man present programs to keep our technical and production work forces busy?" Rather, they could ask, "How much can we do well within our pro-jected staff levels?" Company officials would have less reason to fear informing government agencies of surplus capacity, for the government's reaction would be to assign additional work and load the firm up to its level of effort quota, not to insist that em-ployees be laid off and plants be closed. Such a change in attitude would lead to greatly improved utilization of defense resources.

A philosophy of loading producers to capacity was a significant characteristic of the World War II defense contracting effort, and the results can scarcely be considered unimpressive. Since then, on the other hand, members of the defense industry have repeatedly found themselves in excess capacity situations, and when this happens, competition for survival impels the overmanning of remaining contracts. But this overmanning, while sound competitive tactics for the individual firm, is in large measure waste to the nation as a whole. If surplus resources could be identified and tapped, additional weapons programs could be carried out at an incremental cost only slightly greater than the cost of raw materials and other commodities purchased in competitive markets. Or the over-all level of defense spending could be reduced with no sacrifice of defense output but a gain in output from other sectors for which resources are freed.[33]

Performance Index Problems

Contractor sales or value added would be related to over-all past performance in the incentive systems visualized here. The Program Evaluation Board would supply rankings of contractor performance in each major weapon system and subsystem development program, and it might also evaluate efficiency in production efforts. But these rankings could not be used in raw form for source selection decisions and level of effort projections. Most firms (or autonomous divisions of firms) have several prime contract and major subcontract efforts under way simultaneously. How would the performance rankings of, say, Programs A, B, and C be combined into a single average performance index to determine the Gamma Division's relative position in the competition for new Program D,

---

[33] One might query, why would firms ask to be loaded with work until their allowed resources are fully utilized when the result may be an over-all reduction in defense spending? The reason is analogous to the logic of purely competitive markets. When a firm's in-house sales are fixed on the basis of performance, the decrease in defense spending due to efficiency increases by that firm would be distributed over the whole defense industry, and the individual firm would suffer a negligible sales loss while gaining efficiency-correlated profits as a result of its actions. Only if firms behaved collusively, attempting to maximize joint defense industry sales, would efficiency moves be inhibited by recognition of their possible aggregative effects. But overt or tacit collusion is unlikely, since the number of firms competing for a share of the over-all defense budget is quite large.

or to establish its level of effort for the coming three years? Taking program size as the weighting factor could encourage inadequate attention to small but vital subcontracts.[34] For how many years should performance rankings on completed programs be included in the average performance index? Should tentative evaluations of performance in uncompleted (and for that reason most current) programs be included in the index, despite the increased risk of error due to transient influences? And what would be done if a firm has performed well in its development efforts, but poorly in its production work — in other words, what relative weights would be given to the development and production phases of programs? Detailed answers to all these questions must be hammered out before a system which correlates sales with average past performance can be implemented. As in all index number problems, there is undoubtedly no perfectly satisfactory answer, although fairly workable answers probably can be found.

Summary

In sum, it is proposed that the Program Evaluation Board rank the over-all performance of contractors in major weapon system and subsystem programs. The performance ranks for recent programs would then be combined into an index of average firm or division performance. In one possible incentive approach, these indices would be given substantial weight in new program awards, especially when uncertainty precludes confident choices on the basis of proposed designs and technical approaches. A more far-reaching system of incentives could be established by relating contractors' in-house sales levels for future periods to their average performance in the recent past. The better a firm's performance, the higher its planned rate of growth would be. New development program awards, development and production subcontracts, feasibility study contracts, and diversification opportunities would all be varied to ensure that defense contractors' value added grew at rates warranted by their past performance records.

PUBLICATION OF PROGRAM EVALUATION BOARD RANKINGS

It would also be desirable to publish the Program Evaluation Board's performance rankings, so that all may know which firms

[34] Cf. pp. 91–92 *supra*.

have served the nation best in their weapons work and which have performed least effectively. Given the desire of most large firms to maintain a favorable public image and to win public approbation, this policy would provide an added and perhaps important incentive for good performance. At present no real method of exploiting the public approbation motive is available, since meaningful performance evaluations are neither made nor published. Indeed, firms which have performed poorly often manage to gain acclaim for their achievements through misleading press releases and advertising and through the self-serving statements of government officials who share responsibility for their failures.[35] The publication of Program Evaluation Board rank lists would make such attempts at whitewashing more difficult. It would also yield more effective incentives than such devices as the World War II Army-Navy "E" awards, which tended to be given out rather indiscriminately and hence to lose their prestige value.

ADVANTAGES OF THE AFTER-THE-FACT EVALUATION APPROACH

The after-the-fact evaluation approach offers several advantages as a means of providing incentives for good contractor performance. More exactly, two basic incentive systems employing after-the-fact evaluation — one correlating profit with efficiency and the other sales or some related variable with over-all performance — have been proposed here, and each has its own special attractions.

A most compelling advantage of the after-the-fact evaluation concept is its ability to remove profit determination from the arena of bargaining and place it squarely in the arena of contractor performance. The profit realized by a contractor would vary with actual technical and managerial performance, not with success in padding cost targets (or other targets) or with luck on the outcome of uncertain events essentially beyond the contractor's control. Clear-cut incentives for good performance would therefore be established.

This fundamental advantage would also yield certain auxiliary benefits. Strained buyer-seller relationships due to suspicions of

[35] It is depressing to see service officials testify under oath before congressional committees to the successful execution of their programs, when in private they (or at least their colleagues and subordinates) admit poor performance.

cost-padding and profiteering would be minimized, if not completely eliminated. A better spirit of cooperation between the government and its contractors is likely to result. Profit considerations (e.g., government fears that contractors are compensating for initially optimistic bids) could be left out of engineering change decisions, which ought to be (but sometimes are not) made on strictly technical and economic grounds. The alleviation of suspicions might even inspire government officials to place more trust in contractors, permitting some reduction in the costly, perhaps initiative-deadening detailed government surveillance of contractor operations. A desirable increase in technical flexibility might also be facilitated, since contractors would not be bound to specifications or performance targets whose *raison d'être* is often wiped out by changes in the strategic or technological environment.

If production contract profits were determined through after-the-fact evaluation, the noncumulative reward problem associated with short-term automatic contractual incentives would be avoided. As a result, generally stronger incentives could be obtained from a given range of profit variation.

It is also possible that an after-the-fact evaluation system of profit determination might permit substantial reductions in the cost of contract administration and negotiation. Contract prices, profits, and amendments would not have to be negotiated in detail; budgetary estimates already used to supplement contract data in most large programs would suffice. Although no adequate census has ever been taken, it is estimated that in 1960 the three armed services employed roughly 7,000 military and civilian contract negotiators, price analysts, contract attorneys, and contracting supervisors; along with some 2,300 contract auditors.[36] At least as many persons, and probably far more, are engaged in counterpart activities for contractor organizations. For instance, the Grumman

---

[36] These estimates include only persons in fairly responsible positions (generally, GS-7 and above), excluding supporting secretarial and clerical personnel. They are pieced together from a number of sources, including House, Committee on Armed Services, Subcommittee for Special Investigations, *Hearings, Weapons System Management and Team System Concept in Government Contracting* (1959), pp. 534, 556–588; Senate, Committee on Armed Services, Subcommittee on Procurement Practices, *Hearings Pursuant to Section 4, Public Law 86–89* (1960), pp. 277–278 and 352; and *Congressional Record,* February 2, 1961, p. 1579.

Corporation assigned a team of 60 men to negotiate the cost-plus-fixed-fee contract covering its development work on the Project Apollo lunar "Bug." [37] Even more extensive negotiations are required for multidimensional incentive contracts.[38] If only a modest fraction of these functions could be abolished by the elimination of detailed contract negotiation in programs covered by after-the-fact evaluation, impressive savings would result. This claim of potential savings must be made faintly, however, for the administrative savings promised by proponents of new government policies have a way of failing to materialize. Even if after-the-fact evaluation did make certain contracting functions redundant, it might not make the civil servants performing those functions redundant. On the contrary, contracting office inhabitants might prove remarkably adept at either justifying the preservation of their old duties or proposing new and useful contributions they could make to the national defense effort. Therefore, it must be recognized that a shift to an after-the-fact evaluation system for profit determination might increase administrative costs, rather than reduce them.

The use of performance evaluations in individual source selection decisions or in a more general system of level of effort–performance correlations would generate strengthened competitive incentives for good over-all performance, with emphasis on the time and quality dimensions. As we have seen, the competitive incentives acting upon contractors in most programs are already fairly strong. Still the incentive systems proposed in this chapter, and especially the performance-correlated level of effort determination approach, would do more than merely supplement already powerful existing competitive incentives. They would also mitigate some of their most important deleterious effects, tempering the insecurity of national security contractors and ensuring that survival and growth were correlated not with persistence in sales-getting efforts, surreptitious diversification, and talent-hoarding, but with good performance in the actual execution of research, development, and production assignments. This could be a crucial benefit.

Finally, the application of after-the-fact evaluation to both profit and sales determination offers certain attractions in the realm of

[37] "The Bug + TFX = Billion-dollar Coup for Grumman," *Business Week,* December 1, 1962, p. 96.

[38] Cf. pp. 177–181 *supra.*

fairness and equity. Growth and high profits would go to those who perform well; decline and low profits (or losses) would befall those who consistently squander the nation's resources. Few can deny this as a desirable objective. Yet in present practice the goal is realized very imperfectly, if at all. Inefficient firms typically realize about the same rate of profit (on their high costs) as efficient firms (on their low costs), and except in the most flagrant cases, habitual poor performers have fared about as well in the competition for new programs as good performers. Recognition of these facts is a source of considerable frustration to some defense contractor executives.[39] It is likely that implementation of an after-the-fact evaluation system for profit and sales determination would improve morale in the defense industry, although whether this morale boost would be translated into significant behavioral benefits cannot be predicted.

OBJECTIONS TO THE PROPOSAL: A CRITICAL APPRAISAL

There is no such thing as a perfect solution to complex problems of human motivation and behavior, and we can scarcely expect after-the-fact evaluation to be an exception. Many objections to the idea have been raised. A defense industry study group, for example, reviewed certain after-the-fact evaluation proposals and summarily recommended that they "not be given further consideration."[40] Similarly, industry representatives voiced "complete opposition" to the National Aeronautics and Space Administration's first use of a contract with after-the-fact evaluation provisions for profit determination.[41] Certain of the objections to after-the-fact evaluation appear to have considerable validity; others are of dubious merit. In this section the principal known arguments will be examined critically.

[39] Cf. p. 85 *supra*.

[40] National Security Industrial Association, *Report of Cost Reduction Study* (June 15, 1962), pp. 145, 147. "Summarily" is used because the report devoted less than 350 words of analysis to two after-the-fact incentive system proposals.

[41] Katherine Johnsen, "NASA Sole Judge in New Incentive Plan," *Aviation Week & Space Technology,* June 25, 1962, pp. 28–29.

Socialism and Unilateralism

Some may object to after-the-fact evaluation, and especially to the performance-correlated level of effort incentive approach, because it smacks of socialism — because it would entail conscious government planning and manipulation of an industrial sector occupied mainly by private firms. This is in a sense true. But what are the alternatives? Not planning is impossible. Every time a potentially large contract is awarded, the government consciously or unconsciously alters the weapons industry's structure. A margin of discretion exists only for the criteria on which these structural changes will be based, not for the fact of enriching some firms and rejecting others. The contract award criteria presently emphasized encourage nonoptimal resource allocation and inefficiency, and other incentives have been generally unsuccessful in counteracting these tendencies. In other words, existing incentive systems cannot be counted upon to motivate optimal and efficient program conduct. Recognizing this, the government has turned more and more to an alternative approach: direct controls over contractor operations.[42] And it has seriously considered an even more drastic alternative: in-house conduct of military research and development in government laboratories and arsenals.[43] These alternatives clearly represent longer steps along the road to socialism than a system of industry planning which attempts to harness for efficient government service the self-interest of private firms by relating sales and profits to past performance. Private enterprise, in the strict sense, has not been employed for at least two decades to develop and produce advanced weapon systems, nor is it likely that true private enterprise is possible at all in the nonmarket environment of weapons acquisition. A substantial degree of government intervention — socialism, if you like — is inescapable. The crucial question is whether that socialism will be the socialism of direct controls or the socialism of consciously administered incentives.

Industry representatives have roundly condemned the unilateral

[42] The issue of incentives vs. controls will be discussed further in Chapter 14.

[43] Cf. Bureau of the Budget, *Report to the President on Government Contracting for Research and Development,* reproduced as Document No. 94, Senate Committee on Government Operations (1962), pp. 21–24.

nature of what would be the Program Evaluation Board's judgments.[44]   Granted, the Board's evaluations could hardly be anything but unilateral. If contractors were permitted to contest Board
findings, protracted stalemates would arise and penalizing poor performance would become almost impossible. Although available
under existing defense contract disputes law and the Renegotiation
Act, judicial or quasi-judicial review of Program Evaluation Board
determinations would not be feasible. Appellate courts would be
hard-pressed to achieve the degree of expertise required to judge
performance in even a single program, and to review interprogram
comparisons, substantial familiarity with all the programs ranked
is essential. After-the-fact evaluation would necessarily be a departure from the bilateral tradition of defense contracting, especially
in its profit determination application (although not for source selection, which is already essentially unilateral). All this, however,
is not an inherent flaw. Indeed, a primary merit of an after-the-fact
evaluation approach to profit determination is its avoidance of the
bilateral bargaining problems which frustrate the attainment of
strong automatic contractual incentives. Furthermore, defense
contractors would be placed in no worse position than firms selling
in a market environment, where the unilateral decisions of consum-
ers govern sales levels and indirectly profit margins. An after-the-
fact evaluation system would in effect simulate for the nonmarket
environment of weapons acquisition the kinds of incentives afforded
by consumer sovereignty in a market environment.

The Responsibility Issue

Weapons makers have opposed basing rewards and penalties on
evaluations of their performance because a contractor is seldom
solely responsible for the success or failure of programs on which
it works. Rather, the decisions, actions, and inactions of government program management agencies also have a significant impact
on program outcomes.[45] Yet this does not justify the rejection by
contractors of accountability for their performance. If weapons

[44] Johnsen, "NASA Sole Judge in New Incentive Plan," pp. 28–29; and
National Security Industrial Association, *Report of Cost Reduction Study,*
p. 3.
[45] Cf. pp. 91–101 *supra.*

makers were not held accountable for program outcomes on which they bear only a shared responsibility, a lethargic attitude toward preventing unfavorable outcomes might result.[46] Furthermore, the impersonal market forces which confront firms outside the weapons industry are no more equitable in this respect. The survival and profits of companies in a market environment are affected by consumer tastes, the course of the business cycle, the actions of competitors, tariff policies, and even international relations — factors much less within an individual producer's control than the actions of a defense contractor's partner, a government program management agency.[47]

An after-the-fact evaluation incentive system might also, as a Department of Defense official protested, lead to "another bureaucratic layer." This is partly true, although for best results the Program Evaluation Board should be kept quite small and select. This added "bureaucratic layer" could easily be offset by the elimination of detailed contract negotiation functions, if the problems of retrenchment could be solved. It should be noted that a direct transfer of personnel from government contracting offices to the Program Evaluation Board would be undesirable, since very few of the persons now engaged in contract administration and negotiation have the background and skills needed to make sound after-the-fact contractor performance evaluations.

Criticisms have been directed at the delay which would necessarily ensue between early activities in a development program and the evaluation of those activities, determining program profits. As a National Security Industrial Association study group commented:

> . . . this reward system would make rewards so long after the fact that there would be very little inherent positive incentive on the contractor's personnel during performance. The main incentive would be on the contractor's management personnel long after performance had been completed.[48]

[46] In fact, they *are* presently held accountable at least in terms of follow-on sales and reputation, and so a lethargic attitude toward quality and time outcomes is seldom observed.

[47] Of course, setbacks beyond one's immediate control are undoubtedly more galling when the source of difficulty is a very personal government decision maker instead of an impersonal market.

[48] *Report of Cost Reduction Study,* p. 145. See also p. 149.

The logic of this objection is especially difficult to comprehend. It could represent a special case: those situations in which management for one reason or another heavily discounts sales and profits to be realized a few years hence. But most company managers, our case studies revealed, are not so improvident. They typically assigned great importance to securing follow-on contracts as the result of development — a reward which lags development program performance by a substantial period. It is more likely the argument reflects the fallacy common among defense industry personnel of identifying rewards *per se,* rather than rewards contingent upon some action, as incentives. The logical problems of such an assumption are discussed in Chapter 1.

The Problem of Objectives

Another common criticism is that an after-the-fact evaluation system would not provide sufficiently clear contractual objectives to guide contractor performance into the proper channels. As one industry spokesman said, "If there are no precise and fixed ground rules, how does the contractor know what he should work towards to achieve a reward? . . . It's like telling someone to run a race to 'somewhere.' " [49]

There are several aspects to this problem. For all but the most exploratory efforts (when goals are deliberately left vague to permit creativity) the government does express its wants through general and often specific military requirements documents. These are the objectives toward which contractors must work, choosing the most efficient technical approaches they can devise. To be sure, changes in the strategic situation or technological breakthroughs may suggest deviations from military requirements, and thousands of detailed time-quality-cost tradeoff decisions must be made.[50] But liaison with military decision makers is always possible when questions about the government's precise wants and needs arise.

It is nonetheless conceivable that different military decision makers may not agree on what the government's needs are, and there-

---

[49] Johnsen, "NASA Sole Judge in New Incentive Plan," p. 28.

[50] When warranted, government preferences can be specified in much more detail than the average military requirements document allows without going so far as to negotiate contractual incentive provisions tied to specific targets. See p. 176 *supra.*

fore that contractors will not be sure what objectives they should strive to fulfill. A good example is the conflict experienced by would-be TFX fighter contractors between satisfying Secretary of Defense McNamara's preferences for "commonality" and the military services' preferences for maximum technical performance.[51] Three comments on this understandably vexatious problem are in order. First, the problem is not solved by negotiating specific, detailed contract performance targets which ignore or belie the underlying existence of a conflict. If the conflict cannot be resolved short of actual program execution and perhaps hardware testing, the contractor is forced to make the best of its very real dilemma, possibly choosing a development strategy which preserves flexible options until greater unanimity can be achieved. Second, the Program Evaluation Board most assuredly would not make its after-the-fact evaluations in a vacuum, but as a first approximation would relate its judgments to the military requirements confronting the contractor. In the event of conflicting requirements or government preferences, the Board would need to adopt a consistent point of view. Although this philosophy has definite limitations, one would expect the Board normally to favor the preferences of the highest competent authority involved in a clear-cut conflict — e.g., of the Secretary of Defense when his views conflict with those of military subordinates, as in the TFX case. Third, when less clear-cut objective definition problems arise, the Board should take into account the contractor's difficult position when it evaluates the contractor's performance.

One further point deserves emphasis. It is not always a good thing for the contractor to do exactly what the government tells it to do, and there are grounds for distrusting incentive systems which encourage mechanical compliance with detailed contract targets, tradeoff formulas, and specifications. Government decision makers and negotiators make mistakes, and contractors may on occasion have a better idea of what is needed than their government counterparts, especially when the contractor's appreciation of the technical possibilities and hazards is superior. An after-the-fact evaluation system has the advantage of being able to reward contractors who depart fruitfully from military requirements and specifications.

[51] Cf. R. A. Smith, "The $7-Billion Contract That Changed the Rules," *Fortune,* March 1963, pp. 184–188; and April 1963, p. 110 ff.

Naturally, this sort of behavior involves the risk of error. Faulty perception of consumer wants and needs is a normal risk of doing business, but the close buyer-seller coordination permitted in weapons development reduces this risk to the minimum desirable level.

The Performance Evaluation Problem

Perhaps the strongest industry objection to an after-the-fact evaluation system is that the evaluations would include subjective factors — matters of opinion — as well as objective factors. The attitude of defense contractors is illustrated by these excerpts from the National Security Industrial Association's report on cost reduction:

> Little or no incentive to contractor's personnel on a specific contract or program will be provided unless the measurement of the contractor's performance is completed promptly and is a matter of fact rather than a matter of opinion. . . . Parameters such as efficiency, economy, ingenuity, control of changes, assumption of technical, production, and financial risks, breakthroughs achieved, measures taken to reduce cost, basic knowledge and understanding, and creativeness, are subjective matters of opinion. They cannot be defined or measured sufficiently accurately to be used as the sole basis for rewards and penalties. A continuous search for objective tests should be carried out, and the maximum use of these made. . . . The parameters used in the contracts should be those for which the performance achieved can be measured, and not those where the achievement of the performance is subject to opinion.[52]

It would surely be pleasant for all parties concerned if perfectly objective measures of all parameters relevant to contractor performance in a weapons program could be derived. Such parameters as efficiency, creativity, and ingenuity do have important subjective aspects. Nevertheless, they are crucial dimensions of program performance. Are they to be disregarded simply because they are subjective? And are frequently misleading indicators of efficiency, such as the degree to which cost estimates of questionable validity are underrun, to be used just because they are highly objective? If so, then the whole notion of providing conscious, consistent in-

[52] *Report of Cost Reduction Study,* pp. 149, 150, 137.

centives for good contractor performance might as well be forgotten. If, on the other hand, performance judgments *are* made on the basis of appropriate subjective factors as well as objective considerations, defense contractors will be no worse off than firms in a market environment, where subjective consumer preferences determine the fate of new products.[53]

Yet the issue is not quite that simple. As pointed out repeatedly in this volume, unless a reasonably consistent correlation between rewards/penalties and actual performance is maintained, an administered incentive system will create little incentive for good performance.[54] Therefore, unless the Program Evaluation Board is able to make valid, consistent performance measurements, an after-the-fact evaluation incentive system will not work very well.

At the heart of this proposition is an assumption that there is such a thing as good or poor performance in a weapons development program, and that distinctions can be drawn, however imperfectly, between good and poor performance. This assumption must not be taken on faith. As indicated earlier, it is doubtful whether any operational absolute standards of good performance exist. Rather, performance must be judged relative to what is possible and what is desired. Judgments of what is possible and

[53] There is of course a difference. Consumer markets integrate the independent subjective judgments of very many buyers, while the Program Evaluation Board's performance rankings would reflect the less-than-completely independent judgments of only a few persons. One may object to the analogy because of a philosophical aversion to oligarchy. But decisions determining major weapons makers' sales and profits are necessarily made by a few persons. The oligarchy problem seems unavoidable. What is important is to have these decisions provide incentives for good performance. And in this respect the impersonal competitive market can be emulated to good advantage by a competent, unbiased Program Evaluation Board.

[54] As we have seen, it is necessary not only that such a correlation exist, but that it be perceived. The system proposed here could prove ineffective if contractors, through blind obstinacy or other causes, truly refused to believe that a rewards-performance correlation existed. Obstinacy is not unknown in the defense industry. But as Chapter 4 observed, present reputation incentives are probably stronger than they objectively deserve to be because of faulty perception and contractor overcaution. If anything, we should expect contractors to err on the safe side under an after-the-fact evaluation system, striving to perform efficiently through fear of being penalized for inefficiency.

what is desired necessarily involve subjective elements on which, as the TFX case illustrates, reasonable men may disagree. Two fundamental causes of disagreement or (in a sense) potential error — inherent theoretical problems and human failings — can be singled out.

The principal theoretical problem arises from the multidimensionality of development program performance. If some generally accepted system of weights reflecting objective and subjective judgments of government needs cannot be applied to the individual dimensions of performance, no unambiguous ordinal measurement of over-all performance is feasible. The experimental study of development program performance evaluations discussed in Chapter 4 was explicitly designed to test for this problem. It suggested that multidimensionality did cause measurement problems, manifested in inconsistent (intransitive) individual choices and disagreements among well-informed judges.[55] But these proved much less severe than other problems such as bias and lack of knowledge — problems which can be minimized by various controls.[56] Under favorable conditions — e.g., when the persons evaluating contractor performance are highly knowledgeable and biases are controlled — it would appear that ranking "errors" greater than one quartile are unlikely.[57] That is, when different groups of well-informed judges evaluate over-all contractor performance in a sample, say, of 40 programs, the groups might in especially difficult evaluations disagree by as much as 10 ranks on a given program. More frequently, of course, the range of disagreement would be a good deal less than 10 ranks. And since efficiency has fewer dimensions than over-all performance, one might expect greater consistency in efficiency evaluations, although this hypothesis has not been tested.

The degree of accuracy or consistency implied by the program

[55] Cf. pp. 94–95 *supra*. For the complete analysis, see Peck and Scherer, pp. 554–555, 570–571, and 579–580.

[56] *Ibid.*, p. 570.

[57] *Ibid.*, pp. 579–580. This interpretation is based on the rankings of the most knowledgeable, unbiased groups included in the program evaluation experiment, making slight allowance for the less than ideal conditions under which the experiment was conducted. Additional research on the accuracy or consistency of performance measurement processes is clearly desirable.

evaluation experiment is a far cry from perfection. Still it suggests that serious performance measurement "errors" would not occur, such as assigning a low rank to performance which in some real sense is truly superior or a high rank to clearly inferior performance. Perfect measurement is not essential for an effective incentive system; a fairly consistent correlation of rewards/penalties with performance should suffice. For example, the market for nonmilitary goods and services is far from perfectly consistent in its reward-performance correlations. Producers who have made demonstrably valuable contributions sometimes go unrewarded because of market imperfections, while charlatans sometimes gain fortunes. But for the most part competitive markets do fairly well in providing incentives for the efficient satisfaction of consumer wants — well enough, at least, that we are content to rely upon the market, with only occasional prodding from an antitrust action or congressional investigation. If the Program Evaluation Board could do nearly as well — and there is reason to hope that it could under favorable conditions — its evaluations would permit more consistent incentive correlations than existing weapons sales and profit determination systems, which tend either to reward good and poor performers equally or to relate rewards more closely to bargaining power than to actual performance.

Should these conclusions be incorrect — if performance cannot be evaluated validly after-the-fact — how much more difficult must it be to set valid time, quality, and cost targets before the fact! And since valid performance targets are essential to an effective automatic contractual incentive system, that approach must also be infeasible if an after-the-fact evaluation system is infeasible due to measurement dilemmas. But the program evaluation experiment results suggest that the theoretical problems of performance measurement can be surmounted well enough to administer reasonably consistent, even though inherently imperfect, reward-performance correlations through after-the-fact evaluation.

Frequently, however, there is a gap between what is possible in principle and what can be accomplished on a sustained basis by fallible human beings. What troubles contractors most about after-the-fact evaluation is the fear that a Program Evaluation Board would be too susceptible to serious errors of human judgment. Perhaps this lack of confidence is justified, considering the defense industry's experience with performance evaluations by contract negotiators and the Renegotiation Board.[58]

The Program Evaluation Board's Membership

This leads us directly to the problem of the Program Evaluation Board's composition. The Board's performance evaluations would clearly be no better than the competence, knowledge, objectivity, and judgment of its members. A Board which rated high in these qualifications could be the cornerstone of an effective incentive system. A Board which rated low could do more harm than good.

Although many variations in detail are conceivable, two promising basic organizational alternatives may be identified. As one possibility, the Board might consist of from six to ten well-qualified persons of demonstrated wisdom and sound judgment whose primary responsibility would be to follow the progress of weapons programs and make performance judgments.[59] Members might be drawn from government, the academic community, the legal profession, and industry, although appointing industrial executives who intended in a few years to return to their companies would pose formidable conflict-of-interest problems. Some of the board members should have experience in the conduct and management of research and development.

The foremost problem in this approach would be recruiting the requisite level of individual competence. Persons with the high qualifications implied here usually have many alternative opportunities for employing their talents, typically at higher salary levels than the government could offer. Evaluating organizations' performance and determining their business fortunes are apt to be unappealing to the most constructive types of people. Conversely, those who are attracted to such work are likely to be exactly the wrong types for the Program Evaluation Board. If qualified Board members are to be secured under this approach, it would probably have to be for relatively short terms (four years at most) with stress on the public service nature of the appointment. Even then, it is by no means certain that sufficiently competent and wise persons could be engaged, especially after the novelty of an after-the-fact

---

[58] Cf. pp. 254–255, 261–263, and 286–287 *supra.*

[59] Any smaller number might suppress the diversity needed to bring out valid grounds for disagreement.

evaluation incentive system had faded. Much would depend upon the priority given to implementing an effective system by the Secretary of Defense. If the priority is low, persons of high caliber will not be attracted and the after-the-fact evaluation concept would be doomed to failure.

An alternative possibility would be to exploit the competence and knowledge of persons already holding high positions in the defense establishment. Defense and service assistant secretaries for research and development, materiel, and financial management and the corresponding military assistant chiefs might serve *ex officio* as Board members when performance evaluations are made. Administration of the system would be entrusted to the Board's full-time chairman, acting (for example) as Assistant Secretary of Defense for Program Evaluation and Incentives. The principal problem in this approach would be assuring that Board members have sufficient knowledge of all programs evaluated to make sound judgments. Assistant secretaries tend to come and go more rapidly than development programs. Board members would therefore have to spend a significant amount of time (surely not less than a full month each year) studying historical and other reports on the various programs they are evaluating. This work would naturally conflict with other pressing duties, and the success of the evaluation system would again depend upon the priority given to its implementation.

On balance, the second approach seems more likely to succeed on a sustained basis, although the first alternative cannot be ruled out completely.

With either organizational approach, the Board would need a professional staff to accumulate the information underlying its performance evaluations. This data collection job should not be unmanageable, since available decision-making documents and periodic progress reports permit a trained investigator to "get the feel" of a program and identify questions for further exploration rather quickly. To illustrate, fairly detailed historical case studies of 12 weapons programs — in some ways more detailed than the single objective of evaluating contractor performance would require — were compiled with roughly 70 man-months of effort by members of the Harvard Weapons Acquisition Research Project. A capable and well-trained staff of 15 to 20 persons should be able to cover the 50 or so largest programs sponsored at any given time by the Department of Defense.[60] The staff would prepare analyses of each program for the use of Board members in their evaluations.

As with the Board proper, quality cannot be replaced by quantity on the Board's staff. Indeed, tendencies for the staff to grow much larger than 25 persons would be an indication of incompetence. Yet securing qualified staff members would undoubtedly be less difficult than recruiting senior members for a full-time Board. The work might be attractive to ambitious young engineers and military officers, since it would afford unparalleled insight into the managerial problems of advanced technological development programs.

CONCLUSION

An incentive system based upon after-the-fact evaluation of contractor performance appears to offer important inherent advantages over existing alternatives. In its profit determination application it could ensure that profit variations are correlated with variations in contractor performance, instead of with random variations in the target negotiation process. In its sales determination application it could channel the competitive struggle of weapons makers for survival and growth into fruitful rather than uneconomic modes of behavior. If executed boldly and competently, an after-the-fact evaluation system of incentives would yield substantial benefits. If implemented poorly, on the other hand, it would probably do more harm than good. Much depends upon the willingness of the Department of Defense to recognize the fundamental limitations in existing incentive policies and to place high priority on developing a system of incentives better suited to the environment of technological change and uncertainty in weapons acquisition.

---

[60] Assuming an average time span per development program of five years, this implies that ten programs would be completed and would have to be evaluated each year. Obviously, a single program might include the efforts of several system and major subsystem contractors. It is assumed that staff members would be able to draw upon operating agencies for information on specific questions.

CHAPTER 13

Alternative Policies for
Improved Incentives

A COMPREHENSIVE AFTER-THE-FACT evaluation system of contractual and competitive incentives would plainly be a radical innovation. Perhaps it is too much to contemplate such a break
from traditional government-industry relationships. And as we
have seen, the break could prove disappointing — an incompetently
administered after-the-fact system would probably be worse than
none. Therefore, we must also consider settling for more modest
improvements in existing incentive systems.

One possibility which should not be overlooked is the preservation or at most peripheral modification of the *status quo*. Despite
their defects, existing systems of incentives have not prevented the
United States from building up a weapons arsenal of awesome
power. To be sure, much avoidable inefficiency has been heaped
onto the inefficiencies inherent in the execution of rapid technological change. But inefficiency is not necessarily undesirable. One
might argue that modern weapons are too cheap even when acquired inefficiently. If a much larger share of the gross national
product were required to maintain the present rate of advance in
military technology, the average citizen might become more interested in seeing a deceleration of the arms race. Furthermore,
there are many persons who view continued high levels of weapons
expenditure as an essential ingredient of national and local pros-
perity. If pork-barreling and leaf-raking are valued for their political and pump-priming merits, we should not be too hasty in con-
demning the inefficient conduct of weapons programs.

If, on the other hand, the United States wants to forge an even
more formidable arsenal of defense from its limited resources, or
if it wishes to reallocate resources employed inefficiently for defense to more fruitful nondefense ends, defects in the existing sys-

tem of incentives should be recognized and corrected. Several modest possibilities for improvement deserve attention.

IMPROVED AUTOMATIC CONTRACTUAL INCENTIVES

The Department of Defense should cease encouraging the generalized application of multidimensional incentive contracts to weapon systems development, for in many instances profit-quality and profit-time correlations are redundant. Except in special cases — e.g., when competitive incentives for good performance on the quality and time dimensions are weak — the full range of potential profit rate variation on development contracts should be reserved to correlate with performance on the cost dimension. This implies the use of cost-plus-incentive-fee development contracts permitting zero profits or even losses in the event of severe cost overruns and profit rates as high as 15% if significant underruns are achieved.

Strong profit-cost correlations could, of course, lead to unconscionable profits unless competition affords a safeguard against pessimistic biases in cost estimation. Normally competition does place stringent limits on a contractor's ability to submit excessively high total development program cost estimates at the outset of a program. In fact, competitive pressures usually inspire an optimistic bias. To exploit and at the same time moderate this natural safeguard while securing the benefits of stronger automatic contractual incentives for efficiency, the following specific practices are proposed:

(1) The contract negotiated at the start of a full-scale system development program should cover the complete development effort, not just the first stage or the first year's activity. Only in this way can contractors be discouraged from "buying into" development programs with unrealistically low cost estimates on initial contracts involving relatively small expenditures, expecting to compensate for early profit sacrifices through more pessimistic pricing of larger follow-on development contracts. This practice would also make cost and time incentives work in tandem, since schedule slippages which increase total program cost will lead to profit reductions through the contract's cost incentive provisions. Still full-program contracting of this sort is feasible only when a program's technical objectives are fairly well defined. When technical

requirements cannot be defined clearly in advance, the use of cost-plus-fixed-fee contracts is undoubtedly necessary in the absence of an after-the-fact evaluation profit determination system.

(2) The cost estimates incorporated into contract cost targets should be those submitted by the contractor in its efforts to win the particular development program. Contractors should not be permitted, as they have been in the past, to delay the pricing of development contracts until they have gained a sole-source position. Contractual incorporation of the cost estimates submitted during source selection competitions is especially important for high priority programs which do not have to face severe competition for budgetary support. It is less important for medium or low priority programs, since revealing large increases in expected costs during the first year or two of development is likely to endanger a marginal program's continued budgetary support.

If these changes are carried out, strengthened contractual incentives for development efficiency can be achieved with little additional risk of cost-padding. For all the reasons examined in Chapters 7 and 8, however, the stronger contractual incentives may still be ineffective in motivating substantial efficiency gains. It is probable that increased accuracy in program cost estimation, rather than increased efficiency, would be the most significant benefit of the measures proposed here. In particular, the government might avoid some of the serious resource allocation errors which follow when program decisions are based upon misleadingly low cost estimates.

A general policy of negotiating full development program contracts with relatively strong profit-cost correlations would nonetheless raise certain problems. Ambitious, long-term developments might be discouraged unless their early stages could be covered by CPFF instruments with less pricing risk. Cancellation of a program would probably involve contract termination costs higher than under a short-term contracting policy. Finally, a decrease in flexibility would undoubtedly result, since each change in technical goals would have to be negotiated as a special contract amendment, and marginally desirable changes might be rejected as not worth the negotiation burden.

Thus, even an improved system of automatic contractual incentives for development efficiency appears in many respects to offer less promise than an effectively administered after-the-fact evaluation system. However, the changes suggested here are probably preferable to the situation prevailing during the late 1950's and early 1960's, with its deficient incentives for development efficiency and realistic cost estimation.

Production Contract Incentives

By the time production of an advanced weapon system or subsystem begins, the problem of competitive optimism in contract cost estimates has usually disappeared. The most important contractual incentive problem at this stage is one of securing tight cost targets and at the same time strong profit-cost correlations. In the absence of generally increased government bargaining power, there are no simple ways of achieving greatly strengthened automatic contractual incentives for production efficiency. However, the following measures would yield at least limited improvements:

(1) As a matter of general policy, the government's principal objective in contract sharing proportion negotiations should be efficiency maximization rather than outlay minimization.[1] This implies primary reliance on firm fixed-price contracts or fixed-price incentive contracts with high contractor sharing proportions, even when cost targets have a moderate underrun bias. The use of redeterminable fixed-price contracts should also not be precluded when substantial uncertainties exist and when tight base and ceiling prices can be negotiated. But with all of these three basic contract types, it must be reiterated, achieving strong incentives for production efficiency demands the negotiation of tight cost targets as well as high sharing proportions.

(2) To encourage the acceptance of contracts with high sharing proportions, the government might increase the risk-correlated differential in negotiated target profit rates. This could be accomplished by increasing the average target profit rate negotiated on firm fixed-price and strong fixed-price incentive contracts while leaving CPFF and weak FPI profit rates at current levels; by decreasing the level of CPFF and weak FPI profit rates while leaving firm fixed-price rates at their current average level; or by both re-

[1] Cf. pp. 221–225 *supra*.

ducing the lowest target rates and increasing the highest target rates. However, further study of contractor risk aversion propensities and the over-all sufficiency of defense industry resources is desirable before such a step is initiated. Although the acceptance of stronger profit-cost correlations would tend to strengthen the pressure theory incentive for cost reduction (along with the reward theory incentive), an increase in negotiated fixed-price contract profit margins under the first and third alternatives would weaken it.[2] A decrease in average profit rates under the second alternative might drive capable resources with attractive alternative employment opportunities out of defense work.

(3) Government procurement agencies should build up their capabilities for making thorough independent analyses of contractor cost estimates, especially for the analysis of large noncompetitive follow-on contract cost estimates. Government cost analysts should receive further training. Qualified technical personnel in government laboratories and arsenals should whenever possible be called upon to examine contractor cost structures in major programs.

(4) Threats to break out production items for competitive bidding should be made and carried out whenever the costs of securing competition are not prohibitive and when weapon system quality will not be endangered. However, work should be taken away from the original producer only when a challenger's incremental costs are less than the original producer's incremental costs. Full costs are not a valid basis for competitive bid award decisions when overhead costs will be borne by the government in any event.[3]

(5) The rate of progress payments provided by the government under letter contracts should be reduced sharply in order to enhance the bargaining power of government negotiators by putting financial pressure on contractors attempting to hold out for loose cost targets and low sharing proportions.[4]

The Problem of Renegotiation

No statement of contractual incentives policy is complete without reference to the problem of renegotiation. And there is a problem. When a firm is confronted with even an approximate post-

[2] Cf. pp. 233–234 *supra.*
[3] Cf. pp. 112–114 *supra.*
[4] Cf. p. 217 *supra.*

renegotiation profit ceiling based upon such factors as over-all reasonableness, it cannot expect to retain incentive profits which would raise total profits above the anticipated ceiling. The cost reductions which could generate those incremental profits will therefore not be incited. However, the actual amount of cost reduction discouraged by renegotiation appears to have been slight for two reasons. First, the profits renegotiation recoups may have little marginal utility to the companies affected, superimposed as they are on fairly ample profit margins. Consequently, the prospect of earning those profits would not have major behavioral effects in any case. Second, with profit margins declining during the late 1950's, most weapons vendors had good reason to expect to emerge from renegotiation proceedings unscathed. This latter condition clearly reflects special historical circumstances. It seems reasonable to conclude more generally that renegotiation as currently administered can weaken incentives for incremental cost reduction at least somewhat. In addition, when profits gained through chance cost underruns are recouped in renegotiation, the acceptance of contracts with strong profit-cost correlations is discouraged.

Renegotiation's primary function of thwarting profiteering is also somewhat superfluous in times of less than total mobilization. The government has other ways to discourage profiteering — e.g., tightening up its negotiations with firms which gain windfall profits, insisting upon voluntary refunds, and denying new contracts to firms which refuse to play the game. These checks are quite effective with firms heavily dependent upon continued defense business, and the vast majority of major weapons contractors fall into this category. Indeed, they may be too effective, for they encourage firms to absorb price cushions in the form of cost rather than profit.

Nevertheless, Congress is properly concerned not only with this majority, but also with the small minority of cases in which the government is exploited by short-sighted operators. Occasional instances of successful profiteering can cause disproportionately great damage to taxpayers' confidence in the defense procurement effort. Thus, renegotiation may serve a useful psychological function even in peacetime.

During periods of major military mobilization, when the government's relative bargaining power is low due to its urgent need for suitable industrial capabilities, profit renegotiation appears definitely desirable. The case for renegotiation's continuation under cold war conditions is more marginal. A difficult value judgment is required. The efficiency losses due to renegotiation must be weighed against its political and psychological benefits. Given case study evidence that the efficiency losses have been slight, I would recommend that renegotiation be continued with respect to profits gained under automatic contractual incentive provisions. However, this judgment should be reversed if convincing evidence of significant efficiency losses is uncovered. Renegotiation would clearly be both unnecessary and potentially harmful in an after-the-fact evaluation system of profit determination, and any programs covered by such a system should be exempted from re-negotiation.

This weak vote of confidence does not mean that renegotiation is presently administered as effectively as it could and should be. There are at least three important opportunities for improvement. First, greater emphasis should be placed on actual contractor performance as the reason for variations in allowed profits, and less emphasis should be placed on such factors as over-all reasonableness and "going rates of return." Second (and a necessary prerequisite for the first measure), the Renegotiation Board and the Department of Defense should cooperate to develop much more complete, accurate information permitting valid comparative evaluations of the performance of contractors. Finally, appointments to the Renegotiation Board should be made on the basis of relevant experience and demonstrated good judgment in the actual work of weapons acquisition — not demonstrated good judgment in backing a political candidate.

NEGOTIATED PROFIT RATE INCENTIVES

As happens so frequently in human affairs, the least promising courses of action have commanded the most attention in this chapter. At best, the opportunities for efficiency gains through automatic contractual incentive improvements are quite restricted. A much more fruitful attack on the efficiency problem can be mounted by varying negotiated profit rates to reflect variations in past efficiency. It is more fruitful because at least up to 1963, no progress was made in this direction, whereas the Department of Defense devoted much thought and energy to eliminating the correctable deficiencies in its system of automatic contractual incentives.

In essence, this proposal calls for after-the-fact evaluation of contractor efficiency, but without a formal Program Evaluation Board. The principal problem in implementing such a system is the inability of contract negotiators associated with only one or two large programs to determine whether efficiency has been relatively high or relatively low. For best results, the efficiency determinations should be made by an official or office familiar with a broader spectrum of programs. Fine distinctions between varying degrees of efficiency would be unnecessary. Strengthened incentives would follow quite naturally if only those contractors which have performed with clearly outstanding efficiency are singled out for profit rates several points above the average, while clearly inefficient contractors are penalized by negotiated profit rates several points below the average. In addition, the incentives generated by such a system would have the important advantage of being cumulative — a feature absent in automatic contractual incentive systems with annual negotiation of cost targets.

Past Performance as a Source Selection Criterion

More effective incentives for good over-all performance can be secured by placing greater emphasis on past performance as a source selection criterion. Again, this is possible without a formal Program Evaluation Board. The armed services simply need to make a concerted effort to collect relevant information on contractors' comparative past performance and to communicate that information to officials responsible for source selection decisions. Two types of sales-performance correlations can be administered fairly well through this relatively informal approach. First, firms with especially good past performance records should be favored in the award of feasibility study and exploratory development contracts when technical uncertainties preclude confident choices on the basis of technical proposals. And second, firms which have repeatedly turned in poor performances should be deprived of new contracts and permitted to wither away and die. The occasional dropping of an unsatisfactory performer would serve as a powerful reminder to others that continued participation in the national defense effort demands sustained vigor and competence.

COMPETITION BETWEEN CLOSE SUBSTITUTES

Little can be added over what has already been said in Chapter 2 about the use of competition between close substitute weapon systems and subsystems as a spur to good performance. There are no simple rules of thumb. Competition between substitutes definitely has its benefits, both statistical and behavioral. At the same time, supporting competing programs tends to increase costs by a multiplicative factor. In the early feasibility study and exploratory development stages of advanced weapons programs, the benefits of competition nearly always outweigh the relatively small costs. But unless the technical uncertainties are especially great, it will seldom be necessary or desirable to support more than three or four active competitors during these early stages. Once full-scale development of prototype systems begins, costs mount rapidly. Then the optimal amount and duration of competition depend upon the nature and extent of program uncertainties; the rate at which important uncertainties can be resolved; the value of time and quality increments; the cost of supporting competing alternatives; and the degree to which competition from indirect substitutes and from similar weapons of different generations, competition for budgetary support among nonsubstitutes, competition on the basis of reputation, and profit-performance correlations afford alternate incentives for good performance. As a general rule, unless the statistical benefits promise to be substantial, parallel competition among same-generation close substitutes during the full-scale development and production stages of a program will seldom be justified.

CHAPTER 14

Alternatives to the Incentives Approach

BY FAR THE LARGEST part of all weapons research and development sponsored by the United States government is contracted out to private firms. But when private industry sponsors its own R & D projects, a strikingly different organizational pattern is observed. Only 4% of the $4 billion in company-sponsored research and development performed during 1959 was contracted to outside organizations; the rest was performed in-house.[1] It is quite likely that this tendency of private firms to perform their own research and development work in-house, where it can be subjected to direct managerial control, is in considerable measure a reaction to the fundamental incentive problems of R & D contracting examined in this volume.

The incentives approach is not, however, the only means by which the government can attempt to secure optimal and efficient execution of its weapons programs. It may also emulate the vertical integration tendencies of private industry in two ways. First, it can reserve for itself some of the managerial functions normally performed by autonomous firms, exercising direct technical and financial administration and control over contractor operations. Or alternatively, the government is not forced to rely at all upon private firms to supply its weapons. In-house development and production — the arsenal approach — are also possible.

These alternatives to the incentives approach cannot be overlooked. Each deserves at least as much attention as the incentives approach, but here they must be examined only as a digression from the main theme of this volume. Therefore, it will be possible only to raise some of the principal issues, not to explore them in detail.

[1] U.S. National Science Foundation, *Funds for Research and Development in Industry: 1959* (Washington: 1962), p. 14.

INCENTIVES VS. CONTROLS

Let us begin with some fundamental questions. In what sense are technical administration and controls an alternative to the incentives approach? That is, are direct administrative controls over contractor operations a substitute for incentives, or a complement to them? Can the government compensate for deficient incentive systems through administrative controls? And conversely, does the imposition of controls weaken incentives for good contractor performance?

There is evidence that direct controls have been expanded as an explicit substitute for incentives when the latter have proved ineffective. In its early years of operation, for example, the Atomic Energy Commission emphasized various intangible incentives to motivate desirable contractor performance. This philosophy was defended by David Lilienthal, the AEC's first chairman, as follows:

> What we are trying to do . . . is to develop a new kind of setup in American industrial affairs which is a hybrid of public and private. . . . Now, the other alternative is to pile on top of the industrial operator another set of managers, that is, that the Government should supervise in such detail that every important step taken by the industrial operator should be checked and rechecked and double checked and triple checked by a group of government supervisors. This we do not think is right.[2]

But the incentives influencing AEC contractors proved weak, and dissatisfaction over contractor performance led to a philosophy of tighter control. Richard Tybout summarized the AEC experience in the following words:

> [The early AEC] approach was at odds with the traditional assumption of economists that financial rewards are the prime movers of economic activities. It is consistent with this assumption, and all that flows from it, that the experiment did not succeed. Mr. Lilienthal may very well have been correct in his assertion that close supervision harasses the contractor's staff, but he was

[2] Cited in Richard A. Tybout, *Government Contracting in Atomic Energy* (Ann Arbor, University of Michigan Press, 1956), p. 81, from U.S. Congress, Joint Committee on Atomic Energy, *Hearings, Investigation into the United States Atomic Energy Project* (1949), p. 338.

wrong in thinking that the withdrawal of government supervision, with nothing substituted in its place, was the remedy.[3]

Our case studies disclosed considerable selective application of administrative controls when incentives appeared to fail. Firms in which service officials had high confidence were sometimes given substantial operational and decision-making freedom. On the other hand, firms whose performance was deviating far from the optimum were subjected to all kinds of detailed administrative supervision and controls. More generally, an industry task force observed that:

> . . . many persons with governmental responsibilities favor taut controls and close supervision because they do not believe sufficient motivation or incentives exist within the normal business operations of the defense industries to bring about efficient and economical results. Also they distrust the business manager's aggressive drive for increased profits.[4]

Still more generally, top defense officials attributed the gradual centralization of decision-making and control functions into the Office of the Secretary of Defense to the failure of both contractors and service procurement agencies "to produce useful weapons with sensible lead times, optimum use of personnel, control of design changes, and within the programmed development funds." [5]

Government participation in the internal operations of its weapons contractors is by no means a new phenomenon. The Robertson Committee, for instance, referred in 1956 to the "Service *tradition* of closely supervising the actions of the contractor." [6] Before aviation became a major factor in national defense, most weapons development was done in government arsenals or ship-

---

[3] Tybout, *Government Contracting in Atomic Energy,* p. 87.

[4] National Security Industrial Association, *Report of Cost Reduction Study* (June 15, 1962), p. 3. The report went on to say that such beliefs are "erroneous or uninformed," negating "the basic concepts of our free enterprise system."

[5] Don Zylstra, "DOD Defends Centralized Management," *Missiles and Rockets,* November 12, 1962, p. 15, quoting Assistant Secretary of Defense John H. Rubel.

[6] U.S. Department of Defense, Ad Hoc Study Group, *Manned Aircraft Weapon Systems: A Program for Reducing the Time Cycle from Concept to Inventory* (July 1956), p. 57 (emphasis supplied).

yards. Industrial contractors were hired primarily to perform production assignments, governed by detailed design drawings and specifications and subject to rigorous end-product inspection by military representatives. The rise of air power and then electronic warfare shifted the task of development predominantly to private firms; and at first it was common for contractors to experience considerable autonomy in their development operations, subject mainly to specific operational requirements and general military specifications. But as aircraft, radar, and guided missile programs became more complex and expensive in the years following World War II, three trends emerged.

First, as the military procurement agencies built up staffs familiar with the new technologies, they gradually assumed a more active role in technical decision making and the surveillance of contractor operations. In this respect the autonomy of contractors was reduced. Second, despite increased staffs, the services found themselves unable to cope with the multiplying problems connected with combining technically advanced subsystems and components into an integrated weapon system. Through the so-called weapon system prime contractor approach, responsibility for the detailed work of systems integration was delegated to contractors, while the government retained its supervisory and control functions. This step gave somewhat increased responsibility and autonomy to contractors. However, disenchantment with the weapon system prime contractor approach led to further efforts by government agencies to enhance their in-house or captive technical capabilities, and the job of systems integration then gravitated back toward the government. As a result the government in 1963 generally exercised much more detailed technical and administrative control over the development operations of its contractors than it did before and during World War II.

The trend toward more detailed technical administration and control is epitomized by measures taken in the Air Force ballistic missile development program. As a matter of policy, the Air Force has been inclined to delegate more autonomy to its development contractors than the other two armed services.[7] When the

---

[7] This is not necessarily true as a matter of practice. The Army, for example, despite its advocacy of a modified arsenal approach to development, delegated almost complete weapon system prime contractor responsi-

Atlas ICBM program was accelerated in 1954, officials of Convair
— the original Atlas study program contractor — surmised from
contemporary Air Force policy trends that their duties would be
expanded to include management of the over-all weapon system development effort. But for a variety of reasons, the Air Force chose
instead to entrust technical direction and systems engineering responsibilities to a new firm, the Ramo-Wooldridge Corporation
(later reorganized as Space Technology Laboratories, Inc., or
STL).[8] Convair was limited to the role of airframe prime contractor, and work on other major Atlas subsystems was placed
under separate prime contracts coordinated by STL. STL subsequently assumed similar responsibilities in the Thor IRBM and
the Titan and Minuteman ICBM programs. By late 1960 STL had
built up a staff of approximately 5,500, of whom some 3,500 (including 1,500 scientists and engineers) were assigned to program
management activities for Air Force missile and space programs.[9]
More than 300 STL scientists and engineers were engaged in directing and coordinating the work of Atlas contractors alone at the
peak of that program's activities. In addition, the Air Force in
1960 employed more than 4,000 civil servants and military personnel in its ballistic missile development program management office,
including nearly 900 persons with scientific or engineering training.[10] The allocation of so much talent to program management
functions naturally brought about a very detailed kind of control
over the operations of contractors actually performing development
work. As one major contractor's ballistic missile project manager
related in a case study interview:

> Every contractor expects some surveillance and direction, but
> the efforts of STL are so sweeping and so detailed that we have
> never experienced anything like them before.

---

bilities for the Nike program to Western Electric in 1945 — years before
the Air Force popularized the weapon system prime contractor concept.

   [8] For a fairly comprehensive history of the STL involvement, see House,
Committee on Government Operations, *Eleventh Report, Organization and
Management of Missile Programs* (1959), pp. 69–100.

   [9] House, Committee on Government Operations, *Third Report, Air
Force Ballistic Missile Management* (1961), pp. 28–29.

   [10] *Ibid.* See also House, Committee on Government Operations, *Hearings, Organization and Management of Missile Programs* (1960), pp. 123–
124 and 161–162.

Because of criticisms largely unrelated to the detailed character of its involvement in contractor operations, STL was gradually relieved of its ballistic missile program management responsibilities. Taking its place was the Aerospace Corporation, a nonprofit corporation founded in June 1960 specifically to serve the Air Force. Aerospace was given responsibility for "general systems engineering" and "technical steering" in Air Force ballistic missile and space programs. By mid-1962, Aerospace employed more than 3,000 persons, including 1,255 scientists and engineers.[11] The rapid growth of Aerospace made clear the Air Force's intention to continue exercising significant supervision and control over the technical activities of its major development contractors. Although exact administrative arrangements vary widely, the Army, Navy, and Space Administration, as well as segments of the Air Force not primarily concerned with missile and space work, have also moved toward the creation of either in-house or captive contractor organizations able to exert strong technical supervision over development contractor operations.

The Government's Specific Roles in Program Management

What does this growing army of government technical administrators and controllers do? Is it merely a matter of "everyone watching everyone else," as a critic of Space Technology Laboratories' activities suggested? Or do government program managers make contributions which would be valuable even if an adequate system of incentives for good contractor performance existed? Several specific functions of technical management organizations can be distinguished. These include product decision making, independent research, systems engineering and integration, and administrative review and control.

Few would deny that the government must retain basic responsibility for expressing its qualitative weapon system preferences. This clearly includes the establishment of qualitative military requirements, the choice of preferred technical approaches (often through source selection decisions emphasizing design features),

---

[11] House, Committee on Government Operations, *Hearings, Systems Development and Management,* Part 3 (1962), pp. 960, 1134. In mid-1963, the count was 4,540. Bill Becker, "Space Planners Expanding Role," *New York Times,* August 4, 1963, p. 42.

and the approval of major quality-time-cost tradeoffs and design changes. How far these product decision-making functions should be carried by government agencies is, however, open to debate. Two issues are especially pertinent. First, should qualitative preferences be expressed in terms of performance specifications (required speed, range, accuracy, reaction time, mean time to failure, etc.) or detailed design specifications? Often government personnel review each detail of proposed designs, independently specifying whether, for instance, a certain circuit should employ potentiometers rather than resistors, or what specific ceramic material should be used in a missile radome. Second, should military procurement agencies exercise detailed control over engineering changes? Again, once the contractor's production designs have been approved, each deviation — however slight and however obvious the need — customarily must receive the approval of a government representative.

It is possible to argue that if incentives are working effectively, the thousands upon thousands of minor design decisions required in each weapon system program can safely be left to contractor discretion. The usual reply to this contention is that only the buyer knows exactly what it wants, and it must review contractor designs in detail to ensure that its wants will not be misinterpreted. And frequently, seemingly minor design details are of significant military concern. For example, in one of the programs covered by our case studies, the choice between potentiometers and resistors in a circuit design touched off a heated disagreement between contractor and military technical personnel. The contractor favored resistors to enhance system reliability, while government representatives favored potentiometers because their use permitted more complete field maintenance of the weapon system. This detailed design decision therefore involved nontrivial questions of government preferences, and to the extent that government personnel were best able to weigh military needs against the technical possibilities and consequences, their intervention was useful.

Military personnel *are* undoubtedly better qualified to judge military needs than contractor managers and engineers. But it is doubtful whether they are best able to understand the technical implications of a decision, especially when it involves technological uncertainties. As a rule the best technical understanding resides with the contractor. Military insight, technical competence, and objectivity are all important in design decisions. Military insight and perhaps objectivity considerations pull the locus of detailed product decision making toward government, while technical expertise draws it toward the contractor. Consequently, there is no simple best answer to the question of how detailed the government's participation in product decision making should be. The answer depends upon the relative weights assigned to conflicting criteria.

A rather different function occasionally performed by strong government program management organizations is the pursuit of independent research on the technical problems faced by development contractors. This was a significant role of Space Technology Laboratories in the Air Force ballistic missile program and of the Army Ballistic Missile Agency in the Redstone, Jupiter, and Pershing programs. Once committed to a certain basic technical approach, a development contractor tends to don blinders. It has difficulty recognizing limitations in its own approach and sensing the value of alternative approaches.[12] Even when held to a relatively low level of effort, independent research by a government program management group less deeply committed to the contractor's approach can have important statistical benefits. For example, Space Technology Laboratories' investigations led to major simplifications in two different ICBM guidance system concepts — simplifications which had not occurred to guidance development contractor engineers. Similarly, independent tests by Army Ballistic Missile Agency engineers revealed the nature of Jupiter-Thor-Atlas rocket engine turbopump bearing problems which had been diagnosed only imperfectly by the engine's development contractor.[13] Conducting independent research permits the government to weigh technical alternatives which otherwise might never have been identified.

A third potential function of government technical administration groups — systems engineering and integration — demands more extensive analysis. With the rapid growth of weapon system sophistication and complexity, it has become increasingly important that some one group devote attention to assuring that the various

[12] See also pp. 23–26 *supra.*

[13] Cf. House, Committee on Government Operations, *Eleventh Report, Organization and Management of Missile Programs* (1959), pp. 105–108.

subsystems and components are properly matched and balanced. In part, the problem is one of identification: someone must consider the over-all weapon system plan to define all points of contact and interaction between the components furnished by diverse contractors. When complementary or conflicting interactions are identified, technical decisions on the optimal tradeoff of design goals must be made. To cite only two illustrations, in the Atlas ICBM guidance development effort, the total error tolerance was allocated between the computer and radio subsystem contractors by Space Technology Laboratories engineers. In the Polaris IRBM development, the Navy's Special Projects Office made final decisions on the allocation of umbilical cord connections among various users when the contractors were unable to agree upon a satisfactory plan. And finally, some central organization must attend to the unexciting but vital task of keeping all the parties to a complex development effort informed about what each is doing. All of these jobs must be done. The debate in recent years has focused on who should do them: in-house government technical group, prime contractor, or special (perhaps nonprofit) systems engineering contractor?

Objectivity is one criterion emphasized in the resolution of this question. The general assumption has been that in-house government groups are most objective in performing systems engineering functions, special systems engineering contractors (and especially nonprofit organizations) only slightly less objective, and weapon system prime contractors least objective. Prime contractors, it is alleged, would make tradeoff decisions which ease their own technical problems at the expense of subcontractors if allowed autonomy in systems engineering. Likewise, they would choose technical solutions which maximize their own sales and profits at the expense of subcontractors' production.[14]

These criticisms of the prime contractor approach, if valid, represent a condemnation of existing incentive systems. But our case studies suggested that at least in technical tradeoff decisions, prime contractors generally tended to achieve a fairly high level of objectivity when entrusted with over-all weapon system integration responsibilities. Since their reputations and follow-on sales were

[14] See, for example, House, Committee on Government Operations, *Third Report, Air Force Ballistic Missile Management* (1961), pp. 4–5.

tied to over-all performance of the weapon system, including the performance of subcontracted items, they were anxious to achieve optimal tradeoffs among the various subsystems. Except for the technical approach commitment problem discussed earlier, weapon system prime contractors appeared no less objective in tradeoff decisions than special systems engineering firms. And the latter also exhibited commitment biases. For instance, with a staff of creative and enthusiastic professionals, Space Technology Laboratories tended to slight such mundane but important engineering problems as the design of ground support equipment, and as a result ICBM operational capabilities initially suffered and program costs were increased. Similarly, the Applied Physics Laboratory, nonprofit systems engineering contractor in the Navy Bureau of Ordnance air defense guided missile program, focused nearly all of its attention on the beam rider guidance concept, rejecting the continuous wave doppler homing approach until its merits were clearly demonstrated through independent development efforts sponsored by the Bureau of Aeronautics.

Only in the realm of make vs. buy decisions, where the interests of prime contractors frequently conflicted with the interests of specialist subcontractors and the government, did independent systems engineering organizations appear consistently more objective than weapon system prime contractors. Greater objectivity in task allocation and subcontracting decisions is a significant advantage in its own right for independent systems engineering groups. Yet there is an even more important facet to the problem. Even if the government were willing to tolerate inefficient make vs. buy decisions on the part of weapon system prime contractors, serious coordination difficulties would arise from the prime contractor's efforts to pull work into its own shops. It is difficult for a subcontractor to cooperate closely with a prime contractor it considers to be a competitive threat. During the late 1950's, for example, strained relationships developed between electronic subsystem makers and airframe firms which had revealed a desire to diversify into the electronics business. The electronics firms either refused to become subcontractors, or they were wary about conveying data which the airframe prime contractor needed to perform its systems integration function, but which it might also employ in its efforts to secure electronics production contracts. In several such cases complete coordination breakdowns and even overt hostility arose as a result of competitive suspicions.

This problem dealt a fatal blow not only to certain proposed weapon system prime contractor management arrangements, but also to the Space Technology Laboratories' role as systems engineer and technical director for the Air Force ballistic missile program. STL's contract with the Air Force proscribed its participation in ballistic missile production work, guaranteeing that at least in the short run STL would not compete with the industrial firms whose efforts it was directing and coordinating. But the officers of STL's parent firm made no secret of their intent to build a powerful new competitor in the aerospace field upon the competence acquired by STL. This long-run competitive threat, more than any other aspect of STL's performance, incited the opposition first of industry and then of Congress to STL's privileged relationship with the Air Force. The formation of Aerospace Corporation to replace STL followed directly from the criticisms of STL's position.

The STL experience and the more general resistance to diversification-minded industrial prime contractors reveal clearly that the systems integration role can seldom be performed successfully by organizations competing with the firms whose work they are expected to coordinate. Competitive dilemmas of this sort virtually force the systems integration function upon government agencies or, when the government lacks the requisite in-house technical capability, independent nonprofit systems engineering organizations. Two other factors reinforce such a tendency. First, many large firms consider accepting technical direction as subcontractors from their industrial peers to be status-degrading. They prefer for prestige reasons to be direct prime contractors to the government. Second, by contracting directly with subsystem vendors and assuming the coordination burden itself, the government can avoid the profit override it might otherwise pay to a weapon system prime contractor on subcontracted subsystem work.[15]

For all these reasons, the trend has been toward government assumption of the systems engineering role in weapon system development programs. Still this has not barred contractor efforts to make a parallel systems integration contribution. When the gov-

[15] Cf. pp. 104–107 *supra*.

ernment has retained systems engineering responsibility in-house or delegated it to a special contractor, airframe prime contractors have tended to develop their own counterpart coordination groups to deal with both government and subsystem contractor engineers.[16] The net result has been a substantial, probably unavoidable duplication of functions.

Finally, there is the host of detailed review and control functions performed by government program management groups. These include checks on contractor technical and contractual decisions, management surveys, cost audits, property controls, and a virtual infinity of requirements to submit reports on program status, problems, compliance with government policies, and so forth. Contractors habitually complain that the sum of all such controls is an onerous burden which not only inflates administrative manpower requirements, but also retards the progress of their technical efforts. Anyone who has experienced bureaucratic red tape is necessarily sympathetic, even though the true cost of detailed government controls is difficult to measure. One company official estimated that the engineering effort devoted to administration amounts to as much as 40% of the total engineering hours spent on a project.[17] This estimate, however, apparently includes much of the managerial and coordinating activity inevitable in any complex project. At the other extreme, a major airframe firm found in 1957 that about 1% of its work force was directly engaged in preparing some 212 periodic government reports. This figure excludes all the indirect managerial and technical activity required to develop inputs for those reports, as well as the time consumed in answering special (nonperiodic) requests for information and justification of decisions. The true proportion of effort channeled into compliance with government reviews and controls undoubtedly lies somewhere between these extremes of 1% and 40%. Much of this unknown

[16] In the Atlas program, Space Technology Laboratories objected to Convair's insistence upon direct communication with other Atlas contractors. Its objections were overruled by the Air Force. Convair personnel claimed that as a result, their relations with Atlas associate contractors were not noticeably different from the relations the Convair Fort Worth division had as weapon system prime contractor with its B–58 subcontractors.

[17] "Ground Equipment Costs Show Steady Rise," *Aviation Week & Space Technology,* October 24, 1960, p. 32.

quantity might well be turned to more productive ends if there were an effective system of incentives on which government officials would be willing to rely.

Controls, Initiative, and Responsibility

It is clear that detailed controls and technical administration by the government are, at least to some extent, a substitute for deficient incentives. Is there a further relationship between incentives and controls? In particular, do detailed controls impair existing incentives for good performance, discouraging contractor initiative and the acceptance of responsibility?

There is some evidence that they do, although the problem is singularly resistant to conclusive analysis. Robert Schlaifer observes in his study of aircraft engine development that:

> . . . development was fully successful only when the services gave the firms all possible freedom in deciding on details of design and development. Government intervention in technical details always led to a very considerable delay, and often to a poorer product in the end.[18]

Our case studies did not provide sufficient evidence for determining whether, on balance, weapons contractors exhibited less initiative than firms selling in a market environment. They did show that contractors sometimes simply forgot about potentially desirable product improvements rather than accept the burden of negotiating the requisite amendments to contracts.[19] Similarly, they disclosed several clear instances of contractor refusal to accept responsibility for weapon system performance when a government agency insisted that some objectionable item of equipment or design principle be incorporated. More frequently, however, contractors appeared to exert their most diligent efforts to achieve the desired weapon system performance despite government decisions and controls they considered oppressive. Thus, the evidence is mixed. Detailed government controls probably do lead to some undesirable technical results and bring out certain perverse aspects of human nature, but they do not encourage wholesale abdication of responsibility.

[18] Robert Schlaifer, *Development of Aircraft Engines* (Boston: Division of Research, Harvard Business School, 1950), p. 8.
[19] Cf. pp. 237–239 *supra*.

Technical Administration and Controls: Conclusion

Even if perfectly satisfactory incentive systems could be developed, not all government technical administration and control functions could be eliminated. Product decision making, in more or less detail, must remain a government function. And in all likelihood, continued government participation in the important area of systems integration will be necessary when program collaborators also happen to be potential competitors. Nevertheless, recognition by government officials that existing incentive systems generate strong compulsions for good contractor performance on the quality and time dimensions, even if not on the cost dimension, might permit a beneficial lessening of burdensome controls whose utility is slight. And significantly strengthened incentives should logically lead to a substantial relaxation of the detailed controls presently imposed on contractor operations.

THE ARSENAL SYSTEM OF WEAPONS DEVELOPMENT

Competition, profit incentives, contract negotiations, technical supervision, detailed technical and financial controls — all of these seem necessary to harness private enterprise into effective government service for the development of advanced weapons. We are inclined to ask, "Isn't there a simpler way?" One possible answer is, "Let the government do the job itself."

Advocates of the arsenal approach to weapons development point to a number of fundamental defects in the private enterprise system of weapons development which make industry ill-suited for the task. Most of these, basically related to interactions of the profit motive with an environment of rapid technological change, have already been identified in this volume. They include the propensity for contractors to submit unrealistically optimistic time, cost, and quality promises to secure new contract awards; the squandering of scarce creative talent on competitive efforts; the tendency to do work in-house which could be executed more efficiently by specialist subcontractors; and the hoarding of technical personnel to maintain an advantage in competing for future contracts. A further problem worth pondering is the social and moral issue of firms' strenuous efforts to sell new weapon systems —

efforts which, some have asserted, have contributed to the intensification of the armaments race.[20]

Granting that most, if not all, of these defects actually exist, we must nevertheless inquire: are they unique to private, profit-seeking organizations? The evidence indicates that in many respects, they are not. Arsenals, government laboratories, and captive nonprofit contractors presumably lack the profit maximization motive.[21] But they clearly are affected by the survival motive — an important basis of competitive incentives, as defined in this volume. For example, when confronted with imminent cancellation of the Jupiter IRBM development, its principal project, the Army's in-house missile development group behaved very much as any profit-maximizing contractor would behave. It prepared to pull work which had been "subcontracted" back into its own facilities. And it began "selling" many proposals for new missile and space projects — so many, in fact, that its resources would have been seriously overextended if half the proposals were accepted.[22] Illustrations from the histories of other nonprofit organizations could be multiplied. Few organizations, profit or nonprofit, like to decline and disband.

There may, however, be a significant difference between profit-seeking and nonprofit organizations in another basis of competitive incentives — the growth motive. Our case studies shed little light on the growth aspirations and predilections of government laboratories and arsenals. Much more evidence was obtained on the be-

[20] For a recent statement of this proposition, see Fred J. Cook, *The Warfare State* (New York: Macmillan, 1962). For pre-World War II expositions, see H. C. Engelbrecht, *Merchants of Death* (New York: Dodd, Mead, 1934) and Philip Noel-Baker, *The Private Manufacture of Armaments* (London: Victor Gollancz, 1937).

[21] Paradoxically, many so-called "nonprofit" organizations serving the government as contractors actually receive profits (or strictly speaking, fees) which, given their exemption from federal income taxation, typically turn out to be higher than the fees retained under CPFF contracts by profit-seeking concerns. These profits cannot, however, accrue to the private benefit of stockholders or trustees. Rather, they are used to build facilities, support special research projects, provide scholarships, cover interest costs and other expenditures not allowed under government contracting regulations, and build up working capital.

[22] Cf. J. B. Medaris, *Countdown for Decision* (New York: Putnam's, 1960), pp. 136–137.

havior of nonprofit firms which specialized in performing research and development, systems engineering, and other technical services under contract to government agencies. Although the analogy with in-house government operations is undoubtedly imperfect, these nonprofit organizations (with certain exceptions) appeared generally less eager than profit-seeking firms to exploit their growth opportunities fully. When not faced with actual sales declines, they were more selective in undertaking new projects. They adhered to higher standards in hiring professional personnel. Their officers often had clearly defined ideas as to maximum desired rates of growth, and when government demands forced them to exceed these rates, they sometimes "spun off" whole departments, creating completely autonomous new organizations.[23] And perhaps most important, they were willing to forego the growth opportunities implicit in production contracting — opportunities on which profit-seeking contractors usually place great emphasis.

What is the cause of this apparent difference? Do profit-seeking firms seek growth because growth is the best route to increased long-run profits? Or is growth a goal in its own right? Are nonprofit organizations willing to forego growth opportunities because they have no desire to maximize long-run profits? Or do nonprofit laboratories exhibit a weaker growth drive because they are more frequently dominated by professionally oriented individuals who value other attributes more highly than growth?[24] These are questions of considerable interest to the economist, but they cannot be answered conclusively on the basis of our case study evidence. My interpretation is that each of the suggested explanations is partly valid; that both growth and profits are important, distinguishable goals of the executives of profit-seeking firms.[25]

In any event, the survival motive is common to virtually all

---

[23] This, for instance, was a crucial consideration in the divestiture of what is now called the Systems Development Corporation from The RAND Corporation in 1956. Cf. House, Committee on Government Operations, *Hearings, Systems Development and Management,* Part 3 (1962), pp. 923, 991.

[24] On this point the analogy between in-house government technical organizations and special captive nonprofit contractors may break down. However, it would appear that many (although clearly not all) government laboratories and arsenals have a strong professional orientation.

[25] Cf. also pp. 321–322 *supra.*

organizations, and when survival is threatened, both profit-seeking and nonprofit groups tend to manifest the competitive behavior which complicates weapons acquisition.   But in this connection, still another difference exists between nonprofit arms of the government — especially in-house technical organizations — and profit-seeking contractors.   Most defense contractors believe that the government stands ready to drop them from its list of suppliers if their capabilities lag behind the demands of military technology or (less frequently) if their performance has been unsatisfactory. This belief underlies the insecurity of national security contractors. In contrast, government arsenals, technical centers, shipyards and the like are customarily regarded as a government resource, to be utilized in fair weather and foul.   This difference in the government's attitude toward in-house as compared to private defense resources is in many respects undesirable, but it exists.[26]   Furthermore, political pressures act with greater consistency to insure the survival of government arsenals.   It may be difficult in the current political milieu to shed a major contractor, but it is even more difficult (although not impossible) to close an arsenal or shipyard. Given this relatively greater security, in-house development groups are less likely to indulge in the competitive excesses characteristic of private contractors.

The security and freedom from competitive pressures of arsenals can, of course, have concomitant disadvantages.   Or to put the point positively, competition clearly provides some benefits.   In particular, competition exerts pressures on contractors to adapt, to sustain vigorous technical and managerial efforts, and to innovate which may be lacking in the arsenal case.

Do government arsenals in fact tend to be less innovative and generally less vigorous in developing new weapons than private firms exposed to the full gale of competition?   Certainly, instances of government arsenals' failure to exploit new technologies effectively have been cited frequently enough.   Schlaifer commented in his study of U.S. aircraft engine development that:

> Both the armed services . . . tried on various occasions to develop an engine themselves, but all these attempts were failures, and the record shows clearly that the services were in general in-

[26] Cf. pp. 112–114 and 344–345 *supra.*

capable of successfully developing a complex finished product such as an aircraft engine. . . . The private firm was the only agency which between 1919 and 1939 showed itself capable of developing aircraft engines rapidly enough to reach production before they reached obsolescence.[27]

The experience of the 1930's and 1940's undoubtedly afforded some grounds for the assertion of an aerospace industry journal that "the arsenal concept failed miserably the test imposed by even the comparatively simple technologies of World War-2 type weapons such as subsonic aircraft, tanks, and heavy artillery." [28] On the other hand, in-house government technical groups can also claim many praiseworthy accomplishments, such as the early development of radar during the 1930's (in the Naval Research Laboratories and the Army Signal Corps), creation of the inexpensive but effective Sidewinder infrared homing guided missile (at the Naval Ordnance Test Station), and path-breaking research on the properties and applications of titanium and beryllium (at the Army's Watertown Arsenal). And although possession of the German rocket group under Wernher von Braun was undoubtedly a unique historical accident, the Army's Redstone Arsenal did brilliant pioneering work in the ballistic missile and satellite field while many aircraft industry leaders were insisting that long-range rocket technology had no military potential. On technological frontiers other than rocketry, private firms have also proved singularly resistant to change and innovation at times. Similarly, the many development failures of private contractors cannot be ignored, if the uninspiring history of certain government laboratories and arsenals is to be cited. In short, the record is mixed. Specific examples can be brought forth to support virtually any contention about the relative effectiveness of arsenals and private industry. It is clear that the arsenal system *can* succeed under at least some circumstances, but how frequently these circumstances occur is unknown. Lacking a thorough comparative study of the *average* success records of arsenals and industry — a study which has never been made — no firm conclusions can be offered as

[27] Robert Schlaifer, *Development of Aircraft Engines,* p. 7.

[28] Robert Hotz, "The New Arsenal Concept," *Aviation Week & Space Technology,* July 9, 1962, p. 13. For a similar comment on Army tank development, see House, Committee on Government Operations, *Eleventh Report, Organization and Management of Missile Programs* (1960), p. 50.

to how serious the drawbacks of a noncompetitive arsenal environment are.

The Production Motive and Innovation

Thus far it has been assumed that private firms should tend to be more innovative than arsenals, since they are exposed to more pervasive competitive pressures. But some analysts, notably Professor Kaysen, have suggested that the competitive environment of weapons contracting leads to just the opposite result: less innovation in private industry, rather than more.[29] The argument is as follows. As indicated in this volume, the competitive struggle of weapons vendors is a struggle to maximize sales, and an important element of sales maximization is maximizing production follow-on contract potential. Firms therefore tend to place a good deal of emphasis on production prospects. But, it is alleged, this has two unfavorable effects on the propensity to innovate. First, defense contractors favor those research and development opportunities which have a fairly clear and immediate promise of production orders, slighting the more imaginative, far-reaching projects which may (although with considerable *ex ante* uncertainty) lead to the most dramatic improvements in weapons capabilities. Second, preoccupied with the tangible production consequences of their development efforts, firms behave as if development were not an uncertain process of searching for new knowledge about technical problems. Instead, great stress is placed by production-oriented firms on systems integration. This emphasis, it is argued, leads to early specification of design parameters and components, and given these specification constraints, the introduction of new ideas and new solutions as the development generates new knowledge and insights becomes difficult or impossible. To quote Kaysen:

> Fundamentally, there is an antagonism between compatibility in terms of some preconceived system and novelty, and where compatibility is emphasized, it must have its impact on novelty. Since higher performance rests ultimately on novelty, the result

[29] Carl Kaysen, "Improving the Efficiency of Military Research and Development," *Public Policy,* Vol. XII (Cambridge: Harvard University Graduate School of Public Administration, in press).

will be a sacrifice in performance over what might have been possible in the absence of pre-set demands of compatibility.[30]

With respect to the first point, there are definite indications that defense contractors have sometimes favored development projects with a clear and immediate promise of production orders, neglecting possibilities which ultimately proved to have much greater military value. But in many other cases contractors have undertaken very imaginative long-range development programs — often in response to competitive pressures. Conflicting forces act upon defense contractors, some conducive to innovation and some to conservatism. On balance, there seems to have been no marked shortage of contractors willing to undertake ambitious, far-reaching systems development projects during the 1950's and early 1960's.

Nevertheless, it is quite possible that there *has* been a shortage of really good new technical ideas to exploit through development efforts.[31] Whether this phenomenon is in any way related to the institutional structure of American weapons acquisition is difficult to determine. One might argue that truly significant new technical ideas are largely exogenous in an economic sense; that allocating more resources to their creation would lead to no discernible increase in the number of ideas forthcoming. But this view is too extreme. It is more likely that increased spending on basic and applied research would at least slightly increase the rate of emergence of new concepts and technical possibilities. And in this respect, the record of U.S. weapons makers does appear deficient. In 1959 the aircraft and parts industry — the identifiable sector most exclusively devoted to defense work — allocated only 1.4% of its total research and development outlays to basic research. The average for all industries was 3.6%, and only "fabricated metal products" and "motor vehicles" had poorer percentage records than aircraft and parts. Similarly, aircraft and parts spent only 10.8% of its R & D outlays on applied research, compared to 20.8% for all U.S. industry.[32]

U.S. defense contractors might be criticized from these com-

---

[30] *Ibid.*

[31] Cf. Peck and Scherer, pp. 11–12 and 238.

[32] National Science Foundation, *Funds for Research and Development in Industry: 1959,* p. 65.

parisons, although a more complete analysis would have to determine whether the opportunities open to aircraft firms for useful basic and applied research were less rich than in other sectors. Still it does not follow that, given the supply of unexploited technical possibilities, *development* is approached less innovatively by industry than by government arsenals and laboratories. Basic and applied research may well flourish best in institutions not concerned with the profit motive,[33] supplying concepts to be exploited either by industrial contractors or arsenals — whichever can perform the quite different job of development most effectively.

Failure to distinguish between basic and applied research on the one hand and development on the other, and among the various stages of development, is the principal flaw in Professor Kaysen's second argument: that emphasis on systems integration by private contractors is an undesirable impediment to innovation. It can also be dangerous to draw the distinction too sharply, but this risk must be accepted here to frame the issue concisely.[34] There are times in weapons research and development when design approaches and parameters should not be closely specified and constrained, so that creativity, experimentation, and innovation can hold full sway. These include for the most part what we customarily call applied research, feasibility studies, exploratory development, and some component development. But there are also periods when component and subsystem interactions must be specified, design parameter constraints imposed, and commitments to specific approaches and designs made. These comprise what we

[33] See Richard Nelson, "The Simple Economics of Basic Scientific Research," *Journal of Political Economy,* June 1959, pp. 297–306.

[34] For a more comprehensive and cautious analysis, see Peck and Scherer, pp. 25–45, 225–238, and 306–308. See also the exchange between Burton Klein and myself in Richard Nelson, ed., *The Rate and Direction of Inventive Activity* (National Bureau of Economic Research conference report; Princeton: Princeton University Press, 1962), pp. 497–508.

Kaysen's interpretation of the problems and uncertainties of development is based mainly upon the writings of Klein, Charles J. Hitch, and other RAND Corporation economists. It is interesting to note that Hitch, after becoming Assistant Secretary of Defense, acknowledged in what amounted to a virtual recantation of earlier views the importance of the distinction made here. See House, Committee on Government Operations, *Hearings, Systems Development and Management,* Part 2 (1962), pp. 540–541.

normally call systems development (which, it is important to recognize, consumes the preponderance of resources allocated to the whole process of weapons research and development).[35]

To be sure, complete rigidity of design approaches during development is almost always undesirable. Changes are inevitable. But when there are complex interrelationships among components of a proposed weapon system, changes in one technical area may touch off an extended chain of complementary changes in other areas. It is essential to specify a system in at least enough detail to identify the implications of potential changes, and often changes which appear worthwhile when viewed in isolation may be rejected to avoid adverse chain reactions. Furthermore, organizational and psychological needs compel the establishment of a definite technical plan. There must be some basis for dividing work, defining lines of coordination, and setting quality and time goals. The optimal timing and degree of firmness for technical commitments depends upon particular program circumstances such as the nature of the technical problems faced and the degree of urgency attached to schedules.[36] In general, however, the most favorable time for innovation in a systems development effort is at the very outset, and from that time on the opportunities for adopting new ideas become increasingly constrained as the need for commitment grows.

Thus, attention to the problems of systems integration — perhaps with a loss of the flexibility which permits innovation — is a necessary and important aspect of weapon systems development, whether the work is done by an arsenal or a profit-seeking contractor. The conflict between compatibility and novelty is universal, not unique to contractor organizations. Much more concrete evidence would be required to support Professor Kaysen's inference that contractors are inherently less innovative than government laboratories during development because of their concern for sys-

[35] Roughly 63% of the Defense Department's $6.1 billion fiscal year 1964 research, development, test, and evaluation budget (excluding management and support costs) was for systems development, as defined here. Another 10% was for advanced development, including systems work with technical and operational goals which normally would be specified more flexibly. Cf. "Constant Reviews Yield Sharp Technical Control," *Missiles and Rockets,* March 25, 1963, pp. 47–49.

[36] See Peck and Scherer, p. 307.

tems integration. And at least in this particular respect, his conclusion that "research and development" activities (lumped together, with no distinction) should be organizationally segregated
from production activities is also not supported. "Research"
might very well be separated from "development," but that is a
different matter.

The Development-Production Transition Problem

Let us, despite these objections, grant for the sake of argument
that government arsenals not seeking production orders would in
at least certain circumstances be more efficient and more favorably
disposed toward imaginative development projects than private
contractors. If so, a case might be made for concentrating weapons development in government arsenals, letting private firms serve
mainly as production contractors. But still another issue must
be contemplated: can the development-production transition be
bridged effectively by separate and distinct organizations?

Again, no dogmatic answer is possible. Certainly, an organizational gap between the development and production stages does
create problems. Channels of communication are inevitably
lengthened and perhaps become more formalized, leading to more
complex coordinating structures and possibly to design information
flow breakdowns and program delays. Flexibility in making last-
minute test vehicle configuration changes would probably be reduced. Production engineers may fail to gain sufficient understanding of the product they are expected to produce. Development
and design engineers may lose touch with the realities of production, turning out designs which permit successful fabrication under
laboratory conditions, but which prove impossible or unnecessarily
costly to implement under the distinctly different conditions of a
production operation. These are very real problems even when
development and production are executed under the same roof.
Organizational and geographic separation of development and production groups can only aggravate them. Serious quality deficiencies and schedule slippages have resulted from communications breakdowns between compartmentalized development and
production organizations in some U.S. weapons programs.[37]

[37] The Soviets apparently have experienced similar difficulties due to the
organizational separation of development and production responsibilities in

Nevertheless, in other programs the development-production transition has been accomplished smoothly despite a division of responsibilities between two different organizations. Although it is not an ideal illustration, the Jupiter IRBM airframe production program — the only program with development by a government arsenal and production by a private contractor covered in detail by our case studies — shows how this can be done.[38] A "know-how gap" was avoided by having Chrysler production engineers work directly with Army Ballistic Missile Agency development personnel at Redstone Arsenal during the research and development stages. In addition, a pilot production line (to some extent duplicating Chrysler's facilities) was set up at Redstone Arsenal at an incremental cost of roughly $9 million — about 1% of total program costs. This line permitted quick, flexible prototype fabrication and gave Army development engineers an intimate familiarity with the Jupiter missile's special production problems.

It therefore appears possible — usually at an additional expense small in comparison with total program outlays — to avert many of the pitfalls associated with a development-production transition involving different organizations. But when for some reason good interorganization working relationships prove difficult to establish, realization of this possibility can still be frustrated. In programs with less happy transition experiences, a primary source of trouble was the unwillingness of busy development engineers to "waste their time" talking to production organization representatives. Overcoming this type of resistance may require the intervention of a common management interested in over-all program success. Certainly, there have been enough instances of failure to suggest that separating development organizationally from production is

---

the drug field. See Raymond A. Bauer and Mark G. Field, "Ironic Contrast: US and USSR Drug Industries," *Harvard Business Review,* September–October 1962, pp. 93–94. In the past the Russians also separated some manned aircraft development work from production operations, although little is known on how well the system functioned. A Soviet scientist indicated to me that development and production operations are integrated in the guided missile and space fields.

[38] It is not ideal since, as events turned out, Jupiter production was limited to such small quantities that the whole job could have been accomplished at Redstone Arsenal without the assistance of Chrysler.

problematic, even though under favorable conditions the problems can be overcome.

The Personnel Problem of Government Laboratories

Personnel recruitment is without doubt the Achilles' heel of the arsenal approach to weapons development in the United States. Historically, the scope and quality of government in-house technical operations have been severely limited by the government's inability to attract and retain sufficient numbers of qualified technical personnel. As Director of Defense Research and Engineering Harold Brown observed:

> I think that the amount of work that is done in the in-house laboratories is not unreasonable. It is perhaps 15 or 20 percent of the total research and development. I think its quality has not been as good as it should be and I am afraid that the in-house laboratories have had their competence eroded very substantially over the past 20 years. . . .[39]

Central to this problem is the disparity between government and industry salaries — a disparity increasing over the past two decades.[40] As a committee of top government officials reported to President Kennedy in 1962:

> At the present time we consider that one of the most serious obstacles to the recruitment of first-class scientists, administrators, and engineers in the Government service is the serious disparity between governmental and private compensation for comparable work.[41]

It is doubtful whether this salary disparity can be eliminated in the near future. Two corrective actions were recommended by the so-called Bell Committee: pay reform legislation and the imposition of controls on contractor salary structures.[42] These, however,

[39] House, Committee on Government Operations, *Hearings, Systems Development and Management,* Part 2 (1962), p. 473.

[40] Cf. Peck and Scherer, pp. 90–93.

[41] Senate, Committee on Government Operations, *Document No. 94, Report to the President on Government Contracting for Research and Development Prepared by the Bureau of the Budget* (1962), p. viii. A comparative analysis of industry, government, and university salaries for technical personnel is provided on pp. 47–68 of that report.

[42] *Ibid.,* pp. 9, 20.

have little chance of real success. Pay reform is blocked partly by the reluctance of Congress to authorize Executive Branch salaries higher than the salaries paid to members of Congress. But a more fundamental obstacle is the difficulty of making selective adjustments in a government salary structure covering several million persons. The government's personnel problem is most severe in professional and executive categories, which include only a small proportion of total federal employment. Implementing substantial salary increases in these categories alone could provoke morale problems in other more highly populated classifications. On the other hand, conferring across-the-board increases in federal salaries would be a prohibitively costly way of solving the specific professional and executive talent recruitment problem. At best, only modest gains can be expected through pay reform.

The imposition of stringent controls on contractor salary structures has its own set of dilemmas. If contractors were prevented from paying salaries higher than those offered for comparable work in government, an exodus of the best talent from defense work to civilian activities would undoubtedly follow. If contractors were merely prevented from paying salaries higher than those prevailing in nondefense industry, as the Bell Committee suggested, the disparity between government and contractor salaries will persist.

Given the present institutional constraints, the government's scientific and engineering personnel salary problem appears largely insoluble, at least by direct attacks. Indirect solutions offer more promise. As we have seen, by contracting with nonprofit institutes — both existing university laboratories and specially organized defense-oriented corporations — the government has been able to build up captive substitutes for in-house talent pools. In some cases these nonprofit organizations have proved to be rather good substitutes, identifying closely with government aims and avoiding most of the lapses from efficiency and objectivity common to industrial contractors. In other cases, however, the behavioral differences between special nonprofit and profit-seeking organizations have been slight.

Even though the government may be unable to solve its salary disparity problem directly, it could do a better job of attracting technically competent personnel than it has in certain fields. Money is by no means the only variable influencing professionals in their choice of jobs. The desire to do interesting, useful work is often of equal importance to persons with the most valuable professional talents. Some government agencies have made their technical staff recruitment problems unnecessarily difficult by refusing to support actual research and development work in-house, using their scientists and engineers only for "desk engineering" — e.g., supervising the work of contractors.[43] Such policies drive out many energetic and creative professionals who might otherwise be willing to work for the government at pay scales lower than those in industry. By sponsoring vigorous, stimulating in-house R & D efforts, the armed services can do much to enhance their ability to attract technical personnel. The scientists and engineers employed in this way will not only make worthwhile technical contributions directly, but will also provide a reservoir of independent competence which can be focused on specific questions when the objectivity of industrial firms is open to question. This, perhaps, is the most important reason for active government conduct of weapons research and development work: not to displace industry, but to build and hold a nucleus of independent expertise within government.

Conclusion

There never has been a thorough, dispassionate study of the relative strengths and weaknesses of government arsenals and laboratories in advanced weapons development work. This chapter cannot claim to be the exception. Our case studies — only one of which focused directly on an in-house development by a government arsenal — provided far too little evidence for a thorough analysis. The limitations of space and balance in the present chapter have permitted only a superficial examination of even the available evidence. Nevertheless, it has been possible at least to identify some of the issues relevant to defining the optimal role of arsenals in the U.S. weapons acquisition process.

The principal issue, broadly defined, concerns the efficiency and progressiveness of arsenals as compared to profit-seeking contractor organizations. There is reason to believe that arsenals are less susceptible to the competitive excesses of private firms. Their rela-

---

[43] Cf. Peck and Scherer, pp. 92–93.

tive freedom from competitive pressures may also cause arsenals to be somewhat less efficient and innovative than private firms, although their ability to choose technical approaches without worrying about production follow-on contract potential could create opposite tendencies. Only a careful historical study would be able to show whether the net balance of advantage lies in favor of the arsenal system or the private contractor system.

A significant disadvantage of the arsenal system is the government's apparent inability to offer professional salaries commensurate with those of industry. But the existence of this problem makes it all the more important that the military services sustain a vigorous in-house research and development program, for such an effort will attract many competent scientists and engineers who are motivated more by the desire to do useful, interesting work than by the desire to maximize purely monetary rewards.

CHAPTER 15

Conclusion

IT IS CUSTOMARY to conclude policy-oriented studies with a set of confident, definite recommendations for change and (hopefully) improvement. The present chapter defers to that tradition. Yet it would be less than honest to insist that here will be found the final, correct solution to the government's defense procurement incentive problems. The social sciences are not that powerful, especially when so much depends upon value judgments and the human element in implementation.

The principal innovation suggested by this study is an after-the-fact evaluation system of contractual and competitive incentives. Although many permutations are possible, the following measures are proposed for the realization of a thoroughgoing system of incentives based upon after-the-fact evaluation:

(1) Program evaluation boards should be established by the Department of Defense, the National Aeronautics and Space Administration, and the Atomic Energy Commission. The boards would periodically evaluate on a relative basis the performance of major contractors in the principal development programs sponsored by those agencies.

(2) Development work in programs subject to after-the-fact evaluation should be covered by contracts which guarantee in advance no profit, or at least no more profit than the amount necessary to offset minimum incremental financial costs and other nonreimbursable costs. When the main development effort in a program is completed, the contractor will receive a lump sum profit award. The size of this award will depend upon the contractor's relative efficiency in performing its development program assignment, as evaluated by the program evaluation board. The more efficient the contractor's performance, the higher its profit return will be.

(3) The total in-house sales volume of each major contractor organization should be correlated as closely as possible with the contractor's recent over-all performance record. This will be accomplished by establishing periodically adjusted level of effort quotas to ensure that firms with outstanding performance records grow in sales volume and firms with inferior performance records decline. Given these level of effort quotas, contractor organizations should be viewed as a national defense resource, to be utilized fully up to their quotas by loading them with appropriate development and production prime contracts and subcontracts.

(4) Performance evaluations made by the program evaluation boards should be published, so that the public will know which firms have served the nation well and which have performed poorly.

(5) Until sufficient experience has been gained in the application of after-the-fact evaluation to development programs, automatic contractual incentives should be employed to provide incentives for production efficiency. Ultimately, realized production contract profit rates may also be determined through after-the-fact evaluation of contractors' relative production efficiency.

Preliminary reactions have shown that for many participants in the weapons acquisition process this will seem too strong and unpalatable a dose of medicine. It is for the patient, not the diagnostician, to decide whether the cure is better or worse than the disease. But if the diagnosis in this volume is anywhere near correct, the tendencies toward inefficiency which plague weapons programs will not be checked by much weaker and better tasting medicine. Strong remedies are needed to undermine or overpower the user costs and disutilities blocking cost reduction. Unconventional remedies are needed to deal with the problem of uncertainty in development efforts and to permit flexibility of action unfettered by unreliable and frequently biased initial quality, time, and cost estimates.

Still to carry the medical metaphor one step further, the diagnostician cannot guarantee the success of his prescription. There are definite problems in an after-the-fact evaluation incentive approach. The difficulty of measuring performance in a complex weapons program is one; the possibility of human failure on the part of performance judges is another. Some more detailed problems of implementing an after-the-fact evaluation system have been discussed only fleetingly in this volume, partly to avoid discouraging further consideration, partly to encourage flexibility in adapting the system to specific situations, and partly because the most favorable psychological conditions for carrying out a new policy are undoubtedly created when the responsible organization solves its own problems. Certainly, after-the-fact evaluation is not a perfect solution to the government's incentive needs, just as existing incentive systems are far from perfect. The policy maker's choice must be made from a selection of imperfect alternatives.

It is my best judgment, based upon the analysis and findings of this volume, that a competently administered after-the-fact evaluation system of incentives would prove substantially superior to existing alternatives. The possibility of error in this judgment cannot be denied. A careful and unbiased test would permit a more confident policy decision. Considering the potential benefits of an incentive system inherently better-suited to the environment of weapons acquisition, such a test appears well worth while. Therefore, an experimental after-the-fact evaluation incentive system application along the general lines suggested in this volume is strongly recommended. Many of the fundamental uncertainties connected with after-the-fact evaluation can also be reduced significantly through soundly conceived and carefully executed research not necessarily tied to an actual application of the system.[1] In particular, studies should be made of:

(1) The feasibility of measuring performance in incomplete segments of development programs.

(2) The weights implicitly assigned to time, quality, and cost dimensions in knowledgeable judges' evaluations of over-all performance for a large sample of development programs.

(3) The feasibility of measuring development program cost efficiency on a relative basis through after-the-fact evaluation.

(4) The feasibility of measuring production efficiency on a relative basis through after-the-fact evaluation.

(5) Multiprogram performance index weighting problems.

---

[1] By "soundly conceived and carefully executed" I mean to exclude the 30- or 90-day "crash" studies which seem to underlie so many Department of Defense policy decisions. I also exclude studies which do no more than sample the predetermined opinions of practitioners.

(6) Historical correlations of performance on successive programs conducted by particular contractors, to determine how well future performance can be predicted from past performance.

(7) Optimal distributions of profit and sales growth rate variations, with emphasis on the form of the distribution, its mean, and its range, taking into account both short-run performance incentive objectives and long-run entry and exit requirements.

(8) Problems in securing an optimal balance of quality, time, and cost incentives through variations in the several components of the over-all incentive system.

(9) The possibility of eliminating detailed contract negotiations in major procurement programs.

(10) Administrative aspects of an after-the-fact evaluation incentive system, including the personnel problem.

Only when these studies and experiments yield satisfactory results should after-the-fact evaluation be considered for full-scale implementation.

Despite this cautious assessment of the prospects for improvement, we must not forget the consequences of failing to improve existing incentive systems. The Department of Defense and other government agencies responsible for procuring technologically advanced hardware have reacted to acknowledged incentive system shortcomings by imposing increasingly detailed direct controls over contractor operations. Many of these controls have a high cost in terms of effort diverted from actual productive work to checking, double-checking, and triple-checking. Their cost in terms of suppressed initiative may also be high. Each year the government marches a few paces farther down the controls road. This, in my opinion, is an undesirable trend. It can be reversed only if a vigorous effort is exerted to make the incentives road more passable.

APPENDICES TO CHAPTERS 7 AND 8

Appendix to Chapter 7

A Stochastic User Cost Model

THE PURPOSE of this appendix is to define the concept of user cost more rigorously. User costs reflect the future profit sacrifices resulting from current contract cost reductions which yield current accounting profit increments. As we have seen in Chapter 6, under auto-correlating contracts designed to incite cost reduction, accounting profit is determined by the equation:

$$(7.1) \qquad \pi_A = \pi_T + \alpha(C_T - C_A);$$

where π_A is the amount of accounting profit realized, π_T is the negotiated target profit amount, α is the contractor's sharing proportion, C_T is the negotiated target cost, and C_A is the actual accounting cost charged to the contract.[1] The existence of cost ceilings and floors is ignored. For convenience, it is assumed that all accounting costs represent current outlays and are reimbursed instantaneously, while profit payments are made only at the end of the year. Thus, π_A for the forthcoming contract year is written π_{A1}, and it will be realized $t = 1$ year from the present.

By introducing slightly different notation, equation (7.1) can be rewritten in a more action-oriented context. Let C_1^* be the accounting cost which would result if no new cost-reducing actions are taken, and let π_1^* be the accounting profit realized in this *status quo* case.[2] Then:

$$(7.2) \qquad \pi_{A1} = \pi_1^* + \alpha(C_1^* - C_{A1}).$$

To simplify the exposition, let ΔC_1 measure the departure of actual accounting cost C_{A1} from the *status quo* cost level C_1^*:

$$(7.3) \qquad \Delta C_1 = C_1^* - C_{A1}.$$

A positive value of ΔC_1 indicates that new cost reduction actions have been taken, while a negative value indicates that new cost increases have

[1] For completeness, (7.1) might also include a term $-C_D$, designating actual costs directly connected with the contract, but not allowable under government procurement regulations. As note 3 in Chapter 6 indicated, generally the value of C_D would be quite small.

[2] Any value of C_1^* is permissible, as long as it is predetermined. If the firm will just realize its target profit π_T by undertaking no new cost reduction actions, equations (7.1) and (7.2) are identical. The formulation in equation (7.2) is more general, also covering situations in which the targets have been set at pessimistically high or optimistically low levels.

been permitted. Since C_1^* is predetermined, ΔC_1 is an inverse linear function of C_{A1}. Furthermore, let us call $\alpha \Delta C_1 = \alpha(C_1^* - C_{A1})$ the firm's *incentive profit*, to be distinguished from the profit π_1^* which would be received if no new cost-reducing or cost-increasing actions are taken. When α is fixed, the firm's incentive profit is also an inverse linear function of C_{A1}; the higher the current actual accounting costs C_{A1} incurred, the less the firm's incentive profit $\alpha \Delta C_1$ will be.

Reductions in current actual accounting costs are achieved by cutting corners on quality; letting schedules slip; or eliminating personnel, equipment, and projects which may enhance the firm's future competitive position. In every such case, cost reduction coincides with potential reductions in future sales. Therefore, increases in ΔC_1 and hence in the incentive profit $\alpha \Delta C_1$ coincide with decreases in future sales. Let the true relationship between ΔC_1 and sales in year t be:

$$(7.4) \qquad\qquad \Delta S_t = f_t(\Delta C_1),$$

where ΔS_t is defined as the total amount of sales sacrificed (or if it is negative, gained) as a result of increases (or decreases) in ΔC_1 due to decreases (or increases) in C_{A1}. One possible configuration of the $f(\Delta C_1)$ function suggested by the case study evidence is shown in Figure 7A.1a. As ΔC_1 (and hence the firm's incentive profit) is increased by reducing costs, future sales are sacrificed at an increasing rate. For specific programs the function may reach a limit at the point where follow-on sales in year t are reduced to the zero level. But when the reputation and capability effects of cost reduction on a firm's ability to win future source

FIGURE 7A.1

Possible Configurations of the $f_t(\Delta C_1)$ Function

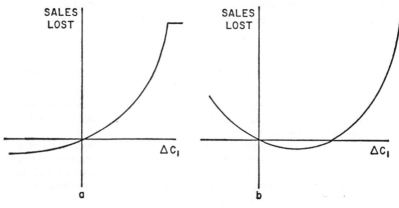

selection competitions are included, the limit will be reached only at the point where over-all company sales are equal to zero. Naturally, other configurations are possible. For example, when opportunity costs are high or when high development costs could lead to program cancellation, the configuration shown in Figure 7A.1b might be encountered.

Contractor executives never know the true shape of the $f_t(\Delta C_1)$ function with certainty. Rather, for any given value of ΔC_1, the best they can do is visualize a prior subjective probability distribution of future sales outcomes $\phi_{t\Delta c}(\Delta S_t)$. This distribution can be of any shape, depending upon the expectations of contractor executives and the degree of confidence they have in their judgments. It need not be unbiased; in fact, contractor personnel may tend to overestimate the sales losses which will result from cost reduction efforts involving the sacrifice of peripheral technical features.

Although it is entirely plausible that they should consider only single-valued "best guess" or modal estimates, let us assume that company executives make their decisions on the basis of expected values. The expected value of ΔS_t for a given value of ΔC_1 is:

$$(7.5) \qquad E(\Delta S_t \mid \Delta C_1) = \int_{-\infty}^{+\infty} \Delta S_t \, \phi_{t\Delta c}(\Delta S_t) \, d\Delta S_t.$$

Associated with this expected sales loss in year t as a result of reducing costs by ΔC_1 in year 1 is a profit margin $P(t)$ on year t's sales.[3] The expected profit loss in this case can be written:

$$(7.6) \qquad E(\Delta \pi_t \mid \Delta C_1) = P(t) \int_{-\infty}^{+\infty} \Delta S_t \, \phi_{t\Delta c}(\Delta S_t) \, d\Delta S_t.$$

The user cost $U_{t\Delta c}$ associated with reducing costs by ΔC_1 in year 1 is the present value of expected profit losses in year t:

$$(7.7) \qquad U_{t\Delta c} = \frac{P(t) \int_{-\infty}^{+\infty} \Delta S_t \, \phi_{t\Delta c}(\Delta S_t) \, d\Delta S_t}{[1 + r(1)][1 + r(2)] \ldots [1 + r(t)]};$$

where $r(t)$ is the discount rate appropriate to year t, reflecting either the firm's cost of capital or its alternative investment opportunities in that year.

[3] In the simple case where the sales sacrificed are follow-on production contract sales only, $P(t)$ will generally be increasing with t to reflect the transition from cost reimbursement to fixed-price incentive to firm fixed-price contracts, each bearing higher negotiated profit margins and generally higher realized profit expectations. In a more complex model, this $P(t)$ profit margin function might also be made stochastic. Further complexity is injected when sales losses due to inability to win source selection competitions are considered, since there need be no uniform time pattern of profit rates.

For the sake of simplicity, the user cost function derived thus far has been for only a single assumed value of ΔC_1 and for a single year. Letting ΔC_1 now be variable, we can write:

$$(7.8) \qquad E(\Delta S_t) = E[f_t(\Delta C_1)].$$

It is not necessary that the probability distribution $\phi_{t\Delta c}(\Delta S_t)$ be identical for all values of ΔC_1. It is in fact more likely that the distribution will be heteroscedastic, fanning out on both sides of $\Delta C_1 = 0$ to reflect the increasing uncertainty of contractor executives as to what the effect of increasingly large cost reductions (or increases) will be on future sales. Such a case is illustrated by the use of confidence bands around the true (known only to the Omniscient) $f_t(\Delta C_1)$ function in Figure 7A.2.

Considering all n years in which sales sacrifices might occur, total user cost U is then defined as:

$$(7.9) \qquad U = \sum_{t=0}^{n} \frac{P(t)\,E[f_t(\Delta C_1)]}{[1 + r(1)][1 + r(2)] \ldots [1 + r(t)]} = U(\Delta C_1).$$

A firm which seeks to maximize its long-run profit π_{LR} should in year 1 maximize the discounted value of accounting profits on the current contract minus user cost:

FIGURE 7A.2

The $f_t(\Delta C_1)$ Function with Confidence Bands

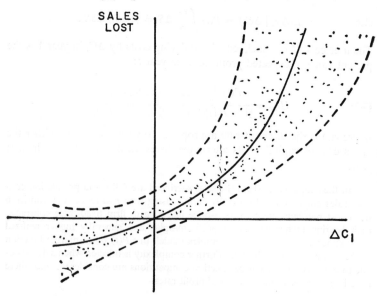

(7.10) $\pi_{LR} = \dfrac{\pi_{A1}}{1 + r(1)} - U(\Delta C_1) = \dfrac{\pi_1{}^*}{1 + r(1)} + \dfrac{\alpha \Delta C_1}{1 + r(1)} - U(\Delta C_1).$

Maximizing with respect to ΔC_1, we obtain as a first order condition:

(7.11) $\dfrac{d\pi_{LR}}{d\Delta C_1} = \dfrac{\alpha}{1 + r(1)} - \dfrac{dU(\Delta C_1)}{d\Delta C_1} = 0.$

(7.12) $\dfrac{dU(\Delta C_1)}{d\Delta C_1} = \dfrac{\alpha}{1 + r(1)}.$

This means that the increase in user cost due to the last dollar's worth of cost reduction should equal the contractor's discounted profit share of that dollar saved. It should be apparent that if the $f(\Delta C_1)$ function is as shown in Figure 7A.1; that is, if cost reduction increases future sales losses and hence user cost at an increasing rate after some point; then the contractor's cost reduction efforts will proceed farther for large values of α (as under firm fixed-price contracts, where $\alpha = 1.0$, if tax considerations are ignored) than for small values. When $\alpha = 0$, as under a CPFF contract, cost reduction will proceed only to the point at which the user cost function is at its minimum, with slope of zero.

If the model were to be elaborated, several different user cost functions might be defined; one reflecting, say, the follow-on sales losses due to quality reduction, one the sales losses due to time increases, one the sales losses due to dismissing personnel valuable in future source selection competitions, and one (with an opposite sign) reflecting the profits foregone when scarce resources are employed in one program at the expense of alternative military or commercial opportunities. When this last opportunity cost term has a substantial value, it will provide a countervailing incentive for cost reduction even under CPFF contracts.

Appendix to Chapter 8

The Optimal Choice of a Sharing Proportion

THE PURPOSE of this appendix is to demonstrate rigorously the optimal choices of the contractor's overrun-underrun sharing proportion α by a profit maximizing contractor and a contract outlay minimizing government buying agency, given some negotiated cost target. It will also determine the conditions necessary for the profit maximization and outlay minimization objectives to be in harmony.

Following the notation used in the Appendix to Chapter 7, the accounting profit π_A on a current contract is given by the equation:

$$(8.1) \qquad \pi_A = \pi_T + \alpha(C_T - C_A),$$

where π_T is the negotiated target profit amount, α is the contractor's sharing proportion, C_T is the negotiated target cost, and C_A is the actual accounting cost charged to the contract. To avoid introducing a time discount rate, it is assumed that π_A is realized instantaneously. Target cost C_T is assumed to have a given value of 100 as a result of already completed negotiations. (The convention $C_T = 100$ permits all other magnitudes to be expressed, as in common practice, as a percentage of target cost.) To simplify the exposition, it is convenient to write:

$$(8.2) \qquad X = C_T - C_A = 100 - C_A,$$

where a positive value of X indicates a contract cost underrun and a negative value a cost overrun.[1] Therefore,

$$(8.3) \qquad \pi_A = \pi_T + \alpha X.$$

The sharing proportion α is assumed variable only between 0 and $+1.0$, reflecting the possibilities available in existing contract types. With a CPFF contract $\alpha = 0$; with a firm fixed-price contract $\alpha = +1.0$; and with FPI and CPIF contracts α can take on values intermediate between 0 and 1.0. It is further assumed that π_T is a monotonically increasing function of the sharing proportion α chosen:

$$(8.4) \qquad \pi_T = k + h\alpha + m\alpha^2.$$

This specification reflects the common government practice of awarding higher negotiated profit rates when the contractor assumes a high financial

[1] X here is a special case of ΔC in the Appendix to Chapter 7.

412

risk — that is, a high share α of potential underruns and overruns — than when risk is shifted to the government, as in CPFF contracts. In the numerical examples which follow, k will be taken to equal 6, since a negotiated profit rate averaging roughly 6% is generally awarded on CPFF contracts, where $\alpha = 0$. It will also be assumed that for firm fixed-price contracts ($\alpha = 1.0$), the negotiated profit rate π_T is always 12, so that variations in h and m affect only the rate at which the risk premium increases with intermediate values of α. Empirical support for these numerical assumptions will be found in Chapter 9.

The Contractor's Profit Maximization Problem

Let us begin with the simplest possible case: a contractor seeking to maximize its expected contract accounting profit π_A under the assumption that the contract will have the specific actual cost outcome $\hat{X}$, defined either fully uniquely in the case of certainty or as a unique expected value in the case of technological uncertainty. We shall also hold m equal to zero in the $\pi_T(\alpha)$ function, so that the negotiated profit is a linear function of α. Given the prior stipulations that $\pi_T = 6$ when $\alpha = 0$ and $\pi_T = 12$ when $\alpha = 1.0$, this requires that $\pi_T = 6 + 6\alpha$. The contractor therefore wishes to maximize:

$$(8.5) \qquad \pi_A = 6 + 6\alpha + \alpha\hat{X}$$

with respect to α. Differentiation shows that there is no local maximum for this function when $\hat{X}$ is specifically anticipated. If $\hat{X} > -6$ (that is, if the contract is expected to show an underrun, or an overrun of less than six percentage points), the contractor will maximize its profits by choosing the highest available α of 1.0. If $\hat{X} < -6$, the contractor should seek CPFF coverage, with $\alpha = 0$. If $\hat{X} = -6$, the optional α is indeterminate; the contractor will maximize its profits at any of the available values of α from 0 to 1.0. Thus, except for the special case where $-\hat{X} = h$, the contractor's optimal choice polarizes between either $\alpha = 1.0$ or $\alpha = 0$.

This first case involves the questionable assumption that the expected cost outcome $\hat{X}$ is uniquely defined, regardless of the value of α chosen. But actually, we should expect X to depend at least to some extent on the value of α; that is, on the strength of the reward theory incentive for cost reduction. If changes in the value of α do have reward theory effects on contractor behavior, there must be some function of X which offsets the incentive profits attainable by increasing X. The cost reduction user cost function is one possibility defined rigorously in the Appendix to Chapter 7. A cost reduction disutility function is another possibility. Here only a user cost function will be employed.[2] The analysis in Chap-

[2] It might be possible to include cost reduction disutility considerations in the user cost function by expressing disutility in terms of user cost equivalents.

ter 7 and its appendix, to be elaborated later in this appendix, suggests that the user cost function should be generally U-shaped. Following the principle of Occam's razor, it will be assumed that user cost U is a quadratic function of the expected amount by which actual accounting costs will be reduced below target cost, with X measuring the expected amount of cost reduction:

$$(8.6) \qquad\qquad U = a + bX + cX^2.$$

Certain knowledge of the user cost function's configuration is assumed here, although as the Appendix to Chapter 7 shows, a more realistic stochastic approach is also possible at the sacrifice of simplicity. It is assumed further that the constant term $a = 0$. This specification has two justifications. First, once the contractor has decided that it will execute the contract, a is irrelevant in determining either X or α. Second, letting $a = 0$ is consistent with the action-oriented nature of the user cost concept. User costs are incurred only by moving from some existing position. In this model the *status quo* is assumed to be letting actual costs neither underrun nor overrun the cost target, so that $X = 0$. For this *status quo* case, user cost should be zero, which occurs only if $a = 0$.

Given the existence of a user cost function and a negotiated cost target, the contractor has a two-stage long-run profit maximization problem. First, an optimal α must be chosen in contract negotiations. Then given α, the contractor must carry its cost reduction efforts just far enough to expect the optimal value of X to result from actual contract performance. It is convenient to anticipate solution of the second maximization problem first. As the Appendix to Chapter 7 has shown, to maximize expected long-run profit π_{LR} the contractor should maximize the following expression:

$$(8.7) \qquad \pi_{LR} = \pi_T + \alpha X - U = \pi_T + \alpha X - (bX + cX^2),$$

where, since α is predetermined in negotiations, π_T is also a predetermined constant. Differentiating with respect to X, we obtain as a first order condition:

$$(8.8) \qquad\qquad \frac{d\pi_{LR}}{dX} = \alpha - b - 2cX = 0.$$

Taking the second derivative shows that when c is positive, $\dfrac{d^2\pi_{LR}}{dX^2}$ is negative, and a local maximum exists. Rearranging terms in (8.8), we find that:

$$(8.9) \qquad\qquad \alpha = b + 2cX.$$

The procedure would require decision makers to ask themselves, "How much profit would I be willing to sacrifice to avoid this particular cost cut?"

Similarly, solving for X in terms of α we find that:

$$(8.10) \qquad X_{opt} = \frac{\alpha - b}{2c}.$$

In contract negotiations, the contractor has a somewhat different problem — attempting to obtain that value of α which maximizes:

$$(8.11) \quad \pi_{LR} = 6 + 6\alpha + \alpha X - U = 6 + 6\alpha + \alpha X - bX - cX^2.$$

It is useful to begin the analysis of this problem with a numerical example. Let the user cost function be:

$$(8.12) \qquad U = .2X + .04X^2,$$

which is illustrated in Figure 8A.1. This configuration is similar to Figure 7A.1a, and it seems fairly representative of reality, although perhaps the curve is somewhat flatter than normal (that is, empirical research might reveal a larger average value for c). The contractor seeks to maximize:

$$(8.13) \qquad \pi_{LR} = 6 + 6\alpha + \alpha X - .2X - .04X^2.$$

Substituting in (8.10) for X, we obtain:

$$(8.14) \quad \pi_{LR} = 6 + 6\alpha + \alpha\left(\frac{\alpha - .2}{.08}\right) - .2\left(\frac{\alpha - .2}{.08}\right) - .04\left(\frac{\alpha - .2}{.08}\right)^2.$$

FIGURE 8A.1

Graph of $U = .2X + .04X^2$

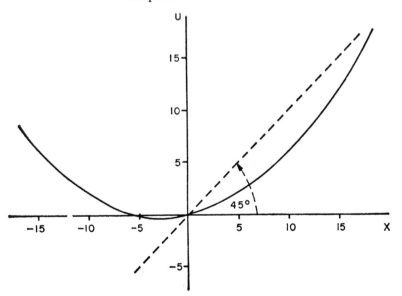

This expression can be reduced to:

(8.15) $$\pi_{LR} = 5.25 + 3.50\alpha + 6.25\alpha^2.$$

Differentiating with respect to α, we get as a first order condition:

(8.16) $$\frac{d\pi_{LR}}{d\alpha} = 3.5 + 12.5\alpha = 0;$$

(8.17) $$\alpha = -.28.$$

This is a vexsome result, since we have specified on institutional grounds that α vary only between 0 and $+1.0$. But the second derivative of π_{LR} is $+12.5$, indicating that $\alpha = -.28$ minimizes rather than maximizes the contractor's long-run profit. Any movement away from $\alpha = -.28$ therefore increases π_{LR}. If a CPFF contract is used, with $\alpha = 0$, we find from (8.10) that:

(8.18) $$X = \frac{\alpha - b}{2c} = \frac{0 - .2}{2(.04)} = -2.5.$$

That is, the contractor would maximize its profits by operating so as to expect an overrun of 2.5 percentage points. At this expected value of X, the contractor's long-run profit is:

(8.19) $$\pi_{LR} = 6 + 6(0) + 0(-2.5) - .2(-2.5) - .04(-2.5^2) = 6.25.$$

But the contractor can do still better by moving farther away from the pessimum $\alpha = -.28$ all the way to $\alpha = 1.0$, accepting firm fixed-price contractual coverage. In this case, the profit maximizing X would be:

(8.20) $$X = \frac{\alpha - b}{2c} = \frac{1.0 - .2}{2(.04)} = +10.0.$$

If this underrun of 10.0 percentage points is anticipated, the firm's expected long-run profit will be:

(8.21) $$\pi_{LR} = 6 + 6(1.0) + 1.0(10.0) - .2(10.0) - .04(10.0^2) = 16.0.$$

We find therefore some indication of the tendency observed earlier for the contractor's choice of α to polarize toward $\alpha = 1.0$. Is this result merely a special case, or is it general? To move toward an answer, let us determine whether there are any user cost functions with which the contractor is indifferent between $\alpha = 1.0$ and $\alpha = 0$, assuming still that $\pi_T = 6 + 6\alpha$. Indifference in this sense implies that equal long-run profits are anticipated with $\alpha = 1.0$ and $\alpha = 0$. Thus:

(8.22) $$\pi_{LR} = 6 + 6(0) + 0(X_o) - bX_o - cX_o^2 = 6 + 6(1) + 1(X_1) - bX_1 - cX_1^2.$$

From (8.10) we know that at the optimum

$$(8.23) \qquad X_o = \frac{0 - b}{2c} = -\frac{b}{2c}; \text{ and}$$

$$(8.24) \qquad X_1 = \frac{1 - b}{2c}.$$

Substituting in (8.23) and (8.24) for X_o and X_1, we have:

$$(8.25) \qquad \pi_{LR} = 6 - b\left(\frac{-b}{2c}\right) - c\left(\frac{-b}{2c}\right)^2$$
$$= 12 + \left(\frac{1-b}{2c}\right) - b\left(\frac{1-b}{2c}\right) - c\left(\frac{1-b}{2c}\right)^2.$$

Solving this equation for b in terms of c, we obtain:

$$(8.26) \qquad b = \tfrac{1}{2} + 12c.$$

Whenever (8.26) holds and when $\pi_T = 6 + 6\alpha$, the contractor will be indifferent between $\alpha = 0$ and $\alpha = 1.0$. To illustrate, let us take from the infinity of possible quadratic user cost functions satisfying (8.26) the function

$$(8.27) \qquad U = 1.10X + .05X^2,$$

which is illustrated in Figure 8A.2. Following the substitution and differentiation procedures used before, we obtain:

$$(8.28) \qquad \pi_{LR} = 6 + 6\alpha + \alpha X - 1.10X - .05X^2.$$

$$(8.29) \qquad \pi_{LR} = 6 + 6\alpha + \alpha\left(\frac{\alpha - 1.10}{.1}\right) - 1.10\left(\frac{\alpha - 1.10}{.1}\right)$$
$$- .05\left(\frac{\alpha - 1.10}{.1}\right)^2.$$

$$(8.30) \qquad \pi_{LR} = 12.05 - 5\alpha + 5\alpha^2.$$

$$(8.31) \qquad \frac{d\pi_{LR}}{d\alpha} = -5 + 10\alpha = 0.$$

$$(8.32) \qquad \frac{d^2\pi_{LR}}{d\alpha^2} = +10.$$

From (8.32) we see that differentiation has again yielded a solution which minimizes, rather than maximizes, the contractor's long-run profit. Solving (8.31), we find that at the minimum $\alpha = .5$. When $\alpha = .5$, the optimal $X = -6$ (an overrun of 6 percentage points), and $\pi_{LR} = 10.80$. By moving in either direction from $\alpha = .5$ the contractor can increase its

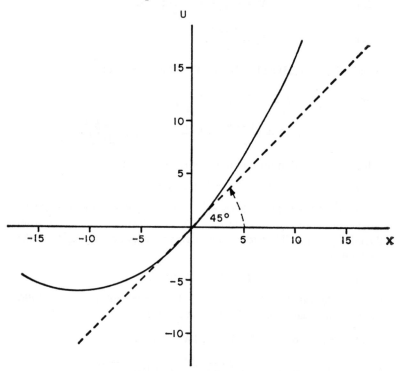

FIGURE 8A.2

Graph of $U = 1.10X + .05X^2$

profits. At $\alpha = 0$, the optimal $X = -11.0$ and π_{LR} is 12.05. At $\alpha = 1.0$, the optimal $X = -1.0$ and π_{LR} is 12.05.[3] Thus, the contractor is indifferent between the two poles $\alpha = 0$ and $\alpha^{\cdot} = 1.0$. It can easily be seen that with $\pi_T = 6 + 6\alpha$ as a negotiated profit function and with a U-shaped quadratic user cost function of the form $U = bX + cX^2$, a profit

---

[3] It is worth emphasizing that an overrun is optimal in this case despite FFP contractual coverage. It is easily seen that an underrun is optimal only if the user cost function's parameters are such that when $X = 0$, the slope of the user cost function is less than $+1.0$. Differentiation shows that this can occur with a U-shaped quadratic user cost function only when $b < 1.0$. And if $b < 1.0$, it will profit the contractor to accept FFP coverage, with $\alpha = 1.0$, and to increase its underrun until the slope of the user cost function rises to $+1.0$.

Thus, when a contractor says a contract is negotiated so tightly that an overrun is likely, it must mean that the slope of the user cost function is greater than $+1.0$ at the target cost level.

maximizing contractor will always prefer firm fixed-price contractual coverage ($\alpha = 1.0$) whenever

$$(8.33) \qquad b < \tfrac{1}{2} + 12c.$$

It will always prefer CPFF coverage ($\alpha = 0$) whenever

$$(8.34) \qquad b > \tfrac{1}{2} + 12c.$$

In sum, under the conditions assumed thus far, we should never find a profit maximizing contractor preferring FPI or CPIF contracts, with values of α between 0 and 1.0.

This conclusion is so inconsistent with actual contractor behavior that we must search further for different conditions under which values of α between 0 and 1.0 might maximize the contractor's profits. Let us first examine the most general case of a linear negotiated profit premium function $\pi_T = k + h\alpha$ and a quadratic user cost function $U = bX + cX^2$. With X expressed in terms of α, the long-run profit function is:

$$(8.35) \quad \pi_{LR} = k + h\alpha + \alpha\left(\frac{\alpha - b}{2c}\right) - b\left(\frac{\alpha - b}{2c}\right) - c\left(\frac{\alpha - b}{2c}\right)^2.$$

When this is differentiated, we obtain:

$$(8.36) \qquad \frac{d\pi_{LR}}{d\alpha} = h - \frac{b}{2c} + \frac{\alpha}{2c}.$$

Taking the second derivative, we get:

$$(8.37) \qquad \frac{d^2\pi_{LR}}{d\alpha^2} = \frac{1}{2c}.$$

We can have a local maximum in terms of α if and only if (8.37) is negative. And given the relationships assumed in (8.35), this is possible only if c is negative. If c is negative, we have an inverted user cost function of the type shown in Figure 8A.3. Does such a function have any empirical validity? It seems most unlikely that it does. If the firm were to operate on the lefthand (increasing) segment of the user cost function, each increment of cost reduction would add to user cost by less than the preceding increment. This seems foolish indeed, for one would expect a rational firm to exploit first those cost reduction opportunities which add little to user cost, leaving the high marginal user cost opportunities until last. It would be even more foolish to leave until last the opportunities on the righthand side of the user cost function. Rather, user cost-decreasing cost reduction opportunities should be exploited first, since they add directly to profits under any kind of contractual coverage. And if a firm were for some strange reason to operate on a user cost function similar to Figure 8A.3, it would maximize profits by reducing costs all

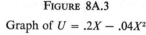

FIGURE 8A.3

Graph of $U = .2X - .04X^2$

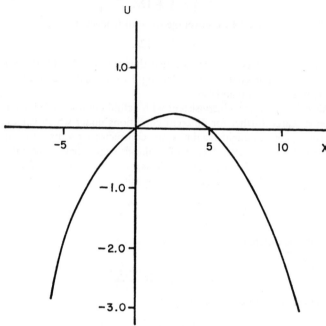

the way to zero unless some physical barriers not recognized by the user cost function intervened. It is reasonable to conclude that a $\cap$-shaped user cost function is improbable, if not impossible, and so a negative value of c is also improbable.

There is, however, a much more likely alternative. Thus far it has been assumed that the negotiated target profit premium is a linear function of α. But if we permit it to be quadratic of the form:

$$(8.38) \qquad \pi_T = k + h\alpha + m\alpha^2,$$

as in (8.4), we obtain as the second derivative of the general form of π_{LR}:

$$(8.39) \qquad \frac{d^2\pi_{LR}}{d\alpha^2} = 2m + \frac{1}{2c}.$$

This can be negative, indicating a local maximum for π_{LR}, when:

$$(8.40) \qquad m < -\frac{1}{4c}.$$

Now there are infinitely many combinations of m and c which satisfy this condition. The quadratic π_T function must also satisfy another condition: that it be monotonically increasing from 6 when $\alpha = 0$, to 12 when $\alpha = 1.0$. There are many combinations of h, m, and c which satisfy this condition along with (8.40), and with considerable empirical relevance. The progression of negotiated target profit premiums actually employed by the U.S. armed services appears to exhibit the sort of diminishing returns consistent with a negative value of m. If the linear risk premium function $\pi_T = 6 + 6\alpha$ were in general use, π_T would be 6.0 for CPFF contracts with $\alpha = 0$, 12.0 for FFP contracts with $\alpha = 1.0$, and 7.2 for FPI contracts with $\alpha = .20$. But in fact, the average adjusted [4] π_T for the 47 Navy FPI contracts covered by Figures 8.3 and 9.2 was 8.4%, with an average α of nearly .20. This relatively high negotiated profit rate for contracts with intermediate values of α suggests a π_T function on the order of:

$$(8.41) \qquad \pi_T = 6 + 10\alpha - 4\alpha^2;$$

which lets $\pi_T = 7.8$ when $\alpha = .20$.[5] In this case we find from (8.40) that a local maximum for π_{LR} will be attained when $c > .0625$.

Let us assume that (8.41) is in fact the risk premium function, $c = .08$, and the complete user cost function is:

$$(8.42) \qquad U = 1.5X + .08X^2.$$

Then the contractor wishes to maximize

$$(8.43) \qquad \pi_{LR} = 6 + 10\alpha - 4\alpha^2 + \alpha X - 1.5X - .08X^2.$$

Substituting, reducing, and differentiating, we obtain:

$$(8.44) \qquad \pi_{LR} = 13.03 + .625\alpha - .875\alpha^2.$$

$$(8.45) \qquad \frac{d\pi_{LR}}{d\alpha} = .625 - 1.75\alpha = 0.$$

$$(8.46) \qquad \frac{d^2\pi_{LR}}{d\alpha^2} = -1.75.$$

[4] The assumption that $\pi_T = 6.0$ reflects Air Force practice more closely than Navy averages. Generally, Air Force negotiated profit rates have been about one-half percentage point lower than Navy rates. Therefore, .5 has been subtracted from the actual Navy FPI sample average of 8.9 to make the illustration more consistent with an assumption that $\pi_T = 6$ when $\alpha = 0$.

[5] It is impossible to find a quadratic function which increases monotonically from 6 to 12 as α increases from 0 to 1.0 and which yields a value of 8.4 at $\alpha = .20$. The early steepness of observed π_T functions is undoubtedly due in part not only to increases in α over the normal range of profit-cost correlation, but also to the imposition of cost ceilings beyond which $\alpha = 1.0$.

It is evident that since (8.46) is negative, differentiation has this time yielded a local maximum. Solving (8.45), we obtain as the optimum $\alpha = .357$, which implies an optimal X of -7.14: an overrun. Thus, we have found at least one case in which a profit maximizing contractor would prefer an intermediate value of α.

Let us try another user cost function which satisfies the condition $c > .0625$:

(8.47) $$U = .8X + .08X^2.$$

Then the contractor wishes to maximize:

(8.48) $$\pi_{LR} = 6 + 10\alpha - 4\alpha^2 + \alpha X - .8X - .08X^2.$$

Substituting, reducing, and differentiating, we obtain:

(8.49) $$\pi_{LR} = 8 + 5\alpha - .875\alpha^2.$$

(8.50) $$\frac{d\pi_{LR}}{d\alpha} = 5.0 - 1.75\alpha = 0.$$

(8.51) $$\frac{d^2\pi_{LR}}{d\alpha^2} = -1.75.$$

Again, (8.51) indicates a local maximum. Solving (8.50), we obtain as the optimal α a value of 2.86, which implies an optimal X of nearly $+13$. But $\alpha = 2.86$ is not an allowable solution.[6] The best the contractor can do is to take $\alpha = 1.0$, maximizing its expected profits by operating so as to make $X = +1.25$.

This numerical result again suggests polarization toward firm fixed-price contractual coverage in underrun situations, even when the negotiated profit premium function is quadratic. It is possible to prove generally that under the profit maximization assumptions adopted thus far, values of $\alpha < 1.0$ will be optimal to the contractor only in overrun situations. But since the proof is rather abstruse, a preliminary intuitive explanation is in order. If an underrun is at all attractive to the contractor, the slope b of the user cost function at $X = 0$ must be less than some attainable value of α. If this were not so, $(\alpha - b)$ in (8.10) would be negative, and so X would also be negative at the optimum. Let us assume that $b = .20$. Then an underrun would be optimal if $\alpha > .20$. But if the contractor expects to underrun at all, it would maximize its profits by going all the way to $\alpha = 1.0$. This is so for three reasons. First, the contractor can get a higher negotiated profit rate by going from, say, $\alpha = .30$ to $\alpha = 1.0$. Second, at $\alpha = 1.0$ the contractor retains the largest

---

[6] It must be rejected not only because α cannot exceed 1.0 on institutional grounds, but also because it implies that (8.41) is not constrained at $\alpha = 1.0$.

possible share of its underrun. And third, with $\alpha = 1.0$ the contractor will find it optimal to achieve a larger underrun than with any lower value of α, and so it will have a larger cost saving to retain (or share 100%) as profit. Only on the overrun side may an $\alpha < 1.0$ begin to look attractive. For then, while the contractor may increase its negotiated profit rate by moving from $\alpha = 0$ to $\alpha = 1.0$, there is an offsetting reduction of realized profit due to the larger share of the overrun absorbed as α increases to 1.0. Thus, a tradeoff must be made between increased profits due to a higher risk premium and reduced profits due to absorbing a higher proportion of the overrun. As we have seen, when the risk premium function is quadratic, this tradeoff may lead to a value of α greater than 0 but less than 1.0.

Let us prove now that X must be negative — that is, an overrun must be anticipated — if the optimal $\alpha < 1.0$. We will employ the most general long-run profit function:

$$(8.52) \qquad \pi_{LR} = k + h\alpha + m\alpha^2 + \alpha X - bX - cX^2.$$

Substituting in (8.10) and differentiating, we obtain as a first order condition:

$$(8.53) \qquad \frac{d\pi_{LR}}{d\alpha} = h - \frac{b}{2c} + 2\alpha \left(m + \frac{1}{4c} \right) = 0.$$

Solving for b, we obtain:

$$(8.54) \qquad b = \alpha + 4cm\alpha + 2ch.$$

From (8.10) we know that at the cost reduction optimum:

$$(8.55) \qquad X = \frac{\alpha - b}{2c}.$$

Substituting (8.54) for b into (8.55), we obtain:

$$(8.56) \qquad X = \frac{\alpha - \alpha - 4cm\alpha - 2ch}{2c} = -2m\alpha - h.$$

We recall that one condition imposed on

$$(8.57) \qquad \pi_T = k + h\alpha + m\alpha^2$$

was that it be monotonic increasing at least up to $\alpha = 1.0$. This requires that:

$$(8.58) \qquad \frac{d\pi_T}{d\alpha} = h + 2m\alpha > 0; \quad \alpha < 1.0.$$

To satisfy this condition it is necessary that:¹

$$(8.59) \qquad -h < 2m\alpha,$$

or in the more convenient form of an equality, that:

(8.60) $$-h = 2m\alpha - \delta,$$

where δ is any positive real number. Substituting (8.60) for $-h$ into (8.56), we obtain:

(8.61) $$X = -2m\alpha + 2m\alpha - \delta = -\delta,$$

which proves that X must be negative at the local optimum for α when all functions are within their constraints. It does not mean that the optimal X cannot be positive, since in an underrun situation the maximum possible α of 1.0 is generally constrained below its optimal value and the π_T function is constrained at its maximum value for $\alpha = 1.0$. Only when the optimal $\alpha \leq 1.0$ does (8.61) hold. But it is precisely the cases where the optimal $\alpha < 1.0$ for which we had to show the necessity of an overrun.

To complete our analysis of the contractor's profit maximization problem, one further complication must be introduced. We have seen in Chapter 8 that high contract profits due to a substantial cost underrun may be recouped by the government through renegotiation or informal pressures. Or if windfall profits are retained, a firm's relationships with government buying agency personnel may deteriorate. In the latter case, positive user costs are incurred as a function of contract accounting profit π_A beyond some value of π_A on the order of 12%. To deal with this problem it would be necessary to maximize a long-run profit function with two user cost terms — one a function of cost reduction X, as emphasized in this appendix, and the other a discontinuous function of π_A. But to keep the analysis as intelligible as we can, let us consider the simpler and almost equivalent case of a constraint on π_A — all accounting profits in excess of, say, 12% are refunded to the government either voluntarily or through renegotiation.[7] Then situations may very well arise in which an underrun is desirable (that is, $b < 1.0$) and the maximum retainable π_A could be realized with values of α less than 1.0 as well as with $\alpha = 1.0$. In this event the firm should as a rule seek to achieve an underrun just sufficient to earn its maximum π_A of 12. But the magnitude of this underrun depends upon the value of α chosen. The less α is, the larger the underrun required to make $\pi_A = 12$. What value of α should be chosen?

We must note initially that up to this point, it has been possible to view the actual cost outcome X as a variable whose *ex ante* value is uniquely defined by the contractor, being foreseen either with certainty or as the

---

[7] This assumption is plainly too simple. Firms can probably retain a higher accounting profit margin under firm fixed-price contractual coverage than under fixed-price incentive or CPFF coverage. However, empirical data needed to specify a more elaborate constraint are not available.

expected value resulting from some prior subjective probability distribution of possible cost outcomes. In other words, the cases of certainty and technological uncertainty have been essentially congruent, assuming that the contractor seeks to maximize the expected value of its long-run profits. But when a constraint related to actually realized (as opposed to expected) contract profits is introduced, this congruence breaks down. To distinguish between expectations and realizations, we shall let unadorned variables (i.e., X) represent the contractor's *ex ante* expectations, while starred variables will represent actually realized values.[8]

Then four cases can be identified. First, with a user cost function monotonically increasing over all values of $X > 0$, as in Figure 8A.1, firm fixed price coverage will always be optimal if the contractor knows with certainty the actual value of $X = X^*$ which will result from its cost reduction efforts. This is so because with FFP coverage the constrained maximum for π_C^* is achieved with the smallest possible underrun, and hence the minimum user cost. And when π_C^* is firmly constrained at its limit, long-run profit is maximized by minimizing user cost.

The problem becomes much more difficult when an element of technological uncertainty with respect to the actual cost outcome X^* exists. Suppose that, as in the first case, the contractor provisionally chooses firm fixed price coverage and plans to operate in such a way as to set the expected cost outcome X at that level which will equate expected contract profit $\pi_C = \pi_T + \alpha X$ with the constraint ($= 12$). Now as a result of uncontrollable contingencies the actual cost outcome X^* is likely to deviate either above or below the expected outcome X, and so the actual π_C^* will deviate above or below the expected π_C. If $X^* > X$; that is, if the actual cost underrun is larger than the expected underrun, all incremental profits $\alpha(X^* - X)$ exceeding the ceiling must be refunded. The best the contractor can do is to retain actual contract profits of 12, which will happen when $X^* = X$. But whenever by chance the actual cost underrun turns out to be *less than* the expected underrun; e.g., whenever $X^* < X$, the contractor will fail to reach the profit ceiling of $\pi_C^* = 12$. And so it is apparent that the contractor's average retained π_C expectation must be less than 12 under this plan. The greater the uncertainty of cost outcomes, the more the expected retainable profit π_C will depart from its maximum possible value of 12. Now by reducing α from 1.0 to 0 and making appropriate changes in X,[9] the contractor can minimize the adverse effect of

[8] I am afraid this presentation of the uncertainty problem is not very satisfactory. For an improved treatment which is stochastic throughout, see my article, "The Theory of Contractual Incentives for Cost Reduction," *Quarterly Journal of Economics*, February 1964.

[9] As α goes from 1.0 to 0, X must initially be increased to maintain π_C at its ceiling of 12. But eventually increases in X will drive user costs up to the point

unexpectedly small underruns. That is, for any X^*, $\alpha(X^* - X)$ will be smaller, the smaller the α. But it is most improbable that the contractor will reduce α all the way to zero, for at $\alpha = 0$ the contractor's contract profit $\pi_C{}^*$ can be no greater than the fixed fee of approximately 6 offered under CPFF contracts. The contractor's optimum will as a rule be found with some kind of incentive contract having an intermediate value of α.[10]

A third distinguishable case occurs when the user cost function is still declining for low positive values of X; e.g., when $b < 0$, as in Figure 7A.1b. Then a value of α less than 1.0 may be optimal even when there is complete certainty with respect to actual cost outcomes. In this case the contractor would normally maximize its long-run expected profit by underrunning to that value of X at which the user cost function attains its minimum, choosing the α which makes π_C equal to the limit of 12 at the intended value of X. It is readily apparent that the greater the optimal X is, the smaller the optimal α will be.

Finally, when $b < 0$ and actual cost outcomes are subject to uncertainty, the contractor's incentive to negotiate a value of $\alpha < 1.0$ despite the expectation of an underrun is likely to be even stronger.

It is clear then that especially in an environment of technological uncertainty, renegotiation and equivalent constraints on profits may lead to a departure from the firm fixed-price contractual coverage optimal in the unconstrained situations explored earlier. How frequently is the value of b and the degree of uncertainty such that contractors face an effective actual or potential constraint on their profits? The bimodal profit distribution tendency illustrated in Figure 8.9 suggests that firms may be holding α to values which just permit expected contract profits to reach some ceiling, although statistical significance tests of this result were inconclusive.[11] Even if the observed bimodal tendency is no statistical accident, it appears to have been generated by only a fairly small proportion of all the contracts. And the qualitative and quantitative evidence recorded in Chapter 8 on renegotiation's effects also suggests that constrained maximization of the sort outlined here was not particularly prevalent during the late 1950's. Nevertheless, the question has important policy implications and clearly deserves further research.

In sum, we find that except in one special but potentially important set of cases, profit maximizing contractors would prefer firm fixed-price con-

---

where with further decreases in α, it will be more profitable to *reduce X* and move away from an expectation of achieving (at least before renegotiation) the ceiling contract profit.

[10] For a more complete statement of the conditions for an optimum, see my *Quarterly Journal of Economics* article.

[11] Cf. pp. 247–249 *supra*.

tractual coverage, with $\alpha = 1.0$, when they anticipate an underrun. Their preferences in an overrun situation may vary from $\alpha = 0$ to $\alpha = 1.0$, depending upon the configuration of the user cost function and the negotiated profit risk premium function. In general, the larger the anticipated overrun, the smaller the optimal α will be when a clear dichotomy between CPFF and FFP is avoided because of a nonlinear risk premium function.

GOVERNMENT OUTLAY MINIMIZATION AND CONFLICTS OF INTEREST

Let us see now what happens when the government seeks to minimize its total contract outlays; that is, cost plus profit. The government's outlay E is the sum of target cost C_T plus target profit π_T less the cost underrun X plus the contractor's share of the underrun αX. From (8.2) we have that $C_T = 100$. Therefore, the government wishes to minimize:

$$(8.62) \qquad E = 100 + \pi_T - X + \alpha X.$$

Let us assume, following (8.4), that π_T is a quadratic function of α. Similarly, we know from (8.10) that X is a function of α. The government therefore seeks to minimize:

$$(8.63) \qquad E = 100 + k + h\alpha + m\alpha^2 - \left(\frac{\alpha - b}{2c}\right) + \alpha\left(\frac{\alpha - b}{2c}\right).$$

Differentiating, we obtain as a first order condition:

$$(8.64) \qquad \frac{dE}{d\alpha} = h - \frac{1}{2c} - \frac{b}{2c} + 2\alpha\left(m + \frac{1}{2c}\right) = 0.$$

Solving for α, we obtain:

$$(8.65) \qquad \alpha = \frac{1 + b - 2ch}{2 + 4cm}.$$

The second derivative is:

$$(8.66) \qquad \frac{d^2E}{d\alpha^2} = 2m + \frac{1}{c}.$$

For a local minimum, (8.66) must be positive. If m is negative, this can occur only when:

$$(8.67) \qquad m > -\frac{1}{2c}.$$

Using these results, we can find the government's outlay minimizing optima for the various contractor profit maximization examples studied earlier. The government and contractor optima for seven examples are compared in Table 8A.1. Inspection immediately suggests that except in

TABLE 8A.1

Government and Contractor Optima under Diverse Assumptions

User Cost |Function	Negotiated Profit Risk Premium Function	Government Optimum		Contractor Optimum	
		α	X	α	X
Outcome fixed at $X > -6$	$6+6\alpha$	0	> -6	1.0	> -6
Outcome fixed at $X = -6$	$6+6\alpha$	$0 \geq \alpha \geq 1.0$	-6	$0 \geq \alpha \geq 1.0$	-6
Outcome fixed at $X < -6$	$6+6\alpha$	1.0	< -6	0	< -6
$.2X+.04X^2$	$6+6\alpha$	.36	$+2.0$	1.0	$+10.0$
$1.1X+.05X^2$	$6+6\alpha$	.75	-3.5	0 or 1.0	-11.0 or -1.0
$1.5X+.08X^2$	$6+10\alpha-4\alpha^2$	1.0	-3.1	.36	-7.1
$.8X+.08X^2$	$6+10\alpha-4\alpha^2$	.28	-3.3	1.0	$+1.3$

special cases, the government outlay minimizing and contractor profit maximizing optima are not the same.

Are there ever any situations involving quadratic user cost and π_T risk premium functions in which the optimal choices of α for contractors and government coincide? For government and contractor preferences to be in harmony under the assumptions made here, it is necessary that the conditions for an optimal α for the government and the contractor be satisfied simultaneously.[12] Solving (8.53) for α, we find that at the contractor's optimum:

$$(8.68) \qquad \alpha_c = \frac{b - 2ch}{1 + 4cm}.$$

Similarly, (8.65) shows that at the government's optimum:

$$(8.69) \qquad \alpha_g = \frac{1 + b - 2ch}{2 + 4cm}.$$

For a mutually compatible optimum, α_g must equal α_c; thus:

$$(8.70) \qquad \frac{b - 2ch}{1 + 4cm} = \frac{1 + b - 2ch}{2 + 4cm}.$$

[12] The problem of a constraint on π_A due to renegotiation or the deterioration of buyer-seller relations is excluded from this analysis.

Solving this equation for b, we find that for a compatible optimum:

$$(8.71) \qquad b = 1 + 2c(2m + h).$$

This condition demonstrates that the α preferences of an unconstrained profit maximizing contractor and an outlay minimizing government are in harmony only when certain special relationships prevail among the parameters of the user cost and negotiated profit risk premium functions.[13] More generally, when:

$$(8.72) \qquad b > 1 + 2c(2m + h),$$

the contractor should want an α lower than the government's optimal α. When:

$$(8.73) \qquad b < 1 + 2c(2m + h),$$

the contractor should prefer an α higher than the government's optimal α.

This relationship is illustrated in Figure 8A.4, which shows the optimal choices of α for the contractor (solid line) and the government (broken

FIGURE 8A.4

Government and Contractor Optimal α as a Function of b

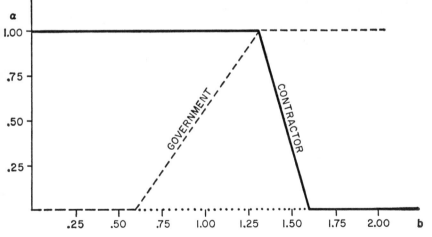

[13] To avoid corner solutions, it is also necessary that c and m assume values which satisfy constraints (8.40) and (8.67). For a mutual local optimum, the combination of these two constraints is quite restrictive. If m is negative, it must lie in the range:

$$-\frac{1}{4c} > m > -\frac{1}{2c}.$$

line) for various values of b, assuming that $c = .08$ and $\pi_T = 6 + 10\alpha - 4\alpha^2$. The functions intersect at $b = 1.32$, where the optimal α is 1.0.[14] When $b > 1.32$, the government prefers firm fixed-price coverage, with $\alpha = 1.0$, while the contractor prefers a lower value of α. The more b exceeds 1.32, the lower is the contractor's optimal α. When $b < 1.32$, the contractor prefers firm fixed-price coverage, while the government prefers a lower value of α. The more b falls short of 1.32. the lower is the government's optimal α.

It is easily shown that the contractor and government optimal α are equal only when the values of b and c are such that both parties prefer firm fixed-price coverage, with $\alpha = 1.0$. Substituting (8.71) into (8.68), we obtain:

$$(8.74) \qquad \alpha_c = \frac{1 + 4cm + 2ch - 2ch}{1 + 4cm} = 1.0.$$

Similarly, substituting (8.71) into (8.69) — the condition for an optimal government α — we obtain:

$$(8.75) \qquad \alpha_g = \frac{1 + 1 + 4cm + 2ch - 2ch}{2 + 4cm} = 1.0.$$

Thus, under the conditions assumed here, it would be impossible for the government and its contractor simultaneously to satisfy the objectives of outlay minimization and unconstrained profit maximization with any kind of CPFF, CPIF, or FPI contract.

We can isolate even further the conditions under which the preferences of the government and its contractor can be in accord, assuming a profit maximization objective for the contractor and an outlay minimization objective for the government. As indicated earlier, the negotiated profit risk premium function must be monotonically increasing at least up to $\alpha = 1.0$. This specification requires, as we have seen in (8.58) and (8.60), that:

$$(8.76) \qquad -h = 2m - \delta,$$

where δ is any positive real number. Substituting (8.76) into (8.71), we obtain:

$$(8.77) \qquad b = 1 + 2c(2m - 2m + \delta) = 1 + 2c(\delta).$$

Since, as we have observed earlier, a positive value of c is generally required for a sensible quadratic user cost function, this result shows that

---

[14] Note that these are not reaction functions, and so the contractor and the government cannot simply move to the joint optimum. Rather, b is essentially fixed once cost targets have been negotiated.

b must be greater than 1. Let us assume that $b = 1 + \epsilon$, where ϵ is any positive real number. We recall from (8.10) that at the contractor cost reduction optimum:

$$(8.78) \qquad X = \frac{\alpha - b}{2c}.$$

For institutional reasons the maximum value of α is 1.0. Substituting in $\alpha = 1.0$ and $b = 1 + \epsilon$, we obtain:

$$(8.79) \qquad X = \frac{1 - 1 - \epsilon}{2c} = \frac{-\epsilon}{2c}.$$

Because c is necessarily positive, this means that X must be negative; an overrun must be expected. Thus, the α preferences of an unconstrained profit maximizing contractor and an outlay minimizing government procurement agency are in harmony only when both parties find an expected cost overrun optimal. It follows that in underrun situations, the α preferences of the government and its contractor cannot be in harmony under the conditions and motivations assumed here.

Since most weapons production contracts are not of the firm fixed-price type, and since the majority of weapon system and subsystem production contracts have tended to end in underruns, these results suggest that a substantial element of conflict would exist in sharing proportion negotiations if contractors attempted to maximize profits and the government attempted to minimize contract outlays.

Selected Bibliography

GOVERNMENT DOCUMENTS

Comptroller General of the United States, *Report, Examination of the Pricing of Selected Department of the Air Force Contracts and Subcontracts*, May 1959.

U. S. Congress, House of Representatives

Committee on Appropriations, *Report, Air Force Intercontinental Ballistic Missile Construction Program*, 87th Cong., 1st Sess. (1961).

Subcommittee of Committee on Appropriations, *Hearings, Department of Defense Appropriations for 1960*, 86th Cong., 1st Sess. (1959).

Hearings, Department of Defense Appropriations for 1961, 86th Cong., 2d Sess. (1960).

Hearings, Department of Defense Appropriations for 1963, 87th Cong., 1st Sess. (1962).

Committee on Armed Services, *Hearings, Aircraft Production Costs and Profits*, 84th Cong., 2d Sess. (1956).

Hearings Pursuant to Section 4, Public Law 86–89, 86th Cong., 2d Sess. (1960).

Subcommittee for Special Investigations, *Hearings, Overpricing of Government Contracts*, 87th Cong., 1st Sess. (1961).

Hearings, Study of Air Force Contract AF 33(038)–18503; General Motors Corp. — Buick-Oldsmobile-Pontiac Assembly Division, 85th Cong., 1st Sess. (1957).

Hearings, Weapons System Management and Team System Concept in Government Contracting, 86th Cong., 1st Sess. (1959).

Committee on Government Operations, *Tenth Intermediate Report, Navy Jet Engine Procurement Program*, 84th Cong., 2d Sess. (1956).

32d Report, Research and Development (Office of the Secretary of Defense), 85th Cong., 2d Sess. (1958).

Eleventh Report, Organization and Management of Missile Programs, 86th Cong., 1st Sess. (1959).

Third Report, Air Force Ballistic Missile Management, 87th Cong., 1st Sess. (1961).

Subcommittee of Committee on Government Operations, *Hearings, Organization and Management of Missile Programs,* 86th Cong., 1st Sess. (1959).

Hearings, Systems Development and Management, 87th Cong., 2d Sess. (1962).

Committee on Naval Affairs, *Report of the Subcommittee Appointed To Investigate the Causes of Failure of Production of Brewster Aeronautical Corporation Under Its Contracts With the Navy,* 78th Cong., 1st Sess. (1943).

Committee on Ways and Means, *Hearings, Extension of the Renegotiation Act,* 85th Cong., 2d Sess. (1958).

U. S. Congress, Senate

Committee on Appropriations, *Hearings, Department of Defense Appropriations for 1957,* 84th Cong., 2d Sess. (1956).

Hearings, Department of Defense Appropriations for 1958, 85th Cong., 1st Sess. (1957).

Committee on Armed Services, Preparedness Investigating Subcommittee, *Hearings, Inquiry Into Satellite and Missile Programs,* 85th Cong., 1st and 2d Sess. (1958).

Procurement Subcommittee, *Hearings, Procurement Study,* 86th Cong., 2d Sess. (1960).

Committee on Government Operations, *Document No. 94, Report to the President on Government Development Prepared by the Bureau of the Budget,* 87th Cong., 2d Sess. (1962).

Permanent Subcommittee on Investigations, *Hearings, Pyramiding of Profits and Costs in the Missile Procurement Program,* 87th Cong., 2d Sess. (1962).

Select Committee on Small Business, *Hearings, Government Procurement — 1960,* 86th Cong., 2d Sess. (1960).

Case Problems in Government Procurement: Report on Government Procurement Problems of Aerosonic Corp., Clearwater, Fla.; and Hastings-Raydist, Inc., Hampton, Va., 86th Cong., 2d Sess. (1960).

U. S. Department of Commerce, *Statistical Abstract of the United States,* 1962.

U. S. Department of Defense, *Armed Service Procurement Regulation.*

Incentive Contracting Guide, prepared under the direction of Office of Assistant Secretary of Defense, Installations and Logistics, by Harbridge House, Inc., August 1962.

Report of Study Project No. 103, June 1961.

Ad Hoc Study Group, *Manned Aircraft Weapon Systems: A Program for Reducing the Time Cycle from Concept to Inventory* (The Robertson Report), July 1956, declassified from confidential in 1960.

Army Air Forces, Air Materiel Command, *Source Book of World War II Basic Data: Airframe Industry,* Vol. 1, 1952.

Office of Secretary of Defense, *Military Prime Contract Awards,* July–September 1960.

Military Prime Contract Awards and Subcontract Payments, July 1961–June 1962.

Statistical Services Center, *Report,* December 20, 1960.

U. S. National Science Foundation, *Funds for Research and Development in Industry: 1959* (1962).

Reviews of Data on Research and Development, August 1961, April 1962, August 1962, September 1962.

U. S. Renegotiation Board, *Annual Report,* 1956–1962.

BOOKS AND REPORTS

Aerospace Industries Association, *Aerospace Facts and Figures: 1962.* Washington: American Aviation Publications, 1962.

Arrow, Kenneth, "Economic Welfare and Allocation of Resources for Invention," in *The Rate and Direction of Inventive Activity: Economic and Social Factors,* National Bureau of Economic Research conference report. Princeton: Princeton University Press, 1962, pp. 609–625.

Asher, Harold, *Cost-Quantity Relationships in the Airframe Industry,* RAND Report R–291. Santa Monica: The RAND Corporation, 1956.

Baumol, William, *Business Behavior, Value, and Growth.* New York: Macmillan, 1959.

Cook, Fred J., *The Warfare State.* New York: Macmillan, 1962.

Gerschenkron, Alexander, "Industrial Enterprise in Soviet Russia," in *The Corporation in Modern Society,* ed. E. S. Mason. Cambridge: Harvard University Press, 1959, pp. 277–300.

Graaff, J. de V., *Theoretical Welfare Economics.* Cambridge: Cambridge University Press, 1957.

Hitch, Charles J. and McKean, Roland N., *The Economics of Defense in the Nuclear Age.* Cambridge: Harvard University Press, 1960.

Jane's All the World's Aircraft. London: S. Low, Marston & Co., annually.

Keynes, John Maynard, *The General Theory of Employment, Interest and Money.* New York: Harcourt Brace, 1936.

Klein, Burton H., "The Decision Making Problem in Development," in
  *The Rate and Direction of Inventive Activity: Economic and So-
  cial Factors,* National Bureau of Economic Research conference
  report. Princeton: Princeton University Press, 1962, pp. 477–
  508.
Logistics Management Institute, *Study of Profit or Fee Policy.* Wash-
  ington: 1963.
Medaris, John B., *Countdown for Decision.* New York: Putnam,
  1960.
Miller, John Perry, *Pricing of Military Procurements.* New Haven:
  Yale University Press, 1949.
Moore, Frederick T., *Military Procurement and Contracting: An Eco-
  nomic Analysis,* RAND Report RM–2948–PR. Santa Monica:
  The RAND Corporation, 1962.
National Security Industrial Association, *Addresses Delivered at the
  NSIA Joint Industry–Defense Department Symposium on the
  Profit Motive and Cost Reduction.* Washington: National Se-
  curity Industrial Association, June 15 and 16, 1961.
——. *Report of Cost Reduction Study,* Washington: National Security
  Industrial Association, June 15, 1962.
Novick, David, *Costing Tomorrow's Weapon Systems,* RAND Report
  RM–3170–PR. Santa Monica: The RAND Corporation, 1962.
——. *Efficiency and Economy in Government Through New Budget-
  ing and Accounting Procedures,* RAND Report R–254. Santa
  Monica: The RAND Corporation, 1954.
Osborn, Richards C., "Background and Evolution of the Renegotia-
  tion Concept," in *Procurement and Profit Renegotiation,* ed.
  J. Fred Weston, San Francisco: Wadsworth, 1960, pp. 13–42.
Papandreou, A. S., "Some Basic Problems in the Theory of the Firm,"
  in *A Survey of Contemporary Economics,* ed. B. F. Haley, Vol.
  II. Homewood: American Economic Association, 1952.
Peck, Merton J., and Scherer, Frederic M., *The Weapons Acquisition
  Process: An Economic Analysis.* Boston: Division of Research,
  Harvard Business School, 1962.
Schlaifer, Robert, *Development of Aircraft Engines.* Boston: Division
  of Research, Harvard Business School, 1950.
Stanford Research Institute, *The Industry-Government Aerospace Re-
  lationship.* Menlo Park: 1963.
Tikhomirov, V. I., *Organizatsiya I Planirovaniye Samoletostroitel'nogo
  Predpriyatiya (Organization and Planning of an Aircraft Con-
  struction Enterprise).* Moscow: 1957, translated by the U. S.
  Air Force Technical Documents Liaison Office.

Tybout, Richard A., *Government Contracting in Atomic Energy.* Ann Arbor: University of Michigan Press, 1956.

Usher, Abbott Payson, *A History of Mechanical Inventions.* Rev. ed. Cambridge: Harvard University Press, 1954.

ARTICLES AND PERIODICALS

Bauer, Peter T., "Notes on Cost," *Economica,* May 1945, pp. 90–97.

Bauer, Raymond, and Field, Mark S., "Ironic Contrast: US and USSR Drug Industries," *Harvard Business Review,* September–October 1962, pp. 89–97.

Baumol, William, "On the Theory of Expansion of the Firm," *American Economic Review,* December 1962, pp. 1078–1087.

"Contractor Evaluation Comments Asked," *Aviation Week & Space Technology,* April 15, 1953, p. 32.

Fellner, William, "The Influence of Market Structure on Technological Progress," *Quarterly Journal of Economics,* November 1951, pp. 556–577.

Gregory, William H., "DOD–NASA Study Common System for Rating Company Performance," *Aviation Week & Space Technology,* February 4, 1963, pp. 95–99.

Johnsen, Katherine, "NASA Sole Judge in New Incentive Plan," *Aviation Week & Space Technology,* June 25, 1962, pp. 28–29.

Kaysen, Carl, "Improving the Efficiency of Military Research and Development," *Public Policy,* Vol. XII. Cambridge: Harvard University Graduate School of Public Administration (in press).

Liberman, E. G., "Planning Production and Standards of Long-Term Operation," *Problems of Economics,* December 1962, pp. 16–22.

McGuire, J. W., Chiu, J. S. Y., and Elbing, A. E., "Executive Incomes, Sales, and Profits," *American Economic Review,* September 1962, pp. 753–761.

"McNamara Explains TFX Award Decision," *Aviation Week & Space Technology,* March 25, 1963, pp. 81–103.

Nelson, Richard, "The Simple Economics of Basic Scientific Research," *Journal of Political Economy,* June 1959, pp. 297–306.

———. "Uncertainty, Learning and the Economics of Parallel Research and Development Efforts," *Review of Economics and Statistics,* November 1961, pp. 351–364.

Patton, Arch, "Annual Report on Executive Compensation," *Harvard Business Review,* September–October 1958, pp. 129–140.

Ramo, Simon, "New Incentive Contract Plan Advanced," excerpts from speech before American Rocket Society, *Aviation Week & Space Technology,* January 8, 1962, pp. 99–103.

Scott, A. D., "Notes on User Cost," *Economic Journal,* June 1953, pp. 368–384.

Simon, Herbert A., "Theories of Decision-Making in Economics and Behavioral Science," *American Economic Review,* June 1959, pp. 253–283.

Smith, R. A., "The $7-Billion Contract That Changed the Rules," *Fortune,* March 1963, p. 96 ff., and April 1963, p. 110 ff.

Taylor, Hal, "System Will Rate Contractors," *Missiles and Rockets,* February 11, 1963, p. 14.

Wilson, George C., "USAF–Defense Research Conflict Aired," *Aviation Week & Space Technology,* August 13, 1962, pp. 32–34.

Zylstra, Don, "DOD Defends Centralized Management," *Missiles and Rockets,* November 12, 1962, p. 15.

Court Decisions

In the Matter of Boeing Airplane Company, 37 U. S. Tax Court Reports 613 (1962).

National Electronic Laboratories, Inc., v. the United States, No. 279–57, U. S. Court of Claims (1960).

In the Matter of North American Aviation, Inc., 39 U. S. Tax Court No. 19 (1962).

INDEX

accounting practices, contractor, 65; efforts to improve, 66, 206; deficiencies of, 207–209

Aerospace Corp., 283, 377

after-the-fact evaluation, as basis for contract awards, 329, 331, 337

after-the-fact evaluation, as basis for sales awards, 339–341, 349–350, 401

Allen, T. J., note 51, 47

Allen, William M., 256–257

Anderson, G. W., 37–38

Apollo, 349

Armed Services Procurement Act, 40, 141

Armed Services Procurement Regulation, 132, 141, 171, 172, 205, 208, 263, 272, 280, 298, 306, 308

Arrow, Kenneth, 45

arsenal approach to development, 351, 372, 374–375; 385; security of, 388; lack of innovation in, 388–389; evidence of innovation in, 389; development-production transition, 394–396; personnel recruitment problems of, 396–399

Asher, Harold, 119, 123–125

aspiration levels, 243–244, 245

Atlas ICBM, 12, 22, 25, 51, 73, 103; program management of, 376, 383

Atwood, J. L., 33–34, 84

B–17, 117, 119, 120, 122

B–24, 117, 119, 120, 122

B–29, 117, 119, 120

B–47, 117, 126, 343

B–52, 109–110

B–58, 12, 25, 103; incentive contract approach in, 136–137; 383

Babcock and Wilcox Co., atomic power plant, 165

Baker, H. D., 126

Bannerman, Graeme C., 173

bargaining power, 11; of contractors, 205–206; subcontractors, 206; example of contractor, 226–228

bargaining power, government, 213–218; lack of by government personnel, 204–206

Bates, William H., 33–34

Baumol, William, 10; sales maximization hypothesis, 10, 161

Bell Aircraft Corp. (Bell Aerospace Corp.), 72–73, 78, 120, 122

Bell Committee, recommendations of, 396–397

bidding, competitive, 26–27, 102, 107–108

Boeing Airplane Co., 29, 37, 38, 120, 122, 126, 176, 343

Bomarc, 13, 22

bonds, performance, 308–309

Braun, Wehrner von, 389

breakout, costs of, 107–112, 117

breakout, definition, 102

breakout, effects, 107–108, 111–112; on R & D, 112–113; on proprietary rights, 114–115; on bargaining power, 115–117; to improve production contract incentives, 367

breakout, types, 104–105

Brewster Aeronautical Corp., 75–76, 81–82, 123, 125

Brewster Corsair (F4U–1), 76, 81, 121, 123, 125

Brown, Harold, 72; note 44, 90; note 7, 303; 396

Buffalo, 75

Bullpup, 126

"buying in," 27, 156, 364

cancellation, program, 36; effect of threat of, 42–49; reasons for in 1957–1960, 56; for default, 306–307

capacity, excess, effect on incentive contracts, 183; development of, 318

case studies, list of, 12–13; limitations of, 14

Chance-Vought Aircraft Inc., 121

change, resistance to, by technically committed personnel, 26

changes, design, 191, 228, 378

changes, engineering, 237–238, 378

Chrysler Corp., 395

"closed loop," 110, 112

collusion, 45–46

commitment to a technical approach, 24–25; difficulty of change in, 26, 379; biases of special systems engineering, 381

"commonality," 37, 70, 355

Commonwealth Edison Co., atomic power plant, 165

competence, technical, government, 29; lack of, 33, 61; in budget estimation, 63, 65, 266–267; in con-

competence (*cont.*)
tract negotiation, 205–206, 209, 287; in performance evaluation, 287–290; suggested improvement in, 367

competition, behavioral effects, 20, 21, 23–25, 28; on management and technical talent morale, 43–44; due to number of competitors, 48–49; on quality, 50

competition, budgetary, 9; incentives from, 52–54, 66; effects of priority on, 55–56; inefficiency in development resulting from, 60–61; effect on government bargaining power, 215–218; effect on efficiency, 320

competition, design, 39; benefits vs. costs, 41; number of competitors, 47–48, 316; benefits, 316; excesses of, 316–317

competition, development stage, types of, 26; misinformation costs of, 27–28, 49; other costs, 49–50; budgetary pressures, 56; inefficiency in development from, 60–61

competition, effect on innovation, 23–24, 49; perception of, 25, 35; effect on tradeoffs, 29; other effects of, 49–50

competition, management, 40; number attracted to, 47; emphasis in, 70

competition, potential, 23–24, 35, 41–42

competition, source selection, 39

competition, statistical benefits of, 19–20, 28; from technical proposals, 41, 49, 50

competitive optimism, reasons for, 26–27; costs of, 27–28; attempts to discourage, 28–29; effect of multidimensional incentive contracts on, 174, 175–176

competitors, number of, optimal, 44–45; effect of variations in, 46–49

conservatism, in technical goal setting, note 44, 178; 180, 302–303

consistency of incentive correlations, 94

Consolidated Edison Co., atomic power plant, 165

contingencies, 209–211, 217

contract administration, costs of, 348–349

contract cost outcomes, distribution of, 192–193; of fixed price type, 194–204

contract cost outcomes, related to contract size, 213–215

contract cost outcomes, related to contract type, 132, 133

contract negotiations, personnel engaged in, 348–349

contract types employed, statistics, 142–144, 146

contracting, annual, results of, 27, 158

contracts, cost plus fixed-fee (CPFF), 11; effect on optimism, 27, 131, 157; definition, 132, 135; amount of, 142; use by Army, 147, 149; contractor preference for, 151–152; overruns in, 154–157; profit role in, 155; opportunity cost effect on efficiency under, 185–186, 188; cost outcomes of production contract sample, 192–193; tendency to overrun, 194; contractor sharing proportion, 218–219

contracts, cost plus incentive-fee, (CPIF), definition, 136; use, 153; profit rate in, 155; effects, 156–158, 166–168; limitations of for development cost reduction, 181–183; contractor sharing, 218

contracts, cost plus-a-percentage-of-cost, definition, 140–141; opportunity cost under, 188

contracts, cost reimbursement, 142–145; use in research and development, 145–147; Air Force stress on, 147; decline in, 149–150; overruns under, 154–157; effect on tradeoff decisions, 157–164

contracts, firm fixed-price (FFP) definition, 132; Army use of, 147, 149; increase in use of, 150; effects on tradeoff decisions in development programs, 164–166; contractor sharing proportion, 218–219; example of, 234–235; effect on quality tradeoffs, 237–239; profit-cost correlation, 230; reward and pressure theory, 231–232; behavioral effects of tight cost targets under, 230–236

contracts, fixed-price incentive (FPI) definition, 134; amount of, 142; Air Force use of, 147; TFX contract, 175; cost outcomes of production contract sample, 192–193; tendency to underrun, 194; contractor sharing, 218; government choice of, 225; behavioral effects of tight cost targets under, 230–236; reward and pressure theory under, 230–232; example, 232–234

contracts, incentive, 134–137

contracts, letter, 141

contracts, level of effort, definition, 154; effects of, 157–158

contracts, multidimensional incentive, negotiation of, 136–137; problems in negotiation of, 177–180; redundancy of, 166–172; Department of Defense enthusiasm for, 172; expected benefits from, 173–174; reservations about, 174–177; application to hardware not development, 175; balance problem of, 325–326

contracts, redeterminable, note 9, 136; definition, 137–138; effects of, 138–140; cost outcomes of production contract sample 192–193; tendency to underrun, 194

contracts, types employed, criteria for choosing, 145–147, 191

controls, technical and financial, expansion of government, 373–377; centralization, 374–375, 377; detailed government, 383; results of, 384–385, 403

Convair Div. of General Dynamics Corp., 73, 119, 120, 122–123; Atlas program management, 376, 383

coordination breakdowns, 110

cost, development, 4; lack of emphasis on, 33–34, 36; effect of multidimensional contracts on, 174–177

cost, opportunity (*see* opportunity cost)

cost padding, 209–210, 323–324; in Soviet Union, 211–213, 323

cost reduction, incentives for, 36; effects of budgetary competition on, 59; incentives for in production phases, 62; disutilities of, 321–322

cost targets, importance of tight, 63; FPI contracts effects on, 190; effect of efficiency maximization on, 224–225, 366–367; behavioral effects of tight, 230–236

cost targets, negotiation of, 134; under multidimensional contracts, 172, 175, 180; under CPIF contracts, 181–182; conflict in, 204; effect of contingency factors on,

209–210; Russian problems with, 212; sequence in, 216–218; effects on contract type, 219

costs, not allowable, 132–133

costs, estimation of, 1, 27; by contractors, 64, 205–206; by subcontractors, 206; problems due to accounting practices, 207–209; problems due to contingency factors, 210–211

costs, excessive, 5; effect of competition on, 26–28; reduction of, 36

costs, incremental, 113

costs, overhead, 60–61, 182–183

costs, user (*see* user cost)

criteria in formal source selection, 69–70, 72

Curtiss-Wright Corp., 78–79, 125

Davis, W. A., 209

default, termination for, 306–307

demand, changes in, 56–58

demand, elasticity of, consumer, 52; of weapon systems, 53, 62

development programs, size of, 168–169

development and production separation, 394–396; Russian experience, note 37, 394–395

development cost, size of, 1

development cost predictions, errors in, 1, 32; effect of competitive optimism on, 27–28

development programs, commercial, 13, 165

development sales, 169–170

diversification of firms, 80, 317–320

Douglas Aircraft Co., 104; Honest John breakout controversy, 114–115; 116, 120, 126; X–22 competition, 73; Skybolt, 73; Nike Hercules, 280; profits on, 281; B–47, 343

duplication, 20; risk reduction of, 21 (*see also* competition, statistical benefits of)

eagerness, 26, 47

Eagle, 22

economies of scale, 127

Emerson Electric Manufacturing Co., 105

efficiency, classification of programs observed, 55

efficiency, definition of, 3, 4; inefficiency, definition of, 60; effect of priority on, 55–56; effects of max-

efficiency (*cont.*)
imization of, 224; pressure theory incentive effect on, 232–234; limitations of contractual incentives on, 239–242, 324; effects of competitive incentives on, 316
efficiency, evaluation of, 92–101; in program sample, 186–188, 287, 335
efficient conduct, weapons program, definition of, 3, 4; results of inefficient development conduct, 59–61; effect of CPIF contracts on, 181–182
entry and exit of firms, 8, 57, 74; due to profits, 224–225; effect of no development profit on, 305–306
expenditures, over-all national defense, 57
expenditures, research and development, 57; by private firms, 372; research, development test and evaluation, 168–169, 393
extra scope, 27, 155, 176

F–84F, profits on, 246
F–86D, 262
F–86F, 262
F–100, 262
F–102, 73
F–105, 12; importance of quality in, 54
F–111 (*see* TFX)
F3H, 77
F4H–1, 12, 48; importance of quality in, 34
F4U–1, 117, 119, 121, 123, 169
F8U–3, 34, 48
facilities, government furnished, 116
Fairchild Engine and Airplane Corp. (Fairchild Stratos Corp.), 79
Falcon, 22
Fellner, William, note 47, 45
follow-on orders, importance of, to defense contractors, 156–162, 169; to commercial contractors, 165–166; development follow-on orders, 169–170
Ford Motor Co., 74, 117, 120

General Accounting Office, 245, 246, 247
General Dynamics Corp., 29, 37, 41, 176
General Electric Co., 118; atomic power plant, 165

General Motors Corp., 74, 117; profits on F–84F, 246
Gershenkron, Alexander, 212
Gilpatric, Roswell L., 73
goals, conflicts of, 61, 134, 204
goals, contractor, 7; conflicts among, 7, 12; effect of incentives on, 10, 11, 22; sales maximization, 51, 61; in development delay acceptance, 60; in production, 63; in cost estimation, 64; for long-run survival, 80, 161; in tradeoff decisions, 159–161; organizational, 321–322
goals, contractor, in contract negotiations, 133, 134, 151–152, 204
goals, government, 29–30; theoretical illustration of, 30–31
goals, government, in contract negotiations, 147, 149–150, 204
gold plating, 318
Goodyear Aircraft Corp., 121
Gross, Robert E., 84–85
growth, organizational, 7, 161–162
Grumman Aircraft Engineering Corp., 349

Hitch, Charles J. and McKean, Roland N., 20, 42, 216, 218, 392
Honest John, breakout of, 105; decision with regard to, 114–115
Horne, C. F., 39

incentives, automatic contractual, definition, 132; development of, 153; effects on tradeoff decisions in development programs, 157–158; redundancy of, 166–168; expected benefits from, 174; problems with, 172–177; limitations on efficient conduct of development programs, 181–184, 189; Russian use of, 211; reward theory of, 231; limitations of, 236; effects on cost reduction, 251–252; effects of renegotiation on, 255–257, 260; limitations of in later production stages, 266–268; weaknesses of, 268–270; limitations of for cost reduction, 322–325
incentives, automatic contractual, suggested improvements, for development contracts, 364–366, 401; for production contracts, 366–367
incentives, competitive, definition, 9; 12, 36; effects on efficiency, 316
incentives, contractual, definition, 9,

12; effects, 154; special contractual, 306–309
incentives, definition, 5–6; correlation with performance, 6, 8; in after-the-fact evaluation, 331
incentives, dimensional balance problem, 325
incentives, non-administrable, 313
incentives, other, 12, 162–163; importance of, 166, 168, 170–171, 175
incentives, pressure theory, 231–234; observed case, 234–235
incentives, reward theory, 231, 234
inefficiency (*see* efficiency)
innovation, definition, 22; effect of competition on, 23–26; lack of in arsenals, 388–389; presence of in arsenals, 389; effect of production motive on, 390–394
insecurity, contractors, 317, 318, 349, 388
investment, as basis for profit awards, 336–337
investment, return on, 275, 278–280
Irvine, Clarence S., 42–43

J–40, 77, 81
J–46, 77
J–47, 117
J–48, 117
J–54, 77
J–57, 117
J–65, 117
Jupiter, 13, 22; competition with Thor, 42–43, 379; effect of cancellation threat of, 386; development and production of, 395

Kaysen, Carl, 390–391, 392, 393–394
Kennedy, John F., 396
Keynes, John M., 158–159
Klein, Burton, note 34, 392
know-how, 114–115, 381

learning curve (*see* progress curve)
level-of-effort incentive system, 341–345, 401
Lilienthal, David, 373
liquidated damages, 308
Lockheed Aircraft Corp., 119, 121, 126, 343
Logistics Management Institute, note 6, 279–280; note 15, 284; note 21, 287
Lord Manufacturing Co., 76

loss, special importance of, 131, 152, 231–236

make vs. buy, 381–382 (*see also* subcontracting)
market vs. nonmarket environment, 2; lack of for weapons acquisition, 1–2
Martin Co., 120
McDonnell Aircraft Corp., 169
McElroy, Neil H., 43
McKean, Roland N. (*see* Hitch, Charles J. and McKean, Ronald N.)
McKee, William F., 38
McNamara, Robert S., 29, 36–38, 172, 176, 178, 290, 315, 325, 355
Medaris, John B., 43
Meteor, 22
Miller, John P., 131, 153, 229, 252–253, 254–255
Minuteman, 22, 51, 308, 376
monopoly, bilateral, in weapons programs, 2, 9, 156
monopsonist, government as, 224
Moore, Frederick T., 151; note 24, 214; note 16, 284
morale, effects of competition on, 42–44, 50
"mouse trapping," 289–290
multidimensionality, in weapons program performance, 3, 94–99, 290–293

National Security Industrial Association, 350, 353, 356
Nelson, Richard R., note 1, 20
Nike Ajax, 13, 25, 103; breakout costs, 107–108; development lead time, 333; weapon system prime contractor approach, note 7, 375–376
Nike Hercules, 13, 25; breakout of, 104–105, 106, 108; profit rates on, 280–281
Nike Zeus, 13; budgetary competition over, 22, 51–52, 53; interpretation of this, 54; breakout, 106
nonprofit organizations, 35; behavior of, 386–388; as substitute for government in-house talent, 397
North American Aviation, Inc., 120, 262
Novick, David, note 21, 65; note 24, 66; note 30, 341

opportunity cost, definition of, 185; effect on efficiency in CPFF con-

opportunity cost (*cont.*)
tracts, 185–186; observed effects in 10 programs, 186–188; effect of contract choice on, 222–223
optimal conduct, weapons programs, 4
optimism, competitive (*see* competitive optimism)
outlay minimization, government, demonstration, 427–431
overhead, 208
overlapping, 171
overruns, cost, 134; definition, 155; under cost reimbursement contracts, 154–157, 192–194; under redeterminable contracts, 202–204; effect on contract choice, 219, 226–227
overstaffing, 239–241

P–47, 119, 121, 125
performance bond, 308–309
performance, dimensions of, 3; weighting of, 95–99
performance, evaluation of contractor, comparability in, 92–94, 328–331; frequency of, 332; objectivity in, 330, 354–356; organizational approaches, 328–339
performance, government, 99–101
performance, indices, 345–346
performance, measurement, feasibility of, 95–99, 287–290
performance, measurement problems, 91–92; answers to, 93–94; of new DOD evaluation system, 288–290; of officials directly involved, 329
performance, multidimensionality of, 94–99, 290–293
performance, past, as criterion in setting profit rates, 284–286; as criterion for profit in after-the-fact evaluation, 332–335
performance, past, as predictor of future performance, 88–89; new Department of Defense emphasis on, 88
performance, past, as source selection criterion, 69, 71–72, 370; lack of emphasis by government on, 72, 79–80, 86, 101; commercial emphasis on, 82–83; contractor perception of, 84–87; conflicts of objectives in, 89–91; as criterion in after-the-fact evaluation, 339–341
performance, technical, military emphasis on, 32, 34, 35, 70, 355; Boeing increments in TFX design, 37, 38; military displeasure over unsatisfactory, 75–77, 81–82
performance evaluation, publication of, 346–347, 401
Pershing, 379
personnel recruitment problem, government, 396–398
PERT/Cost System, 66
Philco Corp., 118
Polaris, IRBM, 12; competition facing, 22; 51, 52, 380
political influence, in source selection, 70–71; on government forcing exit of unsatisfactory performers, 83–84
price ceiling, 218
price determination, 216–218
pricing risk, by contract type, 273; effect on negotiated profit rate, 273–274
priority, program, influence on program budgets, 54–59, 66
priority, program, relationship to efficiency, in development, 59–62; in production, 62
profit, diminishing marginal utility of, 242–252, 269
profit, effects of paying no, 281–282; on development, 300–301; on contractor behavior, 301–304; on exit of resources, 305–306
profit, related to contract type, 132
profit incentive, definition, 132, 135, 149, 241; incremental nature of, 258–260, 321
profit maximization, long-run, 11, 159–162, 163, 189, 218, 321–322; demonstration, 413–427
profit maximization, short-run, 10–11, 158, 159, 189, 268, 321–322
profit rates, distribution of, 248–251; on renegotiable sales, 264–265
profit rates, going, 150
profit rates, negotiated, reasons for variation, 150–151, 273–286; under fixed price contracts, 160; correlation with past performance, 271; variability of, 271–272; criteria for variability, 272–273; due to contract type, 273–274; due to contractor investment, 279; due to subcontracting, 280; by industry, 282; due to bargaining power, 282–283; due to nature of

work performed, 283–284; because of service preference, 284; because of past performance, 284–285; new DOD system, 287–288, and suggestions for improvement of, 291–293; proposed performance correlated variations in, 294–298; some limitations on proposed, 298–299; penalty reduction in, 307–308, 309

profit rates, negotiated, weighted guideline approach, 335–337

profit rates, realized, 150; under CPFF contracts, 185; as a percentage of actual cost, 248–251

profiteering, 245, 323–324

profits, avoidance of high, 245–247

profits, correlated with development performance in after-the-fact evaluation, 332–335, 347, 400; correlated with production performance, 337–338; 349–350

profits, variability in, 182–184

profits, windfall, 133, 134, 245, 247, 324; elimination of in after-the-fact evaluation, 338

program definition effort, 28

program evaluation, objections to, 351–360

Program Evaluation Board, 330–331, 339, 345–347, 352; unilateral judgment, 351–352; personnel of, 353, 360–362; objectives, 354–355; performance measurements, 357–359; establishment by DOD, NASA, AEC, 400

program manager, government as, 377–384; product decision making of, 377–379; independent research of, 379; systems engineering and integration of, 379–380; reasons for, 382–383; detailed reviews and controls of, 383

progress curve, slope under competition, 119–125

progress curve, use in cost estimation, 124–125

progress payments, 279, 367

project manning, effect of competition on, 41–42

proprietary data, definition, 114 (*see also* know-how)

quality, 3; dominance over cost, 33–35; TFX controversy over, 37; behavioral effects of competition on, 50; contractor emphasis on, 159–162

quality, weapon system, 3; importance in evaluation, 315–316

quality maximization, 31–32; emphasis on by contractors, 159–162; by scientists and engineers within firm, 162–164; under cost reimbursement contracts, 157–164; example, 238; under firm fixed-price contracts, 165–166; example, 237

Ramo, Simon, 86, 340–341

Ramo-Wooldridge Corp., 283, 376 (*see also* Space Technology Laboratories)

ranking, 330–331; publication of Program Evaluation Board's, 346–347

Redstone, 379

Redstone Arsenal, 395

Regulus II, 22

renegotiation, effect on contract choice, 261; effect on efficiency, 254–255, 265–266; industry arguments on, 255–257, 265; exemption from in after-the-fact evaluation profit, 338; cost reduction from, 368; suggested improvements in, 368–369

Renegotiation Act, criteria for determining excessive profits, 253–254

Renegotiation Board, composition of, 261; ability to make efficiency evaluations, 261–262; suggested improvements in, 369

Republic Aviation Corp., 117, 121, 125

reputation, importance to contractors, 68

research, basic and applied, outlays on, 391; distinction between this and development, 392

research and development expenditures, 168–169; in-house by private companies, 372

responsibility, rejection of, 111–112

responsibility, shared, 352–354

"reverse engineering," 115

rewards, cumulative, under after-the-fact profit evaluation, 335–339; under after-the-fact sales evaluation, 341–346; noncumulative reward problem, 348

risk, in development, 19

risk, pricing, 273–275

risk, related to contract type, 132

risk, in sharing proportion choice, 221, 226, 228
risk aversion, 133; contractor, 221, 228, 231; example of, 233–234; government, 225; effect on efficiency, 268
Robertson Committee, 374

salaries, government, 396–398
sales, aircraft industry, 58
sales, correlated with performance in after-the-fact evaluation, 339–341, 349–350, 401
sales maximization, weapons contractors, 10–11, 22, 51, 168–169
Schlaifer, Robert, 24, 42, 300, 384, 388–389
Schriever, Bernard A., 70
Schumpeter, Joseph A., 319
second sourcing, 102, 117; objectives of, 117, 118; progress curves under, 123
second sourcing, benefits, 118, 125–126
second sourcing, costs, 127–128
secrecy, in award decisions, 86–87
sharing proportion, as determinant of contract type, 134–135, 226; contractor preference, 218–219, 221; government preference, 217–220; effect of uncertainty on, 221, 228; effect of renegotiation on, 261; for efficiency maximization, 221–225, 366
sharing proportion, optimal choice of, 222–225; demonstration of, 412–431
Sidewinder, 22, 38; development of, 118, 389; second sourcing of, 118–119; cost reduction of, 118–119, 127
Skybolt, 53, 73
Snark, 53
source selection, criteria, conflicts among, 69
Space Technology Laboratories, note 31, 170; program management of Atlas, 376; of Thor, Titan, and Minuteman, 376, 379, 380, 381; end of role as systems engineer, 382, 383
Sparrow I, 22, 38, 116
Sparrow II, 22, 38
Sparrow III, 13; competition facing, 22, 116; development lead time, 333
specifications, contract, 236
Sperry Rand Corp., 116

stretchouts, development program, 60
subcontracting, as factor in setting profit rate, 280–281
subcontracting vs. in-house conduct of work, 281–282
substitutability, degree of between weapon systems, 21–22, 53
substitutes, reasonably close, definition of, 21; example of competition between close, 42–44; example of competition between not reasonably close substitutes, 51–52; bargaining power of government due to close, 213, 215; statistical and behavioral benefits of, 371
sunk costs, 54, 66
systems engineering, government, 379–380; objectivity of, 381; duplication by contractors, 382–383
systems integration, government, 379–380; reasons for, 382

TFX (F–111), 29, 33; quality arguments over, 37, 38; cost of competitive proposals for, 40; deficient proposal of, 41; choice of finalists, 70; criteria used, 70; unrealistic estimates, 176; conflict of objectives, 355; subjective elements, 358
talent, allocation of technical and managerial, 39–40; use in design competitions, 39, 49; in management competitions, 40; effect of number of competitors on, 47–48
talent hoarding, 318
Talos, 13
termination (*see* cancellation)
Thor, 22; competition with Jupiter, 42–43, 48, 376, 379
Thurman, W. T., 230
time, development, 4; military emphasis on, 32, 35, 36; contractor emphasis on, 159–162; average, 333
time, lead (*see* time, development)
Titan, 22, 51
tradeoffs, definition of, 4; observations of, 5; effect of competition on, 29, 38; condition for optimum, 29–32; in commercial development, 35; due to budgetary constraint, 63–64; under cost plus incentive fee contracts, 157–158; effect of user cost on, 159–162

turnover, among top prime contractors, 74–75, 78–79
Tybout, Richard A., 229–230, 373–374

underruns, cost, under fixed-price type contracts, 192–193, 194; reasons for, 210; changes in, 215–216; effect on contract choice, 218–220, 225, 227
user cost, definition of, 158, 185; effect on tradeoff decisions, 159–162, 166; in commercial project, 165; effects on efficiency, 183–184; on development cost reduction, 189; on contract type, 218; on production efficiency, 239; on cost reduction, 321–322
user cost, functions, 407–411
uncertainty, in contract pricing, 191, 221
uncertainty, measure of, 1, 161, 221
uncertainty, strategic (intelligence), 3, 46
uncertainty, technical, 19, 41, 46, 50

Usher, Abbott Payson, 23
utility maximization, 251–252

value, military, 53, 54
Vela Hotel, 170
Vinson, Carl, 209
Vinson-Trammell Act, 252

weapon system prime contractor approach, 281, 375; criticisms, 380–381, 382
weapons acquisition process, definition of, 1; nonmarket envisionment of, 2, 45
weapons programs, optimal conduct of, 4; value maximization theory of, 29–32
Western Electric Corp., 104; profit rates, 280–281
Westinghouse Electric Corp., 78, 81–82; unsatisfactory performance and exit from jet engine field, 77
Wilson, Charles E., 59, 314

X–22, 72–73